P9-BZC-966

The Purloined Poe

The Purloined Poe

Lacan, Derrida & Psychoanalytic Reading

Edited by
John P. Muller &
William J. Richardson

The Johns Hopkins University Press
Baltimore and London

© 1988 The Johns Hopkins University Press
All rights reserved
Printed in the United States of America

Originally published, hardcover and paperback, 1988
Second printing, paperback, 1988

The Johns Hopkins University Press
701 West 40th Street
Baltimore Maryland 21211
The Johns Hopkins Press Ltd., London

Library of Congress Cataloging-in-Publication Data

The Purloined Poe.

    Bibliography: p.
    Includes index.
    1. Poe, Edgar Allan, 1809–49. Purloined letter. 2. Lacan, Jacques, 1901–
1981.—Contributions in criticism. 3. Derrida, Jacques—Contributions in
criticism. 4. Psychoanalysis and literature. I. Muller, John P., 1940–   .
II. Richardson, William J.
PS2618.P83P87   1988   813'.3   87-2760
ISBN 0-8018-3292-6 (alk. paper)
ISBN 0-8018-3293-4 pbk.

❦ Contents

Preface

When asked what scenes from the historical past he would like to witness on film, Vladimir Nabokov reportedly wished he could see the marriage ceremony in which Edgar Allan Poe was wedded to his thirteen-year-old cousin (Hall 1981, 275). In such a scene Nabokov would have been the unseen observer of Poe and his young bride, and in recounting it Nabokov becomes an observer observed in turn (by our own imaginary vision, at least), without being obviously aware of the fact. Such a series of hypothetical scenes tells us something about Nabokov and ourselves, no doubt. But does it tell us anything about psychoanalysis and literary criticism?

The thesis of this book is that it does. At least the double fantasy suggests a striking analogue with Poe's short story "The Purloined Letter" (about an observer being observed without observing that she is being watched in turn), which has evoked a major ongoing debate in contemporary letters. For in 1956 the French psychoanalyst Jacques Lacan made public an interpretation of the Poe story that not only revealed a radically fresh conception of psychoanalysis but also challenged literary theorists. If Lacan is generally counted among the major influences on poststructuralist literary criticism, it is primarily because of this one essay, which he presented for reasons of purely psychoanalytic interest. Its far-reaching claims about language and truth, however, provoked a vigorous response from the French philosopher Jacques Derrida. His critical essay spawned other essays, and the debate was on.

This book has as its purpose, then, to make available essential moments of this debate and dialogue. After reprinting Poe's story, we present a translation of Lacan's essay, the most difficult piece in the book and therefore the one essay for which we provide textual commentary. Next comes a discussion of traditional and contemporary approaches to "psychoanalyzing" texts, followed by Derrida's extended criticism of Lacan's essay. Their conflict and debate, in turn, are discussed and mediated by subsequent chapters. In addition, we include several alternative readings of the same material. The previously published essays have been altered only to remove redundant repetition of the plot of Poe's story. All in all, the book assembles a good part of the existing contemporary scholarship on "The Purloined Letter" and thereby affords a structured exercise in the elaboration of textual interpretation.

But while learning something about Edgar Allan Poe and Jacques Lacan and how some authors read them, readers will also find in this book, we think, a special experience of language. By "special experience of language" we mean "an experience we undergo with language" in Heidegger's sense (1971, 57), where such experience "is something else again than to gather information about language" (58). Such an experience is not an object of study but one in which we are the objects of certain effects:

To undergo an experience with something—be it a thing, a person, or a god—means that this something befalls us, strikes us, comes over us, overwhelms and transforms us. When we talk of "undergoing" an experience, we mean specifically that the experience is not of our own making; to undergo here means that we endure it, suffer it, receive it as it strikes us and submit to it. It is this something itself that comes about, comes to pass, happens. (Heidegger 1971, 57)

In these texts we experience the dynamics of an exchange that has assumed a shape and movement of its own to such an extent that we can perhaps describe the experience as being set in motion by language itself. That is to say, it is language itself that yields and takes back, that covers, uncovers, and recovers itself in and through these texts, in a manner consonant with Heidegger's emphasis that "such withholding is in the very nature of language" (1971, 81) and with Lacan's musings about "the poet's superiority in the art of concealment" (see below, chap. 2).

The anchor text for this display of language is, then, the short story written by Edgar Allan Poe in 1844 titled, in apparent simplicity, "The Purloined Letter." It is the third piece in the Dupin series, following "The Murders in the Rue Morgue" (1841) and "The Mystery of Marie Rogêt" (1842). These stories are generally regarded as inaugurating the genre of detective fiction (Most and Stowe 1983), and the figure of Dupin suggested numerous features of Arthur Conan Doyle's portrayal of Sherlock Holmes (Symons 1981, 223). Dupin's method of "analysis" (and Holmes's subsequent "science of deduction and analysis") has been compared to Peirce's "abduction" as a semiotic method as well as to Freud's psychoanalytic approach as a conjectural science (Eco and Sebeok 1983). Poe himself described "The Purloined Letter" as "perhaps the best of my tales of ratiocination" (see Mabbott's notes to Poe's story in this book, chap. 1).

Edgar Allan Poe was born January 19, 1809, in Boston and died October 7, 1849, in Baltimore, where he was buried. Although to a sizable degree the historical traditions about Poe's life have been controverted, a narrative of poverty and pathos appears to be established.[1] Both his parents were actors. A year after his birth his father disappeared; before he was three years old his mother, Elizabeth Arnold, died of tuberculosis, after acting in New York City, Charleston, and Richmond. An older brother was raised by grandparents. When his mother died Poe was taken in by the Allans, acquaintances of his mother in Richmond, who were childless (and whose friends made a home for Poe's younger sister). The Allans took Poe to Scotland and England, where he attended school from age six to eleven, receiving a classical education that continued in Richmond. When he was seventeen he attended the University of Virginia for eleven months, but his gambling losses led Mr. Allan to stop tuition payments. In desperation, Poe then joined the United States Army, where he served for almost two years before Mr. Allan enabled him to enter the United States Military Academy at West Point, though he was dismissed after eight months for absenteeism. Throughout this period (from age eighteen), he published poetry in Boston, Baltimore, and New York City while struggling with poverty and contending with Mr. Allan over finances. He won a fifty-dollar prize for a short story published in Baltimore in 1833. In 1835 he became an editor at the *Southern Literary Messenger* in Richmond. Here he developed a name as a severe critic, and his reviews and stories led to a marked subscription boost. But a year and a half later, despite warnings, he was fired from the *Messenger* because of alcoholism, whereupon he went to New York City to be coeditor of another journal. In the meantime he had married his thirteen-year-old cousin Virginia, whose mother managed the household details.

In 1838 Poe published *The Narrative of Arthur Gordon Pym,* a major inspiration for *Moby Dick.* He followed with his tales of horror and his stories about detection. In 1845, while he was an editor of the *New York Mirror,* "The Raven" was published, bringing Poe instant national fame. He continued to struggle for money, however, and in 1846 he and his family moved to Fordham in the Bronx, New York City, where he wrote literary gossip sketches that prompted libel suits. In 1847 his wife died of tuberculosis, and he became notably depressed. He continued to write and to drink, and he died in a Baltimore hospital in 1849.

After his death, Poe was nearly forgotten in America. His collected works were subject to strange and conflicting editorships, and his character was vilified, partly a result of his own fabrications. But his writings, especially his views on aesthetics and composition, quickly became influential in France, largely because Baudelaire, whose spirit revived when he read Poe in 1852, found a close kinship with him, translated his works, and wrote long critical introductions from 1852 to 1865. This work, in turn, influenced Mallarmé and played a key role in the development of the Symbolist movement in French poetry.

It is no surprise, therefore, that the classically educated Parisian Jacques Lacan read Poe. Born in 1901, Lacan completed his training in neurology and psychiatry in 1932, then undertook his psychoanalytic formation. During the thirties he also associated with surrealist artists and writers (for whom Poe's work was special; see Balakian 1971), attended the famous lectures on Hegel given by Alexandre Kojève (Miller 1984), studied Freud, and wrote about paranoia, the family, and the origin of the ego. By 1953 Lacan was in dispute with the International Psychoanalytic Association over his training of psychoanalysts and was expelled (Turkle 1978). Many of his colleagues joined him in establishing a new psychoanalytic center in Paris, for teaching and training. He began to give seminars whose theme extended through the year and whose audience soon included the philosophical and literary elite of Paris. These seminars still remain largely unpublished and untranslated, although some have appeared (Lacan 1973, 1975a,b, 1978b, 1981, 1986). Controversy persisted up to and beyond Lacan's death in 1981; additional biographical accounts are available elsewhere (Clément 1983; Schneiderman 1983).

Malcom Bowie tells us: "Lacan reads Freud. This is the simplest and most important thing about him" (1979, 116). But Lacan reads Freud (in German) in a manner shaped by the structural linguistics of Saussure and Jakobson, who afford a framework whereby Lacan can assert that "the unconscious is structured in the most radical way like a language" (Lacan 1977, 159). Lévi-Strauss, in turn, provided a structuralist framework in which the most general laws of mind as well as of social systems are essentially linguistic (Muller and Richardson 1982, 6–9). From the philosophy of Heidegger he obtains what he calls "a propaedeutic reference" (Lacan 1978a, 18) to the relationship between language and being, and he specifically cites Heidegger's notion of truth as the process of unconcealment (1975a, 216; 1966a, 166, 528; and see Lacan's essay below, chap. 2, 37). Lacan also draws extensively on the history of philosophy, especially Plato and Augustine for the problematic of desire and Descartes, Pascal, Kant, Hegel, and Kierkegaard for calling into question substantivist conceptualizations of the subject. He uses Buddhist notions (see, e.g., 1966a, 309) as well as concepts from set theory and topology (e.g., 1966a, 321). But above all, Lacan's perspective is shaped by his own practice of psychoanalysis, for he was always and primarily a psychoanalyst, writing for and teaching other psychoanalysts (Felman 1982). Nevertheless, Bowie writes (1979, 151): "Lacan is widely influential outside psychoanalysis. One of the main reasons for this is that his writing proposes itself consciously as a critique of all discourses and all ideologies." But to position oneself so that ideology and disguise, seduction and self-assurance are made to appear as what they are—isn't this to position oneself as analyst?

Lacan's position, then, is always that of analyst, not literary critic. It is this that leads him to discern the "parallels" that constitute the heart of his interpretation. But the discovery of parallels is infectious, and others find them between Lacan and Hegel, Lacan and Derrida, and so forth. This play of parallels should not surprise us, of course, for as Jakobson (1980, 106) maintained toward the end of his life, "a number of types of literary prose are constructed according to a strict principle of parallelism, but here too one can apply *mutatis mutandis* the remark of Hopkins that the scholar will be amazed to discover the presence of an underlying and latent parallelism even in the relatively free composition of works of prose."

Perhaps readers too will be amazed over the seemingly endless parallels to be discovered in these texts, not to mention the intricate language in which they are expressed. But for any given author, the scope of investigation cannot be endless; it requires delimitation or framing. The notion of setting a frame around a text recurs, especially in the later chapters, and most pointedly in Derrida's critique of Lacan. At this moment we can simply notice that deciding how much to enclose in a frame will affect what parallels are allowed to appear.

The first section of this book (including Poe's story and Lacan's essay) offers its own set of frames, meant to assist readers in working through Lacan's text. These frames include the following: (1) An overview of the Lacan essay that also considers the three untranslated additional pieces he wrote as introduction to or commentary on his own essay ("Présentation de la suite," "Introduction," "Parenthèse des parenthèses"; Lacan 1966a, 41–61). The overview is offered not as a substitute for or paraphrase of Lacan's text, but rather as an effort to contextualize Lacan's discussion of the purloined letter and the intersubjective structure it traverses. (2) An outline or map of the argument that attempts to show the thematic movement of Lacan's text. (3) A set of notes that provide additional information about Lacan's allusions and offer explications when he is obscure. Although obviously not without bias, this manner of approaching Lacan's text has been found to be useful elsewhere (Muller and Richardson 1982; Marcus 1984), and we present it here as no more than a guide to the reading of the text itself, before the other commentators have their say and in advance of the waves of controversy Lacan's essay has provoked. As with Lacan's other texts, we have found it useful to read the material aloud, several times (perhaps alternating with a reading of the overview, the outline, and the notes), when possible with others in seminar fashion. When reading Lacan, one can use whatever help is available.

The second section of the book, "On Psychoanalytic Reading," presents two approaches to the psychoanalytic reading of texts. The classically interpretive approach, often called "applied psychoanalysis," is illustrated by Marie Bonaparte's book *The Life and Works of Edgar Allan Poe: A Psycho-analytic Interpretation,* translated by John Rodker from her 1933 work *Edgar Poe: Etude psychanalytique.* Her analysis of Poe's tales has been called "a compelling fantasy, rather like a strange poem in its own right" (Wright 1984, 44). An alternative approach to psychoanalytic reading, taking Lacan into account, is provided by Shoshana Felman.

Marie Bonaparte (1882–1962) had a long-term, crucial, and often dramatic impact on the history of psychoanalysis in France and elsewhere (for an account of her life and work, and especially her relationship to Freud and the early years of psychoanalysis, see Bertin 1982). She was a descendant of Napoleon and married a Greek prince; after her father's death she pursued analysis with Freud, beginning in 1920 and continuing intermittently for several years. The two became friends, and she used her fortune to help support Freud's publishing house, to begin the first French psychoanalytic society, journal, and training institute, to assist Freud and hundreds of others in escaping from the Nazis, and to purchase and preserve Freud's letters to Wilhelm Fliess. She translated Freud into French and wrote extensively. Her essays on female sexuality, which appeared in 1951 in French and in 1953 in English, were reissued in a French paperback in 1977.

The first selection reprinted here is from the concluding chapters of *The Life and Works of Edgar Allan Poe,* about which Freud wrote in a letter to her: "It seems to me that it is the best part of this good book and the best thing you have ever written. These are not only applications of psychoanalysis but truly enrichments of it" (quoted in Bertin 1982, 184). The second selection, from the same book, deals specifically with "The Purloined Letter" and the role of castration. Bonaparte's analysis is taken up by Derrida, who will charge Lacan with having abused it. Shoshana Felman also examines Bonaparte's approach in order to contrast it with Lacan's new way of conducting psychoanalytic reading.

The third section of the book presents an orientation to Derrida to prepare the reader for Derrida's extensive critique of Lacan's Seminar. In his critique Derrida argues that Lacan has ignored the story's literary context and idealizes the notion of the letter as signifier. Derrida's critique is then examined in a now-classic paper by Barbara Johnson, and Johnson's argument is in turn critically assessed by Irene Harvey. Jane Gallop then offers her own reading of Lacan and Derrida.

In the fourth section we present alternative ways to read Poe's story. Ross Chambers shows us how speakers maintain authority over listeners, Norman Holland argues for a transactional perspective between reader and text, and Liahna Babener examines how the motif of the double runs through the story. François Peraldi opens up the temporal dimension of the tale and its underlying myth of vengeance. John Muller suggests that Lacan's analysis has Hegelian roots, with the notion and practice of negation pervading the Poe story and structuring its effects. In the face of all of this scrutiny, Poe's story maintains its integrity and continues to hold our interest.

Those to whom the editors of this book owe a debt of gratitude are almost beyond number. They count among them, in the first place, members of the staff of the Austen Riggs Center, Stockbridge, Mass., and graduate students of both the University of Massachusetts (Amherst) and Boston College, to whom its subject matter was initially presented. They include, too, the many colleagues of several disciplines who by reaction, comment, and criticism both formally and informally helped clarify for the editors their own intentions. To all these, who must remain nameless here, the editors can only express their sincere thanks. But there are two in particular without whose help the book could never have appeared. The editors wish to express their gratitude in a special way, then, to Daniel P. Schwartz, M.D., medical director of the Austen Riggs Center, for his continued encouragement and generous support of the project from its inception, and Mrs. Elizabeth Thomson, also at the Austen Riggs Center, for the meticulous care and unfailing graciousness with which she typed the manuscript and helped in the chore of proofreading.

NOTE

1. These details have been drawn from Symons (1981), Mabbott (1978), Bonaparte (1933), and *Encyclopedia Britannica,* 15th edition.

O N E   *Poe and Lacan*

1 ❧ Text of "The Purloined Letter," with Notes

THOMAS OLLIVE
MABBOTT

Poe wrote J. R. Lowell on July 2, 1844, that " 'The Purloined Letter,' forthcoming in 'The Gift' is perhaps the best of my tales of ratiocination." Many judicious critics have agreed, some even considering it the best of all Poe's stories. Its great merit lies in the fascination of the purely intellectual plot and in the absence of the sensational.

No exact source for Poe's plot has been pointed out, but Poe remarked on *not* seeking truth in a well in his prefatory "Letter to Mr.———" in *Poems* (1831); in a review of Alexander Slidell's *An American in England* in the *Southern Literary Messenger,* February 1836; and in "The Murders in the Rue Morgue," at note 29 (Mabbott 1978, 2: 572).

The story was apparently hastily completed for the annual in which it was first printed. On May 31, 1844, Poe wrote Edward L. Carey, a publisher, requesting a proof, because "the MS had many interlineations and erasures"—whereas most of his printer's copy was carefully prepared and unusually clean. (The untidy condition referred to is paralleled in the

Reprinted by permission of the publishers from *Collected Works of Edgar Allan Poe,* Volume III: *Tales and Sketches 1843–1849,* Thomas Ollive Mabbott, Ed., Cambridge, Mass.: The Belknap Press of Harvard University Press, Copyright © 1978 by the President and Fellows of Harvard College.

case of "The Murders in the Rue Morgue," but in no other surviving manuscript of a Poe story. The May 31 letter was printed in the first supplement of Ostrom's *Letters of Edgar Allan Poe* [see *American Literature*, November 1952].) The revision for the publication of "The Purloined Letter" in the *Tales* of 1845 was moderate but skillful, and the story was hardly changed at all in the J. Lorimer Graham copy.

The tale was reprinted in *Chambers' Edinburgh Journal* of November 30, 1844, with the following introduction:

The Gift is an American annual of great typographical elegance, and embellished with many beautiful engravings. It contains an article, which, for several reasons, appears to us so remarkable, that we leave aside several effusions of our ordinary contributors in order to make room for an abridgment of it. The writer, Mr. Edgar A. Poe, is evidently an acute observer of mental phenomena; and we have to thank him for one of the aptest illustrations which could well be conceived, of that curious play of two minds, in which one person, let us call him A, guesses what another, B, will do, judging that B will adopt a particular line of policy to circumvent A.

Some students have believed that the abridgment, which is well done, was by the author, but Poe's failure to adopt the version in 1845 argues that the changes were unauthorized. (A separate pamphlet reprint of the abridged text was issued in London in an edition of 325 copies in 1931, with an introduction by Dr. Jacob Schwarz, who wished to regard the Edinburgh version as the earliest—and omitted Chambers's introduction! Actually, *The Gift* was published in the fall of 1844—Wiley and Putnam advertised it for sale in the *New-York Daily Tribune* for September 24—and two or three weeks was ample time for copies to reach Edinburgh.)

Poe knew of the immediate success of his story abroad. In reviewing Poe's *Tales* in his *Aristidean* for October 1845, Dr. English, who had certainly discussed them with the author, wrote: "There is much made of nothing in 'The Purloined Letter,'—the story of which is simple; but the reasoning is remarkably clear, and directed solely to the required end. It first appeared in the 'Gift,' and was thence copied into Chambers' 'Edinburgh Journal,' as a most notable production."

An unsigned translation, "Une lettre volée," was published in the Paris *Magasin Pittoresque* of August 1845, and the story became popular in France. (Later on, a play founded on Poe's story by Victorien Sardou, *Les pattes de mouche* [1860], translated as *A Scrap of Paper* [1861], gave rise to the sinister phrase used contemptuously to describe the treaty broken in 1914 by the invasion of Belgium that began the First World War. See C. P. Cambiaire, *The Influence of Edgar Allan Poe in France* [1927, 286], for a synopsis of the literature on this curious subject.) Although some of the ideas are from books in which Poe was interested and though some of the characters are based on real people, it goes without saying that the real queen of France, Marie Amélie, was not portrayed.

TEXTS

(A) *The Gift: A Christmas, New Year, and Birthday Present,* 1845 (September 1844): 41–61; (B) *Tales* (1845), 200–218; (C) J. Lorimer Graham copy of *Tales,* with manuscript changes of 1849; (D) *Works* (1850), 1:262–80.

The J. Lorimer Graham copy of the *Tales* (C) is followed. Griswold's version (D) is merely a reprint of an unrevised copy of the *Tales* (B) and has no independent authority; it introduces three typographical errors.

Reprints

Chambers' Edinburgh Journal, November 30, 1844, abridged from *The Gift.* The abridgment was copied by: *Littell's Living Age* (Boston), January 18, 1845; the *Spirit of the Times* (Philadelphia), January 20 and 22, 1845; and the *New York Weekly News,* January 25, 1845, labeled "*Chambers' Journal via Littell's Living Age*" (for the last, see G. Thomas Tanselle, *Publications of the Bibliographical Society of America,* second quarter 1962).

🌿 *The Purloined Letter {C}*

Nil sapientiae odiosius acumine nimio.

Seneca

At Paris, just after dark one gusty evening in the autumn of 18—, I was
enjoying the twofold luxury of meditation and a meerschaum,[1] in company with my friend C. Auguste Dupin, in his little back library, or
book-closet, *au troisième,*[a] *No. 33, Rue Dunôt,* Faubourg St. Germain.[2]
For one hour at least we had maintained a profound silence; while each, to
any casual observer, might have seemed intently and exclusively occupied
with the curling eddies of smoke that oppressed the atmosphere of the
chamber. For myself, however, I was mentally discussing certain topics
which had formed matter for conversation between us at an earlier period
of the evening; I mean the affair of the Rue Morgue, and the mystery
attending the murder of Marie Rogêt.[b] I looked upon it, therefore, as
something of a coincidence, when the door of our apartment was thrown
open and admitted our old acquaintance, Monsieur G——, the Prefect
of the Parisian police.[3]

Translation from *Magasin Pittoresque,* August 1845, as "Une lettre volée," reprinted in
L'Echo de la Presse, August 25, 1845.

Motto omitted in A.
[a]troisiême, (A, B, C, D)
[b]Roget. (A)

We gave him a hearty welcome; for there was nearly half as much of the entertaining as of the contemptible about the man, and we had not seen him for several years. We had been sitting in the dark, and Dupin now arose for the purpose of lighting a lamp, but sat down again, without doing so, upon G.'s saying that he had called to consult us, or rather to ask the opinion of my friend, about some official business which had occasioned a great deal of trouble.

"If it is any point requiring reflection," observed Dupin, as he forebore to enkindle the wick, "we shall examine it to better purpose in the dark."

"That is another of your odd notions," said the Prefect, who had a fashion of calling every thing "odd" that was beyond his comprehension, and thus lived amid an absolute legion of "oddities."

"Very true," said Dupin, as he supplied his visiter with a pipe, and rolled towards him a^c comfortable chair.

"And what is the difficulty now?" I asked. "Nothing more in the assassination way, I hope?"

"Oh no; nothing of that nature. The fact is, the business is *very* simple indeed, and I make no doubt that we can manage it sufficiently well ourselves; but then I thought Dupin would like to hear the details of it, because it is so excessively *odd*."

"Simple and odd," said Dupin.

"Why, yes; and not exactly that, either. The fact is, we have all been a good deal puzzled because the affair *is* so simple, and yet baffles us altogether."

"Perhaps it is the very simplicity of the thing which puts you at fault," said my friend.

"What nonsense you *do* talk!" replied the Prefect, laughing heartily.

"Perhaps the mystery is a^d little *too* plain," said Dupin.

"Oh, good heavens! who ever heard of such an idea?"

"A little *too* self-evident."

"Ha! ha! ha!—ha! ha! ha!—ho! ho! ho!" roared^e our visiter, profoundly amused, "oh, Dupin, you will be the death of me yet!"[4]

"And what, after all, *is* the matter on hand?" I asked.

"Why, I will tell you," replied the Prefect, as he gave a long, steady, and contemplative puff, and settled himself in his chair. "I will tell you in

---

^ca very (A)
^dOmitted (D)
^eroared out (A)

a few words; but, before I begin, let me caution you that this is[f] an affair demanding the greatest secrecy, and that I should most probably lose the position I now hold, were it known that I confided it to any one."

"Proceed," said I.

"Or not," said Dupin.

"Well, then; I have received personal information, from a very high quarter, that a certain document of the last importance, has been purloined from the royal apartments. The individual who purloined it is known; this beyond a doubt; he was seen to take it. It is known, also, that it still remains in his possession."

"How is this known?" asked Dupin.

"It is clearly inferred," replied the Prefect, "from the nature of the document, and from the non-appearance of certain results which would at once arise from its passing *out* of the robber's possession;—that is to say, from his employing it as he must design in the end to employ it."

"Be a little more explicit," I said.

"Well, I may venture so far as to say that the paper gives its holder a certain power in a certain quarter where such power is immensely valuable." The Prefect was fond of the cant of diplomacy.

"Still I do not quite understand," said Dupin.

"No? Well; the disclosure of the document to a third person, who shall be nameless, would bring in question the honor of a personage of most exalted station; and this fact gives the holder of the document an ascendancy over the illustrious personage whose honor and peace are so jeopardized."

"But this ascendancy," I interposed, "would depend upon the robber's knowledge of the loser's knowledge of the robber. Who would dare—"

"The thief," said G., "is the Minister D——, who dares all things, those unbecoming as well as those becoming a man. The method of the theft was not less ingenious than bold. The document in question—a letter, to be frank—had been received by the personage robbed while alone in the royal *boudoir*. During its perusal she was suddenly interrupted by the entrance of the other exalted personage from whom especially it was her wish to conceal it. After a hurried and vain endeavor to thrust it in a drawer, she was forced to place it, open as it was, upon a table. The address, however, was uppermost, and, the contents thus unexposed, the letter escaped notice. At this juncture enters the Minister

---

[f]Omitted (D)

D——. His lynx eye immediately perceives the paper, recognises the handwriting of the address, observes the confusion of the personage addressed, and fathoms her secret. After some business transactions, hurried through in his ordinary manner, he produces a letter somewhat similar to the one in question, opens it, pretends to read it, and then places it in close juxtaposition to the other. Again he converses, for some fifteen minutes, upon the public affairs. At length, in taking leave, he takes also from the table the letter to which he had no claim. Its rightful owner saw, but, of course, dared not call attention to the act, in the presence of the third personage who stood at her elbow. The minister decamped; leaving his own letter—one of no importance—upon the table."

"Here, then," said Dupin to me, "you have precisely what you demand to make the ascendancy complete—the robber's knowledge of the loser's knowledge of the robber."

"Yes," replied the Prefect; "and the power thus attained has, for some months past, been wielded, for political purposes, to a very dangerous extent. The personage robbed is more thoroughly convinced, every day, of the necessity of reclaiming her letter. But this, of course, cannot be done openly. In fine, driven to despair, she has committed the matter to me."

"Than whom," said Dupin, amid a perfect whirlwind of smoke, "no more sagacious agent could, I suppose, be desired, or even imagined."

"You flatter me," replied the Prefect; "but it is possible that some such opinion may have been entertained."

"It is clear," said I, "as you observe, that the letter is still in possession of the minister; since it is this possession, and not any employment of the letter, which bestows the power. With the employment the power departs."

"True," said G.; "and upon this conviction I proceeded. My first care was to make thorough search of the minister's hotel;[5] and here my chief embarrassment lay in the necessity of searching without his knowledge. Beyond all things, I have been warned of the danger which would result from giving him reason to suspect our design."

"But," said I, "you are quite *au fait* in these investigations. The Parisian police have done this thing often before."

"O yes; and for this reason I did not despair. The habits of the minister gave me, too, a great advantage. He is frequently absent from home all night. His servants are by no means numerous. They sleep at a distance from their master's apartment,g and, being chiefly Neapolitans, are readily made drunk.6 I have keys, as you know, with which I can open any chamber or cabinet in Paris. For three months a night has not passed, during the greater part of which I have not been engaged, personally, in ransacking the D—— Hotel. My honor is interested, and, to mention a great secret, the reward is enormous. So I did not abandon the search until I had become fully satisfied that the thief is a more astute man than myself. I fancy that I have investigated every nook and corner of the premises in which it is possible that the paper can be concealed."

"But is it not possible," I suggested, "that although the letter may be in possession of the minister, as it unquestionably is, he may have concealed it elsewhere than upon his own premises?"

"This is barely possible," said Dupin. "The present peculiar condition of affairs at court, and especially of those intrigues in which D—— is known to be involved, would render the instant availability of the document—its susceptibility of being produced at a moment's notice—a point of nearly equal importance with its possession."

"Its susceptibility of being produced?" said I.

"That is to say, of being *destroyed,*" said Dupin.

"True," I observed; "the paper is clearly then upon the premises. As for its being upon the person of the minister, we may consider that as out of the question."

"Entirely," said the Prefect. "He has been twice waylaid, as if by footpads, and his person rigorously searched under my own inspection."

"You might have spared yourself this trouble," said Dupin. "D——, I presume, is not altogether a fool, and, if not, must have anticipated these waylayings, as a matter of course."

"Not *altogether* a fool," said G., "but then he's a poet, which I take to be only one remove from a fool."7

"True," said Dupin, after a long and thoughtful whiff from his meerschaum, "although I have been guilty of certain doggerel myself."

"Suppose you detail," I said, "the particulars of your search."8

"Why the fact is, we took our time, and we searched *every where.* I have had long experience in these affairs. I took the entire building, room by room; devoting the nights of a whole week to each. We examined, first, the furniture of each apartment. We opened every possible drawer; and I presume you know that, to a properly trained police agent, such a thing

---

gapartments, (A)

as a *secret* drawer is impossible. Any man is a dolt who permits a 'secret' drawer to escape him in a search of this kind. The thing is *so* plain. There is a certain amount of bulk—of space—to be accounted for in every cabinet. Then we have accurate rules. The fiftieth part of a line could not escape us. After the cabinets we took the chairs. The cushions we probed with the fine long needles you have seen me employ. From the tables we removed the tops."

"Why so?"

"Sometimes the top of a table, or other similarly arranged piece of furniture, is removed by the person wishing to conceal an article; then the leg is excavated, the article deposited within the cavity, and the top replaced. The bottoms and tops of bedposts are employed in the same way."

"But could not the cavity be detected by sounding?" I asked.

"By no means, if, when the article is deposited, a sufficient wadding of cotton be placed around it. Besides, in our case, we were obliged to proceed without noise."

"But you could not have removed—you could not have taken to pieces *all* articles of furniture in which it would have been possible to make a deposit in the manner you mention. A letter may be compressed into a thin spiral roll, not differing much in shape or bulk from a large knitting-needle, and in this form it might be inserted into the rung of a chair, for example. You did not take to pieces all the chairs?"

"Certainly not; but we did better—we examined the rungs of every chair in the hotel, and, indeed, the jointings of every description of furniture, by the aid of a most powerful microscope. Had there been any traces of recent disturbance we should not have failed to detect it instant-ly.[h] A single grain of gimlet-dust,[i] for example, would have been as obvious as an apple. Any disorder in the glueing—any unusual gaping in the joints—would have sufficed to insure detection."

"I presume[j] you looked to the mirrors, between the boards and the plates, and you probed the beds and the bed-clothes, as well as the curtains and carpets."

"That of course; and when we had absolutely completed every particle of the furniture in this way, then we examined the house itself. We

---

[h]*instanter.* (A)
[i]gimlet-dust, or saw-dust, (A)
[j]"I presume/" Of course (A)

divided its entire surface into compartments, which we numbered, so that none might be missed; then we scrutinized each individual square inch throughout the premises, including the two houses immediately adjoining, with the microscope, as before."

"The two houses adjoining!" I exclaimed; "you must have had a great deal of trouble."

"We had; but the reward offered is prodigious."

"You include the *grounds* about the houses?"

"All the grounds are paved with brick. They gave us comparatively little trouble. We examined the moss between the bricks, and found it undisturbed."[k]

"You looked among D———'s papers, of course, and into the books of the library?"

"Certainly; we opened every package and parcel; we not only opened every book, but we turned over every leaf in each volume, not contenting ourselves with a mere shake, according to the fashion of some of our police officers.[9] We also measured the thickness of every book-*cover,* with the most accurate admeasurement, and applied to each[l] the most jealous scrutiny of the microscope. Had any of the bindings been recently meddled with, it would have been utterly impossible that the fact should have escaped observation. Some five or six volumes, just from the hands of the binder, we carefully probed, longitudinally, with the needles."

"You explored the floors beneath the carpets?"

"Beyond doubt. We removed every carpet, and examined the boards with the microscope."

"And the paper on the walls?"

"Yes."

"You looked into the cellars?"

"We did."[m]

"Then," I said, "you have been making a miscalculation, and the letter is *not* upon the premises, as you suppose."

---

[k]*After this are two additional paragraphs:*
   "And the roofs?"
   "We surveyed every inch of the external surface, and probed carefully beneath every
   tile." (A)
[l]them (A)
[m]"We did."/"We did; and, as time and labour were no objects, we dug up every one of
them to the depth of four feet." (A)

"I fear you are right there," said the Prefect. "And now, Dupin, what would you advise me to do?"

"To make a thorough re-search of the premises."

"That is absolutely needless," replied G——. "I am not more sure that I breathe than I am that the letter is not at the Hotel."

"I have no better advice to give you," said Dupin. "You have, of course, an accurate description of the letter?"

"Oh yes!"—And here the Prefect, producing a memorandum-book, proceeded to read aloud a minute account of the internal, and especially of the external appearance of the missing document. Soon after finishing the perusal of this description, he took his departure, more entirely depressed in spirits than I had ever known the good gentleman before.

In about a month afterwards he paid us another visit, and found us occupied very nearly as before. He took a pipe and a chair and entered into some ordinary conversation. At length I said,—

"Well, but G——, what of the purloined letter? I presume you have at last made up your mind that there is no such thing as overreaching the Minister?"

"Confound him, say I—yes; I made the re-examination, however, as Dupin suggested—but it was all labor lost, as I knew it would be."

"How much was the reward offered, did you say?" asked Dupin.

"Why, a very great deal—a *very* liberal reward—I don't like to say how much, precisely; but one thing I *will* say, that I wouldn't mind giving my individual check for fifty thousand francs to any one who could obtain me that letter. The fact is, it is becoming of more and more importance every day; and the reward has been lately doubled. If it were trebled, however, I could do no more than I have done."

"Why, yes," said Dupin, drawlingly, between the whiffs[n] of his meerschaum, "I really—think, G——, you have not exerted yourself—to the utmost in this matter. You might—do a little more, I think, eh?"

"How?—in what way?"

"Why—puff, puff—you might—puff, puff—employ counsel in the matter, eh?—puff, puff, puff. Do you remember the story they tell of Abernethy?"

"No; hang Abernethy!"

"To be sure! hang him and welcome. But, once upon a time, a certain

---

[n]which (D) *misprint*

rich miser conceived the design of spunging upon this Abernethy for a medical opinion. [10] Getting up, for this purpose, an ordinary conversation in a private company, he insinuated his case to the physician, as that of an imaginary individual.

" 'We will suppose,' said the miser, 'that his symptoms are such and such; now, doctor, what would *you* have directed him to take?'

" 'Take!' said Abernethy, 'why, take *advice,* to be sure.' "

"But," said the Prefect, a little discomposed, "I am *perfectly* willing to take advice, and to pay for it. I would *really* give fifty thousand francs° to any one who would aid me in the matter."

"In that case," replied Dupin, opening a drawer, and producing a check-book, "you may as well fill me up a check for the amount mentioned. When you have signed it, I will hand you the letter."

I was astounded. The Prefect appeared absolutely thunderstricken. For some minutes he remained speechless and motionless, looking incredulously at my friend with open mouth, and eyes that seemed starting from their sockets; then, apparently recovering himself in some measure, he seized a pen, and after several pauses and vacant stares, finally filled up and signed a check for fifty thousand francs, and handed it across the table to Dupin. The latter examined it carefully and deposited it in his pocket-book; then, unlocking an *escritoire,* took thence a letter and gave it to the Prefect. This functionary grasped it in a perfect agony of joy, opened it with a trembling hand, cast a rapid glance at its contents, and then, scrambling and struggling to the door, rushed at length unceremoniously from the room and from the house, without having uttered aᴾ syllable since Dupin had requested him to fill up the check.

When he had gone, my friend entered into some explanations.

"The Parisian police," he said, "are exceedingly able in their way. They are persevering, ingenious, cunning, and thoroughly versed in the knowledge which their duties seem chiefly to demand. Thus, when G—— detailed to us his mode of searching the premises at the Hotel D——, I felt entire confidence in his having made a satisfactory investigation—so far as his labors extended."

"So far as his labors extended?" said I.

"Yes," said Dupin. "The measures adopted were not only the best of their kind, but carried out to absolute perfection. Had the letter been

---

°francs, every *centime* of it, (A)
ᴾa solitary (A)

deposited within the range of their search, these fellows would, beyond a question, have found it."

I merely laughed—but he seemed quite serious in all that he said.

"The measures, then," he continued, "were good in their kind, and well executed; their defect lay in their being inapplicable to the case, and to the man. A certain set of highly ingenious resources are, with the Prefect, a sort of Procrustean bed,[11] to which he forcibly adapts his designs. But he perpetually errs by being too deep or too shallow, for the matter in hand; and many a schoolboy is a better reasoner than he. I knew one about eight years of age, whose success at guessing in the game of 'even and odd' attracted universal admiration. This game is simple, and is played with marbles. One player holds in his hand a number of these toys, and demands of another whether that number is even or odd. If the guess is right, the guesser wins one; if wrong, he loses one. The boy to whom I allude won all the marbles of the school. Of course he had some principle of guessing; and this lay in mere observation and admeasurement of the astuteness of his opponents. For example, an arrant simpleton is his opponent, and, holding up his closed hand, asks, 'are they even or odd?' Our schoolboy replies, 'odd,' and loses; but upon the second trial he wins, for he then says to himself, "the simpleton had them even upon the first trial, and his amount of cunning is just sufficient to make him have them odd upon the second; I will therefore guess odd;— he guesses odd, and wins. Now, with a simpleton a degree above the first, he would have reasoned thus: 'This fellow finds that in the first instance I guessed odd, and, in the second, he will propose to himself, upon the first impulse, a simple variation from even to odd, as did the first simpleton; but then a second thought will suggest that this is too simple a variation, and finally he will decide upon putting it even as before. I will therefore guess even;'—he guesses even, and wins. Now this mode of reasoning in the schoolboy, whom his fellows termed 'lucky,'—what, in its last analysis, is it?"

"It is merely," I said, "an identification of the reasoner's intellect with that of his opponent."

"It is," said Dupin; "and, upon inquiring of the boy by what means he effected the *thorough* identification in which his success consisted, I received answer as follows: 'When I wish to find out how wise, or how stupid, or how good, or how wicked is any one, or what are his thoughts at the moment, I fashion the expression of my face, as accurately as possible, in accordance with the expression of his, and then wait to see what thoughts or sentiments arise in my mind or heart, as if to match or

correspond with the expression.'[12] This response of the schoolboy lies at
the bottom of all the spurious profundity which has been attributed to
Rochefoucault,[q] to La Bruyère,[r] to Machiavelli, and to Campanella."[13]

"And the identification," I said, "of the reasoner's intellect with that of
his opponent, depends, if I understand you aright, upon the accuracy
with which the opponent's intellect is admeasured."

"For its practical value it depends upon this," replied Dupin; "and the
Prefect and his cohort fail so frequently, first, by default of this identification, and, secondly, by ill-admeasurement, or rather through non-ad-
measurement, of the intellect with which they are engaged. They consider only their *own* ideas of ingenuity; and, in searching for anything
hidden, advert only to the modes in which *they* would have hidden it.
They are right in this much—that their own ingenuity is a faithful
representative of that of *the mass;* but when the cunning of the individual
felon is diverse in character from their own, the felon foils them, of
course. This always happens when it is above their own, and very usually
when it is below. They have no variation of principle in their investigations; at best, when urged by some unusual emergency—by some extraordinary reward—they extend or exaggerate their old modes of *practice,* without touching their principles. What, for example, in this case of
D——, has been done to vary the principle of action? What is all this
boring, and probing, and sounding, and scrutinizing with the microscope, and dividing the surface of the building into registered square
inches—what is it all but an exaggeration of *the application* of the one
principle or set of principles of search, which are based upon the one set of
notions regarding human ingenuity, to which the Prefect, in the long
routine of his duty, has been accustomed? Do you not see he has taken it
for granted that *all* men proceed to conceal a letter—not exactly in a
gimlet-hole bored in a chair-leg—but, at least, in *some* out-of-the-way
hole or corner suggested by the same tenor of thought which would urge
a man to secrete a letter in a gimlet-hole bored in a chair-leg? And do you
not see also, that such *recherchés*[s] nooks for concealment are adapted only
for ordinary occasions, and would be adopted only by ordinary intellects;
for, in all cases of concealment, a disposal of the article concealed—a
disposal of it in this *recherché* manner,—is, in the very first instance,

---

[q]*In all texts*
[r]Bougive, (A, B, C, D) *corrected editorially*
[s]recherches (A)

ᵗpresumable and presumed;ᵗ and thus its discovery depends, not at all upon the acumen, but altogether upon the mere care, patience, and determination of the seekers; and where the case is of importance—or, what amounts to the same thing in the policial eyes, when the reward is of magnitude—the qualities in question have *never* been known to fail. You will now understand what I meant in suggesting that, had the purloined letter been hidden any where within the limits of the Prefect's examination—in other words, had the principle of its concealment been comprehended within the principles of the Prefect—its discovery would have been a matter altogether beyond question. This functionary, however, has been thoroughly mystified; and the remote source of his defeat lies in the supposition that the Minister is a fool, because he has acquired renown as a poet. All fools are poets; this the Prefect *feels;*[14] and he is merely guilty of a *non distributio medii*[15] in thence inferring that all poets are fools."

"But is this really the poet?" I asked. "There are two brothers, I know; and both have attained reputation in letters. The Minister I believe has written learnedly on the Differential Calculus. He is a mathematician, and no poet."

"You are mistaken; I know him well; he is both. As poet *and* mathematician, he would reason well;ᵘ as mere mathematician, he could not have reasoned at all, and thus would have been at the mercy of the Prefect."

"You surprise me," I said, "by these opinions, which have been contradicted by the voice of the world. You do not mean to set at naught the well-digested idea of centuries. The mathematical reason has long beenᵛ regarded as *the* reason *par excellence.*"

"*'Il y a à parier,'* "ʷ replied Dupin, quoting from Chamfort, " *'que toute idée publique, toute convention reçue, est une sottise, car elle a convenuˣ au plus grand nombre.'*ʸ[16] The mathematicians, I grant you, have done their best to promulgate the popular error to which you allude, and which is none the less an error for its promulgation as truth. With an art worthy a better

---

ᵗ . . . ᵗpresumed and presumable; (A)
ᵘwell; as poet, profoundly; (A)
ᵛlong been/been long (A)
ʷ*parièr,'* (A, B, C, D) *accent deleted editorially*
ˣ*convenue* (A, B, C, D) *corrected editorially*
ʸ*This sentence not italicized* (A)

cause, for example, they have insinuated the term 'analysis' into application to algebra. The French are the originators of this particular deception; but if a term is of any importance—if words derive any value from applicability—then 'analysis' conveys 'algebra' about as much as, in Latin '*ambitus*' implies 'ambition,' '*religio*' 'religion,' or '*homines honesti,*' a set of *honorable* men." [17]

"You have a quarrel on hand, I see," said I, "with some of the algebraists of Paris; but proceed." [18]

"I dispute the availability, and thus the value, of that reason which is cultivated in any especial form other than the abstractly logical. I dispute, in particular, the reason educed by mathematical study. The mathematics are the science of form and quantity; mathematical reasoning is merely logic applied to observation upon form and quantity. The great error lies in supposing that even the truths of what is called *pure* algebra, are abstract or general truths. And this error is so egregious that I am confounded at the universality with which it has been received. Mathematical axioms are *not* axioms of general truth. What is true of *relation*—of form and quantity—is often grossly false in regard to morals, for example. In this latter science it is very usually *un*true that the aggregated parts are equal to the whole. In chemistry also the axiom fails. In the consideration of motive it fails; for two motives, each of a given value, have not, necessarily, a value when united, equal to the sum of their values apart. There are numerous other mathematical truths which are only truths within the limits of *relation.* But the mathematician argues, from his *finite truths,* through habit, as if they were of an absolutely general applicability—as the world indeed imagines them to be. Bryant, in his very learned 'Mythology,' mentions an analogous source of error, when he says that 'although the Pagan fables are not believed, yet we forget ourselves continually, and make inferences from them as existing realities.' [19] With the algebraists, [z] however, who are Pagans themselves, the 'Pagan fables' *are* believed, and the inferences are made, not so much through lapse of memory, as through an unaccountable addling of the brains. In short, I never yet encountered the mere mathematician who could be trusted out of equal roots, or one who did not clandestinely hold it as a point of his faith that $x^2 + px$ was absolutely and unconditionally equal to q. Say to one of these gentlemen, by way of experiment, if you please, that you believe occasions may occur where $x^2 + px$ is *not* al-

---

[z]algebraist, (A)

together equal to q, and, having made him understand what you mean, get out of his reach as speedily as convenient, for, beyond doubt, he will endeavor to knock you down.

"I mean to say," continued Dupin, while I merely laughed at his last observations, "that if the Minister had been no more than a mathematician, the Prefect would have been under no necessity of giving me this check.aa I knew him, however, as both mathematician and poet, and my measures were adapted to his capacity, with reference to the circumstances by which he was surrounded. I knew him as a courtier, too, and as a bold *intriguant*. Such a man, I considered, could not fail to be aware of the ordinary policial modes of action. He could not have failed to anticipate—and events have proved that he did not fail to anticipate—the waylayings to which he was subjected. He must have foreseen, I reflected, the secret investigations of his premises. His frequent absences from home at night, which were hailed by the Prefect as certain aids to his success, I regarded only as *ruses,* to afford opportunity for thorough search to the police, and thus the sooner to impress them with the conviction to which G——, in fact, did finally arrive—the conviction that the letter was not upon the premises. I felt, also, that the whole train of thought, which I was at some pains in detailing to you just now, concerning the invariable principle of policial action in searches for articles concealed—I felt that this whole train of thought would necessarily pass through the mind of the Minister. It would imperatively lead him to despise all the ordinary *nooks* of concealment. *He* could not, I reflected, be so weak as not to see that the most intricate and remote recess of his hotel would be as open as his commonest closets to the eyes, to the probes, to the gimlets, and to the microscopes of the Prefect. I saw, in fine, that he would be driven, as a matter of course, to *simplicity,* if not deliberately induced to it as a matter of choice. You will remember, perhaps, how desperately the Prefect laughed when I suggested, upon our first interview, that it was just possible this mystery troubled him so much on account of its being so *very* self-evident."

"Yes," said I, "I remember his merriment well. I really thought he would have fallen into convulsions."

"The material world," continued Dupin, "abounds with very strict analogies to the immaterial; and thus some color of truth has been given

---

aa*After this* Had he been no more than a poet, I think it probable that he would have foiled us all. (A) to the rhetorical dogma, that metaphor, or simile, may be made to strengthen an argument, as well as to embellish a description. The principle of the *vis inertiae,*[20] for example,[bb] seems to be identical in physics and metaphysics. It is not more true in the former, that a large body is with more difficulty set in motion than a smaller one, and that its subsequent *momentum*[cc] is commensurate with this difficulty, than it is, in the latter, that intellects of the vaster capacity, while more forcible, more constant, and more eventful in their movements than those of inferior grade, are yet the less readily moved, and more embarrassed and full of hesitation in the first few steps of their progress. Again: have you ever noticed which of the street signs, over the shop-doors, are the most attractive of attention?"

"I have never given the matter a thought," I said.

"There is a game of puzzles," he resumed, "which is played upon a map. One party playing requires another to find a given word—the name of town, river, state or empire—any word, in short, upon the motley and perplexed surface of the chart. A novice in the game generally seeks to embarrass his opponents by giving them the most minutely lettered names; but the adept selects such words as stretch, in large characters, from one end of the chart to the other. These, like the over-largely lettered signs and placards of the street, escape observation by dint of being excessively obvious; and here the physical oversight is precisely analogous with the moral inapprehension by which the intellect suffers to pass unnoticed those considerations which are too obtrusively and too palpably self-evident. But this is a point, it appears, somewhat above or beneath the understanding of the Prefect. He never once thought it probable, or possible, that the Minister had deposited the letter immediately beneath the nose of the whole world, by way of best preventing any portion of that world from perceiving it.[21]

"But the more I reflected upon the daring, dashing, and discriminating ingenuity of D——; upon the fact that the document must always have been *at hand,* if he intended to use it to good purpose; and upon the decisive evidence, obtained by the Prefect, that it was not hidden within the limits of that dignitary's ordinary search—the more satisfied I became that, to conceal this letter, the Minister had resorted to the comprehensive and sagacious expedient of not attempting to conceal it at all.

[bb]example, with the amount of *momentum* proportionate with it and consequent upon it, (A)

[cc]*impetus* (A)

"Full of these ideas, I prepared myself with a pair of green spectacles,[22] and called one fine morning, quite by accident, at the Ministerial
hotel. I found D—— at home, yawning, lounging, and dawdling, as
usual, and pretending to be in the last extremity of *ennui*. He is, perhaps,
the most really energetic human being now alive—but that is only when
nobody sees him.

"To be even with him, I complained of my weak eyes, and lamented
the necessity of the spectacles, under cover of which I cautiously and
thoroughly surveyed the[dd] apartment, while seemingly intent only upon
the conversation of my host.

"I paid especial attention to a large writing-table near which he sat,
and upon which lay confusedly, some miscellaneous letters and other
papers, with one or two musical instruments and a few books. Here,
however, after a long and very deliberate scrutiny, I saw nothing to excite
particular suspicion.

"At length my eyes, in going the circuit of the room, fell upon a
trumpery fillagree card-rack of pasteboard, that hung dangling by a dirty
blue ribbon[ee] from a little brass knob just beneath the middle of the
mantel-piece. In this rack, which had three or four compartments, were
five or six visiting cards and a solitary letter. This last was much soiled
and crumpled. It was torn nearly in two, across the middle—as if a
design, in the first instance, to tear it entirely up as worthless, had been
altered, or stayed, in the second. It had a large black seal, bearing the
D—— cipher *very* conspicuously, and was addressed, in a diminutive
female hand, to D——, the minister, himself. It was thrust carelessly,
and even, as it seemed, contemptuously, into one of the upper[ff] divisions
of the rack.

"No sooner had I glanced at this letter, than I concluded it to be that of
which I was in search. To be sure, it was, to all appearance radically
different from the one of which the Prefect had read us so minute a
description. Here the seal was large and black, with the D—— cipher;
there it was small and red, with the ducal arms of the S—— family.
Here, the address, to the Minister, was diminutive and feminine; there
the superscription, to a certain royal personage, was markedly bold and
decided; the size alone formed a point of correspondence. But, then, the
radicalness of these differences, which was excessive; the dirt; the soiled

---

[dd]the whole (A, B, D)
[ee]riband, (A)
[ff]uppermost (A, B, D)

and torn condition of the paper, so inconsistent with the *true* methodical habits of D——, and so suggestive of a design to delude the beholder into an idea of the worthlessness of the document; these things, together with the hyperobtrusive situation of this document, full in the view of every visiter, and thus exactly in accordance with the conclusions to which I have previously arrived; these things, I say, were strongly corroborative of suspicion, in one who came with the intention to suspect.

"I protracted my visit as long as possible, and, while I maintained a most animated discussion with the Minister, on*gg* a topic which I knew well had never failed to interest and excite him, I kept my attention really riveted upon the letter. In this examination, I committed to memory its external appearance and arrangement in the rack; and also fell, at length, upon a discovery which set at rest whatever trivial doubt I might have entertained. In scrutinizing the edges of the paper, I observed them to be more *chafed* than seemed necessary. They presented the *broken* appearance which is manifested when a stiff paper, having been once folded and pressed with a folder, is refolded in a reversed direction, in the same creases or edges which had formed the original fold. This discovery was sufficient. It was clear to me that the letter had been turned, as a glove, inside out, re-directed, and re-sealed.[23] I bade the Minister good morning, and took my departure at once, leaving a gold snuff-box upon the table.

"The next morning I called for the snuff-box, when we resumed, quite eagerly, the conversation of the preceding day. While thus engaged, however, a loud report, as if of a pistol, was heard immediately beneath the windows of the hotel, and was succeeded by a series of fearful screams, and the shoutings of a*hh* mob. D—— rushed to a casement, threw it open, and looked out. In the meantime, I stepped to the card-rack, took the letter, put it in my pocket, and replaced it by a *fac-simile*[ii] (so far as regards externals)[ii] which I had carefully prepared at my lodgings;[jj] imitating the D—— cipher, very readily, by means of a seal formed of bread.

"The disturbance in the street had been occasioned by the frantic behavior of a man with a musket. He had fired it among a crowd of women and children. It proved, however, to have been without ball, and the fellow was suffered to go his way as a lunatic or a drunkard. When he had gone, D—— came from the window, whither I had followed him

---

immediately upon securing the object in view. Soon afterwards I bade him farewell. The pretended lunatic was a man in my own pay."

"But what purpose had you," I asked, "in replacing the letter by a *fac-simile?* Would it not have been better, at the first visit, to have seized it openly, and departed?"

"D——," replied Dupin, "is a desperate man, and a man of nerve. His hotel, too, is not without attendants devoted to his interests. Had I made the wild attempt you suggest, I might[kk] never have left the Ministerial presence alive. The good people of Paris might[ll] have heard of me no more. But I had an object apart from these considerations. You know my political prepossessions. In this matter, I act as a partisan of the lady concerned. For eighteen months the Minister has had her in his power. She has now him in hers;[mm] since, being unaware that the letter is not in his possession, he will proceed with his exactions as if it was. Thus will he inevitably commit himself, at once, to his political destruction. His downfall, too, will not be more precipitate than awkward. It is all very well to talk about the *facilis descensus Averni;*[24] but in all kinds of climbing, as Catalani[nn] said of singing, it is far more easy to get up than to come down.[25] In the present instance I have no sympathy—at least no pity—for him who descends. He is that *monstrum horrendum,*[26] an unprincipled man of genius. I confess, however, that I should like very well to know the precise character of his thoughts, when, being defied by her whom the Prefect terms 'a certain personage,' he is reduced to opening the letter which I left for him in the card-rack."

"How? did you put any thing particular in it?"

"Why—it did not seem altogether right to leave the interior blank—that would have been insulting. D——,[oo] at Vienna once, did me an evil turn, which I told him, quite good-humoredly, that I should remember. So, as I knew he would feel some curiosity in regard to the identity of the person who had outwitted him, I thought it a pity not to give him a clue. He is well acquainted with my MS., and I just copied into the middle of the blank sheet the words—

——Un[pp] dessein si funeste,
S'il n'est digne d'Atrée, est digne de Thyeste.

They are to be found in Crébillon's 'Atrée.' "[27]

[kk]should (A)

[mm]hers;/hers—(A, B, D)

[oo]To be sure, D——, (A)

[ll]would (A)

[nn]Catalini (A) *misprint*

[pp]——Un/ " '—— ——Un (B, D)

NOTES

Motto: The Latin quotation ascribed to Seneca has not been located. Poe used it first in the 1843 version of "The Murders in the Rue Morgue," near the end of the tale, but he omitted it in later texts. It means "Nothing is more hateful to wisdom than too much cunning." Compare Dupin's comment: "The Parisian police, so much extolled for *acumen,* are cunning but no more."

1. A meerschaum pipe is also mentioned in "The Light-House."

2. Dupin lived up three flights of stairs, on what we call the fourth floor. The name of the street is imaginary, as are a number of the street names in Poe's other Dupin stories.

3. The chief of police in Paris from 1831 to 1836 was Henri-Joseph Gisquet, who died in February 1866.

4. Compare *Politian* 2.3–4, "I shall die, Castiglione, I shall die . . . of laughing!"

5. Hôtel means mansion or town residence; the word is capitalized later when used in connection with the owner's name.

6. Compare getting rid of the servants in "The Cask of Amontillado."

7. See *Midsummer Night's Dream,* 5.1.7–8, "The lunatic, the lover, and the poet / Are of imagination all compact."

8. The method of search described may come from some account of Napoleon's detective Vidocq.

9. In a letter of August 28, 1849, Poe instructed Mrs. Clemm how to excuse the loss of a drawing of Elmira Shelton: "Just copy the following words in your letter: I . . . cannot find it anywhere. I took down all the books and shook them one by one."

10. The great British surgeon John Abernethy (1764–1831) was very gruff, but Dupin's story is told about another surgeon, Sir Isaac Pennington (1745–1817), at p. 31 of *Nuts to Crack* (Philadelphia, 1835), a jest book Poe reviewed in the *Southern Literary Messenger* [hereafter cited as *SLM*], December 1835.

11. Procrustean bed—rigorous, ruthless, and arbitrary limits—derived from Procrustes, a legendary Attic robber, slain by Theseus, who fitted his victims to a bed by stretching the short and cutting the feet off the tall.

12. The system of mind reading used by the schoolboy has long been attributed to Tommaso Campanella. An account of how he uncovered his inquisitor's thoughts appears in the *Voyage to the Moon* of Cyrano de Bergerac (1619–55), a work referred to in Poe's "Hans Phaall." [S. L. Varnado, in *Poe Newsletter,* October 1968, quotes a description by Edmund Burke of Campanella's system.] Horace Binney Wallace, in *Stanley* (1838), a book Poe drew on frequently, said (2:242):

It was remarked by the ingenious Campanella that when he wished to discover the leading characteristics of any one whom he saw, he arranged his features into a similitude with theirs and then observed what emotions rose within his heart to *play up,* as it were, to that expression of countenance; in the same manner, if we dispose our interests, and wishes, which may be called the features of feeling, into a conformity with those of others, we shall find that their thoughts and counsels start naturally up in our mind.

"The Duc de L'Omelette" contains references to its hero's use of physiognomy.

13. Poe's spelling (Rochefoucault) for François de la Rochefoucauld (1630–80) is found in the first edition of his maxims listed in the British Museum Catalogue as carrying the author's name on the title page: *Reflexiones ou sentences et maximes morales de Monsieur de la Rochefoucault* . . . (Amsterdam, 1705); in Isaac D'Israeli's *Curiosities of Literature,* so frequently used by Poe; and in *The Duke de la Rochefoucault's Maxims and Moral Reflections* (New York: G. and C. Carvill, 1835), which was apparently based on an "improved edition" (with the same spelling) issued in Edinburgh in 1796. "La Bougive," which I have emended to La Bruyère, is undoubtedly a printer's error, from a misreading of Poe's manuscript. Poe spelled the name correctly in crediting the motto for "The Man of the Crowd" and in his review of Longstreet's *Georgia Scenes* (*SLM,* March 1836), where he also mentioned Rochefoucault. Machiavelli was mentioned in Satanic company in "Bon-Bon," along with Rochefoucault and Seneca in the introduction to "Pinakidia" (*SLM,* August 1836, reworked in "Marginalia," no. 46, *Democratic Review,* December 1844, 581); with Campanella was represented on the bookshelves of the House of Usher (*Burton's Magazine,* September 1839); and with Rochefoucault was mentioned in a review of *The Canons of Good Breeding* (*Burton's,* November 1839).

14. In "Lionizing" we read that "Sir Positive Paradox . . . observed that all fools were philosophers, and that all philosophers were fools."

15. *Non distributio medii*—the fallacy of the undistributed middle—is ignoring the fact that if all A's are B's, all B's may not necessarily be A's.

16. Poe quotes from the French cynic Sébastien-Roch Nicolas, called Chamfort (1740–94), *Maximes et pensées,* 2:42: "It is safe to wager that every idea that is public property, every accepted convention, is a bit of stupidity, for it has suited the majority." Poe had already used the French quotation in reviewing J. P. Robertson's *Solomon Seesaw* in *Burton's,* September 1839, *Writings of Charles Sprague* in *Graham's,* May 1841, and Longfellow's *Ballads and Other Poems* in *Graham's,* March 1842; he used it again later in "Marginalia," no. 250 (*SLM,* June 1849, 338).

17. In classical Latin *ambitus* means seeking office, *religio* is superstition, and *homines honesti* is Cicero's term for men of his party. Poe also referred to *religio* in the first version of "Metzengerstein" and in "Marginalia," no. 176 (*Graham's,* November 1846, 246).

18. J. J. Cohane, in his book list, April 1859 (item 86, catalogue 30), pointed out that Poe's source for Dupin's argument in the following paragraph is Horace Binney Wallace's novel *Stanley* (cited in no. 12 above), 1:206–8:

As a means . . . of cultivating the intellect . . . I consider mathematics as a study of little value as compared with moral logic. . . . The axioms of mathematics are not axioms of general truth; they are derived from the consideration of form and quantity, and it does not follow that what is true of form and quantity is true of moral principles or of human motives. . . . In morals, things are considered and compared by their categories or qualities, whereof each thing has many, according to the view and purpose in reference to which the thing is looked at; what is affirmed of a thing in contemplation of one category is not true of it in respect of another, nor true in respect of that category in reference to all considerations. . . . Thus, the position, that two things being equal to a third are equal to one another, may be true universally if we define "equal" with absolute strictness, but, in use, will constantly lead to the logical fallacy of an undistributed middle term; and if you will examine the logic of a mathematician you will find the error of a non-distribu~d medii very often committed. Another mathematical axiom which is not true in the scope of general reason is, that all the parts taken together are equal to the whole. This is not always true of physical science, and is generally false in morals. It is not true in chymical combination, and the instinct of a chymist's mind would be to deny the axiom; it is not necessarily true that if two motives separately have given values, these motives united will have a value equal to their sum. . . . I might name to you many other principles of mathematical science which are not true beyond the boundaries of that science. In truth, mathematics is a composite science . . . and not a fundamental exhibition of reason; it is *logic applied to the sciences of form and quantity*. . . . There is danger that the mathematician will mistake the axioms of his science for the principles of reason, and will apply universally what is true only of a particular system.

19. The remark of Jacob Bryant comes from *A New System of Ancient Mythology*, 3d ed. (1807), 2:173. Poe referred to it in "Pinakidia," no. 70 (*SLM*, August 1836, 577), and used it again in *Eureka*.

20. *Vis inertiae* is the force of inertia.

21. Compare: "Just as the moderately-sized shop-signs are better adapted to their object than those which are Brobdignagian, so, in at least three cases out of five, is a fact or a reason overlooked solely on account of being excessively obvious. It is almost impossible to see a thing that is immediately beneath one's nose" ("Does the Drama of the Day Deserve Support?" in *Evening Mirror,* January 9, and *Weekly Mirror,* January 18, 1845).

22. Green spectacles are mentioned also in "The Folio Club," "Bon-Bon," and "The Mystery of Marie Rogêt."

23. The letter was on an old-fashioned four-page sheet, with text on the first and address on the last page, and so could be turned inside out. The minister erred in using his own seal.

24. *Facilis descensus Averno*—"The descent to Hades is easy"—comes from Vergil *Aeneid* 6.126. Poe used the Latin words earlier in a criticism of Miss Sedgwick's *Tales and Sketches* in *SLM,* January 1836.

25. Where the remark of Angelica Catalani (1779–1849), Italian opera star and teacher, is recorded is not known. Poe used her name punningly in "A Decided Loss."

26. "A terrifying monster" is from the *Aeneid* 3.658 and is also quoted in "The System of Doctor Tarr and Professor Fether."

27. The quotation, "So baleful a plan, if unworthy of Atreus, is worthy of Thyestes," comes from *Atrée et Thyeste* (1707), 5.4.13–15, by Prosper-Jolyot de Crébillon (1674–1762). Poe had used it previously in a review of Thomas Campbell's *Life of Petrarch* in *Graham's Magazine*, September 1841, and earlier had quoted Crébillon's *Xerxes* in the motto to "Epimanes" and referred to the play in "The Murders in the Rue Morgue." A brief comment on Crébillon is quoted in "Pinakidia," no. 129 (*SLM*, August 1836, 580) and repeated in "Marginalia," no. 24 (*Democratic Review*, November 1844, 488).

2 ❧ Jacques Lacan, Seminar on "The Purloined Letter"

Translated by
JEFFREY MEHLMAN

Und wenn es uns glückt,
Und wenn es sich schickt,
So sind es Gedanken.

Our inquiry has led us to the point of recognizing that the repetition automatism (*Wiederholungszwang*) finds its basis in what we have called the *insistence* of the signifying chain. We have elaborated that notion itself as a correlate of the *ex-sistence* (or: eccentric place) in which we must necessarily locate the subject of the unconscious if we are to take Freud's discovery seriously. As is known, it is in the realm of experience inaugurated by psychoanalysis that we may grasp along what imaginary lines the human organism, in the most intimate recesses of its being, manifests its capture in a *symbolic* dimension.

The lesson of this seminar is intended to maintain that these imaginary incidences, far from representing the essence of our experience, reveal only what in it remains inconsistent unless they are related to the symbolic chain which binds and orients them.

We realize, of course, the importance of these imaginary impregnations (*Prägung*) in those partializations of the symbolic alternative which give the symbolic chain its appearance. But we maintain that it is the

Reprinted by permission from *French Freud: Structural Studies in Psychoanalysis, Yale French Studies* 48 (1972):39–72.

specific law of that chain which governs those psychoanalytic effects that are decisive for the subject: such as foreclosure (*Verwerfung*), repression (*Verdrängung*), denial (*Verneinung*) itself—specifying with appropriate emphasis that these effects follow so faithfully the displacement (*Entstellung*) of the signifier that imaginary factors, despite their inertia, figure only as shadows and reflections in the process.

But this emphasis would be lavished in vain, if it served, in your opinion, only to abstract a general type from phenomena whose particularity in our work would remain the essential thing for you, and whose original arrangement could be broken up only artificially.

Which is why we have decided to illustrate for you today the truth which may be drawn from that moment in Freud's thought under study—namely, that it is the symbolic order which is constitutive for the subject—by demonstrating in a story the decisive orientation which the subject receives from the itinerary of a signifier.

It is that truth, let us note, which makes the very existence of fiction possible. And in that case, a fable is as appropriate as any other narrative for bringing it to light—at the risk of having the fable's coherence put to the test in the process. Aside from that reservation, a fictive tale even has the advantage of manifesting symbolic necessity more purely to the extent that we may believe its conception arbitrary.

Which is why, without seeking any further, we have chosen our example from the very story in which the dialectic of the game of even or odd—from whose study we have but recently profited—occurs. It is, no doubt, no accident that this tale revealed itself propitious to pursuing a course of inquiry which had already found support in it.

As you know, we are talking about the tale which Baudelaire translated under the title "La lettre volée." At first reading, we may distinguish a drama, its narration, and the conditions of that narration.

We see quickly enough, moreover, that these components are necessary and that they could not have escaped the intentions of whoever composed them.

The narration, in fact, doubles the drama with a commentary without which no mise en scène would be possible. Let us say that the action would remain, properly speaking, invisible from the pit—aside from the fact that the dialogue would be expressly and by dramatic necessity devoid of whatever meaning it might have for an audience: in other words, nothing of the drama could be grasped, neither seen nor heard, without, dare we say, the twilighting which the narration, in each scene, casts on the point of view that one of the actors had while performing it.

There are two scenes, the first of which we shall straightway designate the primal scene, and by no means inadvertently, since the second may be considered its repetition in the very sense we are considering today.

The primal scene is thus performed, we are told, in the royal *boudoir,* so that we suspect that the person of the highest rank, called the "exalted personage," who is alone there when she receives a letter, is the Queen. This feeling is confirmed by the embarrassment into which she is plunged by the entry of the other exalted personage, of whom we have already been told prior to this account that the knowledge he might have of the letter in question would jeopardize for the lady nothing less than her honor and safety. Any doubt that he is in fact the King is promptly dissipated in the course of the scene which begins with the entry of the Minister D——. At that moment, in fact, the Queen can do no better than to play on the King's inattentiveness by leaving the letter on the table "face down, address uppermost." It does not, however, escape the Minister's lynx eye, nor does he fail to notice the Queen's distress and thus to fathom her secret. From then on everything transpires like clockwork. After dealing in his customary manner with the business of the day, the Minister draws from his pocket a letter similar in appearance to the one in his view, and, having pretended to read it, he places it next to the other. A bit more conversation to amuse the royal company, whereupon, without flinching once, he seizes the embarrassing letter, making off with it, as the Queen, on whom none of his maneuver has been lost, remains unable to intervene for fear of attracting the attention of her royal spouse, close at her side at that very moment.

Everything might then have transpired unseen by a hypothetical spectator of an operation in which nobody falters, and whose *quotient* is that the Minister has filched from the Queen her letter and that—an even more important result than the first—the Queen knows that he now has it, and by no means innocently.

A *remainder* that no analyst will neglect, trained as he is to retain whatever is significant, without always knowing what to do with it: the letter, abandoned by the Minister, and which the Queen's hand is now free to roll into a ball.

Second scene: in the Minister's office. It is in his hotel, and we know— from the account the Prefect of Police has given Dupin, whose specific genius for solving enigmas Poe introduces here for the second time—that the police, returning there as soon as the Minister's habitual, nightly absences allow them to, have searched the hotel and its surroundings from top to bottom for the last eighteen months. In vain—although everyone can deduce from the situation that the Minister keeps the letter within reach.

Dupin calls on the Minister. The latter receives him with studied nonchalance, affecting in his conversation romantic ennui. Meanwhile Dupin, whom this pretense does not deceive, his eyes protected by green glasses, proceeds to inspect the premises. When his glance catches a rather crumpled piece of paper—apparently thrust carelessly into a division of an ugly pasteboard card rack, hanging gaudily from the middle of the mantelpiece—he already knows that he's found what he's looking for. His conviction is reinforced by the very details which seem to contradict the description he has of the stolen letter, with the exception of the format, which remains the same.

Whereupon he has but to withdraw, after "forgetting" his snuffbox on the table, in order to return the following day to reclaim it—armed with a facsimile of the letter in its present state. As an incident in the street, prepared for the proper moment, draws the Minister to the window, Dupin in turn seizes the opportunity to snatch the letter while substituting the imitation and has only to maintain the appearances of a normal exit.

Here as well all has transpired, if not without noise, at least without any commotion. The quotient of the operation is that the Minister no longer has the letter, but far from suspecting that Dupin is the culprit who has ravished it from him, knows nothing of it. Moreover, what he is left with is far from insignificant for what follows. We shall return to what brought Dupin to inscribe a message on his counterfeit letter. Whatever the case, the Minister, when he tries to make use of it, will be able to read these words, written so that he may recognize Dupin's hand: ". . . *Un dessein si funeste / S'il n'est digne d'Atrée est digne de Thyeste,*" whose source, Dupin tells us, is Crébillon's *Atrée.*

Need we emphasize the similarity of these two sequences? Yes, for the resemblance we have in mind is not a simple collection of traits chosen only in order to delete their difference. And it would not be enough to retain those common traits at the expense of the others for the slightest truth to result. It is rather the intersubjectivity in which the two actions are motivated that we wish to bring into relief, as well as the three terms through which it structures them.

The special status of these terms results from their corresponding simultaneously to the three logical moments through which the decision is precipitated and the three places it assigns to the subjects among whom it constitutes a choice.

That decision is reached in a glance's time.[1] For the maneuvers which follow, however stealthily they prolong it, add nothing to that glance, nor does the deferring of the deed in the second scene break the unity of that moment.

This glance presupposes two others, which it embraces in its vision of the breach left in their fallacious complementarity, anticipating in it the occasion for larceny afforded by that exposure. Thus three moments, structuring three glances, borne by three subjects, incarnated each time by different characters.

The first is a glance that sees nothing: the King and the police.

The second, a glance which sees that the first sees nothing and deludes itself as to the secrecy of what it hides: the Queen, then the Minister.

The third sees that the first two glances leave what should be hidden exposed to whoever would seize it: the Minister, and finally Dupin.

In order to grasp in its unity the intersubjective complex thus described, we would willingly seek a model in the technique legendarily attributed to the ostrich attempting to shield itself from danger; for that technique might ultimately be qualified as political, divided as it here is among three partners: the second believing itself invisible because the first has its head stuck in the ground, and all the while letting the third calmly pluck its rear; we need only enrich its proverbial denomination by a letter, producing *la politique de l'autruiche,* for the ostrich itself to take on forever a new meaning.

Given the intersubjective modulus of the repetitive action, it remains to recognize in it a *repetition automatism* in the sense that interests us in Freud's text.

The plurality of subjects, of course, can be no objection for those who are long accustomed to the perspectives summarized by our formula: *the unconscious is the discourse of the Other.* And we will not recall now what the notion of the *immixture of subjects,* recently introduced in our reanalysis of the dream of Irma's injection, adds to the discussion.

What interests us today is the manner in which the subjects relay each other in their displacement during the intersubjective repetition.

We shall see that their displacement is determined by the place which a pure signifier—the purloined letter—comes to occupy in their trio. And that is what will confirm for us its status as repetition automatism.

It does not, however, seem excessive, before pursuing this line of inquiry, to ask whether the thrust of the tale and the interest we bring to it—to the extent that they coincide—do not lie elsewhere.

May we view as simply a rationalization (in our gruff jargon) the fact that the story is told to us as a police mystery?

In truth, we should be right in judging that fact highly dubious as soon as we note that everything which warrants such mystery concerning a crime or offense—its nature and motives, instruments and execution, the procedure used to discover the author, and the means employed to convict him—is carefully eliminated here at the start of each episode.

The act of deceit is, in fact, from the beginning as clearly known as the intrigues of the culprit and their effects on his victim. The problem, as exposed to us, is limited to the search for and restitution of the object of that deceit, and it seems rather intentional that the solution is already obtained when it is explained to us. Is *that* how we are kept in suspense? Whatever credit we may accord the conventions of a genre for provoking a specific interest in the reader, we should not forget that "the Dupin tale"—this the second to appear—is a prototype, and that even if the genre were established in the first, it is still a little early for the author to play on a convention.

It would, however, be equally excessive to reduce the whole thing to a fable whose moral would be that in order to shield from inquisitive eyes one of those correspondences whose secrecy is sometimes necessary to conjugal peace, it suffices to leave the crucial letters lying about on one's table, even though the meaningful side be turned face down. For that would be a hoax which, for our part, we would never recommend anyone try, lest he be gravely disappointed in his hopes.

Might there then be no mystery other than, concerning the Prefect, an incompetence issuing in failure—were it not perhaps, concerning Dupin, a certain dissonance we hesitate to acknowledge between, on the one hand, the admittedly penetrating though, in their generality, not always quite relevant remarks with which he introduces us to his method and, on the other, the manner in which he in fact intervenes.

Were we to pursue this sense of mystification a bit further we might soon begin to wonder whether, from that initial scene which only the rank of the protagonists saves from vaudeville, to the fall into ridicule which seems to await the Minister at the end, it is not this impression that everyone is being duped which makes for our pleasure.

And we would be all the more inclined to think so in that we would recognize in that surmise, along with those of you who read us, the definition we once gave in passing of the modern hero, "whom ludicrous exploits exalt in circumstances of utter confusion."[2]

But are we ourselves not taken in by the imposing presence of the amateur detective, prototype of a latter-day swashbuckler, as yet safe from the insipidity of our contemporary *superman?*

A trick . . . sufficient for us to discern in this tale, on the contrary, so perfect a verisimilitude that it may be said that truth here reveals its fictive arrangement.

For such indeed is the direction in which the principles of that verisimilitude lead us. Entering into its strategy, we indeed perceive a new drama we may call complementary to the first, insofar as the latter was what is termed a play without words whereas the interest of the second plays on the properties of speech.[3]

If it is indeed clear that each of the two scenes of the real drama is narrated in the course of a different dialogue, it is only through access to those notions set forth in our teaching that one may recognize that it is not thus simply to augment the charm of the exposition, but that the dialogues themselves, in the opposite use they make of the powers of speech, take on a tension which makes of them a different drama, one which our vocabulary will distinguish from the first as persisting in the symbolic order.

The first dialogue—between the Prefect of Police and Dupin—is played as between a deaf man and one who hears. That is, it presents the real complexity of what is ordinarily simplified, with the most confused results, in the notion of communication.

This example demonstrates indeed how an act of communication may give the impression at which theorists too often stop: of allowing in its transmission but a single meaning, as though the highly significant commentary into which he who understands integrates it, could, because unperceived by him who does not understand, be considered null.

It remains that if only the dialogue's meaning as a report is retained, its verisimilitude may appear to depend on a guarantee of exactitude. But here dialogue may be more fertile than it seems, if we demonstrate its tactics: as shall be seen by focusing on the recounting of our first scene.

For the double and even triple subjective filter through which that scene comes to us: a narration by Dupin's friend and associate (henceforth to be called the general narrator of the story) of the account by which the Prefect reveals to Dupin the report the Queen gave him of it, is not merely the consequence of a fortuitous arrangement.

If indeed the extremity to which the original narrator is reduced precludes her altering any of the events, it would be wrong to believe that the Prefect is empowered to lend her his voice in this case only by that lack of imagination on which he has, dare we say, the patent.

The fact that the message is thus retransmitted assures us of what may by no means be taken for granted: that it belongs to the dimension of language.

Those who are here know our remarks on the subject, specifically those illustrated by the countercase of the so-called language of bees: in which a linguist[4] can see only a simple signaling of the location of objects, in other words: only an imaginary function more differentiated than others.

We emphasize that such a form of communication is not absent in man, however evanescent a naturally given object may be for him, split as it is in its submission to symbols.

Something equivalent may no doubt be grasped in the communion established between two persons in their hatred of a common object: except that the meeting is possible only over a single object, defined by those traits in the individual each of the two resists.

But such communication is not transmissible in symbolic form. It may be maintained only in the relation with the object. In such a manner it may bring together an indefinite number of subjects in a common "ideal": the communication of one subject with another within the crowd thus constituted will nonetheless remain irreducibly mediated by an ineffable relation.

This digression is not only a recollection of principles distantly addressed to those who impute to us a neglect of nonverbal communication: in determining the scope of what speech repeats, it prepares the question of what symptoms repeat.

Thus the indirect telling sifts out the linguistic dimension, and the general narrator, by duplicating it, "hypothetically" adds nothing to it. But its role in the second dialogue is entirely different.

For the latter will be opposed to the first like those poles we have distinguished elsewhere in language and which are opposed like word to speech.

Which is to say that a transition is made here from the domain of exactitude to the register of truth. Now that register—we dare think we needn't come back to this—is situated entirely elsewhere, strictly speaking at the very foundation of intersubjectivity. It is located there where the subject can grasp nothing but the very subjectivity which constitutes an Other as absolute. We shall be satisfied here to indicate its place by evoking the dialogue which seems to us to merit its attribution as a

Jewish joke by that state of privation through which the relation of signifier to speech appears in the entreaty which brings the dialogue to a close: "Why are you lying to me?" one character shouts breathlessly. "Yes, why do you lie to me saying you're going to Cracow so I should believe you're going to Lemberg, when in reality you *are* going to Cracow?"

We might be prompted to ask a similar question by the torrent of logical impasses, eristic enigmas, paradoxes, and even jests presented to us as an introduction to Dupin's method if the fact that they were confided to us by a would-be disciple did not endow them with a new dimension through that act of delegation. Such is the unmistakable magic of legacies: the witness's fidelity is the cowl which blinds and lays to rest all criticism of his testimony.

What could be more convincing, moreover, than the gesture of laying one's cards face up on the table? So much so that we are momentarily persuaded that the magician has in fact demonstrated, as he promised, how his trick was performed, whereas he has only renewed it in still purer form: at which point we fathom the measure of the supremacy of the signifier in the subject.

Such is Dupin's maneuver when he starts with the story of the child prodigy who takes in all his friends at the game of even and odd with his trick of identifying with the opponent, concerning which we have nevertheless shown that it cannot reach the first level of theoretical elaboration; namely, intersubjective alternation, without immediately stumbling on the buttress of its recurrence.[5]

We are all the same treated—so much smoke in our eyes—to the names of La Rochefoucauld, La Bruyère, Machiavelli, and Campanella, whose renown, by this time, would seem but futile when confronted with the child's prowess.

Followed by Chamfort, whose maxim that "it is a safe wager that every public idea, every accepted convention is foolish, since it suits the greatest number" will no doubt satisfy all who think they escape its law, that is, precisely, the greatest number. That Dupin accuses the French of deception for applying the word *analysis* to algebra will hardly threaten our pride since, moreover, the freeing of that term for other uses ought by no means to provoke a psychoanalyst to intervene and claim his rights. And there he goes making philological remarks which should positively delight any lovers of Latin: when he recalls without deigning to say any more that "*ambitus* doesn't mean ambition, *religio,* religion, *homines honesti,* honest men," who among you would not take pleasure in remembering . . . what those words mean to anyone familiar with Cicero and Lucretius. No doubt Poe is having a good time. . . .

But a suspicion occurs to us: Might not this parade of erudition be destined to reveal to us the key words of our drama? Is not the magician repeating his trick before our eyes, without deceiving us this time about divulging his secret, but pressing his wager to the point of really explaining it to us without us seeing a thing? *That* would be the summit of the illusionist's art: through one of his fictive creations to *truly delude us*.

And is it not such effects which justify our referring, without malice, to a number of imaginary heroes as real characters?

As well, when we are open to hearing the way in which Martin Heidegger discloses to us in the word *aletheia* the play of truth, we rediscover a secret to which truth has always initiated her lovers, and through which they learn that it is in hiding that she offers herself to them *most truly*.

Thus even if Dupin's comments did not defy us so blatantly to believe in them, we should still have to make that attempt against the opposite temptation.

Let us track down [*dépistons*] his footprints there where they elude [*dépiste*] us.[6] And first of all in the criticism by which he explains the Prefect's lack of success. We already saw it surface in those furtive gibes the Prefect, in the first conversation, failed to heed, seeing in them only a pretext for hilarity. That it is, as Dupin insinuates, because a problem is too simple, indeed too evident, that it may appear obscure, will never have any more bearing for him than a vigorous rub of the ribcage.

Everything is arranged to induce in us a sense of the character's imbecility. Which is powerfully articulated by the fact that he and his confederates never conceive of anything beyond what an ordinary rogue might imagine for hiding an object—that is, precisely the all too well known series of extraordinary hiding places: which are promptly cataloged for us, from hidden desk drawers to removable tabletops, from the detachable cushions of chairs to their hollowed-out legs, from the reverse side of mirrors to the "thickness" of book bindings.

After which, a moment of derision at the Prefect's error in deducing that because the Minister is a poet, he is not far from being mad, an error, it is argued, which would consist, but this is hardly negligible, simply in a false distribution of the middle term, since it is far from following from the fact that all madmen are poets.

Yes indeed. But we ourselves are left in the dark as to the poet's superiority in the art of concealment—even if he be a mathematician to boot—since our pursuit is suddenly thwarted, dragged as we are into a thicket of bad arguments directed against the reasoning of mathematicians, who never, so far as I know, showed such devotion to their formulae as to identify them with reason itself. At least, let us testify that unlike what seems to be Poe's experience, it occasionally befalls us—with our friend Riguet, whose presence here is a guarantee that our incursions into combinatory analysis are not leading us astray—to hazard such serious deviations (virtual blasphemies, according to Poe) as to cast into doubt that "$x^2 + px$ is perhaps not absolutely equal to q," without ever—here we give the lie to Poe—having had to fend off any unexpected attack.

Is not so much intelligence being exercised then simply to divert our own from what had been indicated earlier as given, namely, that the police have looked *everywhere:* which we were to understand—vis-à-vis the area in which the police, not without reason, assumed the letter might be found—in terms of a (no doubt theoretical) exhaustion of space, but concerning which the tale's piquancy depends on our accepting it literally? The division of the entire volume into numbered "compartments," which was the principle governing the operation, being presented to us as so precise that "the fiftieth part of a line," it is said, could not escape the probing of the investigators. Have we not then the right to ask how it happened that the letter was not found *anywhere,* or rather to observe that all we have been told of a more far-ranging conception of concealment does not explain, in all rigor, that the letter escaped detection, since the area combed did in fact contain it, as Dupin's discovery eventually proves?

Must a letter then, of all objects, be endowed with the property of *nullibiety:* to use a term which the thesaurus known as *Roget* picks up from the semiotic utopia of Bishop Wilkins?[7]

It is evident ("a little *too* self-evident")[8] that between *letter* and *place* exist relations for which no French word has quite the extension of the English adjective *odd. Bizarre,* by which Baudelaire regularly translates it, is only approximate. Let us say that these relations are . . . *singuliers,* for they are the very ones maintained with place by the *signifier.*

You realize, of course, that our intention is not to turn them into "subtle" relations, nor is our aim to confuse letter with spirit, even if we receive the former by pneumatic dispatch, and that we readily admit that one kills whereas the other quickens, insofar as the signifier—you perhaps begin to understand—materializes the agency of death. But if it is first of all on the materiality of the signifier that we have insisted, that materiality is *odd* [*singulière*] in many ways, the first of which is not to admit partition. Cut a letter in small pieces, and it remains the letter it is—and this in a completely different sense than *Gestalttheorie* would account for with the dormant vitalism informing its notion of the whole.9

Language delivers its judgment to whoever knows how to hear it: through the usage of the article as partitive particle. It is there that spirit—if spirit be living meaning—appears, no less oddly, as more available for quantification than its letter. To begin with meaning itself, which bears our saying: a speech rich with meaning ["plein *de* significa-tion"], just as we recognize a measure of intention ["*de* l'intention"] in an act, or deplore that there is no more love ["plus *d'amour*"]; or store up hatred ["*de la* haine"] and expend devotion ["*du* dévouement"], and so much infatuation ["tant *d'*infatuation"] is easily reconciled to the fact that there will always be ass ["*de la* cuisse"] for sale and brawling ["*du* rififi"] among men.

But as for the letter—be it taken as typographical character, epistle, or what makes a man of letters—we will say that what is said is to be understood *to the letter* [*à la lettre*], that *a letter* [*une lettre*] awaits you at the post office, or even that you are acquainted with *letters* [*que vous avez des lettres*]—never that there is *letter* [*de la lettre*] anywhere, whatever the context, even to designate overdue mail.

For the signifier is a unit in its very uniqueness, being by nature symbol only of an absence. Which is why we cannot say of the purloined letter that, like other objects, it must be *or* not be in a particular place but that unlike them it will be *and* not be where it is, wherever it goes.

Let us, in fact, look more closely at what happens to the police. We are spared nothing concerning the procedures used in searching the area submitted to their investigation: from the division of that space into compartments from which the slightest bulk could not escape detection, to needles probing upholstery, and, in the impossibility of sounding wood with a tap, to a microscope exposing the waste of any drilling at the surface of its hollow, indeed the infinitesimal gaping of the slightest abyss. As the network tightens to the point that, not satisfied with shaking the pages of books, the police take to counting them, do we not see space itself shed its leaves like a letter?

But the detectives have so immutable a notion of the real that they fail to notice that their search tends to transform it into its object. A trait by which they would be able to distinguish that object from all others.

This would no doubt be too much to ask them, not because of their lack of insight but rather because of ours. For their imbecility is neither of the individual nor the corporative variety; its source is subjective. It is the realist's imbecility, which does not pause to observe that nothing, however deep in the bowels of the earth a hand may seek to ensconce it, will ever be hidden there, since another hand can always retrieve it, and that what is hidden is never but what is *missing from its place,* as the call slip puts it when speaking of a volume lost in a library. And even if the book be on an adjacent shelf or in the next slot, it would be hidden there, however visibly it may appear. For it can *literally* be said that something is missing from its place only of what can change it: the symbolic. For the real, whatever upheaval we subject it to, is always in its place; it carries it glued to its heel, ignorant of what might exile it from it.

And to return to our cops, who took the letter from the place where it was hidden, how could they have seized the letter? In what they turned between their fingers what did they hold but what *did not answer* to their description. "A letter, a litter": in Joyce's circle, they played on the homophony of the two words in English. [10] Nor does the seeming bit of refuse the police are now handling reveal its other nature for being but half torn. A different seal on a stamp of another color, the mark of a different handwriting in the superscription are here the most inviolable modes of concealment. And if they stop at the reverse side of the letter, on which, as is known, the recipient's address was written in that period, it is because the letter has for them no other side but its reverse.

What indeed might they find on its obverse? Its message, as is often said to our cybernetic joy? . . . But does it not occur to us that this message has already reached its recipient and has even been left with her, since the insignificant scrap of paper now represents it no less well than the original note.

If we could admit that a letter has completed its destiny after fulfilling its function, the ceremony of returning letters would be a less common close to the extinction of the fires of love's feasts. The signifier is not functional. And the mobilization of the elegant society whose frolics we are following would as well have no meaning if the letter itself were content with having one. For it would hardly be an adequate means of keeping it secret to inform a squad of cops of its existence.

We might even admit that the letter has an entirely different (if no more urgent) meaning for the Queen from the one understood by the Minister. The sequence of events would not be noticeably affected, not even if it were strictly incomprehensible to an uninformed reader.

For it is certainly not so for everybody, since, as the Prefect pompously assures us, to everyone's derision, "the disclosure of the document to a third person, who shall be nameless" (that name which leaps to the eye like the pig's tail twixt the teeth of old Ubu) "would bring in question the honor of a personage of most exalted station, indeed that the honor and peace of the illustrious personage are so jeopardized."

In that case, it is not only the meaning but the text of the message which it would be dangerous to place in circulation, and all the more so to the extent that it might appear harmless, since the risks of an indiscretion unintentionally committed by one of the letter's holders would thus be increased.

Nothing then can redeem the police's position, and nothing would be changed by improving their "culture." *Scripta manent:* in vain would they learn from a deluxe-edition humanism the proverbial lesson which *verba volant* concludes. May it but please heaven that writings remain, as is rather the case with spoken words: for the indelible debt of the latter impregnates our acts with its transferences.

Writings scatter to the winds blank checks in an insane charge. And were they not such flying leaves, there would be no purloined letters.

But what of it? For a purloined letter to exist, we may ask, to whom does a letter belong? We stressed a moment ago the oddity implicit in returning a letter to him who had but recently given wing to its burning pledge. And we generally deem unbecoming such premature publications as the one by which the Chevalier d'Eon put several of his correspondents in a rather pitiful position.

Might a letter on which the sender retains certain rights then not quite belong to the person to whom it is addressed? Or might it be that the latter was never the real receiver?

Let's take a look: we shall find illumination in what at first seems to obscure matters: the fact that the tale leaves us in virtually total ignorance of the sender, no less than of the contents, of the letter. We are told only that the Minister immediately recognized the handwriting of the address and only incidentally, in a discussion of the Minister's camouflage, is it said that the original seal bore the ducal arms of the S—— family. As for the letter's bearing, we know only the dangers it entails should it come into the hands of a specific third party, and that its possession has allowed the Minister to "wield, to a very dangerous extent, for political purposes," the power it assures him over the interested party. But all this tells us nothing of the message it conveys.

Love letter or conspiratorial letter, letter of betrayal or letter of mission, letter of summons or letter of distress, we are assured of but one thing: the Queen must not bring it to the knowledge of her lord and master.

Now these terms, far from bearing the nuance of discredit they have in bourgeois comedy, take on a certain prominence through allusion to her sovereign, to whom she is bound by pledge of faith, and doubly so, since her role as spouse does not relieve her of her duties as subject, but rather elevates her to the guardianship of what royalty according to law incarnates of power: and which is called legitimacy.

From then on, to whatever vicissitudes the Queen may choose to subject the letter, it remains that the letter is the symbol of a pact and that, even should the recipient not assume the pact, the existence of the letter situates her in a symbolic chain foreign to the one which constitutes her faith. This incompatibility is proven by the fact that the possession of the letter is impossible to bring forward publicly as legitimate, and that in order to have that possession respected, the Queen can invoke but her right to privacy, whose privilege is based on the honor that possession violates.

For she who incarnates the figure of grace and sovereignty cannot welcome even a private communication without power being concerned, and she cannot avail herself of secrecy in relation to the sovereign without becoming clandestine.

From then on, the responsibility of the author of the letter takes second place to that of its holder: for the offense to majesty is compounded by *high treason*.

We say the *holder* and not the *possessor*. For it becomes clear that the addressee's proprietorship of the letter may be no less debatable than that of anyone else into whose hands it comes, for nothing concerning the existence of the letter can return to good order without the person whose prerogatives it infringes upon having to pronounce judgment on it.

All of this, however, does not imply that because the letter's secrecy is indefensible, the betrayal of that secret would in any sense be honorable. The *honesti homines,* decent people, will not get off easily. There is more than one *religio,* and it is not slated for tomorrow that sacred ties shall cease to rend us in two. As for *ambitus:* a detour, we see, is not always inspired by ambition. For if we are taking one here, by no means is it stolen (the word is apt), since, to lay our cards on the table, we have borrowed Baudelaire's title in order to stress not, as is incorrectly claimed, the conventional nature of the signifier, but rather its priority in relation to the signified. It remains, nevertheless, that Baudelaire, despite his devotion, betrayed Poe by translating as "la lettre volée" (the stolen letter) his title: the purloined letter, a title containing a word rare enough for us to find it easier to define its etymology than its usage.

To *purloin,* says the Oxford dictionary, is an Anglo-French word, that is: composed of the prefix *pur-,* found in *purpose, purchase, purport,* and of the Old French word: *loing, loigner, longé.* We recognize in the first element the Latin *pro-,* as opposed to *ante,* insofar as it presupposes a rear in front of which it is borne, possibly as its warrant, indeed even as its pledge (whereas *ante* goes forth to confront what it encounters). As for the second, an Old French word: *loigner,* a verb attributing place *au loing* (or, still in use, *longé*), it does not mean *au loin* (far off), but *au long de* (alongside); it is a question then of *putting aside,* or, to invoke a familiar expression which plays on the two meanings: *mettre à gauche* (to put to the left; to put amiss).

Thus we are confirmed in our detour by the very object which draws us on into it: for we are quite simply dealing with a letter which has been diverted from its path; one whose course has been *prolonged* (etymologically, the word of the title), or, to revert to the language of the post office, a *letter in sufferance.*

Here then, *simple and odd,* as we are told on the very first page, reduced to its simplest expression, is the singularity of the letter, which as the title indicates, is the *true subject* of the tale: since it can be diverted, it must have a course *which is proper to it:* the trait by which its incidence as signifier is affirmed. For we have learned to conceive of the signifier as sustaining itself only in a displacement comparable to that found in electric news strips or in the rotating memories of our machines-that-think-like-men, this because of the alternating operation which is its principle, requiring it to leave its place, even though it returns to it by a circular path. [11]

This is indeed what happens in the repetition automatism. What Freud teaches us in the text we are commenting on is that the subject must pass through the channels of the symbolic, but what is illustrated here is more gripping still: it is not only the subject, but the subjects, grasped in their intersubjectivity, who line up, in other words our ostriches, to whom we here return, and who, more docile than sheep, model their very being on the moment of the signifying chain which traverses them.

If what Freud discovered and rediscovers with a perpetually increasing sense of shock has a meaning, it is that the displacement of the signifier determines the subjects in their acts, in their destiny, in their refusals, in their blindness, in their end and in their fate, their innate gifts and social acquisitions notwithstanding, without regard for character or sex, and that, willingly or not, everything that might be considered the stuff of psychology, kit and caboodle, will follow the path of the signifier.

Here we are, in fact, yet again at the crossroads at which we had left our drama and its round with the question of the way in which the subjects replace each other in it. Our fable is so constructed as to show that it is the letter and its diversion which governs their entries and roles. If *it* be "in sufferance," *they* shall endure the pain. Should they pass beneath its shadow, they become its reflection. Falling in possession of the letter—admirable ambiguity of language—its meaning possesses them.

So we are shown by the hero of the drama in the repetition of the very situation which his daring brought to a head, a first time, to his triumph. If he now succumbs to it, it is because he has shifted to the second position in the triad in which he was initially third, as well as the thief— and this by virtue of the object of his theft.

For if it is, now as before, a question of protecting the letter from inquisitive eyes, he can do nothing but employ the same technique he himself has already foiled: Leave it in the open? And we may properly doubt that he knows what he is thus doing, when we see him immediately captivated by a dual relationship in which we find all the traits of a mimetic lure or of an animal feigning death, and, trapped in the typically imaginary situation of seeing that he is not seen, misconstrue the real situation in which he is seen not seeing.

And what does he fail to see? Precisely the symbolic situation which he himself was so well able to see, and in which he is now seen seeing himself not being seen.

The Minister acts as a man who realizes that the police's search is his own defense, since we are told he allows them total access by his absences: he nonetheless fails to recognize that outside of that search he is no longer defended.

This is the very *autruicherie* whose artisan he was, if we may allow our monster to proliferate, but it cannot be by sheer stupidity that he now comes to be its dupe.

For in playing the part of the one who hides, he is obliged to don the role of the Queen, and even the attributes of femininity and shadow, so propitious to the act of concealing.

Not that we are reducing the hoary couple of *Yin* and *Yang* to the elementary opposition of dark and light. For its precise use involves what is blinding in a flash of light, no less than the shimmering shadows exploit in order not to lose their prey.

Here sign and being, marvelously asunder, reveal which is victorious when they come into conflict. A man man enough to defy to the point of scorn a lady's fearsome ire undergoes to the point of metamorphosis the curse of the sign he has dispossessed her of.

For this sign is indeed that of woman, insofar as she invests her very being therein, founding it outside the law, which subsumes her nevertheless, originarily, in a position of signifier, nay, of fetish. In order to be worthy of the power of that sign she has but to remain immobile in its shadow, thus finding, moreover, like the Queen, that simulation of mastery in inactivity that the Minister's "lynx eye" alone was able to penetrate.

This stolen sign—here then is man in its possession: sinister in that such possession may be sustained only through the honor it defies, cursed in calling him who sustains it to punishment or crime, each of which shatters his vassalage to the Law.

There must be in this sign a singular *noli me tangere* for its possession, like the Socratic sting ray, to benumb its man to the point of making him fall into what appears clearly in his case to be a state of idleness.

For in noting, as the narrator does as early as the first dialogue, that with the letter's use its power disappears, we perceive that this remark, strictly speaking, concerns precisely its use for ends of power—and at the same time that such a use is obligatory for the Minister.

To be unable to rid himself of it, the Minister indeed must not know what else to do with the letter. For that use places him in so total a dependence on the letter as such, that in the long run it no longer involves the letter at all.

We mean that for that use truly to involve the letter, the Minister, who, after all, would be so authorized by his service to his master the King, might present to the Queen respectful admonitions, even were he to assure their sequel by appropriate precautions—or initiate an action against the author of the letter, concerning whom, the fact that he remains outside the story's focus reveals the extent to which it is not guilt and blame which are in question here, but rather that sign of contradiction and scandal constituted by the letter, in the sense in which the Gospel says that it must come regardless of the anguish of whoever serves as its bearer,—or even submit the letter as document in a dossier to a 'third person' qualified to know whether it will issue in a Star Chamber for the Queen or the Minister's disgrace.

We will not know why the Minister does not resort to any of these uses, and it is fitting that we don't, since the effect of this non-use alone concerns us; it suffices for us to know that the way in which the letter was acquired would pose no obstacle to any of them.

For it is clear that if the use of the letter, independent of its meaning, is obligatory for the Minister, its use for ends of power can only be potential, since it cannot become actual without vanishing in the process—but in that case the letter exists as a means of power only through the final assignations of the pure signifier, namely: by prolonging its diversion, making it reach whomever it may concern through a supplementary transfer, that is, by an additional act of treason whose effects the letter's gravity makes it difficult to predict—or indeed by destroying the letter, the only sure means, as Dupin divulges at the start, of being rid of what is destined by nature to signify the annulment of what it signifies.

The ascendancy which the Minister derives from the situation is thus not a function of the letter, but, whether he knows it or not, of the role it constitutes for him. And the Prefect's remarks indeed present him as someone "who dares all things," which is commented upon significantly: "those unbecoming as well as those becoming a man," words whose pungency escapes Baudelaire when he translates: "ce qui est indigne d'un homme aussi bien que ce qui est digne de lui" (those unbecoming a man as well as those becoming him). For in its original form, the appraisal is far more appropriate to what might concern a woman.

This allows us to see the imaginary import of the character, that is, the narcissistic relation in which the Minister is engaged, this time, no doubt, without knowing it. It is indicated, as well, as early as the second page of the English text by one of the narrator's remarks, whose form is worth savoring: the Minister's ascendancy, we are told, "would depend upon the robber's knowledge of the loser's knowledge of the robber." Words whose importance the author underscores by having Dupin repeat them literally after the narration of the scene of the theft of the letter. Here again we may say that Baudelaire is imprecise in his language in having one ask, the other confirm, in these words: "Le voleur sait-il? . . ." (Does the robber know?), then: "Le voleur sait . . ." (the robber knows). What? "que la personne volée connaît son voleur" (that the loser knows his robber).

For what matters to the robber is not only that the said person knows who robbed her, but rather with what kind of a robber she is dealing; for she believes him capable of anything, which should be understood as her having conferred upon him the position that no one is in fact capable of assuming, since it is imaginary, that of absolute master.

In truth, it is a position of absolute weakness, but not for the person of whom we are expected to believe so. The proof is not only that the Queen dares to call the police. For she is only conforming to her displacement to the next slot in the arrangement of the initial triad in trusting to the very blindness required to occupy that place: "No more sagacious agent could, I suppose," Dupin notes ironically, "be desired or even imagined." No, if she has taken that step, it is less out of being "driven to despair," as we are told, than in assuming the charge of an impatience best imputed to a specular mirage.

For the Minister is kept quite busy confining himself to the idleness which is presently his lot. The Minister, in point of fact, is not *altogether* mad. That's a remark made by the Prefect, whose every word is gold: it is true that the gold of his words flows only for Dupin and will continue to flow to the amount of the fifty thousand francs worth it will cost him by the metal standard of the day, though not without leaving him a margin of profit. The Minister then is not *altogether* mad in his insane stagnation, and that is why he will behave according to the mode of neurosis. Like the man who withdrew to an island to forget, what? he forgot—so the Minister, through not making use of the letter, comes to forget it. As is expressed by the persistence of his conduct. But the letter, no more than the neurotic's unconscious, does not forget him. It forgets him so little that it transforms him more and more in the image of her who offered it to his capture, so that he now will surrender it, following her example, to a similar capture.

The features of that transformation are noted, and in a form so characteristic in their apparent gratuitousness that they might validly be compared to the return of the repressed.

Thus we first learn that the Minister in turn has *turned the letter over,* not, of course, as in the Queen's hasty gesture, but, more assiduously, as one turns a garment inside out. So he must proceed, according to the methods of the day for folding and sealing a letter, in order to free the virgin space on which to inscribe a new address. [12]

That address becomes his own. Whether it be in his hand or another, it will appear in an extremely delicate feminine script, and, the seal changing from the red of passion to the black of its mirrors, he will imprint his stamp upon it. This oddity of a letter marked with the recipient's stamp is all the more striking in its conception, since, though forcefully articulated in the text, it is not even mentioned by Dupin in the discussion he devotes to the identification of the letter.

Whether that omission be intentional or involuntary, it will surprise in the economy of a work whose meticulous rigor is evident. But in either case it is significant that the letter which the Minister, in point of fact, addresses to himself is a letter from a woman: as though this were a phase he had to pass through out of a natural affinity of the signifier.

Thus the aura of apathy, verging at times on an affectation of effeminacy; the display of an ennui bordering on disgust in his conversation; the mood the author of the philosophy of furniture[13] can elicit from virtually impalpable details (like that of the musical instrument on the table), everything seems intended for a character, all of whose utterances have revealed the most virile traits, to exude the oddest *odor di femina* when he appears.

Dupin does not fail to stress that this is an artifice, describing behind the bogus finery the vigilance of a beast of prey ready to spring. But that this is the very effect of the unconscious in the precise sense that we teach that the unconscious means that man is inhabited by the signifier: Could we find a more beautiful image of it than the one Poe himself forges to help us appreciate Dupin's exploit? For with this aim in mind, he refers to those toponymical inscriptions which a geographical map, lest it remain mute, superimposes on its design, and which may become the object of a guessing game: Who can find the name chosen by a partner?—noting immediately that the name most likely to foil a beginner will be one which, in large letters spaced out widely across the map, discloses, often without an eye pausing to notice it, the name of an entire country. . . .

Just so does the purloined letter, like an immense female body, stretch out across the Minister's office when Dupin enters. But just so does he already expect to find it, and has only, with his eyes veiled by green lenses, to undress that huge body.

And that is why without needing any more than being able to listen in at the door of Professor Freud, he will go straight to the spot in which lies and lives what that body is designed to hide, in a gorgeous center caught in a glimpse, nay, to the very place seducers name Sant' Angelo's Castle in their innocent illusion of controlling the City from within it. Look! between the cheeks of the fireplace, there's the object already in reach of a hand the ravisher has but to extend. . . . The question of deciding whether he seizes it above the mantelpiece as Baudelaire translates, or beneath it, as in the original text, may be abandoned without harm to the inferences of those whose profession is grilling.[14]

Were the effectiveness of symbols to cease there, would it mean that the symbolic debt would as well be extinguished? Even if we could believe so, we would be advised of the contrary by two episodes which we may all the less dismiss as secondary in that they seem, at first sight, to clash with the rest of the work.

First of all, there's the business of Dupin's remuneration, which, far from being a closing pirouette, has been present from the beginning in the rather unselfconscious question he asks the Prefect about the amount of the reward promised him, and whose enormousness, the Prefect, however reticent he may be about the precise figure, does not dream of hiding from him, even returning later on to refer to its increase.

The fact that Dupin had been previously presented to us as a virtual pauper in his ethereal shelter ought rather to lead us to reflect on the deal he makes out of delivering the letter, promptly assured as it is by the checkbook he produces. We do not regard it as negligible that the unequivocal hint through which he introduces the matter is a "story attributed to the character, as famous as it was eccentric," Baudelaire tells us, of an English doctor named Abernethy, in which a rich miser, hoping to sponge upon him for a medical opinion, is sharply told not to take medicine, but to take advice.

Do we not in fact feel concerned with good reason when for Dupin what is perhaps at stake is his withdrawal from the symbolic circuit of the letter—we who become the emissaries of all the purloined letters which at least for a time remain in sufferance with us in the transference. And is it not the responsibility their transference entails which we neutralize by equating it with the signifier most destructive of all signification; namely money.

But that's not all. The profit Dupin so nimbly extracts from his exploit, if its purpose is to allow him to withdraw his stakes from the game, makes all the more paradoxical, even shocking, the partisan attack, the underhanded blow, he suddenly permits himself to launch against the Minister, whose insolent prestige, after all, would seem to have been sufficiently deflated by the trick Dupin has just played on him.

We have already quoted the atrocious lines Dupin claims he could not help dedicating, in his counterfeit letter, to the moment in which the Minister, enraged by the inevitable defiance of the Queen, will think he is demolishing her and will plunge into the abyss: *facilis descensus Averni,*[15] he waxes sententious, adding that the Minister cannot fail to recognize his handwriting, all of which, since depriving of any danger a merciless act of infamy, would seem, concerning a figure who is not without merit, a triumph without glory, and the rancor he invokes, stemming from an evil turn done him at Vienna (at the Congress?) only adds an additional bit of blackness to the whole.

Let us consider, however, more closely this explosion of feeling, and more specifically the moment it occurs in a sequence of acts whose success depends on so cool a head.

It comes just after the moment in which the decisive act of identifying the letter having been accomplished, it may be said that Dupin already *has* the letter as much as if he had seized it, without, however, as yet being in a position to rid himself of it.

He is thus, in fact, fully participant in the intersubjective triad, and, as such, in the median position previously occupied by the Queen and the Minister. Will he, in showing himself to be above it, reveal to us at the same time the author's intentions?

If he has succeeded in returning the letter to its proper course, it remains for him to make it arrive at its address. And that address is in the place previously occupied by the King, since it is there that it would reenter the order of the Law.

As we have seen, neither the King nor the police who replaced him in that position were able to read the letter because that *place entailed blindness*.

Rex et augur, the legendary, archaic quality of the words seems to resound only to impress us with the absurdity of applying them to a man. And the figures of history, for some time now, hardly encourage us to do so. It is not natural for man to bear alone the weight of the highest of signifiers. And the place he occupies as soon as he dons it may be equally apt to become the symbol of the most outrageous imbecility.[16]

Let us say that the King here is invested with the equivocation natural to the sacred, with the imbecility which prizes none other than the Subject.

That is what will give their meaning to the characters who will follow him in his place. Not that the police should be regarded as constitutionally illiterate, and we know the role of pikes planted on the *campus* in the birth of the State. But the police who exercise their functions here are plainly marked by the forms of liberalism, that is, by those imposed on them by masters on the whole indifferent to eliminating their indiscreet tendencies. Which is why on occasion words are not minced as to what is expected of them: "*Sutor ne ultra crepidam,* just take care of your crooks. We'll even give you scientific means to do it with. That will help you not to think of truths you'd be better off leaving in the dark."[17]

We know that the relief which results from such prudent principles shall have lasted in history but a morning's time, that already the march of destiny is everywhere bringing back—a sequel to a just aspiration to freedom's reign—an interest in those who trouble it with their crimes, which occasionally goes so far as to forge its proofs. It may even be observed that this practice, which was always well received to the extent that it was exercised only in favor of the greatest number, comes to be authenticated in public confessions of forgery by the very ones who might very well object to it: the most recent manifestation of the preeminence of the signifier over the subject.

It remains, nevertheless, that a police record has always been the object of a certain reserve, of which we have difficulty understanding that it amply transcends the guild of historians.

It is by dint of this vanishing credit that Dupin's intended delivery of the letter to the Prefect of Police will diminish its import. What now remains of the signifier when, already relieved of its message for the Queen, it is now invalidated in its text as soon as it leaves the Minister's hands?

It remains for it now only to answer that very question, of what remains of a signifier when it has no more signification. But this is the same question asked of it by the person Dupin now finds in the spot marked by blindness.

For that is indeed the question which has led the Minister there, if he be the gambler we are told and which his act sufficiently indicates. For the gambler's passion is nothing but that question asked of the signifier, figured by the *automaton* of chance.

"What are you, figure of the die I turn over in your encounter (*tyché*) with my fortune?[18] Nothing, if not that presence of death which makes of human life a reprieve obtained from morning to morning in the name of meanings whose sign is your crook. Thus did Scheherazade for a thousand and one nights, and thus have I done for eighteen months, suffering the ascendancy of this sign at the cost of a dizzying series of fraudulent turns at the game of even or odd."

So it is that Dupin, *from the place he now occupies,* cannot help feeling a rage of manifestly feminine nature against him who poses such a question. The prestigious image in which the poet's inventiveness and the mathematician's rigor joined up with the serenity of the dandy and the elegance of the cheat suddenly becomes, for the very person who invited us to savor it, the true *monstrum horrendum,* for such are his words, "an unprincipled man of genius."

It is here that the origin of that horror betrays itself, and he who experiences it has no need to declare himself (in a most unexpected manner) "a partisan of the lady" in order to reveal it to us: it is known that ladies detest calling principles into question, for their charms owe much to the mystery of the signifier.

Which is why Dupin will at last turn toward us the medusoid face of the signifier nothing but whose obverse anyone except the Queen has been able to read. The commonplace of the quotation is fitting for the oracle that face bears in its grimace, as is also its source in tragedy: ". . . Un destin si funeste, / S'il n'est digne d'Atrée, est digne de Thyeste."

So runs the signifier's answer, above and beyond all significations: "You think you act when I stir you at the mercy of the bonds through which I knot your desires. Thus do they grow in force and multiply in objects, bringing you back to the fragmentation of your shattered childhood. So be it: such will be your feast until the return of the stone guest I shall be for you since you call me forth."

Or, to return to a more moderate tone, let us say, as in the quip with which—along with some of you who had followed us to the Zurich Congress last year—we rendered homage to the local password, the signifier's answer to whoever interrogates it is: "Eat your Dasein."

Is that then what awaits the Minister at a rendezvous with destiny? Dupin assures us of it, but we have already learned not to be too credulous of his diversions.

No doubt the brazen creature is here reduced to the state of blindness which is man's in relation to the letters on the wall that dictate his destiny. But what effect, in calling him to confront them, may we expect from the sole provocations of the Queen, on a man like him? Love or hatred. The former is blind and will make him lay down his arms. The latter is lucid, but will awaken his suspicions. But if he is truly the gambler we are told he is, he will consult his cards a final time before laying them down and, upon reading his hand, will leave the table in time to avoid disgrace.

Is that all, and shall we believe we have deciphered Dupin's real strategy above and beyond the imaginary tricks with which he was obliged to deceive us? No doubt, yes, for if "any point requiring reflection," as Dupin states at the start, is "examined to best purpose in the dark," we may now easily read its solution in broad daylight. It was already implicit and easy to derive from the title of our tale, according to the very formula we have long submitted to your discretion: in which the sender, we tell you, receives from the receiver his own message in reverse form. Thus it is that what the "purloined letter," nay, the "letter in sufferance," means is that a letter always arrives at its destination.

NOTES

1. The necessary reference here may be found in "Le temps logique et l'assertion de la certitude anticipée," *Ecrits* (1966a, 197).

2. Cf. "Fonction et champ de la parole et du langage" in *Ecrits* (1966a, 244); "The Function and Field of Speech and Language in Psychoanalysis," in *Ecrits: A Selection* (1977, 36).

3. The complete understanding of what follows presupposes a rereading of the short and easily available text of "The Purloined Letter."

4. Cf. Emile Benveniste, "Communication animale et langage humain," *Diogène,* no. 1, and our address in Rome, *Ecrits* (1966a, 297; 1977, 84). [See Benveniste 1971, 49–54.]

5. Cf. *Ecrits* (1966a, 58). "But what will happen at the following step (of the game) when the opponent, realizing that I am sufficiently clever to follow him in his move, will show his own cleverness by realizing that it is by playing the fool that he has the best chance to deceive me? From then on my reasoning is invalidated, since it can only be repeated in an indefinite oscillation."

6. We should like to present again to M. Benveniste the question of the antithetical sense of (primal or other) words after the magisterial rectification he brought to the erroneous philological path on which Freud engaged it (cf. *La Psychanalyse,* 1:5–16). For we think that the problem remains intact once the instance of the signifier has been evolved. Bloch and Von Wartburg date at 1875 the first appearance of the meaning of the verb *dépister* in the second use we make of it in our sentence. [See Benveniste 1971, 65–75.]

7. The very one to which Jorge Luis Borges, in works which harmonize so well with the phylum of our subject, has accorded an importance which others have reduced to its proper proportions. Cf. *Les Temps Modernes,* June–July 1955, 2135–36 and October 1955, 574–75.

8. Underlined by the author.

9. This is so true that philosophers, in those hackneyed examples with which they argue on the basis of the single and the multiple, will not use to the same purpose a simple sheet of white paper ripped in the middle and a broken circle, indeed a shattered vase, not to mention a cut worm.

10. Cf. *Our Examination Round His Factification for Incamination of Work in Progress* (Shakespeare & Co., 12 rue de l'Odéon, Paris, 1929).

11. See *Ecrits* (1966a, 59): "It is not unthinkable that a modern computer, by discovering the sentence which modulates without his knowing it and over a

long period of time the choices of a subject, would win beyond any normal proportion at the game of even and odd."

12. We felt obliged to demonstrate the procedure to an audience with a letter from the period concerning M. de Chateaubriand and his search for a secretary. We were amused to find that M. de Chateaubriand completed the first version of his recently restored memoirs in the very month of November 1841 in which the purloined letter appeared in *Chambers' Journal*. Might M. de Chateaubriand's devotion to the power he decries and the honor which that devotion bespeaks in him (*the gift* had not yet been invented), place him in the category to which we will later see the Minister assigned: among men of genius with or without principles?

13. Poe is the author of an essay with this title.

14. And even to the cook herself.

15. Virgil's line reads: *facilis descensus Averno*.

16. We recall the witty couplet attributed before his fall to the most recent in date to have rallied Candide's meeting in Venice: "Il n'est plus aujourd'hui que cinq rois sur la terre, / Les quatre rois des cartes et le roi d'Angleterre." (There are only five kings left on earth: / the four kings of cards and the king of England.)

17. This proposal was openly presented by a noble lord speaking to the Upper Chamber in which his dignity earned him a place.

18. We note the fundamental opposition Aristotle makes between the two terms recalled here in the conceptual analysis of chance he gives in his *Physics*. Many discussions would be illuminated by a knowledge of it.

3 ❧ Lacan's Seminar on "The Purloined Letter": Overview

[handwritten margin notes:] Pleasure principle — Seeking / Pleasure — and its pain

Lacan chose his "Seminar on 'The Purloined Letter'" to introduce the collection of his *Écrits* (1966a), whose essays otherwise appear in chronological order. The essay was written out in its present form in the summer of 1956, but its content had been presented a year earlier (April 26, 1955) as part of his weekly seminar (1954–55) that bore the general title "The Ego in the Theory of Freud and in the Technique of Psychoanalysis" (1978b). In fact, the whole seminar was a year-long commentary on Freud's *Beyond the Pleasure Principle* (1955a [1920]).

In this work Freud addresses the problem of the "repetition automatism,"[1] that is, the tendency of many patients to mechanically repeat unpleasant experiences (e.g., dreams that repeat war traumata) in disregard of the so-called pleasure principle. His solution, as we know, was to propose the hypothesis of a force in the human psyche more fundamental than (hence, "beyond") the pleasure principle—the so-called death instinct. For his part, Lacan maintains (in the "Introduction" to his "Seminar on 'The Purloined Letter'") that the examination of the problem of "repetition" in 1920 was actually the renewal of an old question—one about the nature of memory as it emerged in the "Project for a Scientific Psychology" (1954b [1895]). There, Lacan insists, Freud conceives of his system *psi* (predecessor of what would later be called the unconscious) as caught up in the effort to find an irretrievably lost object (1966a, 45). This movement takes the form not of a reminiscence of that object but of some kind of a repetition (unconscious, to be sure) of the losing of it. The repetition, however, is a "symbolic" one (since it is only through the symbol that presence in absence is attained), and the "order of the symbol can no longer be conceived as constituted by man but as constituting him" (1966a, 46).

Just how the "order of the symbol" "constitutes" a human being is the issue that engages Lacan's entire enterprise. It is elaborated in the Seminar from which the present essay is taken and finds expression in the entire collection of *Ecrits,* to which it serves as an introduction. It is not our intention to repeat an exposition that is offered elsewhere.[2] We must be content merely to summarize in lapidary form the essentials of Lacan's position. Freud's discovery in the experience of the "talking cure" was an insight into the way language works. Hence, the unconscious that he postulated to account for the cure was "structured like a language" (Lacan 1977, 234/594),[3] even though Freud, whose discovery antedated but anticipated the work of Saussure and the structural linguists, was unable to articulate it as such and was constrained to conceive it in terms of nineteenth-century science. Lacan accepted from Saussure the distinction between language (as structure) and speech (as act), the distinction in a linguistic sign between the signifier (speech sound) and signified (mental image), and the arbitrary nature of the relation between the two. Moreover, he insisted on this arbitrariness to such an extent that, for him, individual signifiers refer not to individual signifieds but rather to other signifiers (a function of the diacritical nature of the signifying system) under which the signified "slides" (1977, 154/503).

From Saussure's followers (e.g., Roman Jakobson), Lacan accepts the principle that signifiers relate to each other along either an axis of "combination" or an axis of "selection," the former making possible what rhetoricians call "metonymy," the latter what they call "metaphor." Moreover, Lacan accepts (in his own way) Jakobson's suggestion that it is the axis of combination that makes possible what Freud calls "displacement" and the axis of selection that makes possible "condensation" in the unconscious process of "dreamwork." It is in such fashion that the "unconscious is structured like a language." Jakobson had a marked influence on Lévi-Strauss (Lévi-Strauss 1978), who in turn recognized the utility of structural linguistics as a paradigm for a kind of periodic table for all social relationships and suggested to Lacan (Lacan 1977, 73/285) the usefulness of the same paradigm for discovering "universal laws which regulate the unconscious activities of the mind" (Lévi-Strauss 1963, 58–59).

How laws such as these permeate the sedimentation of language that surrounds an infant when it comes into the world and thereby constitute what Lévi-Strauss (and Lacan after him) calls the "symbolic order"; how this order constitutes an "ex-centric" center, that is, a "center" excentric to the "conscious" center of the subject that would therefore be an *unconscious* subject (or "subject of the unconscious"); how the infant is introduced into this "excentric place" (28/11),[4] and how the symbolic order thus conceived is even "constitutive" (29/12) of the subject—all this Lacan presupposes in this essay as familiar to his readers. What he proposes here is to illustrate the whole business by means of a literary example in which we may see "in a story the decisive orientation which) χ the subject receives from the itinerary of a signifier" (29/12).

As for the story itself, it is straightforward enough, and Lacan offers his own synopsis of it 30–31/12–14) that we can accept as sufficient for our purposes.

The main thrust of Lacan's interpretation of this story focuses on two issues: the anomalous nature of the letter, which serves as the "true subject" of the story; and the pattern of intersubjective relationships that remain constant in the tale, despite the interchanging terms of the relationships, the interchange itself generating the principal interest of the tale.

THE LETTER

One is struck, indeed, by how little we know about the nature of the letter, either about its sender or about its contents: "love letter or conspiratorial letter, letter of betrayal or letter of mission, letter of summons or letter of distress, we are assured of but one thing: the Queen must not bring it to the knowledge of her lord and master" (42/27). And why? Because this letter of its very nature is the "symbol of a pact," and even if the Queen refuses the pact the very existence of the letter "situates her in a symbolic chain foreign to the one which constitutes her [fealty to the King]" (42/28) and in that way compromises her. As the letter passes from the Queen to the Minister to Dupin to the Prefect back to the Queen, the content remains irrelevant, and the shifting parameters of power for the subjects concerned derive from the different places where the letter is diverted along this "symbolic circuit" (49/37).

Every one is defined in their relationship to the letter

If we transpose all this into Saussurian terms of the distinction between signifier and signified, it becomes clear that the "stolen" letter functions as a signifier whose signified (i.e., content) is irrelevant to the proceedings. This is how we understand Lacan's designation of it as a "pure signifier" (32/16), that is, completely independent of its signified, serving, by its displacement, as a movable pivot around which revolves a shifting set of human relations. It functions not only independent of its content, therefore, but also independent of the subjects through whose hands it passes.

To whom, then, does the letter belong: To the sender? To the addressee? Lacan raises the question without answering it as such but rather addresses another form of it: What is the proper "place" of the letter? Here he focuses on the nature of the letter as a signifier, but in doing so he plays on the ambiguity in the notion of "letter" itself, which may be taken as a typographical character as well as an epistle. As a typographical character, understood in the most material sense, it is essentially indivisible, incapable of "partition" of any kind (39/24). The English translator reminds us that in this typographical sense "the letter is a unit of signification without any meaning in itself. In this it resembles the 'memory trace,' which for Freud is never the image of an event, but a term that takes on meaning only through its differential opposition to other traces" (Lacan 1972b, 38). This recalls, of course, Saussure's remark to the effect that "in language there are only differences" (1966, 120; cited by Mehlman [Lacan 1972b, 54n.]), that is, between signifiers that are constituted as such precisely by this differentiation. Moreover, the signifier is for Lacan "by nature symbol only of an absence." We are able to follow his shift to the consideration of the letter as signifier in the sense of epistle when he adds: "which is why we cannot say of the purloined letter that, like other objects, it must be *or* not be in a particular place but that unlike them it will be *and* not be where it is, wherever it goes" (39/24).

For the "place" of the signifier is determined by the symbolic system within which it is constantly dis-placed. It is only in terms of a symbolic order, for example, that one may speak of the signifier as "symbol of an absence" the way a slip of paper—or even an empty space—may symbolize the absence of a book on a library shelf. Conversely, "what is hidden is never but what is missing from its place" like a book misplaced on another shelf (40/25). In Lacan's reading of the Poe tale, the fateful letter is not stolen so much as dis-placed, that is, "purloined" in the sense of "pro-longed" or "diverted from its path" along the circuits of the symbolic order. That is why it is best described as a "letter in sufferance" (43/29). According to Lacan's conception, these circuits function automatically according to the same laws of binary alternation as govern computers: "For we have learned to conceive of the signifier as sustaining itself only in a displacement comparable to that found in electric news strips or in the rotating memories of our machines-that-think-like-men, this because of the alternating operation which is its principle, requiring it to leave its place, even though it returns to it by a circular path" (43/29).

In summary, then, the letter in Poe's tale operates as a signifier whose signified is irrelevant; it is not subject to divisibility; it can have and lose its place only in the symbolic order; and its displacement-and-return has much in common with binary circuits.

INTERSUBJECTIVITY

Given the letter as shifting pivot around which a pattern of human relationships rotates, let us now consider that pattern more in detail. As Lacan reads the story, the essentials of the pattern consist in an interplay between three subjective positions: one subject sees nothing, hence is "blind" to the situation in which he finds himself; a second subject "sees" that the first subject sees nothing but "deludes himself as to the secrecy" of what he hides, that is, is unaware of being "seen" in turn; a third subject sees that the first two subjects leave "what should be hidden exposed to whomever would seize it" and capitalizes on this fact (32/14). As the story proceeds, different members of the cast of characters occupy these different positions in what Lacan describes as two successive "scenes." The story ends with still another constellation of relationships that might be called (though Lacan does not explicitly do so) a third "scene."

Scene 1

In the first, "primal scene," the "blind" personage is the King, the unaware seer is the Queen, and the perspicacious "robber" is the Minister.

1. The role of the "blind" is played by the King, who, as such, signifies the "order of the Law" (50/38) that is challenged by the sheer existence of the letter. And no matter whose hands the letter falls into

(even the Queen's), nothing concerning its existence "can return to good order without the person whose prerogative it infringes upon having to pronounce judgment upon it" (42/28). Such are the demands of the (symbolic) order of the Law, even though the King himself, as individual subject, remains blind to it all (50/38).

2. In the role of the "seer" in this first scene we find the Queen, who is compromised by the very existence of the letter. Possession of the letter cannot be legitimized by acknowledging its existence before the Law (i.e., the King), yet to have this possession respected, she "can invoke but her right to privacy, whose privilege is based on the honor that possession violates" (42/28). That is why she is helpless to prevent violation of that right by the Minister, who sees her predicament and takes advantage of her helplessness.

3. The role of perspicacious profiteer in the first scene is played by the Minister, whose retention of the letter gives him political power as long as he does not "use" it as a means to attain an end beyond the sheer retention of it as a threat. The threat here is a function not of the letter as such but of the role it constitutes for the Minister (46/33), not simply as a robber but the kind of robber he is, "capable of anything" (46/33). Be that as it may, the use of the letter by the Minister "for the ends of power can only be potential, since it cannot become actual without vanishing in the process" (46/32).

Scene 2

In the second "scene," the role of the "blind" subject is played by the Queen, the role of unaware "seer" by the Minister, and the role of profiteer ("robber") by Dupin.

1. The "blind" personage here has become the Prefect of Police who now undertakes the Queen's cause and thereby stands for the Queen. It is important for Lacan's argument that he be "unable to see," hence the insistence that the Prefect's methods of search explored a kind of "space" that indeed encompassed the letter as "real" but failed to discern it as the letter in question, because as *signifier* the letter belonged not to the order of sensible reality but to the order of the symbolic (39–40/24–25).

2. The role of the complacent "seer" now is played by the Minister. But what does he see? Himself as not being seen. For in resorting to the Queen's ruse of "hiding" the letter by leaving it in the open, the Minister "realizes that the police's search is his own defense . . . [but] . . . fails

to recognize that outside of that search he is no longer defended" (44/31). In other words, just as in scene 1 the Queen's defense against the King does not protect her from the "lynx eye" of the Minister, so in scene 2 the Minister's defense against the police does not protect him from being "seen" by Dupin. Thus he is caught up in the typically imaginary situation "which he himself was so well able to see [in scene 1], and in which he is now seen seeing himself not being seen [by Dupin]" (44/31).

3. The role of astute "robber" now is played by Dupin, comprising as it does two separate phases that may be considered as one—the moment of discovery of the fateful letter hanging from the mantelpiece and the moment of substitution the following day, prepared for by the construction of a facsimile with its carefully chosen inscription and by the collaboration of an accomplice.

Scene 3

In the third "scene," with which the story closes, the pattern remains the same, but there are some changes in the cast: the role of the "blind" is now played by the Minister, the role of the self-absorbed "seer" by Dupin, and the role of the one who "sees" "what should be hidden exposed" and takes advantage of it (as the "robber," so to speak) by the (psycho)analyst/Lacan.

1. Without knowing it, and until in one way or another he becomes aware of the substitution, the Minister now assumes the mask of the "blind" personage unable to "see" the situation of fact, that is, that the facsimile in his possession is perfectly innocuous. Under what conditions will he come to "see"? Dupin predicts a humiliating scene with the Queen that will precipitate his "political destruction," but Lacan suggests that his gambler's instincts may save him yet: "If he is truly the gambler we are told he is, he will consult his cards a final time before laying them down and, upon reading his hand, will leave the table in time to avoid disgrace" (52/41).

2. But now Dupin himself assumes the role of the complacent "seer," who himself is seen for what he is, not by himself but by Lacan. For what characterizes this second position is the "typically imaginary" situation of being captured by one's own controlling self-image to the disregard of the symbolic situation of which one is a part. Lacan notes two aspects of this capture of Dupin by the imaginary. In the first place, his preoccupation with reward compromises the detachment that we expect to charac-

terize his intentions (49/37). In the second place, the explosion of anger that leads him to cite the spiteful lines from Crébillon's *Atrée* in the substituted facsimile indicates precisely that he does *not* withdraw from the symbolic circuit but rather thereby becomes "in fact, fully partici-pant in the intersubjective triad, and, as such, in the median position previously occupied by the Queen and Minister" (50/37).

3. But in thus assuming the second position, Dupin yields to another his place as the far-seeing "robber" who perceives the full import of the symbolic situation, namely to the (psycho)analyst (Lacan himself), who thus sees Dupin as failing to see himself as being seen. It is the analyst's (Lacan's) function to discern for us the symbolic structure of the entire tale and to reveal its import for psychoanalysis.

"The Purloined Letter" and Psychoanalysis

It is clear that Lacan's interest in this tale serves as a parable for his conception of psychoanalysis, according to which "the unconscious is the discourse of the Other" (32/16). More specifically, he illustrates how "it is the symbolic order which is constitutive for the subject by demonstrat-ing in [the Poe] story the decisive orientation which the subject receives from the itinerary of a signifier" (29/12). In this story the signifier is obviously the letter, and the "subject" in question is the triadic pattern of intersubjective relationships the story deals with.

Thus—and here the thesis of the essay rejoins the theme of the larger Seminar of which it is a part—it is the "*insistence* of the signifying chain" (Lacan's emphasis, 28/11) through the "intersubjective module" (32/15), whose pivot is the "pure signifier" of the "purloined letter" that accounts for the automatism of repetition (32/16). Hence the force of the analogy of the three ostriches, "the second believing itself invisi-ble because the first has its head stuck in the ground, and all the while letting the third calmly pluck its rear" (32/15); for, like the ostriches, the three subjects, "more docile than sheep, model their very being on the moment of the signifying chain which traverses them" (43/30). It is the traversing of the subjects by the signifying chain that constitutes them precisely as the kind of subjects they are, and Lacan proclaims this principle explicitly in all its radicalness:

If what Freud discovered and rediscovers with a perpetually increasing sense of shock has a meaning, it is that the displacement of the signifier determines the subjects in their acts, in their destiny, in their refusals, in their blindnesses, in their end and in their fate, their innate gifts and social acquisitions notwithstanding, without regard for character or sex, and that, willingly or not, everything that might be considered the stuff of psychology, kit and caboodle, will follow the path of the signifier. (43–44/30)

Lacan wonders, indeed, whether it is not the sense that everyone in the story is being "duped"—the French reads *joué* ("played," i.e., determined in his action by a signifying chain beyond his power to control)—that all but reduces the proceedings to a vaudeville show and makes the story amusing (33/17). Be that as it may, we get here a clearer sense of why Lacan says that "the unconscious means that man is inhabited by the signifier." We understand, too, how he can say that if the Minister (for example) forgets the letter, "the letter, no more than the neurotic's unconscious, does not forget him" (47/34), for it "transforms" him, unbeknown to himself, into the "image" of the Queen, placing him as it does in the position of the seer unaware of himself being seen. This transformation may be thought of in terms of the "return of the repressed" (47/34), that is, the perduring dynamic of the module.

With this much clear as a fundamental thesis, Lacan suggests other points of comparison between the story and the psychoanalytic process:

1. In the first place, there appears to be a certain correlation between the position of the "blind" personage and the real, between the position of the self-absorbed "seer" and the imaginary, and between the position of the perspicacious "robber" and the symbolic. But the term "real" here is decidedly ambiguous, for the specifically Lacanian sense (as the "impossible" to symbolize or imagize) yields in this text to a more normal usage signifying a naively empiricist objectivism that is oblivious of the role of symbolic structures in the organization of "reality." Hence the "realist's imbecility" (40/26), say, of the police. As for the imaginary quality of the second position, it is to be understood in terms of the narcissism (and its ruses) implied in the subject's "seeing" but failing to see that he is seen.

What correlates the third position with the symbolic is the fact that it discerns the role of structure in the situation and acts accordingly. The paradox is that, in the Poe story as told, the "acting accordingly" of the third position tends to catch the subject up in the dynamics of repetition that drag him into the second position, and so forth, without any conscious intention on his part. Thus, because the power that derives to the Minister from the holding of the letter depends on the non-use of that power, he is forced willy-nilly into the passivity of the second position.

Accordingly, "in playing the part of the one who hides, he is obliged to don the role of the Queen" (44/31). Result: "a man man enough to defy to the point of scorn a lady's fearsome ire undergoes to the point of metamorphosis the curse of the sign he has dispossessed her of" (45/31). Hence he fails to see the symbolic situation that he was once so able to see and in which "he is now seen seeing himself as not being seen" (44/31). Rather than his possessing the letter, the letter possesses him.

In similar fashion Dupin, instead of using the monetary exchange as a means (by reason of its "neutralizing" power) of "withdrawal from the symbolic circuit" (49/37), himself enters into that very circuit by the vindictive message enclosed in his substituted letter. Thus he is dragged, as if by undertow, into the second position of the triad (50/37–38). The mechanism of the module operates inexorably. When Lacan speculates that the Minister, prudent gambler that he is, may indeed "leave the table in order to avoid disgrace," the translator observes: "Thus nothing shall [have] happen[ed]—the final turn in Lacan's theater of lack" (Lacan 1972b, 72), and the module remains intact. It is this transcending power of the signifying chain, dominating the intersubjective interchange, that we take to be the thrust of Lacan's closing remark: "What the 'purloined letter,' nay, the 'letter in sufferance,' means is that a letter always arrives at its destination" (53/41).

If there is inexorability here, then what is the function of psychoanalysis? Presumably to help the subject discern this dynamic and thus attain the third position in the triad. To be sure, the task is not achieved without doing violence to the self-imaging integrity of the subject's ego, whose usual state consists in being "captivated by a dual relationship" (44/30) and engrossed in "specular mirage[s]" (47/34). This violence may even be thought of as a kind of rape (48/36). At any rate, the subject's reconciliation with the inevitabilities that permeate him is described by Lacan elsewhere in the 1954–55 seminar: "The game is already played, the dice are already cast. . . with this exception, that we may take them in hand again and cast them once more. . . . Don't you find something ridiculous and laughable in the fact that the dice are [already] cast?" (Lacan 1978b, 256).

2. A second correlation with Lacan's conception of psychoanalysis is suggested by his highly sensuous imagery, for it recalls his frequent allusion to the problem of femininity in the latter part of this essay. Not only is the second position in the triad the initial position of the Queen, but there appears to be something specifically feminine about it. Thus

"in playing the part of the one who hides, [the Minister] is obliged to don the role of the Queen, and even the attributes of femininity [*la femme*] and shadow, so propitious to the act of concealing" (44/31). The sign that the Minister steals from the Queen "is indeed that of woman [*la femme*] insofar as she invests her very being therein, founding it outside the law, which subsumes her nevertheless, originally, in a position of signifier, nay, of fetish" (45/31). Again:

It is significant that the letter which the Minister, in point of fact, addresses to himself is a letter from a woman: as though this were a phase he had to pass through out of a natural affinity of the signifier. Thus the aura of apathy, verging at times on an affectation of effeminacy; the display of an ennui bordering on disgust in his conversation; the mood the author of the philosophy of furniture can elicit from virtually impalpable details (like that of the musical instrument on the table), everything seems intended for a character, all of whose utterances have revealed the most virile traits, to exude the oddest *odor di femina* when he appears. (48/35)

Furthermore, Dupin, when drawn into the second position of the triad in the denouement of the story, experiences a rage against the Minister that is "of manifestly feminine nature" (51/39–40). And finally, "it is known that ladies detest calling principles into question, for their charms owe much to the mystery of the signifier" (52/40).

All of these texts, taken in sum, add up, it seems, to an enigmatic statement about the nature of femininity and imply a specific theory about the role of the phallus as a signifier in the sexual differentiation of the subject. For example, Mehlman notes with regard to the correlation of woman and fetish: "The fetish, as replacement for the missing maternal phallus, at once masks and reveals the scandal of sexual difference. As such it is the analytic object *par excellence*" (Lacan 1972b, 62). At issue here, of course, is not simply the phallus but the imaginary loss of it, that is, castration—whether the absence of penis is actual (as in the female) or potential (as in the male)—with all that this implies for Lacan in terms of the infant's separation from its mother and the ineluctable finitude to which it testifies. How Lacan conceived the function of castration in the constitution of the subject through primary repression as well as in its sexualization is thematized elsewhere, for example, in "The Signification of the Phallus" (Lacan 1977, 281–91/685–95). The question raised by the present text is: What precisely is being said here, where the phallus is never mentioned? Though the matter remains unexplicated by Lacan, it becomes a central issue for several of the commentators (e.g., Derrida et al.).

3. There are other issues the author raises in passing that call for examination in a much broader scope than this essay provides. One of these is the important question about the nature of truth in psychoanalysis. Clearly it is to be found on a different level of experience than that of "exactitude," with all this implies about the reduction of the real to an object of investigation controllable by the techniques of science and technology (35/20; 39–40/25). Rather, at this stage of Lacan's thought, truth apparently is to be thought of in terms of re-velation, as this term emerges out of Heidegger's analysis of the original Greek notion of truth as *a-letheia:* "When we are open to hearing the way in which Martin Heidegger discloses to us in the word *aletheia* the play of truth, we rediscover a secret to which truth has always initiated her lovers, and through which they learn that it is in hiding that she offers herself to them *most truly*" (37/21; Lacan's emphasis).

The self-hiding of truth, however, raises a complex set of problems concerning the negativity ingredient to truth as such. For example, elsewhere Lacan remarks: "the man who in the act of speaking breaks the bread of truth with his counterpart also shares the lie" (1966a, 379); and "the discourse of error, its articulation in acts, could bear witness to the truth against evidence itself" (1977, 121/409), and so on. A careful consideration of this negativity that is essential to truth as such for Lacan should precede the evaluation of any critique made of his treatment of the "meaning" of truth by the commentators. The matter has been discussed more fully elsewhere (Richardson 1983b, 149–52).

4. Still another theme that Lacan alludes to tangentially and that warrants further reflection is the role of death in psychoanalysis. For example, Lacan remarks in passing, "You realize, of course, that our intention is not . . . to confuse letter with spirit . . . and that we readily admit that one kills whereas the other quickens, insofar as the signifier—you perhaps begin to understand—materializes the agency of death" (38/24). A still more figurative (though more enigmatic) allusion comes later when the Minister, phantasied as gambler, is presumed to address the die he is about to cast: "What are you, figure of the die I turn over in your encounter (*tychē*) with my fortune? Nothing, if not that presence of death which makes of human life a reprieve obtained from morning to morning in the name of meanings whose sign is your crook"

(51/39). At the base of these allusions, we believe, is the fundamental notion that death for Lacan is, as it was for Heidegger, the ultimate sign of limit, experienced profoundly at the moment of symbolic castration when the subject submits to the law of the signifier in primary repression. It is this that constitutes the "division" of the subject, which will become so central a theme for subsequent writings in the *Ecrits* (1966a, 10).

There are other themes to single out, of course, whether they are indicated obliquely in passing or echoed by allusion, but let this much suffice to indicate the general orientation of Lacan's essay, together with the density and richness that characterize it. The heart of the matter, we repeat, is simply the primacy of the signifier over the subject. Lacan emphasizes it once more as he brings the essay to an end:

So runs the signifier's answer, above and beyond all significations: "You think you act when I stir you at the mercy of the bonds through which I knot your desires. Thus do they grow in force and multiply in objects, bringing you back to the fragmentation of your shattered childhood. So be it: such will be your feast until the return of the stone guest I shall be for you since you call me forth. (52/40)

RETROSPECTIVE PROSPECT: LACAN'S COMMENTARY ON HIS SEMINAR

The French text (1966) appends to the original essay a series of dense propaedeutic essays, somewhat repetitious of each other, that have not been translated into English. The first, entitled "Presentation of the Following," appeared in the first edition of the *Ecrits* (1966) but apparently was written earlier. It is polemic in tone, directed at unnamed adversaries, and serves as preface to the second, which bears the formal title "Introduction." The latter is succeeded by the third essay, entitled "Parenthesis of Parentheses," which redevelops the principal theses of the "Introduction" as the latter is being readied for publication.[5]

Enigmatic as these essays are, their purpose at least is clear. Much later, Lacan will tell us explicitly: "Mathematical formalism is our aim, our ideal. Why? Because it alone is *matheme*, i.e., capable of being transmitted integrally" (Lacan 1975b, 108), but already in these texts we can see that ideal struggling for articulation. Given that the theme of the entire Seminar is that the automatism of repetition is accounted for by the primacy of the signifier over the subject, Lacan tries to transpose that thesis into formal language by showing how this automatism (he now calls it "memoration") is not to be understood, in a properly Freudian conception, as a function of "memory" "insofar as that would be the property of a living being," but rather as the result of the "ordered chains of a formal language." Hence "the program that is traced out for us [here] is to know how a formal language determines the subject" (1966, 42). It is the function of the "Introduction" that follows to suggest how the "syntax" of such a language might be conceived.

Lacan's "Introduction," whose original function was to introduce his Seminar in volume 2 of *La Psychanalyse* (1956), begins by repeating themes that are familiar to us now: that *Beyond the Pleasure Principle,* with its address to the problem of the automatism of repetition and recourse to the hypothesis of a "death instinct," was but the updating of an old problematic that first found expression in Freud's *Project for a Scientific Psychology* (1954b [1895]) concerning the nature of memory. There the system *psi,* predecessor of the unconscious, "could only be satisfied by *finding again the object that had been radically lost*" (1966a, 45; Lacan's emphasis), hence is caught up in a process of "repetition" from the very beginning that extends beyond the processes of life, and in that sense may be called the "death instinct" (46).

The term "repetition" invites comparison with Kierkegaard's use of the same word in a specifically "modern" sense (as opposed to the Greek use of "recollection") to refer to the interior transformation of human existence in which consciousness, by implication, plays a part. But Freud, as opposed to Kierkegaard, refuses to identify the necessity characteristic of repetition with consciousness in the human agent. "The repetition being symbolic repetition, Freud maintains that the order of the symbol can no longer be conceived as constituted by man but as constituting him" (46). It is into this order that the child is introduced in the first experience of the phonemes, as in the *Fort-Da* phenomenon "at point zero of desire" (46), and becomes determined in both synchronic and diachronic terms (47).

To give some sense of how this determination functions, Lacan suggests that we let plus (+) represent presence and minus (−) represent absence, and then arrange a random series of them, for example: + + +

− + + − − + −. Now Lacan argues that such a series, despite the
"chance" character of its composition, manifests a strict symbolic pattern. For example, if we designate by the numeral 1 a series of three
identical signs (+ + + or − − −), by the numeral 3 a series of three
alternating signs (+ − + or − + −), and by the numeral 2 a series of
two similar signs followed or preceded by a different sign (+ + −, − −
+, − + +, or + − −), then the relationships between these different
series can be plotted on a graph to show the basic symbolic pattern that
governs them.

But first let us recall a word about graphs. Any graph is basically a set
of points and couplings of points related to each other either by lines or
(to indicate direction) arrows. The most comprehensive graph is that
between two points (e.g., A and B), where the possible relationships are
between A and B (AB), B and A (BA), A and itself (AA), B and itself (BB)
(fig. 1).

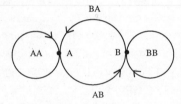

Let us suppose, however, that we complicate the graph by adding two
more points of reference, C and D (fig. 2).

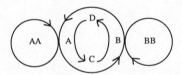

Then, in addition to the relationships we already have we shall have a
relationship between C and D, between D and C—plus, of course,
between A and C, and so on. Accordingly, we would be able to follow a
path between A-C-D-A-AA, or A-C-B-D-A, and so on, but not A-C-D-B
or A-D-C-A. Hence, as the graph becomes more complicated, certain
constraints are added.

With this much as preparation, let us come back to the graph (fig. 3)
Lacan proposed to show the relationship between the three series of pluses
and minuses (48).

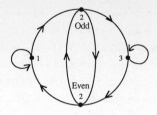

We notice that series 1 can be followed by series 2-odd, and this in turn can be followed either by series 3 or by series 2-even. The latter can be followed by series 1 or series 2-odd, but not by series 3 and so on. Note that the built-in constraints constitute a kind of "memory" as they also constitute a "law." If the different relationships in the graph may be thought of as "words," then the constraints ("memory," "law") may be regarded as "syntax."

Such then is Lacan's fundamental paradigm. He quickly lifts it to a new level of complexity (48–52) that invites comparison with the probability theories of Poincaré and Markov (51). It cannot be our purpose to follow the argument in detail, but we can grasp the general sense of the move if, for example, we make the following equivalences. Let passage from 1 to 1, 1 to 3, 3 to 1, and 3 to 3 be represented by alpha; passage from 1 to 2 and 3 to 2 be represented by beta; passage from 2 to 2 be represented by gamma; return from 2 to 1 and from 2 to 3 be represented by delta. The result will be the graph shown in figure 4.

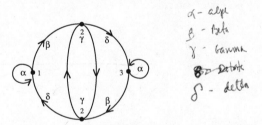

You will notice that after the repetition of a great number of *alpha*'s, if we had a *beta* before it, there can only emerge a *delta*. There you have a primitive symbolic organization. . . . In some fashion, the series of *alpha* remembers that it cannot express anything but a *delta*, if a *beta*, no matter how distant, was produced before the series of *alpha*'s. . . . From the beginning (*origine*) and independently of all attachment to any supposedly real bond of causality whatever, the symbol is already at play and engenders of itself its necessities, its structures, its organizations. (Lacan 1978b, 228)

Some of these necessities, structures, and organizations are spelled out in the present text.

More important for us than the details of the analysis is to underline the purpose of this whole exercise. The point is that what determines the Freudian subject for Lacan is of a "symbolic" nature (rather than "real"— we shall return to this distinction below) and that the symbolic order (with all its "laws") is autonomous. It is only according to such a conception that we can account for the theory and practice of free association as Freud conceives it, not according to the conventional forms of philosophical, psychological, or experimental "associationism" (Lacan 1966a, 52). Moreover, it is the conservation of the "exigencies of the symbolic chain" that permits us to situate and explain the "indestructible persistence" of unconscious desire (52). And it is surely to the autonomy of the symbolic order that Freud makes recourse when, in *Beyond the Pleasure Principle* (1955a [1920]), he attempts to explain the automatism of repetition by postulating some dimension of the human phenomenon that is "prevital" and "transhistorical" (52).

It is essential to understand, however, that the symbolic order is not the creation of human consciousness, as might be inferred if one's purview were limited to the purely imaginary interaction between an ego and its counterpart. Rather, we must think of a human being as seized (*pris*) "in his [very] being" by the symbolic order and as entering into it actively in the guise of subject only by passing through the "radical defile" of speech, such as we see happening in the *Fort-Da* experience. This formulation suggests a schematization (fig. 5) that is the most fundamental of all Lacan's schemata (scheme L, 53).

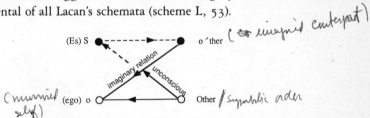

In an initial reading of this diagram that represents for Lacan the psychoanalytic situation:

S: designates the subject, and the parenthesized homophonic *Es* (*Id*, It, *Ça*)—the French retains the German spelling—suggests that the subject here is the subject of the unconscious;

o: designates the other of the subject in the sense of its own alienated image in a mirror reflection;

o': designates the other of the subject in the sense of an imaged counterpart (in the psychoanalytic situation such an other would be the analyst experienced as other ego, and the solid line connecting o and o′ would indicate an essentially imaginary relationship);

O: designates the Other as symbolic order, whose place the analyst holds.

Although Lacan does not allude here to the frequently cited text of Freud, *Wo es war soll ich werden* ("Where It was I must come to be," e.g., Lacan 1977, 171), the schema offers a convenient way to illustrate it: Whereas the subject has always been "spoken" by the unconscious, the task of the analysand, with the help of the analyst holding the place of the Other, is first to discover itself as a subject, that is, to distinguish itself from its own ego caught up in imaginary intercourse with other egos, and then to discover within itself the difference between being subject of the "enunciated" and subject of the "enunciation." It is in guise of the latter that the subject functions as subject of the unconscious and has finally come to be "where It was."

Lacan refers to such an exchange as a "dialectic of intersubjectivity" (1966a, 53), but is it really that? Hardly. What takes place is less a reciprocal exchange between two subjects than the attunement of one subject (the analysand) to the discourse of the Other coursing through it, with the help of another subject (the analyst). It is understandable, then, why Lacan soon completely drops the term "intersubjectivity" from his vocabulary. It is understandable, too, why he speaks disparagingly of a practice of psychoanalysis that remains caught on the level of the purely imaginary, such as one that overidealizes the paragon of "so-called genital love," or one that exaggerates the function of "object relations" in the process. Both neglect the fact that the Freudian unconscious is essentially the "discourse of the Other." In any case, it is the primacy of the Other over all subjectivity that accounts for the "veritable gymnastics" of intersubjective relationships on which the Seminar dwells (54).

The third installment of this postfactum propaedeutic to the Seminar receives the title "Parenthesis of Parentheses" with reference to the fact that the basic paradigm for the symbolic chain already raised to a second degree of sophistication in the Introduction is now transposed into a different key, a sequence of o's and 1's, scanned by parentheses and parentheses within parentheses (behind this is an argument made more fully elsewhere).[6] The language of o's and 1's is the binary language of absence/presence proper to combinatorial analysis, and as Lacan sees it, this was initially made possible through the development of calculus by Pascal. Whereas modern science in the classical sense had always been concerned with attempting to give a place in the symbolic order (with "exactitude") to the real—that is, to what is always found "at the same place"—the calculus of possibilities made it possible to think that symbolic "place" for itself both as presence and as absence. "Instead of the science of what is found at the same place, there is thus substituted the science of the combination of places as such" (Lacan 1978b, 345). The search for the laws that govern this combination has culminated in the science of cybernetics. The apogee of such a science would be the hypothesis (and the contemporary explosion of computer science would seem to confirm it) that "anything can be written in 0 and 1" (1978b, 346). Thus, by way of example, we can see (fig. 6) how the fundamental paradigm of the Introduction can be written (56 n. 2).

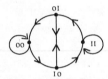

Be that as it may, it is essential to Lacan's argument that "the chain of possible combinations . . . can be studied as such, as an order that subsists with its own rigor, independently of all subjectivity" (1978b, 350). As such it is the foundation of any theory of games, laws of chance, and science of strategy. It is this sense that we understand Lacan to have in mind when he speaks of the symbolic order as the "absolute Other" (58).

Given this cybernetic subtext, the thrust of the argument remains the same as heretofore: that the symbolic order determines the subject according to laws that govern a finite number of possibilities, even for what appear to be matters of "chance." Here the emphasis is on the significance of Poe's account in the original story of the youngster's success with the game of "even and odd." The point is to distinguish clearly a purely dyadic (essentially imaginary) intersubjectivity between child and adversary from "veritable subjectivity" (57), which implies the third dimension of the "absolute Other" (58). Lacan points out that the identification of the child (i.e., "player") with his adversary through mimicry and projection of internal attitudes is essentially "imaginary," though pertaining to the "symbolic" to the extent that it is identification with the reasoning process of the adversary. If the adversary is simple and his reasoning naive, it is fairly easy for the player to outguess him by assuming a kind of analogy with himself. But what if the adversary is as sophisticated as the player himself? If the game remains on the level of reciprocal identification, the outcome will be the result of oscillating guesswork between them (1978b, 213–14). The intersubjectivity here remains dyadic. But if both players resort to "reason," then a third dimension is introduced: the function of the symbolic. For recourse is made to some sort of operating principle (Lacan calls it "law") that guides the choices involved. Then the task of one player will be to conceal that "law" from his opponent by whatever ruse he can, the task of the other to discover it. Once the true pattern of choice, no matter how complex, of one player is discovered, the other is bound to win. For example, Lacan relates how a colleague, experimenting with this game, resorted to a pattern of choice based upon the transposition into conventional terms of letters from a verse of Mallarmé (see Lacan 1978b, 224). "But if the game had lasted the length of a whole poem, and if, miraculously, the adversary had been able to recognize it [for what it was], he [i.e., the adversary] would have won every time [à tout coup]" (59).

If, then, there is such a thing as the Freudian unconscious—at least as we are given to understand it, say, in *The Psychopathology of Everyday Life* (Freud 1960b [1901]), where nothing happens by pure "chance"—then it must be conceived of as being a "law" of that kind. That is why it is not altogether unthinkable that a modern calculator, "by disengaging the phrase that modulates the long-term choices of a subject without his knowing it (à son insu et à long terme) might come to win the game of 'even and odd' beyond all customary proportions" (Lacan 1966a, 59). There is a paradox in this, however, for we would refuse to qualify such a mechanism as a "thought machine" (machine-à-penser), not because it lacks human consciousness, but because it does not "think" any more than the ordinary human does. "We don't think either at the moment that we perform an operation. We follow exactly the same mechanisms as the machines" (1978b, 350), that is, the pattern of the signifying system as such (appels du signifiant) (1966a, 59–60). This is what we take to be the absolute Other.

Note that "thought/think" here are used in a more restricted sense than Lacan uses them elsewhere to refer to "signifying mechanisms" only (e.g., 1977, 165–66/517). Note, too, that in passing from the example of the "law" in a poem of Mallarmé to the notion of "law" as the unconscious of Freud, Lacan has moved from a level of intersubjectivity to one of transsubjectivity, the dimension of the "absolute Other." This will have certain consequences, of course, for the manner of conceiving the nature of the subject that is determined by this law, but that is not the issue here. In any case, if analysts find such a conception of the unconscious disturbing, that can only be because they fail to realize that it is precisely such a notion of unconscious determination—or overdetermination—that accounts for so-called free association (1966a, 60).

But such determination—and Lacan insists on it—is not "real" but "symbolic." We take him to mean that the determination in question does not function on the level where science gives symbolic structure to the real, hence on the level of observable, scientifically calculable "reality," in such a way as to jeopardize the laws of chance as science or mathematics discerns them (see 1978b, 340–45). Rather, it functions on the level of the "symbolic," the "chain of possible combinations," antecedent to any human observability and independent of all subjectivity, making the laws of chance possible. At any rate, this absolute Other, by determining the subject as a signifying system, dominates it. This, for Lacan, is the "bottom line."

It was to illustrate this domination that Lacan chose to analyze the Poe story that contains the account of the game of "even and odd." Since the anecdote makes clear that more is involved in the child's expertise than a simple matter of chance, Lacan finds in Poe a kindred spirit, who gave evidence by his account that he anticipated the laws of combinatorial analysis and strategy. It was because his auditors found the exposition of the Poe text helpful that Lacan, in response to their request, decided to publish it separately (1966a, 61).

NOTES

1. Lacan prefers this translation to "repetition compulsion" for *Wiederholungszwang*. His reasons will appear shortly.

2. See Lacan, *Ecrits: A Selection* (1977); Muller and Richardson (1982).

3. In this mode of citation, the first page number refers to the English translation (here, of *Ecrits: A Selection* [Lacan 1977]), the second to the French original (Lacan 1966a).

4. In these citations with no date, the first page number refers to the English translation by Mehlman (chap. 2) of Lacan's "Seminar on 'The Purloined Letter,'" the second to the French original (Lacan 1966a).

5. Three years later (1969), a two-volume paperback edition of selections from the *Ecrits* appeared in the "Points" collection of Seuil and included (7–12) an untitled foreword addressed to some unnamed other. It repeats certain major themes of the Seminar with some interesting new formulations, but it is largely

polemic in tone, offering Lacan a chance to respond to his critics. Since it was not retained in subsequent editions of the *Ecrits*, we have not given it formal treatment here. Reference to it will be made by commentators.

6. See "Psychanalyse et cybernétique, ou de la nature du langage," in *Le séminaire, II* (1954–55), *Le moi dans la théorie de Freud et dans la technique de la psychanalyse* (1978b, 339–54). Lacan speaks of this lecture as the "dialectical point of everything that we instigated (*amorcé*) by the work of the year" (362).

4   🌿 Lacan's Seminar on "The Purloined Letter": Map of the Text

I.   "The Purloined Letter" and the structure of repetition.*

  A.   Freudian repetition is based on the insistence of the letter.

    1.   This is correlative to the subject's ex-centric structure,

      a)   which, in turn, reveals a correlation between the imaginary and the symbolic registers.

    2.   Imaginary features are subordinate to the symbolic register,

      a)   especially in those structures that determine the subject,

      b)   such as foreclosure, repression, and denial.

      c)   But we must not be misled by abstractions.

    3.   The truth of Freud's thought is demonstrated in a story showing how the subject is determined by the course of a signifier.

      a)   This truth makes fiction possible.

  B.   Poe's story is structured as a narration.

    1.   Without this narration the drama would be unintelligible to an observer,

---

*The major headings accompanied by roman numerals (I–VII) correspond to the sections marked by the unnumbered but distinct breaks in the French text.

      a)   for the narration casts light on the actors' perspectives.

  2.   Two scenes are narrated.

      a)   The first may be called the primal scene,

      b)   while the second is its repetition.

  3.   In the first scene the Queen, in the King's presence, is robbed of a compromising letter by the Minister,

      a)   who deftly replaces it with a substitute,

      b)   in full view of the silent Queen and without the King's knowledge.

  4.   In the second scene, after an unsuccessful police search, Dupin retrieves the stolen letter

      a)   and leaves a substitute,

      b)   without the Minister's knowledge.

C.   The two scenes share a common intersubjective structure of action.

  1.   Three terms are operative in the decisive action,

      a)   corresponding to three logical moments

      b)   and assigning the shifting subjects to three places,

      c)   based on three glances.

  2.   Such structured action warrants our invoking Freud's notion of repetition, even though more than one subject is involved.

      a)   As a discourse the unconscious is always intersubjective.

      b)   The displacement of the subjects is a function of the place occupied by the letter.

II.   "The Purloined Letter" as mystery story.

A.   It would be misleading to read Poe's story as a simple police mystery.

  1.   The conventional aspects of the detective story do not keep us in suspense,

      a)   for the criminal details are known from the start,

      b)   and the genre itself is not yet well established.

  2.   Nor is it a morality fable.

B.   Perhaps the mystery concerns Dupin.

  1.   We sense a discordance between his remarks and his behavior.

  2.   Perhaps we enjoy the tricks played on everyone, including ourselves.

  3.   But the joke reveals the fictive structure of truth.

C.   We are led to see the two scenes as complementary dramas.

  1.   The first is narrated as a play without words,

      a)   while in the second our interest is held by the narrative's discourse,

      b)   whose features indicate the drama is sustained in the symbolic order.

  2.   The first scene, filtered through multiple narrators, gives the impression of exactness

      a)   and illustrates the limitations of simplistic notions of communication theory.

  3.   But the retransmission of the first scene is in the order of language,

      a)   unlike the signaling of bees,

      b)   which is a function in the imaginary order,

      c)   as is group identification with a common object of hatred.

D.   The role of narration in the second scene brings about a transition from the field of exactitude to the register of truth.

  1.   This register is at the basis of intersubjectivity,

      a)   where the subject can lay hold of only the very subjectivity constituting an Other.

  2.   The effect of Freud's joke about lying is repeated by Dupin's exposition of his method,

      a)   which tricks us partly because we hear it from a disciple

      b)   and because the expository display itself serves to hide the truth from us,

      c)   echoing Heidegger's notion of the hiddenness of truth.

  3.   The narration, however, does provide us with some clues to the truth,

      a)   in stating that what is simple is most obscure,

      b)   in raising a hint about the superiority of the poet in the matter of concealment,

      c)   and in the simplistic notion of spatial concealment held by the police.

E.   The relations between place and letter are best described as odd.

  1.   In a sense the letter has the property of nowhereness.

  2.   Although the signifier is material, it remains what it is even when cut into pieces.

  3.   It is never conjoined with a partitive adjective.

  4.   As symbol of an absence, it is and is not wherever it may be.

  5.   The truly hidden is what is missing from its place,

      a)   and such placing is a function of the symbolic order.

F.   The police, even while examining the torn letter, could not re-
     ceive the message on its reverse.
     1.   The letter did not fit the description they had of it,
          a)   and thus for them the letter had only one side.
     2.   However, its message has already reached its destination,
          a)   since the torn letter represents it as well as the original did.
     3.   The signifier cannot be reduced to its function of communicat-
          ing a message,
          a)   otherwise love letters would not be returned,
          b)   and spoken words would not be associated with transference.
III.   The letter's possession.
   A.   A stolen letter seems to imply an owner.
        1.   We know that letters are returned,
             a)   implying the sender has a claim on them,
             b)   and that perhaps the addressee was never the true destined
                    receiver.
        2.   Poe's story reveals neither the letter's content nor its sender.
   B.   For the Queen, the letter symbolizes a pact.
        1.   It puts into question her honorable relation to the King,
             a)   for it situates her in another chain of signifiers.
        2.   Whoever holds the letter is likewise affected by it
             a)   and is subject to the judgment of the King.
   C.   The word "purloin" implies a diversion or misplacement.
        1.   This suggests the signifier has a proper course,
             a)   one marked by displacement,
             b)   as in thinking machines that operate by symbolic
                    alternation.
IV.   The Freudian notion of repetition is confirmed in Poe's story.
   A.   We must, intersubjectively, follow the grid of the symbolic
        order,
        1.   even modeling our being on particular moments in which we
             are crossed by the signifying chain.
   B.   This path of displacement of the signifier determines who we are,
        1.   even more than native, social, or psychological factors.
V.   In possession of the diverted letter, the minister is put in the
     Queen's place.
   A.   He too conceals the letter by leaving it exposed.
        1.   For he too is lured into a dual relation,
             a)   in which he believes that while seeing he is unseen.

  2. He thus loses his former perspective,
   a) as the third in a symbolic situation.
 B. As the one who hides the letter, he even takes on the Queen's womanly and shadowy characteristics.
  1. The letter is a sign of the woman,
   a) for she puts her worth in it,
   b) founding her being outside the law,
   c) but in her origins the law holds her in position as a signifier,
   d) even as a fetish.
  2. By maintaining immobility in its shadow,
   a) she feigns mastery through inactivity.
  3. The Minister's inactivity is likewise a consequence of the letter,
   a) whose power lies in its non-use,
   b) an effect of the prolonged diversions of a pure signifier.
  4. The Minister's power thus comes not from the letter but from the role it gives him
   a) in a narcissistic, dual, imaginary relation to the Queen.
   b) But, separated from the letter, the Queen has assumed the King's slot.
  5. The Minister, so transformed, even repeats the Queen's actions,
   a) which are deciphered by Dupin.
VI. Dupin, in turn, is affected by the letter's possession.
 A. Two episodes reveal that he too shifts from the symbolic to the imaginary perspective,
  1. while we analysts now occupy the third position.
 B. He trades the letter for money,
  1. thus destroying its significance,
  2. returning it to the place of blindness,
  3. and reinforcing the status of the police.
 C. His message to the Minister is an act of revenge,
  1. making his exploit inglorious,
  2. for he too is caught in a dual, imaginary relation.
VII. The Minister, like the gambler, questions the meaning of the die as signifier without signification.
 A. Dupin, like the place of the woman he now occupies, resists such a question,
  1. for the signifier reveals death's presence,
  2. marks our destiny,

    3.   and structures our desire by articulating and thus fragmenting it.

B.   Because our message returns to us in inverted form,

    1.   a letter always reaches its destination.

5 🌿 Lacan's Seminar on "The Purloined Letter": Notes to the Text

The first of each pair of page numbers below refers to the English translation of Lacan's seminar by Mehlman (Lacan 1972b) as it is reprinted in this book (chap. 2), and the second refers to the French version in *Ecrits* (Lacan 1966a). The letters designate the paragraph, beginning from the top of each page. For other references to *Ecrits*, the first page number refers to the English translation by Alan Sheridan (Lacan 1977) and the second to the French original (1966a).

28/11 The epigraph is from the "Witches' Kitchen" scene of Part One of Goethe's *Faust* (lines 2458–60), which Kaufmann translates:

And if we score hits
And everything fits,
It's thoughts that we feel.

(Goethe 1963, 245)

Why does Lacan begin with this quotation? He does not tell us. We can wonder, however, about the correlation in Freud and Lacan between "es" and the unconscious and take these lines to suggest that our views and behavior are governed by unconscious processes. (The source of the quotation was identified by Don Eric Levine, Department of Comparative Literature, University of Massachusetts, Amherst.)

28a/11a Experience is inscribed semiotically on many levels, some of which, given repression, are not directly available to consciousness. Such unconscious inscription repeatedly insists on being recognized through dream images, fantasies, parapraxes, and so forth, but is experienced as foreign to and decentered from the conscious ego. The French text has "excentrique" for what the English translates as "eccentric" and indicates that the "subject of the unconscious" occupies a place whose center is other than that of the conscious ego. For further elaboration of the Lacanian subject, see Richardson (1983a).

28b/11b The seminar will show that whatever relations individuals maintain, however they represent themselves to one another, all of these are subordinate to the position and structure given them by the symbolic order.

28c/11c The word *Prägung* denotes the impression of an image stamped on a coin. The French text says the imaginary impregnations give the signifying (not "symbolic") chain its "allure," more than is given by the English translation's use of "appearance." This would refer to the attracting, captivating qualities of images.

These "psychoanalytic effects" are defined and clarified in Laplanche and Pontalis (1973). *Foreclosure* is the central mechanism in psychosis whereby a central signifier fails to be inscribed in the unconscious; *repression* itself is a failure in translation from one level of inscription to another; denial (better translated "denegation" for *la dénégation*) involves the use of the signifier "not" in order to maintain the mechanism of repression while allowing its content to enter consciousness. The word *Entstellung* more properly means "distortion" and is used by Freud in *The Interpretation of Dreams*. There he describes the process of dream formation, one of whose twin governing principles is that of displacement (*Verschiebung*). Lacan is emphasizing that these fundamental psychological processes are structured by the concatenation of signifiers (the chaining of linguistic elements) and not by the parade of images (with which they are conjoined), whose presence serves primarily to cast shadows or reflections rather than give direction or meaning to the process.

29e/12c In *Le séminaire: Livre II* (Lacan 1978b [1954–55]), when Lacan first presented his analysis of "The Purloined Letter" (225–40), he devoted several sessions to "the even and the odd" (207–24). We refer to this discussion in the Overview (chap. 3).

29h/12f The text here uses the rhetorical device of repetition: without narration, the action would be "invisible," the speech devoid of meaning; in other words, nothing of the drama would be comprehensible to sight or sound ("ne pourrait apparaître ni à la prise de vues, ni à la prise de sons"). Thus we prefer to translate the French *outre que* not as "aside from the fact that," but rather as "moreover, that the dialogue," thus setting up the meaning/sound pair to parallel the action/sight pairing.

Rather than "without, dare we say, the twilighting which the narration, in each scene, casts on the point of view," we prefer to translate as "without the twilighting, dare we say, which the narration of the point of view gives to each scene" ("sans l'éclairage à jour frisant, si l'on peut dire, que la narration donne à chaque scène du point de vue." The "twilighting" echoes Dupin's not lighting the lamp at the beginning of the story.

30a/12g The English "and by no means inadvertently" translates "et non pas par inattention." The same word (*l'inattention*) is repeated in the following paragraph as a feature of the King; Lacan here is (perhaps "inadvertently," shall we say?) tracing both a negation of and an identification with the position of the King. Lacan's knowing/not knowing will take on some importance in the critical pieces to follow.

The designation "primal scene" ("scène primitive") may be an allusion to what has been called a "classic essay" (Most and Stowe 1983, 13), namely, "Detective Stories and the Primal Scene," by Geraldine Pederson-Krag, first published in the *Psychoanalytic Quarterly* in 1949 (reprinted in Most and Stowe 1983, 14–20).

30e/13d "The Purloined Letter" (1844) is the third and final detective story involving Dupin, following "The Murders in the Rue Morgue" (1841) and "The Mystery of Marie Rogêt" (1842). Therefore it is not the "second time" that Dupin's "specific genius for solving enigmas" is introduced by Poe, as Lacan says here and repeats later (33c/16g).

31b/14b The English word "gaudily" translates "retenant l'oeil de quelque clinquant." This lure of the eye proper to the imaginary order is, as it were, checked by Dupin, whose eyes are "protected" by green glasses, underlining his ability to correctly "read" the situation from another perspective (that of the symbolic order). The contrasts between light/darkness, deception/seeing occur throughout the Poe story. Dupin's first quoted words in the story are: "If it is any point requiring reflection . . . we shall examine it to better purpose in the dark."

31d/14d The phrase "quotient of the operation" repeats words used in an earlier paragraph, "an operation . . . whose quotient" (30c/13b).

That usage was followed (30d/13c) by the word "remainder" (*reste;* italicized in French). Here the use of "remainder" is absent in the English, but it appears in the French as a verb: "ce qui lui reste en main." Lacan considers the action of the thief (the Minister in scene 1, Dupin in scene 2) under the rubric of an arithmetic operation—namely division, from which there results a quotient in each case (the changed position of the former occupant of the letter) as well as a remainder (the substituted letters). Such "mathematization" of the action of the two scenes, giving them an identical structure, supports the thesis he next develops that the "similitude" between the two goes well beyond the collection of common "traits" and rests instead on what he calls "the intersubjective complex" (32f/15h).

Mehlman (Lacan 1972b, 43) notes: " 'So infamous a scheme, / If not worthy of Atreus, is worthy of Thyestes.' The lines from Atreus's monologue in Act V, Scene V, of Crébillon's play refer to his plan to avenge himself by serving his brother the blood of the latter's own son to drink."

31e/14e The French text refers not to "two sequences" but rather to "deux actions," and it is *their* differences that would be deleted by a selfserving selection of common traits. Such post hoc listing of descriptive features, discredited in a structuralist framework, is no guarantee of any truth. Truth can emerge only from structural laws of transformation (see Piaget's *Structuralism* [1970]).

The English "through which it structures them" suffers from a chronic problem in translating Lacan, namely, the ambiguity of pronouns. Here the "it" refers to intersubjectivity, while "them" refers to the two actions. In the next paragraph the "it" refers to "the decision" that deals out the subjects to the three places ("sujets qu'elle départage," translated in the English by "the subjects among whom it constitutes a choice," which is somewhat confusing, since, as assigned, the subjects precisely have *no* choice).

32a/15c We prefer to read that the maneuvers following the decisive moment add nothing to the glance moment. For a useful summary of Lacan's earlier essay on time, see Wilden (1981, 105, n. 47).

32f/15h Mehlman (Lacan 1972b, 44) notes: "*La politique de l'autruiche* condenses ostrich (*autruche*), other people (*autrui*), and (the politics of) Austria (*Autriche*)."

32g/15i Although "modulus" (which correctly translates the French "module") denotes mathematical properties, it is perhaps more simply rendered as "module" (as in the French, "Le module intersubjectif"). This would signify the interchangeability of the repeated actions, but at the cost of not emphasizing its mathematical properties ("modulus" being defined as "some constant multiplier, coefficient, or parameter involved in a given function of a variable quantity, by means of which the function is accommodated to a particular system or base" (Webster's unabridged dictionary, 1980 edition).

32h/16a For further elaboration of the phrase "the unconscious is the discourse of the Other," see Muller and Richardson (1982, 110–11, 116, 209, 368). Its laconic use here calls attention to the essentially intersubjective character of unconscious processes. The notion of the "immixture of subjects" was featured by Lacan in his essay "Of Structure as an Inmixing of an Otherness Prerequisite to Any Subject Whatever" (1972a) and was introduced earlier in his discussion of the Irma dream in Seminar II (1978b, 192), where it is given the following sense: "An unconscious phenomenon that unfolds on a symbolic plane, as such decentered in relation to the ego, takes place always between two subjects." For an interpretation of Lacan's analysis of the Irma dream (in contrast to Erikson's analysis of the same dream) see Richardson (1983a).

32j/16c At the end of this paragraph the French text makes the first of its six breaks. Lacan returns to this theme (of the subjects' replacing each other) after the fourth break (44b/30c).

33e/17b One critic has remarked: "We ought to have been warned by the very name Dupin (which does not quite conceal the French verb meaning 'to dupe')" (Most 1983, 344).

33f/17c For the phrase "that everyone is being duped" the French text has "que tout le monde soit joué," calling attention to the "play" of language, whether as the "jeu des signifiants" (Lacan 1977, 196/551) in the history of a given subject or the "jeu combinatoire" (1973, 24) of the science of linguistics. The notion of our being "played with" or "played out" by language is a recurrent theme for Lacan. He repeats the verb "jouer" three times on the next page (1966a, 18).

34f/18d Here the "it" refers to "but a single meaning." The point seems to be that because the Prefect is literal minded and misses shades of ambiguity, the overall effect on the reader of his deafness to Dupin's remarks is to minimize the importance of the apparently incidental comments, for example, about the Minister being a poet and a fool, as context that provides meaning for the dialogue (see the Poe text earlier).

35c/19c Benveniste (1971, 54) describes the communication of bees as "not a language but a signal code," because the subject matter is fixed, because the message is invariable and related to a single set of circumstances, because of its "unilateral transmission," and because it is impossible to separate the message's components.

Lacan later specified that a point-to-point visual correspondence is characteristic of functions in the imaginary order (1978a, 86). The communication of bees, Lacan wrote earlier, "is distinguished from language precisely by the fixed correlation of its signs to the reality that they signify" (1977, 84/297). He adds, furthermore, that the bee's message is never retransmitted. This much, at least, the Prefect is capable of doing, since he is a speaking human.

35e–f/19e–f Rather than translating as "by those traits in the individual each of the two resist," we can read "by those traits of being which each of the two shun" ("par les traits de l'être auquel l'une et l'autre se refusent"). The point here seems to be that there is a type of identification with a denied (hated) or idealized (loved) feature that binds individuals: such communion is governed primarily by the imaginary order and is not, as such, articulable.

There may be an allusion here to Gustave Le Bon, who wrote in 1895: "A crowd thinks in images, and the image itself immediately calls up a series of other images, having no logical connection with the first" (1960, 41). Le Bon described the individual in a crowd as follows: "We see, then, that the disappearance of the conscious personality, the predominance of the unconscious personality, the turning by means of suggestion and contagion of feelings and ideas in an identical direction, the tendency immediately to transform the suggested ideas into acts; these, we see, are the principal characteristics of the individual forming part of a crowd" (32). In *Group Psychology and the Analysis of the Ego* (1921) Freud reviewed Le Bon's work and specified the mechanism of identification with a common object or quality. Summarizing, and comparing group psychology with being in love and hypnosis, Freud writes: "*The group* multiplies this process; it agrees with hypnosis in the nature of the instincts which hold it together, and in the replacement of the ego ideal by the object; but to this it adds identification with other individuals, which was perhaps originally made possible by their having the same relation to the object" (1955b, 143).

35g/19g Speech repeats signifiers (not natural signs), and so do symptoms.

35h/19h The English "sifts out" translates the French "décante," meaning to pour off gently, separate, or simplify. The narrative act gives us,

Lacan says, a ready access to the linguistic dimension in part 1 of the story, but in contrast the second narration is full of verbal tricks.

35j/20b Lacan creates a parallel between first dialogue (Prefect and Dupin)—speech—exactitude and second dialogue (Dupin and friend)—word—truth. The relation of signifier to speech is one of impoverishment ("dépouillement," translated as "state of privation"), insofar as one cannot ascertain the truth simply in this relation; truth exists in between speaking subjects; it is dialogic and presupposes the Other, a structural perspective not reducible to an aspect of oneself or to a mirroring of oneself (and hence "absolute").

The initial dialogue between the Prefect and Dupin is marked by the pretension to "exactitude" (even down to the "fiftieth part of a line"), while the subsequent dialogue between Dupin and the narrator opens up the process of truth as concealment and unconcealment insofar as we are or are not duped by Dupin's words. (For they too might prompt us to ask, as in Freud's joke, "Why are you lying to me?")

Mehlman (Lacan 1972b, 49) notes: "Freud comments on this joke in *Jokes and Their Relation to the Unconscious* (1960a, 115 [1905]): 'But the more serious substance of the joke is what determines the truth. . . . Is it the truth if we describe things as they are without troubling to consider how our hearer will understand what we say? . . . I think that jokes of that kind are sufficiently different from the rest to be given a special position: What they are attacking is not a person or an institution but the certainty of our knowledge itself, one of our speculative possessions.' Lacan's text may be regarded as a commentary on Freud's statement, an examination of the corrosive effect of the demands of an intersubjective communicative situation on any naive notion of 'truth.'"

36b/20c The word *éristiques* means disputatious or marked by spurious reasoning.

Lacan's discrediting of the witness (who presumably possesses a kind of one-to-one fidelity and exactitude that blinds us to the register of truth) whose testimony cannot be criticized may be a reference to Marie Bonaparte, who appears to be the subject of a derisory footnote later in the text (48/36). For a brief historical survey of her role in Lacan's "excommunication" from the International Psychoanalytic Association in 1953, see Turkle (1978).

36d/20e An alternative reading is that by relying solely on visual identification "he cannot reach the first level of his mental elaboration." As in Freud's joke, you can't figure it out if you remain locked solely in a dual relation, for you must invoke the symbolic dimension of the Other (in this case, to formulate rules of sequencing).

36e/20f François duc de La Rochefoucauld (1613–80) is the author of moral maxims and witty epigrams. Lacan refers to him with favor in earlier texts (1977, 54, 119/264, 407).

Jean de La Bruyère (1645–96) translated Theophrastus from the classical Greek, wrote character sketches and maxims as a social critic, defended the classics, and was a member of the French Academy.

Niccolò Machiavelli (1469–1527) replaced mercenaries with a citizens' army in the Republic of Florence in 1506. He wrote *The Prince* in 1532. Tommaso Campanella (1569–1639) was a Dominican philosopher. His utopian *Civitas solis* (*The City of the Sun*) is modeled on Plato's *Republic.* His emphasis on perception and experimentation anticipated scientific empiricism.

Sebastien Roch Nicolas Chamfort (1740–94) is another French author of maxims and epigrams.

We are indebted for this and other information to *The New Columbia Encyclopedia,* 1975 edition.

36f/21b Among other meanings, according to Lewis and Short (1955), *ambitus* can mean a going-around or periphery, *religio* is conscientiousness or exactness, and *honesti* means respectable or becoming. Clearly Lacan himself is having a good time here and is implicated in Dupin's charge that the mathematicians "have insinuated the term 'analysis' into application to algebra. The French are the originators of this particular deception," with Lacan taking the lead in using topology and set theory in conceptualizing psychoanalysis.

37b/21c The French text (1966a, at least in the later printings) has the following note regarding the "master words": "Regarding these three words, I had at first considered the meaning each would have as a commentary on the story, in case its structure was not enough. But I dropped these unfinished hints for this edition when I reread my essay; moreover, someone told me too late that someone else has done it in a more explicit way—he can have a place off this page."

37d/21e The French text has the Greek word *alēthēs,* literally, the "unconcealed." The phrase "the play of truth" translates "le jeu de la vérité." See M. Heidegger, "On the Essence of Truth" (1977, 113–41).

37e/21–22a This paragraph abounds in alliteration in French (e.g., "la tentative contre la tentation contraire").

37h/22c The point is not of earthshaking importance, but the fact is that the Prefect does not suffer from a "false distribution of the middle term," as far as we can see. His argument would seem to be: All poets are fools. But the Minister is a poet. Therefore, the Minister is ["one remove from"] a fool. The major premise may be untrue, but the middle term ("poets") is at least properly "distributed," that is, it covers all members of the class it denotes in at least one premise (here, the major). The conclusion may be false, but the reasoning is correct. Dupin's version ("All fools are [some] poets. . . . Therefore all poets are [some] fools") does indeed involve a sloppy "distribution," but since it is unduly attributed to the poor prefect, who already has quite enough troubles of his own, it may say more about the pretentiousness of Dupin than about the poor reasoning of the prefect.

38c/23c John Wilkins (1614–72) was an English mathematician and philosopher who wrote *Mathematical Magic* (1648) and probed the nature of language as the crucial epistemological issue for science. For an extensive review of his ideas, see Aarsleff (1982). *Roget's International Thesaurus* (1961 edition) includes "nullibicity, nullibiety, and nullibility" as synonyms for "nowhereness" under the heading "Absence." The "Roget" here also alludes to the second Dupin story.

38e/24a The signifier "materializes the agency of death" insofar as, according to Lacan following Hegel (see Kojève 1969, 140 ff.), the word is "the murder of the thing" (Lacan 1977, 104/319). The word negates the immediate physical presence of things by providing them with a symbolic presence that enables things to become articulable and subject to mediated relationships. Words enable things to be substitutes in desire: but words also thereby constitute a distance from things. For further elaboration see Paz (1981) and Muller and Richardson (1982, 120). Lacan quotes Saint Paul, "the letter killeth while the spirit giveth life" (2 Cor. 3:6) in "The Agency of the Letter in the Unconscious" (1977, 158/509).

Instead of "The vitalism informing its notion of the whole," the translation should read "The vitalism inhabited by its notion of the whole" (i.e., "vitalisme larvé de sa notion du tout"). For an elaboration of the role of "the whole" in Gestalt theory, see Kanizsa (1979). Lacan appears to say that the letter's indivisibility is not due to the unifying dynamism forming wholes in Gestalt theory.

In his footnote to this paragraph, Lacan refers to philosophical arguments "à partir de l'un et du plusieurs," meaning the perennial problem of "the one and the many," beginning with Parmenides (see Kirk and Raven 1983) and crystallized in Plato's *Parmenides* (see Cornford 1957). The issues at stake are the relation of beings to Being, creatures to the

Creator, individuation, the changing world as illusory veil covering an unchanging reality, and so forth.

38c n.7/23n.1 Borges's interest in detective fiction is noted by Holquist (1983, 171–72). Borges has his detective Lönnrot compare himself to Dupin in the opening paragraph of "Death and the Compass" (1967, 1).

39d/24d Earlier in the *Discourse at Rome* Lacan described the word as "a presence made of absence" (1977, 65/276). This will have relevance for Derrida's critique of "phallogocentrism" and its presumed "metaphysics of presence."

39e/25a Space "sheds its leaves" (*s'effeuiller*) insofar as it is stripped by the police, like a tree losing its leaves or a book being stripped of its pages (also *feuilles* in French).

39f/25b Once again, the antecedents of the pronouns and possessives may be ambiguous. The way the police view the real tends to transform it (the real as space "shedding its leaves") into the object of their search, namely the letter. By thus objectifying the letter in their realist way, they hope to find it located among other objects and to differentiate it from them. The French text has "perhaps would be able to distinguish" ("peut-être ils pourraient"). Of course, it is their literalness that blinds them to the letter's presence once its appearance has been altered (or so we are led to believe).

40a/25c The key proposition should read: "For it can *literally* be said that something is missing from its place only of what can change its place, only of the symbolic" ("C'est qu'on ne peut dire *à la lettre* que ceci manque à sa place, que de ce qui peut en changer, c'est-à-dire du symbolique"). The real has no relations (for some elaboration of the Lacanian notion of the real see Richardson 1985, 1987; Muller 1987); the imaginary has point-to-point fixed relations; the symbolic has arbitrary, multilevel relations that allow what was formerly of the real to enter symbolic articulation.

40b/25d The French word *saisir* (translated by "seized") can be translated by "grasped" to connote the sense of "comprehended" as distinct from "took." The police picked up the letter in their physical search of the Minister's premises without grasping that it was what they were after.

Lacan devoted attention to Joyce in his 1975–76 seminar titled "Le sinthome."

40d/26c "The signifier is not functional" with regard to simply communicating a message. Lacan had written, in the *Discourse at Rome,* "The function of language is not to inform but to evoke" (1977, 86/299).

41a/26e The letter would not be incomprehensible to the King, the Prefect insists, were he to read it. The reference to Ubu recalls the figure in the play *Ubu Roi* by Albert Jarry (1873–1907), first presented publicly in 1896 and judged to be the first play in the theatre of the absurd (other Ubu plays followed). The character of Ubu grew out of a student's spoof (Lycée de Rennes, 1888) and came to symbolize the quintessence of egotistical, and eminently stupid, power. Jarry influenced the dadaists and surrealists (see LaBelle 1980).

41c/26g The Latin phrase "Scripta manent sed verba volant" ("What is written remains but spoken words fly away") is a legal maxim with no author attribution (Mencken 1942, 1328).

41d/27b Mehlman (Lacan 1972b, 56–57) notes:

The original sentence presents an exemplary difficulty in translation: "Les écrits emportent au vent les traites en blanc d'une cavalerie folle." The blank (bank) drafts (or transfers) are not delivered to their rightful recipients (the sense of *de cavalerie, de complaisance*). That is: in analysis, one finds absurd symbolic debts being paid to the "wrong" persons. At the same time, the mad, driven quality of the payment is latent in *traite,* which might also refer to the day's trip of an insane cavalry. In our translation, we have displaced the "switch-word"—joining the financial and equestrian series—from *traite* to *charge.*

Flying leaves (also fly-sheets) and *purloined letters*—*feuilles volantes* and *lettres volées*—employ different meanings of the same word in French.

41e/27c The second break in the French text occurs just before this paragraph.

The Chevalier d'Eon was Charles de Beaumont (1728–1810), an officer and spy of Louis XV stationed at the courts of Russia and London. He first disguised himself as a woman in Russia in order to gain access to the empress and subsequently "disguised" himself as a man. Recalling him later from London, where his gallantries risked compromising the English court, the French government insisted that he maintain his female disguise and that he surrender certain compromising papers. He had maintained a confidential correspondence with Louis XV on political matters and left behind his thirteen-volume *Loisirs du Chevalier d'Eon* (1775). Lacan may also be referring to correspondence published in Paris in 1778 titled "Pièces relatives aux démêlés entre Mademoiselle d'Eon de Beaumont, chevalier de l'Ordre roial & militaire de Saint Louis & ministre plénipotentiare de France, &c. &c. &c. et le Sieur Caron, dit de Beaumarchais &c. &c. &c" (Pierre Augustin Caron de, 1732–99). After his death a physical examination proved he was in fact a man (see Cox 1961).

42c/28b Earlier Lacan wondered if the letter's addressee were not its true recipient (*le vrai destinataire*); here he appears to be saying that whoever the letter is addressed to is its recipient (*sa destinataire*). Are we to distinguish, then, apparent or temporary recipient from "final" or "true" recipient?

42e/28d For "compounded," the French has "doubled" (*doubler*). The theme of treason (*trahison*) is repeated on the next page when Lacan charges Baudelaire with having betrayed Poe (*a trahi Poe*).

43b/29b *The Oxford English Dictionary* indeed has the following in its entry for "purloin": "AF [Anglo-French] *purloigner* = OF [Old French] *porloigner* . . . , f[ormed on] *por-*, *pur-* : − L[atin] *pro* − + *loing, loin* : − L. *longe* far; hence, 'to put far off or far away, to put away, to do away with.' The sense 'make away with, steal' appears to be of English development."

43e/30a For the phrase "the subject must pass through the channels of the symbolic," the French text has "le sujet suit la filière du symbolique." The word "filière" means an implement with holes for making vermicelli and also a spinneret and, by extension, a channel, series, or ordeal. Lacan repeats the same verb (*suivra*) in the following paragraph when he says everything will follow the path of the signifier.

44b/30c We left "our drama and its round" on 32j/16c–d with the first break in the French text.

44d/30e The dual relation in which the Minister is captivated is with the Prefect: The Prefect's way is to search for what is presumably hidden in secret recesses, and this is mirrored by the Minister, who acts as if he has nothing to hide; that is, who finds a way to hide it without recourse to secret recesses—his best defense, as long as no one else comes along to question the initial premise. In the French text "And what does he fail to see?" continues the preceding paragraph and is not set off separately as in the English.

44g/31c Mehlman (Lacan 1972b, 61) notes: "*Autruicherie* condenses, in addition to the previous terms [see note 32f], deception (*tricherie*)."

44h/31d Here begins the most obscure part of Lacan's Seminar. What is at stake is his view of the relations between "woman" and language as well as between women and men. This vast topic can be further explored in the following: Mitchell and Rose (1982), Gallop (1982), Irigaray (1985), Marks and Courtivron (1981), and de Lauretis (1984).

A broad paraphrase may orient the reader: what is concealed by veiling "woman" (a construct of our phallocentric discourse and desire) is castration, taken as the condition of radical human finitude.

45c/31g In Poe's story the letter is a sign of the Queen's disloyalty to the King and thereby places her "outside the law." The position of woman as signifier recalls Lévi-Strauss's thesis (e.g., 1969, 496) regarding the prohibition of incest: that the origin of language and culture involved establishing pacts by means of the exchange of women between groups (for whom the women then symbolized the pacts). But this assumes that women occupied a distinct place before the establishment of such pacts, a place therefore prior to or "outside" the ensuing law.

Woman's "simulation of mastery in inactivity" ("simulation de la maîtrise du non-agir") places the issue of woman's "passivity" into an active, determining, tactical context; it thus is not to be taken as a "biological given."

45e/31i Mehlman (Lacan 1972b, 62) quotes from Plato's *Meno:*

[Socrates,] At this moment I feel you are exercising magic and witchcraft upon me and positively laying me under your spell until I am just a mass of helplessness. If I may be flippant, I think that not only in outward appearance but in other respects as well you are exactly like the flat sting ray that one meets in the sea. Whenever anyone comes into contact with it, it numbs him, and that is the sort of thing that you seem to be doing to me now. (Plato 1963, 363)

45h/32d The biblical reference is presumably to Matt. 18:6–9.

46d–o/33c The "narcissistic relation" is enacted in the mirroring of consciousnesses as expressed in "The robber's knowledge of the loser's knowledge of the robber," one of whose imaginary features is taken to be the attribution of absolute mastery supposedly leading to immediate action.

47a/33d For "in fact" the French reads *réellement*.

47d/34c By "return of the repressed" we understand the survival of a signifying system, that is (here), the dynamic power of the triadic module in which the Minister, having defeated the Queen's strategy, falls victim to the letter's influence.

47e n.12/34 n.1 Poe's story appeared in *Chambers' Edinburgh Journal* in November 1844 (not 1841, as Lacan notes) following its 1844 publication in the American annual *The Gift* (Mabbott 1978, 3:972).

46d–e/36a Mehlman (Lacan 1972b, 67 n.38) uses the metaphor of rape to interpret these two paragraphs. We suggest another reading: the Queen's letter, forgotten and repressed in its non-use by the Minister, occupies and transforms him so that he acts like the Queen. Just as a name stretches over an entire region on a map, signs of the Minister's transformation pervade his apartment like an immense female body, serving to camouflage the letter's presence.

48f/36b This paragraph receives further attention in later papers. At this point it may be argued that Lacan's dramatization presents a parody of Marie Bonaparte's approach that culminates in his footnote to this paragraph, a footnote that Lacan added to his text after the original publication in *La Psychanalyse* (1956), where it does not appear.

In her own book on Poe, Marie Bonaparte gives her résumé of "The Purloined Letter," quotes the Poe text in French, and corrects Baudelaire's translation by stating: "L'inexactitude de la traduction de Baudelaire, en ce qui concerne cette phrase, apparaît. En particulier, *beneath* (*au-dessous*), y est rendu par *au-dessus,* qu'il ne saurait en aucun cas signifier" (1933, 600). Her footnote is omitted from the English translation that appears later in this book (chap. 6).

A chimney and mantelpiece figure prominently in Marie Bonaparte's earliest reported dream (Bertin 1982, 28, 160).

The fifth break in the French text occurs here.

49a/36c In doubting that the effectiveness of symbols ends "there" where Marie Bonaparte left her psychoanalytic reading of Poe, Lacan is also, in his allusion to Lévi-Strauss (he made the same allusion elsewhere, e.g., 1977, 3/95), making his own this much of the structuralist position. He refers to the symbolic "debt" in the *Discourse at Rome* (1977, 67/278).

49b/36d The phrase "a closing *pirouette*" translates "un jeu de la fin."

50a/37d Mehlman (Lacan 1972b, 68) notes: "Cf. Corneille, *Le Cid* (2.2): 'A vaincre sans péril, on triomphe sans gloire' (To vanquish without danger is to triumph without glory)."

50e/38b The French text has *devait rentrer* for "would reenter," and therefore includes the notion of "ought to."

50g/38d "Rex et augur" literally means "king and soothsayer." In ancient Rome the king had priestly duties and dignities. After the kings were expelled the title "rex" continued to be given in religious language to priests who performed these duties, of which soothsaying was one.

50h/38e The word "equivocation" translates *l'amphibologie,* meaning "ambiguity." As a figure of speech, amphiboly means "Ambiguity arising from the uncertain construction of a sentence or clause, of which the individual words are unequivocal: Thus distinguished by logicians from equivocation, though in popular use the two are confused" (*Oxford English Dictionary*).

50i/38f In the *Discourse at Rome* Lacan inquired about the origin of language and noted the function of "lances stuck into the ground" as signifiers of a pact (1977, 61–62/272).

There is an ellipsis here of the verb: the sense of the Latin quotation is that a cobbler should not *go* "beyond his sole." Don Eric Levine provides the following sources for the Latin quotation:

1) Pliny *Natural History* 35.85;
2) Erasmus *Adgia* 1.6.16, "Let not the shoemaker go beyond his shoe [or last]."
3) *Romeo and Juliet*, 1.2.39: "It is written that the shoemaker should meddle with his yard and the tailor with his last, the fisher with his pencil and the painter with his nets."
4) The entry in Larousse presents these as words spoken by a painter in response to a shoemaker's criticisms of how he painted a sandal.

51a/39a Rather than "to forge its proofs," the French text has *en forger-
. . . les preuves,* "to forge their proofs." The sense here seems to be that liberal humanism has quickly been followed by (and perhaps as a result) statist revisioning of history.

51e/39e The French word translated by "gambler" is *joueur.* For Lacan's discussion of automaton and *tychē,* see Lacan (1973, 51–54). The sixth and final break in the French text occurs at the start of this paragraph.

51g/40a The French text has *L'image de haute volée* for "The prestigious image."

52a/40b For "ladies" the French text has *les dames.*

52c/40e Rhyming with *destin* the French text has *festin* for "feast." In his analysis of the Don Juan legend, Otto Rank devotes a chapter to the motif of the Stone Guest (1975, 61–77). A French revision appeared that incorporated Rank's work on the theme of the double (Rank 1932).

53a/41b For "always arrives at its destination" the French text has "arrive toujours à destination." The English text omits "according to the very formula of intersubjective communication" ("selon la formule même . . . de la communication intersubjective").

This formula is a favorite, for Lacan repeats it (1977, 85/298, 131/420, 305/807). Its sense appears to be that the good listener resonates with what is unconscious in the speaker's conscious communication, and his or her response thus consists in returning to the speaker (by way of "inverting" and making the unconscious conscious) what was left unsaid in what the speaker said (see Muller and Richardson 1982, 83).

TWO   *On Psychoanalytic Reading*

6 🎋 *Selections from* The Life and Works of Edgar Allan Poe: A Psycho-analytic Interpretation

MARIE BONAPARTE

LITERATURE: ITS FUNCTION AND ELABORATION

Before embarking on our analysis of Poe's tales, we wrote: "Works of art or literature profoundly reveal their creators' psychology and, as Freud has shown, their construction resembles that of our dreams. The same mechanisms which, in dreams or nightmares, govern the manner in which our strongest, though most carefully concealed desires are elaborated, desires which often are the most repugnant to consciousness, also govern the elaboration of the work of art." Freud, in *The Relation of the Poet to Day-dreaming* (1948b {1908}), has demonstrated the links which bind the daydreams of adolescents or adults—so nearly related to the dreams of the night—to the play activities of children; both being fictive fulfillments of wishes. There, too, Freud shows how daydreams and creative writing resemble each other, since the latter gratifies the artist's deepest infantile, archaic, and unconscious wishes in imaginary and, more or less, disguised form. Literary works might thus be ranged according to a

From Marie Bonaparte, *The Life and Works of Edgar Allan Poe: A Psycho-analytic Interpretation,* trans. John Rodker (New York: Humanities Press, 1971). Reprinted by permission of Humanities Press, Inc., Atlantic Highlands, N.J. 07716.

scale of subjectivity. At one extreme, we should find the writings of a Maupassant or Zola, works written almost impersonally, as it were, in which the author is a spectator merely recording the panorama of existence: such, so to speak, would be works of "viewers" of genius, resembling certain unusual forms of daydreaming, however different, at first sight, they might seem from the average night or day dream. In every case, however, we should have to determine the extent to which the author's personality, split into psychic elements seeking to embody themselves in different characters, permits the author to re-embody himself in each of the characters observed. So, too, in mythological subjects, which would seem a source of external inspiration to the dramatist or poet, and which represent humanity's collective phylogenetic daydreams, an author's ontogenetic complexes will always seek ways of expression in the choice of theme and its elaboration.

It is thus possible, through infinite gradations, to pass from what appear purely objective works to others altogether subjective, which last would seem the original form of creative writing. In this latter the author's complexes, more or less masked, project themselves into the work.

It is works that are wholly subjective, loaded with their creator's unconscious memories or, as we would say, with his complexes, which resemble not only adolescent daydreams but even the night dreams of man. Thus, at one end of our scale we might place the works of a Poe or Hoffman which not only resemble the dream in the fashion they are elaborated, but often reproduce the shape and construction of our nightmares. Moreover, addiction to drugs, doubtless, played its part in the creations of both men.

* * * * * * * * *

The deep infantile sources from which Poe's inspiration was drawn have, we trust, been made clear in the earlier portions of this study. It now remains for us to show, as in Poe's tales, what psychic mechanisms, as such, generally govern the manner in which works of literature are elaborated.

In his *The Interpretation of Dreams,* that foundation stone of modern psychology, the only psychology worth the name, that which probes the unconscious, Freud, concluding his chapter on dream elaboration, wrote:

It [the dreamwork] may be exhaustively described if we do not lose sight of the conditions which its product must satisfy. This product, the dream, has above all to be withdrawn from the censorship, and to this end the dreamwork makes use of the *displacement of psychic intensities,* even to the transvaluation of all psychic values; thoughts must be exclusively or predominantly reproduced in the material of visual and acoustic memory-traces, and from this requirement there proceeds the *regard of the dream-work for representability,* which it satisfies by fresh displacements. Greater intensities have (probably) to be produced than are at the disposal of the night dream-thoughts, and this purpose is served by the extensive *condensation* to which the constituents of the dream-thoughts are subjected. Little attention is paid to the logical relations of the thought-material; they ultimately find a veiled representation in the *formal* peculiarities of the dream. The *affects* of the dream-thoughts undergo slighter alterations than their conceptual content. As a rule, they are suppressed; where they are preserved, they are freed from the concepts and combined in accordance with their similarity. Only one part of the dream-work— the revision, variable in amount, which is effected by the partially awakened conscious thought—is at all consistent with the conception which the writers on the subject have endeavoured to extend to the whole performance of dream-formation. (1953b, 468–69)

Starting from this résumé of the conditions which must be satisfied by the dream product and which imply the processes which govern its formation, we shall see that these processes, in varying aspects and degrees, are identical with those by which the unconscious content of a literary work, using preconscious thought as a between stage, is able to pass into the conscious product of the written work. We shall find nothing to surprise us in this fact, since these mechanisms and laws are none other than those which universally govern the human psyche.

* * * * * * * * *

Before, however, we study the diverse processes which govern the elaboration of a literary work, let us seek to formulate a more precise idea of the different psychic states to which we have referred.

What are we to understand, first, by unconscious memories, representations or affects which, let there be no mistake, denote happenings which pass totally unperceived or even suspected by consciousness? Our earliest infantile memories always remain in this condition, as do the representations associated with them. They thus form, with the atavistic sum total of our instincts, the nucleus of what we term the unconscious, from which only their unconscious *affects* succeed in emerging into the preconscious, though displaced on other objects. Thus, it is, that our infantile unconscious continues to govern our lives by imposing its choice of those representations most fitted to effect such displacements.

Preconscious representations may be described as those which, though generally unconscious, may nevertheless emerge into consciousness given suitable occasion. Thus, in effect, we distinguish between two types of unconscious; on one hand the unconscious proper which can never be brought to the surface, composed of the original storehouse of our instincts and earliest infantile experiences, and on the other, the preconscious compounded of later memories and representations which, though generally unconscious, may, under favoring conditions, be brought into consciousness.

As for consciousness, its part is very limited, although psychology once included every psychic function in this category. It would appear to be merely our capacity for apperception but, here, turned inward to happenings in the psyche. And, just as our capacity for external perception, via the senses, can only perceive phenomena without probing their essence, so our faculty of inner perception can only observe surface movements and gleams of happenings in the inaccessible depths of our unconscious. Thus our conscious ego is never but the more or less watchful spectator of ourselves.

When dreams or literary works are elaborated what generally happens, as indeed with all our psychic products, is that first there has been an external perception. During the day, however, our attention, to adapt us to reality, requires to move from object to object. Thus, the beginnings and ends of certain trains of association, during the day, sink into the preconscious. There they continue until their affect is dispersed and vanishes. But, also, they may encounter a link which, by association with some unconscious memory, leads to the unconscious. The entire preconscious chain of association is then swept into the unconscious and charged with the incomparable energy inherent in archaic repressed affects which remain resistant to time, because to consciousness. Reinforced by this affect, they then emerge into consciousness as a night or day dream. It is when this "sinking into the unconscious" takes place, and before they emerge in new guise, that the preconscious thoughts are subjected to the curious processes, processes very different from those of logical thought, which we shall now consider.

But before we do so, a further remark is necessary. Although language forces us to speak of *sinking* into the unconscious and passing from the unconscious to the preconscious, we must beware of imagining unconscious, preconscious, or conscious as localized regions of the psyche, for they are but diverse *conditions* of the latter.

* * * * * * * * *

By sinking into the unconscious, thought pictures (representations) are, first, able to *lose* their affect, which then slips on to more or less allied representations. Examples of such *displacement of psychic intensity* are so numerous, in the tales we have studied, that they constitute, so to speak, the warp and woof of the writer's fabric. To mention only the most striking: in the series of tales of the "live-in-death mother," for instance, displacement is generally confined to transferring the predominant affect, originally attached to the mother, to the imaginary figures endowed with the attributes which pertained to the dead woman. Berenice, Morella, Ligeia, Madeline, are as morbid, as evanescent as advanced consumptives, while their sylphlike motions seem, already, to exhale an odor of decay. Nevertheless, this simple displacement served to keep Poe ignorant, as for almost a century his readers, that these ailing sylphs were but forms of Elizabeth Arnold. At the most, it was sometimes guessed that Virginia might be a surrogate of Elizabeth.

With "The Fall of the House of Usher," however, a greater degree of displacement strikes us. There, the "live-in-death mother" is represented not only by Madeline's human form but as a building—a house whose walls, whose atmosphere, breathe putrefaction. To effect this gross displacement, Poe employs one of man's universal symbols—that which represents a woman as a building.

In "Metzengerstein" the mother is represented, totemically, by a horse. It is on this that the incestuous libidinal emphasis, which originally belonged to the mother, is displaced. Whoever would have found his way through all this but for the keys, the laws, revealed by Freud in his *The Interpretation of Dreams?* Intellectually that is, for it is just because our unconscious so well *recognizes,* under the strangeness of the manifest tale, the depth and reality of the tragedy latently enacted, that each of Poe's stories stirs our instincts so deeply, however puerile they at times seem.

With the tales of the "mother-as-landscape," the displacement of psychic intensities manifests itself in ever more forms and on a yet vaster scale. Our primary bent, to absorb the universe narcissistically, enables the libido with which we invest objects to attach itself to all our senses perceive, however microscopic or large—the seas, the earth's depths, the stars. Thus the mother, the first object we learn to differentiate from ourselves, is represented in *The Narrative of Arthur Gordon Pym* not only by ships, or the strange white totem animal Tekeli-li, but also by the ocean, one of her universal symbols.

Again, in the burial fantasy of *The Narrative of Arthur Gordon Pym* and more, even, of "The Gold-Bug," the earth also symbolizes the mother, and its "bowels," her bowels or womb. In its turn, too, in "The Unparalleled Adventures of One Hans Pfaall," the pale, cold moon represents the mother, while the son's yearning for these symbolic mothers is revealed in the passion with which Poe's various heroes seek to explore and win the earth, the sky, the seas. In Poe's three sea stories, the sea yawns into vast funnels down which the son precipitously returns to the place wherefrom he issued.

In that strange tale "Loss of Breath," with its indirect confession of Poe's impotence, it will not surprise us to discover many and varied instances of such displacements. The basic displacement, here, is that whereby affect is transferred from the natural concern felt by all men in connection with their sexual potency to a concern for lungs and breath. Here, too, Poe has resorted to one of humanity's consecrated symbols, for many theogonies attribute creative powers to their deities' divine breath. It would be beyond our scope to recall here all the displacements with which this tale abounds. The first "guilty" aggressive sex attack by Mr. Lacko'breath was, as we saw, replaced by verbal aggression which resulted in his punishment; namely, the loss of breath inflicted by the castrating father in shape of Mr. Windenough; his being crushed by the fat gentleman in the diligence; his being dismembered by the surgeon and, again, his being perforated by the undertaker's screw; all so many variants of the same theme. On the other hand, he is *rephallized* in the form of hanging. And erection is depicted by an endless swelling of the hero's body after he is hanged. Thus, the libidinal emphasis properly attached to the phallus is displaced on this swelling, which now appears as anxiety and the antithesis of the pleasures so much feared by Poe. Perhaps the only *motif* which appears almost unchanged is that of Elizabeth Arnold's "guilty" love letters, doubtless because, thus *isolated* in a distorted context, they seemed sufficiently disguised. This whole tale, which confesses Poe's tragedy, his impotence, is characterized by its reversed affect: it is a tragedy masquerading as burlesque. Representation by opposites, by which we disguise what we dare not openly express— which device we shall later discuss—dominates this tale. Nor is it by chance that even *rephallization* is represented, ironically, by a limp, dangling body.

In the tales of the "murdered mother," displacement of affect is clearly revealed. The slayer-father, as imaged in the infantile sadistic concept of coitus, here appears as the mysterious unknown, the man of the crowd, "type and genius of profound crime" as, also, in the orangoutang of "The Murders in the Rue Morgue." In one case a dagger symbolizes the piercing phallus; in the other, a razor. There is displacement, too, in the locked room of the rue Morgue—which represents the mother as much as does old Madame L'Espanaye—and displacement once more in the chimney, which figures the maternal cloaca into which the daughter is thrust. Further displacements are the gouged-out eye of "the black cat" symbolizing the castration wound, the cat's *rephallization* in the form of hanging, and the cat as widespread symbol of woman and her genital organs.

In the tales of "revolt against the father," the psychic emphasis properly attached to the phallus is attached to "The Tell-Tale Heart," while that in "The Cask of Amontillado," proper to the maternal bowels, is shifted upon Montresor's vaults. Indeed, all representations by courtiers, princes, or kings, of the parents we knew as children, as in "Hop-Frog" or "The Red Death," are so many displacements designed to render them unrecognizable for what they are, so that, unsuspecting, they may play their "guilty," libidinal parts.

The devil who bets and wins Mr. Dammit's head, and the symbolic bridge which beheads him with its iron bracings, were, as we saw, displacements first of the avenging father and then, of the danger-fraught vagina with its imaginary, fearsome teeth. Innumerable are the displacements which went to construct "The Pit and the Pendulum" nightmare. The cell as the contractile womb of the mother, the vaginal pit, and the penis-scythe of Time, are but the most striking. Finally, what shall we say of the sidereal displacements of that androgynous system *Eureka* or of its God who, like all great deities, is a displacement of the father on infinity; or of the primal ejaculation of that God; or again, of the Particle Proper, that first spermatozoon from which, through irradiation or cellular fission, the universe, child of God, was born?

But here we must interrupt our recital of these examples of displacement in the stories we have analyzed. To instance them all would be almost to rewrite this book.

Of all the devices employed by the dreamwork, that of the *displacement of psychic intensities*—apart from one exception—is the most freely used in the elaboration of works of art, doubtless because such displacement is generally dictated by the moral censor, which is more active in our waking thoughts than in sleep. The conceiving and writing of literary works are conscious activities, and the less the author guesses of the hidden themes in his works, the likelier are they to be truly creative.

* * * * * * * * *

The moral censor, as we see, employs displacement to veil from authors, as from dreamers, the nature of the instincts which dreams, or works of art, reveal. But there is yet another condition which creative work must satisfy, namely, *regard for representability,* although in less degree than is required by dreams or the plastic arts. This *regard for representability,* as Freud wrote in the passage earlier quoted, leads to fresh displacements which, in dreams, attach themselves to latent elements too abstract to fulfill the regard for representability needed to create dreams. Yet, in literature, we frequently find chains of abstract thought which would, with difficulty, find their way into dreams—as, for instance, Dupin's reasoning at the beginning of "The Murders in the Rue Morgue" or Legrand's deductions in "The Gold-Bug." The dream, for instance, in the former, would have represented the comparison of the "ingenious" chess player with the more "analytic" whist player by simultaneously, or successively, presenting people playing whist and chess, the superiority of the whist players being conveyed in a final presentation of the latter. Nevertheless, the tendency to replace abstract concepts by sensory images, mainly visual, is apparent even in the elaboration of imaginative works. The appearance of the Red Death in Prince Prospero's palace, intended to represent the invading epidemic, is depicted by the entrance of a masked, blood-spattered, human form which strikingly, and visually, characterizes the plague's symptoms. The Angel of the Odd also, in its way, "visualizes" unconscious memories of the real fluid nourishment the child absorbed from its mother. Also, by a process of *condensation* which we shall soon meet again, the story similarly "visualizes" the wish for other imagined excreted bodily foods which the child, later, wished to receive from the father who, then, had become the love object. One of the substitutes, later, for this food, in the unconscious, is drinking with bosom cronies. All this, which could not be said directly, is visually expressed by the angel's appearance—a creature composed of bottles and kegs of nourishing fluids, which it lavishes on the narrator while belaboring him with blows. Thus it recalls Poe's upbringing by John Allan.

In "Metzengerstein," the son's incestuous union with the mother is magnificently visualized in the rider's mad rush while glued to his inseparable, symbolic charger. In "The Descent into the Maelstrom," the return to the womb has all the immensity of a vertiginous plunge into the ocean's yawning chasm. Similar examples of intensely visualized displacements can be endlessly found, and described, in Poe's tales.

* * * * * * * * *

But here we shall pause to turn to another problem, observing that, of the four kinds of displacement mentioned as needed to fulfill the regard for representability, three are direct representations of the human body or certain of its parts.

May not, also, the first example, the plague figured as "The Masque of the Red Death," be traced back to a human prototype? For the masker who sows the pestilence or red death is, as we saw, identical with the murdered Oedipal father who, by the talion law returns, in his turn, to become the slayer.

The other displacements with which we first dealt, resulting from the behests of the moral censor, also mostly end by representing human beings in one shape or other. These generally human symbols, invariably derived from the human body, we have throughout found enlisted in the service of the displacement mechanism made necessary by the moral censor.

To the reader, our analyses may at times have seemed overmuch to stress these symbolic devices which, monotonously, bring everything in the universe back to the same human prototypes—father, mother, child, our members and organs, and, in particular, the genitals. The fault, however, is not ours. We cannot help it that the unconscious monotonously reiterates certain themes, governed as it is by our most primitive memories and our most archaic instincts.

Now, of the two great instincts that govern our lives, hunger and love, hunger is much the less *psychological,* doubtless because the nutritive instinct is only in slight degree "compressible." He who eats not, dies! This imperative instinct thus demands to be more or less satisfied and, as a result, has small opportunity to provide psychic substitutes for itself. But what turns the libidinal instinct, the libido, into the *psychological* instinct in excelsis, that whose derivatives and substitutes engage the whole psyche, is not only its compressibility (man, at need, may live without direct satisfaction of his erotism) but doubtless, also, the biological fact that the libido, like the psyche, stands in a specially close relation to the nervous system. So closely interwoven is the erotic instinct, and its dynamics, with other aspects of the psyche, that they seem quite impossible to separate out, as we see from that universal phenomenon sublimation, on which all our civilizations have been raised.

The initial autoerotism of the nursling, with its diffused seekings for gratification, eventually enters a narcissistic phase where the child takes itself as its first love object. In this phase, the child does not as yet distinguish its own body from the breast which suckles it, nor from the mother's soft, warm body; only later does the mother become its first awareness of the outer world. By degrees its father, brothers and sisters, then the outer world, materialize behind the mother and, under the growing pressure of reality, become accepted by the child. The unconscious, however, finds means to revenge itself for thus being robbed of its omnipotence, and the outer world, which destroys our primary, nar-cissistic illusions is, in its turn, *narcissized* by the unconscious. In this process, the child, ontogenetically similar here to our remote ancestors, passes through an animistic stage whose symbols still rule our souls, whether we be primitives or highly civilized—symbols which, doubt-less, are its ineradicable vestige.

Thus it is that symbols for the body, the mother and father, their genitals and ours, throng the unconscious and are projected into what-ever the psyche produces, whether we sleep or wake. For, as instances from every domain of the spirit show:

We need not assume that any special symbolizing activity of the psyche is operative in dream-formation; . . . on the contrary, the dream makes use of such symbolizations as are to be found ready-made in unconscious thinking, since these, by reason of their ease of representation, and for the most part by reason of their being exempt from the censorship, satisfy more effectively the requirements of dream-formation. (Freud 1953b, 332)

Symbols succeed in satisfying both the conditions required for displace-ment; namely, the demands of morality and concreteness. Thus, we find they abound in mythology, art, and religion as, also, in dreams.

Poe's opus, which, in any case, comes as near to the dream as is possible for any successfully conceived conscious production, is found to be especially rich in symbols; these help to instill that intense and visual eloquence which communicates direct from the unconscious of one indi-vidual to that of another.

* * * * * * * * *

Contrary to *displacement, condensation,* that other primary mechanism in the elaboration of dreams, appears to be less active in the elaboration of literary works than of dreams. In particular, it is responsible far less often for those nonsensical products that seem to defy all logic, which we know as nonsense dreams: products resulting from drastic condensation of convergent and, even, divergent thoughts. That difference, doubtless, inheres in the fact that literary creation is the product of the waking psyche. When we are awake, preconscious and conscious thoughts domi-nate, with their strivings for logic, and the unconscious is deeply buried. It is only, however, in the unconscious that condensation takes place. The unconscious, alone, is the crucible into which the preconscious thoughts, once they have sunk there, automatically, as it were, form those strange and at times ridiculous amalgams we know as "condensations." It need not surprise us, therefore, to find that Poe's tales, though at times so similar to dream products, show less condensation than our dreams.

Condensation appears when, despite the conscious thought of the tale, deep unconscious processes are at work. Poe's women, with their "supernatural aura" were, as we saw, condensations of many of the women he loved: Berenice, Madeline, and Eleonora, especially, reveal characteristics of Virginia, his small cousin, as much as of his mother Elizabeth. The Marchesa Aphrodite, in "The Assignation," with her "statuelike" figure, condenses Mrs. Stanard, Elmira, Frances Allan, and Elizabeth Arnold. The Marchese Mentoni, that grim avenger on his palace steps, recalls Judge Stanard and John Allan. Furthermore, the old man in "The Tell-Tale Heart" was shown to condense David Poe, his suppositious successor in Elizabeth's affections and, also, John Allan. Many such instances could be given, were we to seek out, in Poe's works, all those composite figures which—by overdetermination, condensation, and the fusion of many people's attributes into one—result in a general underlining of certain characteristics and, so, in the creation of those intense, almost mythical paternal or maternal figures which so strongly affect our minds. In effect, the purpose condensation fulfills is to produce affects more intense than those found in our latent thoughts, to which end it picks up and concentrates the scattered preconscious thoughts as they sink into the unconscious.

Suffice it if we again recall the figure that seems to come at the end of our scale, that of the Angel of the Odd, which condenses the father concept (John Allan and his whippings), the mother (bottle = breasts) and milk (alcohol) as well as various bodily secretions, female or male, (again alcohol).

Passing to other types of condensation we find that, though the Marchesa Aphrodite and Poe's other composite figures are built up after "the method employed by Galton in producing family portraits"—by superimposing family likenesses one on another, "so that the common features stand out in stronger relief, while those which do not coincide neutralize one another and become indistinct" (Freud 1953b, 282–83), condensation may also create hippogriffs and chimeras. The fantastic Tekeli-li in *The Narrative of Arthur Gordon Pym,* by its cat's head, reminds us of the mother and her genitals and, by its whiteness, of her milk. By its scarlet teeth and claws it also reminds us of the cannibal wishes which develop in the child with its growing teeth, and of the talion for its guilty wishes which the child imagines may be exacted by her teeth, or even vagina, in punishment not, now, for its cannibal wishes but for its incestuous desires. As to the long and prominent rat's tail, that doubtless is an offshoot of the *penis* which the child originally attributes to the mother, while the doglike ears of the strange "cat" are perhaps borrowed from Tiger, Pym's dog, with its mother characteristics.

Again, a single manifest element may represent several which remain latent: Mr. Lacko'breath's lost breath, for instance, represents both creative male potency and intestinal flatus. In "The Gold-Bug," the treasure is strongly overdetermined and represents several hidden and implied sets of ideas. First, all of the fantasies of real wealth which occupied Poe as the son of poor strolling players and, later, as the disinherited "son" of John Allan, reflect themselves in Captain Kidd's dazzling treasure. But beneath its superficial glamour, deep and unconscious drives lend power and conviction to the treasure theme. The unconscious memory of little Rosalie, born shortly before he visited the Carolina coast for the first time with his mother, and his ruminations on her birth, are what unconsciously inspire Legrand's inductions. As for the buried treasure they reveal, this emerges as a substitute for the infant sister whose sojourn in his mother's womb he had guessed.

The treasure itself, with its gold and precious stones, we saw revealed as symbols of the child's first "gifts"; the feces which, in return for his own "generosity" in yielding his, she will exchange for a similar gift. We may recall in this connection the symbolic maternal animals which in "Peau d'Ane" and so many other legends, excrete gold in place of feces. So too, it was from Frances Allan that Edgar desired these anal gifts, gifts expressed in "The Gold-Bug" in the classic, symbolic form of gold and jewels. Yet this gold was not Frances's, but John Allan's. When Frances heaped luxuries on her foster son, it was her husband's wealth which allowed her to do so. The child who, at first, had seen only the "mother's" generosity, must soon have seen from a dispute, word, or gesture that the money she spent came, in fact, from the man. Whence the equating of gold with the father's male potency and, so, penis.

Thus, as a result of factors specific to Poe's childhood and early life, the ancient and universal equation *feces* $=$ *gold* $=$ *child* $=$ *penis* declares itself, in this model tale, in the greatly condensed and sole theme of treasure.

* * * * * * * * *

Another psychic process however, the opposite, as it were, of condensation, even more frequently manifests itself in creative writing than in dreams—that by which one individual is split into several.

In Morella, Ligeia, and Eleonora, the manifest forms of the first wives begin as condensations of the images of Elizabeth and Virginia; they then, however, split to represent, separately, once more distinct from each other, the two images originally separate in the latent thought of the tale. The process to which we allude is thus only apparently at work, for the second act, which restores the second Morella, Rowena, or Ermengarde, merely resolves the earlier condensation.

In "The Black Cat," however, we do, in fact, see the mother split into several characters: the slayer's wife, Pluto, and the second cat all reproduce this one prototype. But, as ever in the unconscious, the diverse mechanisms involved in psychic elaboration function simultaneously. Through *displacement,* the psychic emphasis that belongs to the mother is shifted on the unrecognizable cats or on the murderer's anonymous wife. Through *condensation,* in each of these three protagonists, the poet's mother Elizabeth has been fused with Virginia his wife and, what is more, has incorporated Catterina, Poe's cat, in two of them.

Also, the mechanism by which one character is split into several equally affects their derivatives. The mother, for instance, in whom other elements are so fused as to be no longer recognized, is also split into three. And each of these mothers has her own characteristics, as well as others common to all three. Though all three are symbolically castrated, either genitally or by loss of an eye, thus declaring themselves all mothers, there was a time when Pluto had perfect eyes, a time of more virility than the second cat ever knew, though likewise a male. Thus, the three forms of the mother, in the tale, paint the mother from different angles. Pluto is first the phallic mother, at the time the small boy really believed in his mother's penis. But once Pluto has been symbolically castrated by the man, once the mother has been punished for introducing castration into the world, as witnessed by her body, the second cat appears with the large white splotch on its chest. This second cat represents the nursing mother pleading for pardon by her milk, by her life-giving breasts in lieu of the penis. Finally, in the murderer's wife, we see the mother's original human form emerge from under its totemic cat disguise, in the same way that, with the ancient gods, the original form of the father reappears under their primitive totemic guises. And the double murder, that of the wife after Pluto, clearly reveals who, in the first instance, in cat form, was slain.

As for the father, we see him *multiplied* rather than *subdivided* in "Loss of Breath," in the series of castrating fathers. In *The Narrative of Arthur Gordon Pym,* the father is split into the two classic categories of good and bad father; on the one hand the good but weak captains, Barnard and Guy and, on the other, the rebellious mate and Too-wit, both evil but both eventually rendered impotent like the wicked grandfather with his futile cane. The only survivor, save for Pym, is Peters, himself split off from the author's *ego* and, so to speak, his heroic *ego-ideal*.

Nevertheless, the possibilities of such splittings of the father are limited: he can never be identified with matter in general—the earth and water. Per contra, the mother, as we saw in "The Fall of the House of Usher," appears doubly determined as Madeline and the manor while, in "The Black Cat," she appears as the wife, as both cats, and, again, as the house with its cellar. Again, in "The Murders in the Rue Morgue" she appears both as a woman (the murdered old woman) and then as a room which, though all its orifices are sealed, is nevertheless forced open. In *The Adventures of Arthur Gordon Pym,* this defusion of the mother's entity possibly reaches its highest point, so generally is it attached to all objects for, though she is not revealed in her real form save as the white phantom which closes the tale, we nevertheless find her split up on every page and attached to all objects in nature: the sea and its waves, the earth and its streams and chasms, not to mention the symbolic ships, the dog Tiger, and the Tekeli-li, each of which represents the mother, though with varying attributes.

When defusion attains such proportions, we may wonder, however, whether we can still, properly, speak of *splitting*—a term reserved for the splitting between individuals—for this special psychic mechanism, like a river confined, then loses itself in the vast and general ocean of symbolism.

The splitting up of a single personality, moreover, seems far more appropriate to serve multiple representations of the ego than to depict either father or mother.

Freud writes, in *The Interpretation of Dreams,*

There are also dreams in which my ego appears together with other persons who, when the identification is resolved, once more show themselves to be my ego. . . . I may also give my ego multiple representation in my dream, either directly or by means of identification with other people. (1953b, 308–9)

Again, in "The Relation of the Poet to Day-dreaming," he says,

It has struck me in many so-called psychological novels, too, that only one person—once again the hero—is described from within; the author dwells in his soul and looks upon the other people from outside. The psychological novel in general probably owes its peculiarities to the tendency of modern writers to split up their ego by self-observation into many component egos, and in this way to personify the conflicting trends in their own mental life in many heroes. (1948b, 180)

One can hardly apply the term "psychological novelist" to Poe in its literal sense, but in his eminently egocentric productions many examples of splitting the ego start to the eye.

First and foremost, "William Wilson." We saw, in analyzing this tale, how clearly Poe himself appears in the two William Wilsons; one, personifying his deepest instincts, the id, the other his superego or conscience; this last, derived by introjection from John Allan, the father. This instance is almost schematic and the fact that the author himself was partly aware of its conscious implications lends the tale a certain lack of warmth. Of more significance to us, because of the unconscious mechanisms at work, are the frequent examples where the ego is split in "The Murders in the Rue Morgue." We have already seen that Dupin, the infallible ratiocinator, is Poe in person, the world decipherer of cryptograms and puzzles; a Poe who, in a field apparently purely intellectual, took his revenge for the sexual investigations in which, as a child, he had failed. But Dupin's friend the narrator, who observes and admires the infallible ratiocinator is once again Poe, this time as spectator, from outside, of his own final triumph. It is in the soul of this narrator, present in "The Mystery of Marie Rogêt," "The Purloined Letter," and "The Gold-Bug" that, as Freud says, the author dwells and looks out upon the other characters, father, mother, or split-off ego. The sailor, the owner of the orangoutang, is Poe again, but now the infant present at the parental sex act, sadistically conceived. Thus, part of Poe's ego has attached itself to the father-figure orangoutang in his desire to identify himself with the father to whom the mother belongs. But only the merest allusion indicates this—the creature's youth.

Examples of such splitting-off of the ego might be multiplied in Poe's tales, a mechanism frequently employed in the representation found in creative writing. At its base, moreover, is found the displacement which helps to bring this about and, also, to achieve the *regard for representability* of the writer's material. Such splittings-off enable specific aspects and qualities of the ego to be personified and made concrete and visual. Thus, in "The Murders in the Rue Morgue," the sailor visually embodies Poe's infantile curiosity, Dupin, his eager infantile investigations and the narrator his, doubtless, precocious bent toward self-observation.

* * * * * * * * *

So far, we have seen the same classic mechanisms at work, more or less, in the elaboration of imaginative literature and dreams: condensation, displacement, and regard for representability; this last, like the moral censor, using displacement for its ends. The splitting of a single latent personality, in particular the author's ego, into several manifest characters was found to be one way of obtaining *representability,* itself controlled by *displacement.*

When, however, we come to deal with the way in which literary creation seeks to express the *logical relation* of its themes, manifest or latent, we naturally expect to find it differ greatly from the construction of dreams. Literary creation, being a conscious product, is subject to reason and logic.

So, indeed, at first sight it appears, for the dream has no obvious means by which to represent logical relations (Freud 1953b, 296 ff.), while literature may command the whole range of conjunctions and prepositions. Thus, imaginative writing seems in general to obey the laws of logic and, in many cases, to be coherent to a high degree. Nevertheless, it must not be forgotten that though, on the surface, a literary work relates a manifestly coherent story, intertwined with it and simultaneously, another and secret story is being told which, in fact, is the basic theme. Though, therefore, the manifest tale normally obeys the rules of logic, this deeper current is subject to other laws.

In this respect the work of art resembles every product of the human psyche in which the two great forces which dominate the psyche—the preconscious and unconscious proper—are simultaneously at work, though in different degrees. The contradiction between the preconscious latent dream thoughts, for instance, coherent and logical as they are, and the alogical incoherence imposed on the same thoughts by the dream-work once they have entered the unconscious, has been emphasized by Freud (1953b, 545). This same contradiction is found in creative writing, and the degree in which the latent thought, itself coherent, appears incoherent and illogical will depend on how nearly the work approaches the dream. Poe's works, in effect, fall into that category of literature which presents dream and nightmare characteristics in high degree. It need not therefore, at times, surprise us to see some loosening of the surface logic reveal the deeper alogical unconscious structure and the strange representations employed.

In "Ligeia," for instance, the latent preconscious content of the tale seeks to express the theme: "*Because* I continue fixated to my mother, I cannot love another woman." But before these preconscious thoughts could be represented, they had to sink with the unconscious where, as a result of the infantile, archaic desire with which they were linked—that of refinding the mother who forever dwells there—they acquired the power to emerge in the imagery of art. Thereafter, exactly as with dreams and their hallucinatory processes, the logical relation between two terms will only be expressed representationally, as in the substitution of the ghostly Ligeia's image for that of the dead Rowena. "It is *because* I am always there," the mother seems to be saying, "that it is as though other women did not exist for you." This is as though Poe himself were to declare: "*Because* I am still fixated on my mother, I cannot love another woman." Here, literature uses one of the dream's classic devices, the substitution of one person for another to express a causal relation. "*Causation*," says Freud, "is represented by succession, sometimes by the succession of dreams, sometimes by the immediate transformation of one image into another" (1953b, 302). Thus Rowena-Virginia turns into Ligeia-Elizabeth; thus the first Berenice, the little cousin, at first dark of complexion and glowing with health, almost as suddenly, in the library, is metamorphosed into the corpselike Berenice, whose haunting teeth and yellow hair recall the nightmare "life-in-death" of the Ancient Mariner. In both cases, the transformation is intended to express the same causal relation, the same ban upon women which his mother fixation imposed on Poe. It is meant to express the same *because*.

In this passage from *The Interpretation of Dreams* which we have quoted, Freud shows how, in dreams, causation may also be expressed by succession in the different parts of the dream, the former and shorter portion being, as it were, the prologue to the main dream. May we not see an example of this type of causal representation in "The Murders in the Rue Morgue"? Let us recall the episode concerning Chantilly which so arbitrarily, it seems, appears to precede the history of the ape's crime. There Dupin, from various clues, guesses the train of thought which, at that moment, had led his friend to think of the actor and, from the narrator's thoughts, evokes the ridiculous Chantilly. Earlier, however, we identified Chantilly as the second-rate player David Poe, Edgar's father. Thus, disguised as Chantilly, David Poe is represented to us as, in all respects, impotent. Immediately afterward, without transition, there follows the tale of the crime whose victims were Mme. L'Espanaye and her daughter. The deep logical and causal relation between these portions of the tale, one being but the prologue to the other, seems thus suppressed; the only apparent link between them is the ingenuity Dupin displays in both instances.

Here, succession, once more, doubtless represents the causal relation. What needs inserting between the incident regarding Chantilly and the crime of the orangoutang is, again, a *because!* Poe's preconscious thoughts, sinking into the unconscious and losing their stiffening of logic, must have been something like this: "*Because* father David was impotent my mother yielded to the mighty X." As we say, the ape doubtless represented that unknown lover, and the riddle set by the crime in the rue Morgue was, doubtless, displaced from the riddle set the child Poe by the dubious fatherhood of his sister, Rosalie.

"The Murders in the Rue Morgue" provides other interesting instances of thoughts similarly presented piecemeal, though coherent enough in their latent content and manifest expression; coherent, that is, though in different ways, at the origin and end-point of the elaborative process.

What, indeed, could be more rational, seemingly, than the picture of an old lady living in her room? Yet as we saw, the old woman, like the room, represents one and the same person in the story's latent content; that is, the mother, although it would seem absurd that someone inhabit herself.

Contradictions, however, never disturb the unconscious, and juxtaposition, and even superimposition of different elements, is only one of the ways it expresses an actual relation between them. The room, so generally a woman symbol, here represents, given its *hollowness,* the female genitals, into which the ape enters after forcing (violating) the window. We then get a reversal frequent in the unconscious; a *turning inside out,* with the contents substituted for the receptacle. The woman is then represented as inside this cloaca which, in effect, is inside her; at the same time its dimensions are greatly magnified, as though to throw into relief what was most stressed, psychically, in the author's preconscious; the woman's genitals rather than the woman.

Again, the cloaca reappears, in the same context, as the chimney into which Mlle. L'Espanaye's body is thrust. The mother is thus thrice represented; once in her human form and twice as an aperture in a building. But it is not the same cloaca that is thus twice represented, for, while the room represents the *violated* cloaca—as the headless old lady represents the castrated mother—the chimney represents the pregnant cloaca. Mlle. L'Espanaye here, as it were, is the fetus, conceived via the phallic arm of the mighty ape.

Here we see the process of *isolation* in operation, a mechanism which separately represents each idea of a given context and each incident of one representation, linked only by juxtaposition or superimposition. Only in the preconscious do time and space appear. The juxtapositions and super-impositions which result from the treatment to which the latent thoughts are subjected in the unconscious, per contra, are heedless of both logic and contradictions, as of time and place; thus, they express themselves in ways that seem absurd, if we relate them to the story's hidden content. However, these absurdities disappear in the manifest tale, for it is nowise absurd that an old lady lives in a room or that that room should have a chimney; it is even possible, at need, for an ape to perform everything with which it is credited in these murders in the rue Morgue. But again, the deeper preconscious thoughts which inspire the tale and succeed in achieving expression via the strange elaborative mech-anisms described are also, in their way, entirely coherent. One might formulate them thus: *So my mother was the victim of a man's (the suppositious lover's) aggression. He forced his way into her genitals and there, with his mighty penis, implanted my sister.*

* * * * * * * * *

We shall now observe the manner in which the unconscious treats such forms of conscious and logical thought as compose *negation, contrariety,* and *identity.*

Latent and preconscious dream thoughts which involve contradiction or opposition, once they have passed into the unconscious, lose their power to express these relations directly since, for the unconscious, *negation* does not exist. Also, in creative writing (as in the creation of neurotic symptoms) whenever, within the unconscious, some profound unconscious infantile wish attracts a train of preconscious thoughts—and subjects them to the operations of the unconscious—such thoughts are found to be stripped of their negative aspect when they reappear in the conscious content.

One example of this process may be seen in the hanging themes in "Loss of Breath" and "The Black Cat" where, in both cases, the victim represents the penis. The hanged man thus represents the *rephallization* of one who is genitally impotent. In the former, it is the author himself as Mr. Lacko'breath; in the latter, the mother in shape of the cat. The hanged man or animal all the more readily represents the phallus, in that it is popularly thought that hanging is accompanied by erection in extremis. But, from another angle, the fact that the body *hangs* makes it, again, represent incapacity to achieve erection and, thus, the very negation of potency. In this hanging theme, therefore, we find two diametrically opposed ideas condensed; virility and its negation.

Here we are reminded that many languages, in the remote past, attached opposite meanings to one and the same word. Ancient Egyptian offers many examples of this, and modern languages, also, retain traces of the same primitive way of condensing contraries in a single form, thus associating them by contrast (Freud 1948a). Both literature and dreams take full advantage of this mechanism already present in the unconscious. In "Loss of Breath" and "The Black Cat," however, it seems introduced as a way of expressing deep irony. For though, true enough, hanging the wife or woman, or again the impotent man, on the one hand expresses the fantasy wish: "Were it but otherwise!" on the other, owing to the mechanism of representation by contraries also included here, a mechanism which expresses derision in excelsis, this reattribution of the phallus to Mr. Lacko'breath and the black cat is something like adorning a cuckolded husband with horns; a mighty but derisive phallic symbol (Bonaparte 1927).

So, too, with the eternal wandering to which the guilty father is condemned. The Man of the Crowd, the Wandering Jew, the Flying Dutchman, and the Wild Huntsman, all, by contrariety, namely immortality, represent their death and the son's deep wish for that death.

As for cases where the manifest content of a tale shows the real situation reversed and opposite, these may serve, as in dreams, to express the wish for a similar reversal of the situation and the unconscious wish: "If only it were the other way round!" The best example of this in Poe is when M. Valdemar is hypnotized *in articulo mortis*. Here, Valdemar or Valdemar-Griswold-the-Father is represented as utterly and passively subject to the son, who only keeps him alive the better to kill him; whereas, in reality, it was Poe who was passive toward the father.

Thus the tale, through its imagery, almost openly expresses its unconscious intent. The fusion of many individuals into one personage, which thus produces a composite image as, for instance, that of the Marchesa Aphrodite in which Mrs. Stanard, Frances Allan, Elmira Royster, and Elizabeth Arnold are all condensed, similarly expresses and represents the underlying identity which links these different individuals in the writer's psyche. Indeed, owing to its predilection for condensation, the unconscious seems better fitted to express *identity* than other relations.

* * * * * * * * *

What of tales such as "The Assignation" and its absurdities, even in the manifest content? It will be recalled that the Marchesa Aphrodite—in such despair when her babe falls into the canal and in such delight when the "stranger," her lover, restores it to her—decides, in gratitude, to die with the rescuer next morning, at the same hour, though not in the same place. This is manifestly absurd, for the Marchesa would thus abandon her passionately loved babe to her husband, the stern old Marchese, as no Niobe, as she first seemed, would ever have done. A second absurdity also strikes us, for, in rescuing the infant, the stranger plunges into the canal wrapped in a heavy cloak. Yet, as we saw when analyzing this tale, these apparent absurdities are only the distorted expression of a perfectly coherent criticism by the preconscious. For, in the unconscious, the stranger's rescue of the drowning child was equated with his giving her a child. The stranger, however, represents Poe, as the Marchesa represents his mother. Thus, this absurdity in the manifest content, in its way, expresses the following pronouncement in the latent content: "It is absurd to think I could have had a child by my mother. We can never be united except in death." So strong, indeed, is the incest prohibition that even though they die at the same moment, the lovers cannot die in the same place.

This way of expressing criticism is often encountered in dreams, and we see that it is also to be found in literature. In dreams, it appears independent of the criticism and conscious judgments which may be expressed in the literary product composed, as that is, in the waking state.

However, we must certainly not think that every coherent train of thought in creative writing—especially in Poe's tales—has its validity. We must not, for instance, allow ourselves to be dazzled by the ratiocination which marks the opening of "The Murders in the Rue Morgue" in connection with exactly how much ingenuity is needed for chess or mathematics or the analytic function, that superior faculty which, by sure and subtle observation, permits us to guess the thoughts, feelings, and acts of others. True, there is here a conscious echo (only partly true, however, for chess has nothing to do with mathematics) of the two main divisions of mind; the *geometric faculty* and the *faculty of discrimination*. [1] Predominantly, however, the echo is of something very different, namely memories of the small Edgar's infantile sexual investigations. For this highly developed analytical faculty which he attributes to Dupin would, indeed, have been necessary to the child he then was, in order to solve the mysterious feelings and acts of adults. Strive as his childish curiosity might, that secret eluded him. It is the memory of this to some extent unsatisfied sex curiosity which is here compensated by the triumphs of Dupin the ratiocinator.

Thus we see that the "ratiocinations" scattered through Poe's works are not to be taken at their face value and that even his passion for cryptography, shared with Legrand, may represent something different. We may conclude, therefore, that reasoning in literature, as in life, may be traversed by unconscious memories very remote from what reason, apparently, dictates.

* * * * * * * * *

What happens, respectively, to feeling, *affect* as we say, in dreams and literature? About dreams, psychoanalysis tells us that "*the ideational contents have undergone displacements and substitutions, while the affects have remained unchanged*" (Freud 1953b, 426). Thus, dreams whose manifest content should imply terror may, nevertheless, totally lack that affect should the latent dream thoughts, displaced on this part of the dream, in themselves be pleasurable. For example, Freud cites a woman's dream of three lions advancing upon her in which she had no feeling of fear. And with good reason, for, actually, the lions represented her charming father, who had a manelike beard, her English teacher, Miss Lyons, and the composer, Loewe, who had just made her a present of some ballads. Contrariwise, some particular element in the manifest dream, apparently unimportant, may release a powerful affect if the latent thoughts it represents were originally invested with such affect. Affect would thus appear to be a constant but transferable (*labile*) emotional charge, able freely to displace itself along the dream's associative paths without loss of original intensity.

In other cases, however, the affect seems to expend itself in this process. Should the latent thought be powerfully charged with emotion the manifest dream will lack affect. (The converse, however, never happens.) This is because conflicting affects have neutralized each other, producing what Freud calls "peace after battle."

Another way in which affect is dealt with in the latent thoughts causes reversal of the latter into their contraries. The law of association by contraries provides an ample basis for this mechanism, one which is much employed by the moral censor, as, also, by our wishes. Thus affects which seem morally objectionable to us may be transformed into their opposites, as may painful affects into pleasant.

Rather than adduce instances of dreams illustrating these various mechanisms, I refer the reader to the chapter in *The Interpretation of Dreams* from which I have quoted. I shall confine myself to demonstrating that these mechanisms may be found in literature and in Poe.

"Loss of Breath" provides a typical instance of reversed affect. What more tragic, indeed, for one who is impotent than the loss of potency? Yet Poe's story, in which this confession of impotence is made, is saturated with buffoonish affect. At times, this buffoonery rings false and the basic and tragic affect manages to pierce through.

Again, the affect of great sadness doubtless experienced by Poe in connection with his addiction to alcohol, with all the profound infantile fixations and frustrated primal loves that covered, undergoes the same reversal into its opposite in "The Angel of the Odd," a tale also intentionally buffoonish and extravagant, and far more successfully than "Loss of Breath." In general, all Poe's tales, intended by him as burlesques, have similar foundations: a tragic affect, by reversal, is converted into its opposite and comic affect. As it happens, however, these reversals are never wholly successful; Poe's laughter is anything but contagious; it is always a ghastly grin.

Per contra, that other mechanism, the apparent *suppression* of affect, is dealt with successfully in "The Mystery of Marie Rogêt," though to the prejudice of the dramatic effect. Possibly, this is because it is Poe's only tale in which the theme is manifestly sexual. Here, that mighty adversary, instinct, has thrown aside its disguise, whereupon all the forces of the moral censor draw up in line; the result is that a too equally matched struggle ensues and, as a result, that "peace after battle" which we have already noted. Thus, this story of the raped and strangled scent-shop assistant leaves us indifferent, whereas in "The Murders in the Rue Morgue" we are moved to the depths by gripping instinctual affects which have succeeded in evading the censor in the simian or other disguises they were able to adopt.

Possibly why certain works leave us cold when, to the author, they seem full of fire and inspiration, is because a similar conflict between opposed affects has neutralized them out.

Nevertheless, the process to which affects are subjected, that which we meet most generally in Poe, especially in his finest stories, is of a wholly different order. In dreams and their elaboration, we regularly find that the unconscious affects originally bound to significant but repressed representations, are transferred to representations which have generally arisen during the foregoing day. Often it is as though their very unimportance determined the selection of the recent representations to which such affects are transferred, a phenomenon which, for ages, has attracted the notice of those interested in dreams. Freud has demonstrated that such a choice, in fact, appears to be determined by the moral censor, in order that the latent meaning of the dream be concealed. Nonetheless, what remains of the day's experiences and links up with our earliest, strongest, and most repressed wishes, must conceal some associative bond with the deeper desires which are seeking expression.

In Poe's works, as doubtless in creative art generally—where the artist's purpose is, as it were, to instill his own unconscious affect into the unconscious of his audience or, more exactly, to make both unconsciouses vibrate as one—what is of prime importance is that, as perceived, this transposition should be as close as possible, in affect, to the degree of affect it is intended to pass on. A *massing* of affects then takes place, a massing utilized by the censor to distribute affect as it will. No instance better reveals this mechanism than "The Pit and the Pendulum," where the deep and unconscious affects which are to enter the very unconscious of the reader are, in effect, linked with representations of an especially infantile and deeply repressed nature; wish fantasies to possess the mother in intracloacal fashion and passive homosexual wish fantasies toward the father. All this, the inner inspiration of the tale and doubtless its original source, could never be conveyed, unchanged, to the reader, since, far from pleasing him, his own repressions would cause him to shrink as, doubtless, many of our readers have already shrunk from our interpretations. Thus, the censor demands a displacement, but the process or *instance,* to which we shall later revert, which in our half-waking dreams determines the secondary elaboration of the dream and which, during the day, merges with our preconscious waking thoughts, this instance determines a displacement on objects endowed with affects analogous to the profound affect it is intended to release. These new manifest representations will still betray, to those with eyes to see, the deeper and original underlying representations; the phallic swinging pendulum and the cloacal pit. But the mighty and primal wish affects bound up with these representations, once they have been repressed, cannot again emerge save as painfully charged anxiety. Thereupon, the wished-for pendulum, and the longed-for pit, must themselves be invested with anxiety and must convey terror. In this manner, affect is piled up with maximum effect, and the manifest content of the tale will contain a sort of *preliminary premium of anxiety* to serve as the magnet to draw out and explode the deep, unconscious anxiety thus liberated. Meanwhile, the censor's behest is also obeyed and carried out, for the reader may think that the terror released by the tale is merely what anyone would feel in the cells of the Inquisition.

A certain analogy may be noted here with what happens in the formation of many neurotic symptoms. The phobia of fearing to cross streets because of automobiles, for instance, is rational in part, since motor cars kill people. People with this phobia thus manage to justify themselves as regards their affect. But the *quantity* of this affect is not justified by the manifest representation of such a problematic disaster and can only be explained by overdetermined affect, resulting from affects which have reemerged from deep and hidden sources in the unconscious.

The overwhelming anxiety with which all Poe's greatest tales are charged issues exclusively from this source. In each instance the preconscious selects a manifest representation associated with painful affect, as a result of which *preliminary premium of anxiety,* the underlying unconscious anxiety can be discharged. In such manner were liberated the mighty affects we feel, for instance, in "Berenice," "Ligeia," "The Fall of the House of Usher," "The Murders in the Rue Morgue," "The Tell-Tale Heart," and "The Black Cat."

Of the last and remaining factor in dream formation, *secondary elaboration,* we may say that, in creative writing, it is entirely merged with the processes of preconscious waking thought and that a derivative process is the more or less wakeful residue of the day's thoughts, active in dreams. It is this *secondary elaboration* which, in dreams, when the opportunity offers, corrects too-flagrant absurdities and establishes a new and manifest coherence between the latent and scattered thoughts which often differs greatly from their original latent coherence: in short, it subjects the dream to the censorship of logic and criticism. As regards the inner coherence, however, of literary works, this is established by the waking preconscious thoughts which select or reject the elements suggested in the primary unconscious elaboration of the latent thoughts, eliminate what is too absurd or shocking, and set up new logical connections between what is kept. In short, they are incessantly at work criticizing and constructing in order to fit, to our most deeply repressed desires, that conscious, logical, and aesthetic façade which we call creative writing and which, it must never be forgotten, generally presents itself with a coherence very different from that which prevails in the preconscious and primitive thoughts which inspire works of art.

* * * * * * * * * *

Nevertheless, despite the essential differences which mark off literary from dream creation—the lesser mental and psychic regression which materializes even the most abstract thought as hallucination; the egotism, so far better masked than in dreams; the aesthetic pleasure premium which allows repressed desires to manifest themselves with impunity and with equal impunity be experienced by others—despite these differences which make creative writing, contrary to the dream, a *social* product which all may share, dreams and art fulfill an analogous function as regards the human psyche. Both, in fact, act as safety valves to humanity's overrepressed instincts.

At night, when sleep commands immobility, we can dream with impunity, to others or ourselves, of all we covet and are refused by life; murder even, or incest. During the day, we can also abandon ourselves to our daydreams and be similarly immobile, thus inhibiting our dangerous motor activities. But there are men with a mysterious gift who can clothe these daydreams and fictive instinctual gratifications in forms which allow others, also, to dream their dreams with them. How this is done, and what is the nature of the pleasure premium of form and beauty which draws their fellows, is an aesthetic problem still unsolved. Nor has psychoanalysis really succeeded in explaining it, despite the depths to which it has probed the psyche. Freud merely asks us to note that aesthetic feeling seems related to erotic emotion, though sublimated, it is true.[2] This, Plato has already divined in the *Phaedrus,* where the love of beautiful youths was suggested as the first step to love of the Beautiful.

Meanwhile, psychoanalysis has taught us that, throughout our lives, emotively and in disguised ways we repeat the affective experiences of our childhood. The artist, who creates beauty, is no less subject to this law and, possibly, is even more so than others, due to his essentially narcissistic makeup. We may therefore well assume that his particular aesthetic will be colored by his first love relations. Since for all human beings the first love object was the nurturer or mother, it will not surprise us to observe that the aesthetic ideal of an artist presenting necrophilist features, such as Poe, for instance, wears the hues of the mother's death. In the most literal sense, all beauty, for Poe, whether in woman or nature, in faces or scenes, was "drawn from the cheeks" of the cherished and dying mother.

We agreed that there are artists whose aesthetic ideal appears less directly derived from the concrete qualities of an infantile love object; artists with whom we could not thus hark back to the source. Nor need the mother, indeed, be the only origin of the artist's aesthetic ideal. The love which every child, at some time or other, feels for the father must contribute distinctively masculine and active characteristics to any aesthetic ideal, as we find also in Poe.

Nor must we forget the further fact that all love feeling is dual and comprises the loved object and loving subject. Earlier, we dealt with the qualities the artist's aesthetic ideal borrowed from his infancy's love objects. But there are also differences in the manner in which people love; differences conditioned by constitution, heredity, and infantile happenings which modify the developing libido and by the greater, or less, congenital strength of one or other libidinal factors such as sadism, voyeurism, and the rest. We must therefore distinguish between the *kind of aesthetic emotion* in a given artist, and the *nature of his aesthetic ideal*.

Clearly, the former is least accessible to our inquiries as containing factors impossible to trace; factors such as the original strength of the libido and its diverse elements and their greater, or less, resistance or plasticity to educative pressure and their greater, or less, capacity for sublimation: in short, all those hereditary and constitutional biological and sexual factors before which psychoanalytic investigation must, perforce, halt.

* * * * * * * * *

Nevertheless, whatever the artist's primary makeup and however the form of his aesthetic—that glittering veil which he wraps about his and our own deepest instincts, instincts which his contemporaries would often condemn—the elaboration, like the function of the work of art, is always the same.

With the elaboration mechanisms in creative writing we have already dealt at length. Their function, as we have shown, is that of a safety valve for our overrepressed instincts. It now remains for us to show, with Poe as our example, that this safety valve operates under waking conditions exactly as do dreams in respect to our instincts.

To that end, we once more revert to Freud's famous comparison dealing with dream formation. Recent events in the sleeper's life—the so-called residue of the day—may be likened to the entrepreneur of economic theory. But the entrepreneur can accomplish nothing without capital! The *capital* of the dream is furnished by the ancient, archaic, infantile wishes reactivated by the happenings of the day, for these last, even when most vivid in consciousness, of themselves would be unable to activate the dream activity. The genesis of works of art may be similarly described.

Whereas, in many of Poe's tales, the elements in this partnership perforce elude us, insofar as concerns the factors which inspired the creative process, in others it stands clearly revealed.

From the available evidence, it would seem clear that "Berenice," "Morella," and "Ligeia" came into being as a result of the carnal temptations experienced by Poe at finding himself near to his young cousin Virginia, when first staying with his aunt, Mrs. Clemm. Another man, however, might have seen Virginia without wishing to marry her, or being inspired to write "Berenice" or "Ligeia." Virginia here, therefore, represents the entrepreneur, but the capital for the undertaking could only have been furnished by Poe's rich store of buried sadistic, necrophilist, infantile memories which, with his mother's corpse, lurked deep in his unconscious.

So, too, with "The Black Cat." The residual material of the day, in this nightmare tale, came from his family life with the dying Virginia. Was not Catterina, the cat, her constant companion in their cottage? When, in winter, they lacked fuel and the poor, weak, blood-spitting consumptive was forced to remain in bed, would not the cat curl on her bosom as if to warm her? Nevertheless, touching and pitiful though this was, it would never have inspired "The Black Cat," had not the treasure of stored-up, ancient, sadistic urges bound, in Poe's unconscious, with his dead or dying mother been stored up already in his soul to furnish the Virginia-Catterina enterprise with that once amassed capital.

The actual impetus to write "The Gold-Bug" was doubtless communicated to Poe by his poverty, and the wish to change it for something better. Did he not, in fact, write it to compete for a prize of $100, a competition in which he was successful? Yet all his real desires for riches would never have lent such glamour to Captain Kidd's treasure but for its latent meaning, one so intimately bound with his deepest, most primitive, instincts. For, beyond the memory of Frances Allan and her motherly generosity, there still lay the mystery surrounding the birth of Rosalie, who, as a babe, had accompanied him, and their mother, to the very shores where Kidd once buried his treasure.

Thus, works of art, like dreams, reveal themselves as phantom presences which tower over our lives, with one foot in the past and one in the present. The phantom's face, however, turns to the future, due to the sovereign wish it embodies; a wish which inspires our every activity. That is why dreams, at times, seem prophetic; namely, when our more or less unconscious efforts succeed in achieving the wish they express. But, since such wishes are still more generally condemned by our consciences than externally thwarted, few of our dreams, indeed, come to pass! The same prohibitions are at work in art. Though "The Gold-Bug" may have won Poe $100 and, next to "The Raven," his greatest success, he would never, in fact, be able to gratify the murderous, sadistic urges he expresses in "The Black Cat." Nevertheless, by choosing an obviously consumptive girl for his wife, the dreamer-necrophilist Poe found means to stage the sadistic drama, for himself, of an agonizing death like that he had watched so breathlessly as a child. Thus his heroines, Berenice, Morella, Ligeia, Madeline, and Eleanora, seem prophetically to anticipate his own adored wife's fate.

Edgar Allan Poe, doubtless, had never any clear realization of the memories he thus immortalized in his works, or of the fearful nature of his own sexuality. True, he did, at times, say he was haunted by a "terrible mystery," but what that was he could not say. As to sex, he denied and suppressed, in himself, every sexual manifestation to a love object, though "etherealizing" its every grim aspect in his works.

Yet, what lay deepest below Poe's works was as clearly sensed by others as it was little understood by Poe. Plead chastity's cause as it might, Poe's opus, to many, seemed to embody all evil, perversity, and crime. To some, indeed, Poe seemed little better than a confirmed criminal. Apart from the bad poet's natural envy of the good, and the old male rivalry for Mrs. Osgood's diaphanous graces, much of the same sincere indignation doubtless dictated the ex-cleric's, Rufus Griswold's, condemnatory attitude to Poe. This is the only circumstance that extenuates Griswold's malevolent publication of the "Ludwig Article" (1849) the very day after his death, and his issue of the venomous *Memoir* (Griswold 1853, 176 n.2), which, as executor, he prefaced to the posthumous edition of Poe's works.

Nevertheless, the supreme, forbidden, instinctual urges thus sung by Poe; urges which he himself hardly comprehended and which exceed those our love instinct is permitted to gratify, cast such a spell on mankind that even in his life there rose a chorus of adulation.

Women, in particular, were conquered by his works, as, indeed, they are so often by sadism. Mrs. Whitman and Mrs. Shelton would have wedded the raven and Mrs. Shew and Mrs. Richmond mothered and consoled him.

Soaring far over the Atlantic, Poe's sadonecrophilist genius was destined to awake, in other countries and hearts, the same mighty and eternal instincts of those who recognized themselves in him.[3]

* * * * * * * * *

Other tales by Poe also express, though in different and less aggressive fashion, regret for the missing maternal penis, with reproach for its loss. First among these, strange though it seem, is "The Purloined Letter."

The reader will remember that, in this story, the Queen of France, like Elizabeth Arnold, is in possession of dangerous and secret letters, whose writer is unknown. A wicked minister, seeking a political advantage and to strengthen his power, steals one of these letters under the Queen's eyes, which she is unable to prevent owing to the King's presence. This letter must at all costs be recovered. Every attempt by the police fails. Fortunately Dupin is at hand. Wearing dark spectacles with which he can look about him while his own eyes are concealed, he makes an excuse to call on the Minister and discovers the letter openly displayed in a card rack, hung "from a little brass knob just beneath the middle of the mantelpiece."

By a further subterfuge, he possesses himself of the compromising letter and leaves a similar one in its place. The Queen, who will have the original restored to her, is saved.

Let us first note that this letter, very symbol of the maternal penis, also "hangs" over the fireplace, in the same manner as the female penis, if it existed, would be hung over the cloaca which is here represented—as in the foregoing tales—by the general symbol of fireplace or chimney. We have here, in fact, what is almost an anatomical chart, from which not even the clitoris (or brass knob) is omitted. Something very different, however, should be hanging from that body!

The struggle between Dupin and the Minister who once did Dupin an "ill turn"—a struggle in which the latter is victorious—represents, in effect, the oedipal struggle between father and son, though on an archaic, pregenital, and phallic level, to seize possession, not of the mother herself, but of a part: namely, her penis.

We have here an illustration of that "partial love" and desire, not for the whole of the loved being but for an organ, which characterizes one stage of infantile libidinal development.

Yet though the Minister, impressive father figure and "man of genius" as he is, is outwitted by the ratiocinatory and so more brilliant son, he presents one outstanding characteristic which recalls that very "son," for he, too, is a poet! He is a composite figure, combining characteristics of the two "wicked" fathers; first of Elizabeth Arnold's unknown lover, her castrator in the child's eyes, and then of John Allan.

For did not John Allan, too, appear to the child as the ravisher castrator of a woman, Frances, Edgar's beloved and ailing "Ma"? More still, had he not impugned his true mother's virtue and injured her reputation, as the blackmailing Minister planned to do with the Queen's?

The Minister also reminds us of John Allan by his unscrupulous ambition. And it was John Allan again, who, to Poe as a child, represented that *"monstrum horrendum*—an unprincipled man of genius," not far removed from the "criminal" of "vast intelligence" figured in the Man of the Crowd. So does the father often appear to the small boy, at once admired and hated.

Most striking of all, the Minister exhibits Poe's outstanding feature, his poetic gift. And here Poe, in fact, identifies himself with the hated though admired father by that same gift of identification whose praises he sings in "The Purloined Letter" as being the one supremely effective way of penetrating another's thoughts and feelings.

Poe, impotent and a poet, could never so wholly identify himself with the orangoutang in "The Murders in the Rue Morgue," for there the father conquers the mother only by reason of his overwhelming strength. But, in his unconscious, Poe could achieve this with the Minister, for though the latter, once more, triumphs by superior strength, this time it is of the intellect.

As to the King whom the Queen deceives, he must again be David Poe, Elizabeth's husband. Small wonder that Dupin, embodying the son, should declare his "political sympathies" with the lady! Finally, in return for a check of 50,000 francs, leaving to the Prefect of Police the fabulous reward, Dupin restores the woman her symbolic letter or missing penis. Thus, once more, we meet the equation gold = penis. The mother gives her son gold in exchange for the penis he restores.[4]

NOTES

1. "Différence entre l'esprit de géometrie et l'esprit de finesse," Pascal, *Pensées*, 1.1.2.4.

2. "I have no doubt that the conception of the 'beautiful' is rooted in the soil of sexual stimulation and signified originally that which is sexually exciting. The more remarkable, therefore, is the fact that the genitals, the sight of which provokes the greatest sexual excitement, can really never be considered 'beautiful.'" Freud, *Three Contributions to the Theory of Sex* (New York: Nervous and Mental Disease Publishing Company, 1930), 20n. Translated from *Drei Abhandlungen zur Sexualtheorie* (1905), in *Gesammelte Werke*, vol. 5.

Freud has returned to the same idea on other occasions in the same work. See also chapter 2 of *Civilisation and Its Discontents* (London: Hogarth Press, 1930). Translated from *Das Unbehagen in der Kultur* (1930), in *Gesammelte Werke,* vol. 14.

3. The preceding material is excerpted from Bonaparte (1971, 639–68).

4. The last selection is from Bonaparte (1971, 483–84).

7 ❧ On Reading Poetry: Reflections on the Limits and Possibilities of Psychoanalytical Approaches

SHOSHANA FELMAN

To account for poetry in psychoanalytical terms has traditionally meant to analyze poetry as a symptom of a particular poet. I would here like to reverse this approach, and to analyze a particular poet as a symptom of poetry.

No poet, perhaps, has been as highly acclaimed and, at the same time, as violently disclaimed as Edgar Allan Poe. The most controversial figure on the American literary scene, "perhaps the most thoroughly misunderstood of all American writers,"[1] "a stumbling block for the judicial critic,"[2] Edgar Allan Poe has had the peculiar fortune of being at once the most admired and the most decried of American poets. In the history of literary criticism, no other poet has engendered as much disagreement and as many critical contradictions. It is my contention that this critical disagreement is itself symptomatic of a *poetic effect,* and that the critical

This essay is a slightly different version of chapter 2, "The Case of Poe: Applications—Implications of Psychoanalysis," appearing in *Jacques Lacan and the Adventure of Insight* by Shoshana Felman (Cambridge, Mass.: Harvard University Press). Copyright © 1980, 1987 by the President and Fellows of Harvard College. Originally published in *The Literary Freud,* Joseph H. Smith, ed. (New Haven: Yale University Press, 1980).

contradictions to which Poe's poetry has given rise are themselves indirectly significant of the nature of poetry.

THE POE-ETIC EFFECT: A LITERARY CASE HISTORY

No other poet has been so often referred to as a "genius," in a sort of common consensus shared even by his detractors. Joseph Wood Krutch, whose study of Poe tends to belittle Poe's stature and to disparage the value of his artistic achievement, nevertheless entitles his monograph *Edgar Allan Poe: A Study in Genius.* So do many other critics, who acknowledge and assert Poe's "genius" in the very titles of their essays, and proposing to study "The Genius of Poe" (Robertson 1926–27), *Le génie d'Edgar Poe* (Mauclair 1925), *Edgar Allan Poe: His Genius and His Character* (Dillon 1911), *The Genius and Character of Edgar Allan Poe* (Thompson 1929), *Genius and Disaster: Studies in Drugs and Genius* (Marks 1925), "Affidavits of Genius: French Essays on Poe" (Alexander 1961). "It happens to us but few times in our lives," writes Thomas W. Higginson, "to come consciously into the presence of that extraordinary miracle we call genius. Among the many literary persons whom I have happened to meet, . . . there are not half a dozen who have left an irresistible sense of this rare quality; and among these few, Poe" (1966, 67). For Constance M. Rourke, "Poe has become a symbol for the type of genius which rises clear from its time" (1966, 167); the English poet A. Charles Swinburne speaks of "the special quality of [Poe's] strong and delicate genius" (1966, 63); the French poet Stéphane Mallarmé describes his translations of Poe as "a monument to the genius who . . . exercised his influence in our country" (1945, 223); and the American poet James Russell Lowell, one of Poe's harshest critics, who, in his notorious versified verdict, judged Poe's poetry to include "two fifths sheer fudge," nonetheless asserts: "Mr. Poe has that indescribable something which men have agreed to call *genius.* . . . Let talent writhe and contort itself as it may, it has no such magnetism. Larger of bone and sinew it may be, but the wings are wanting" (1966, 11).

However suspicious and unromantic the critical reader might wish to be with respect to "that indescribable something which men have agreed to call genius," it is clear that Poe's poetry produces, in a uniquely striking and undeniable manner, what might be called a *genius effect:* the impression of some undefinable but compelling *force* to which the reader is subjected. To describe "this power, *which is felt,*" as one reader puts it (see Cooke 1966, 23), Lowell speaks of "magnetism"; other critics speak of "magic." "Poe," writes George Bernard Shaw, "constantly and inevitably *produced magic* where his greatest contemporaries produced only beauty" (1966, 98).[3] T. S. Eliot quite reluctantly agrees: "Poe had, to an exceptional degree, the feeling for the incantatory element in poetry, of that which may, in the most nearly literal sense, be called 'the magic of verse' " (1966, 209).

Poe's "magic" is thus ascribed to the ingenuity of his versification, to his exceptional technical virtuosity. And yet the word *magic,* "in the most nearly literal sense," means much more than just the intellectual acknowledgment of an outstanding technical skill; it connotes the effective action of something that exceeds both the understanding and the control of the person who is subjected to it; it connotes a force to which the reader has no choice but to submit. "No one could tell us what it is," writes Lowell, still in reference to Poe's genius, "and yet there is none who is not *inevitably aware* of . . . its power" (1966, 11). "Poe," said Shaw, "*inevitably* produced magic." There is something about Poe's poetry which, like fate, is experienced as *inevitable,* unavoidable (and not just as irresistible). What is more, once this poetry is read, its inevitability is there to stay; it becomes lastingly inevitable: "it will *stick to the memory* of everyone who reads it," writes Cooke (1966, 23). And Eliot: "Poe is the author of a few . . . short poems . . . which do somehow *stick in the memory*" (1966, 207–8).

This is why Poe's poetry can be defined, and indeed has been, as a poetry of *influence* par excellence, in the sense emphasized by Harold Bloom: "to inflow" = to have power over another. The case of Poe in literary history could in fact be accounted for as one of the most extreme and most complex cases of "the anxiety of influence," of the anxiety unwittingly provoked by the "influence" irresistibly emanating from this poetry. What is unique, however, about Poe's influence, as about the "magic" of his verse, is the extent to which its action is unaccountably insidious, exceeding the control, the will, and the awareness of those who are subjected to it. "Poe's influence," writes T. S. Eliot, is "puzzling":

In France the influence of his poetry and of his poetic theories has been immense. In England and America it seems almost negligible. . . . And yet one cannot be sure that one's own writing has *not* been influenced by Poe. (1966, 205; Eliot's italics)

Studying Poe's influence on Baudelaire, Mallarmé, and Valéry, Eliot goes on to comment:

Here are three literary generations, representing almost exactly a century of French poetry. Of course, these are poets very different from each other. . . . But I think we can trace the development and descent of one particular theory of the nature of poetry through these three poets and it is a theory which takes its origin in the theory . . . of Edgar Poe. And the impression we get of the influence of Poe is the more impressive, because of the fact that Mallarmé, and Valéry in turn, did not merely derive from Poe through Baudelaire: each of them subjected himself to that influence directly, and has left convincing evidence of the value which he attached to the theory and practice of Poe himself. . . .

I find that by trying to look at Poe through the eyes of Baudelaire, Mallarmé and Valéry, I become more thoroughly convinced of his importance, of the importance of his *work* as a whole. (1966, 206, 219; Eliot's italics)

Curiously enough, while Poe's worldwide importance and effective influence are beyond question, critics nonetheless continue to protest and to proclaim, as loudly as they can, that Poe is *un*important, that Poe is *not* a major poet. In an essay entitled "Vulgarity in Literature" and taxing Poe with "vulgarity," Aldous Huxley argues:

Was Edgar Allan Poe a major poet? It would surely never occur to any English-speaking critic t⌐ say so. And yet, in France, from 1850 till the present time, the best poets of each generation—yes, and the best critics, too; for, like most excellent poets, Baudelaire, Mallarmé, Paul Valéry are also admirable critics—have gone out of their way to praise him. . . . We who are speakers of English . . . , we can only say, with all due respect, that Baudelaire, Mallarmé, and Valéry were wrong and that *Poe is not one of our major poets*. (1966, 160)

Poe's detractors seem to be unaware, however, of the paradox that underlies their enterprise: it is by no means clear why anyone should take the trouble to write—at length—about a writer of no importance. Poe's most systematic denouncer, Ivor Winters, thus writes:

The menace lies not, primarily, in his impressionistic admirers among literary people of whom he still has some, even in England and in America, where a familiarity with his language ought to render his crudity obvious, for these individuals in the main do not make themselves permanently very effective; *it lies rather in the impressive body of scholarship.* . . . When a writer is supported by a sufficient body of such scholarship, a very little philosophical elucidation will suffice to establish

him in the scholarly world as a writer whose greatness is self-evident.
(1966, 177)

The irony that here escapes the author is that, in writing his attack on
Poe, what the attacker is in fact doing is adding still another study to the
bulk of "the impressive body of scholarship" in which, in his own terms,
"the menace lies"; so that, paradoxically enough, through Ivor Winters's
study, "the menace"—that is, the possibility of taking Poe's "greatness
as a writer" as "self-evident"—will indeed increase. I shall here precisely
argue that, regardless of the value judgment it may pass on Poe, this
impressive bulk of Poe scholarship, the very quantity of the critical
literature to which Poe's poetry has given rise, is itself an indication of its
effective poetic power, of the strength with which it drives the reader to
an *action,* compels him to a *reading act.* The elaborate written denials of
value, the loud and lengthy negations of his importance, are therefore
very like psychoanalytical negations. It is clear that if Poe's text in effect
were unimportant, it would not seem so important to proclaim, argue,
and prove that he is unimportant. The fact that it so much *matters* to
proclaim that Poe *does not matter* is but evidence of the extent to which
Poe's poetry is, in effect, a *poetry that matters.*

Poe might thus be said to have a *literary case history,* most revealing in
that it incarnates, in its controversial forms, the paradoxical nature of a
strong *poetic effect:* the very poetry that, more than any other, is experienced as *irresistible* has also proved to be, in literary history, the poetry
most *resisted,* the one that, more than any other, has provoked resistances.

This apparent contradiction, which makes of Poe's poetry a unique
case in literary history, clearly partakes of the paradoxical nature of an
analytical effect. The enigma it presents us with is the enigma of "the
analytical" par excellence, as stated by Poe himself, whose amazing
intuitions of the nature of what he calls "analysis" are strikingly similar to
the later findings of psychoanalysis: "The mental features discoursed of as
the analytical are, in themselves, but little susceptible of analysis. *We
appreciate them only in their effects.*"[4]

Because of the very nature of its strong "effects," of the reading *acts*
that it provokes, Poe's text (and not just Poe's biography or his personal
neurosis) is clearly an analytical case in the history of literary criticism, a
case that suggests something crucial to understand in psychoanalytic
terms. It is therefore not surprising that Poe, more than any other poet,
has been repeatedly singled out for psychoanalytical research, has per-
sistently attracted the attention of psychoanalytic critics.

The Psychoanalytic Approaches

The best known and most influential psychoanalytic studies of Poe are the 1926 study by Joseph Wood Krutch, *Edgar Allan Poe: A Study in Genius,* and the 1933 study by Marie Bonaparte, *Edgar Poe: Etude psychanalytique,* later to appear in English as the *Life and Works of Edgar Allan Poe.*[5] More recently, Jacques Lacan has published a more limited study of one tale by Poe, "The Seminar on 'The Purloined Letter,' " first published in 1966.[6]

Joseph Wood Krutch: Ideological Psychology, or the Approach of Normative Evaluation

For Joseph Wood Krutch (1926), Poe's text is nothing other than an accurate transcription of a severe neurosis, a neurosis whose importance and significance for "healthy" people is admittedly unclear in Krutch's mind. Poe's "position as the first of the great neurotics has never been questioned" (208), writes Krutch ambiguously. And less ambiguously, in reply to some admiring French definitions of that position: "Poe 'first inaugurated the poetic conscience' only if there is no true poetry except the poetry of morbid sensibility" (210). "He must stand or fall with that whole body of neurotic literature of which his works furnish the earliest complete example" (212). Since Poe's works, according to Krutch, "bear no conceivable relation . . . to the life of any people, and it is impossible to account for them on the basis of any social or intellectual tendencies or as the expression of the spirit of any age," the only possible approach is a biographical one, and "any true understanding" (210) of the work is contingent upon a diagnosis of Poe's nervous malady. Krutch thus diagnoses in Poe a pathological condition of sexual impotence, the result of a "fixation" on his mother, and explains Poe's literary drive as a desire to compensate for, on the one hand, the loss of social position of which his foster father had deprived him, through the acquisition of literary fame, and on the other hand, his incapacity to have normal sexual relations, through the creation of a fictional world of horror and destruction in which he found refuge. Poe's fascination with logic would thus be merely an attempt to prove himself rational when he felt he was going insane; and his critical theory would be merely an attempt to justify his peculiar artistic practice.

The obvious limitations of such a psychoanalytic approach were very sharply and very accurately pointed out by Edmund Wilson (1966, 142–51) in his essay "Poe at Home and Abroad." Krutch, argues Wilson, seriously misunderstands and undervalues Poe's writings, in

> *complacently caricaturing them*—as the *modern school of social psychological biography,* of which Mr. Krutch is a typical representative, *seems inevitably to tend to caricature the personalities of its subjects.* We are nowadays being edified by the spectacle of some of the principal ornaments of the human race exhibited exclusively in terms of their most ridiculous manias, their most disquieting neurosis, and their most humiliating failures. (1966, 144)

It is, in other words, the reductionist, stereotypical simplification under which Krutch subsumes the complexities of Poe's art and life that renders this approach inadequate:

> Mr. Krutch quotes with disapproval the statement of President Hadley of Yale, in explaining the refusal of the Hall of Fame to accept Poe among its immortals: "Poe wrote like a drunkard and a man who is not accustomed to pay his debts"; and yet Mr. Krutch himself . . . is almost as unperceptive when he tells us, in effect, that Poe wrote like a dispossessed Southern gentleman and a man with a fixation on his mother. (Wilson 1966, 145)

Subscribing to Wilson's criticism, I would like to indicate briefly some further limitations in this type of psychoanalytic approach to literature. Krutch himself, in fact, points out some of the limits of his method, in his conclusion:

> We have, then, traced Poe's art to an abnormal condition of the nerves and his critical ideas to a rationalized defense of the limitations of his own taste. . . . The question whether or not the case of Poe represents an exaggerated example of the process by which all creation is performed is at best an open question. The extent to which all imaginative works are the result of the unfulfilled desires which spring from either idiosyncratic or universally human maladjustments to life is only beginning to be investigated, and with it is linked the related question of the extent to which all critical principles are at bottom the systematized and rationalized expression of instinctive tastes which are conditioned by causes often unknown to those whom they affect. The problem of finding an answer to these questions . . . is the one distinctly new problem which the critic of today is called upon to consider. He must, in a word, endeavor to find the *relationship which exists between psychology and aesthetics.* (1926, 234–35)

This, indeed, is the real question, the real challenge that Poe *as poet* (and not as psychotic) presents to the psychoanalytic critic. But this is the very question that is bracketed, never dealt with, in Krutch's study. Krutch discards the question by saying that "the present state of knowledge is not such as to enable" us to give any answers. This remark, however, presupposes—I think mistakenly—that the realm of "aesthetics," of literature and art, might not itself contain some "knowledge" about, precisely, "the relationship between psychology and aesthetics"; it presupposes knowledge as a *given*, external to the literary object and imported into it, and not as a result of a reading process, that is, of the critic's work upon and with the literary text. It presupposes, furthermore, that a critic's task is not to question but to answer, and that a question that cannot be answered can also therefore not be asked; that to raise a question, to articulate its thinking power, is not itself a fruitful step which takes some work, some doing, into which the critic could perhaps be guided by the text.

Thus, in claiming that he has traced "Poe's art to an abnormal condition of the nerves" and that Poe's "criticism falls short of psychological truth," Krutch believes that his own work is opposed to Poe's as health is opposed to sickness, as "normality" is opposed to "abnormality," as truth is opposed to delusion. But this ideologically determined, clear-cut opposition between health and sickness is precisely one that Freud's discovery fundamentally unsettles, deconstructs. In tracing Poe's "critical ideas to a rationalized defense of the limitations of his own taste," Krutch is unsuspicious of the fact that his *own* critical ideas about Poe could equally well be traced to "a rationalized defense of the limitations of his own taste"; that his doctrine, were it to be true, could equally well apply to his own critical enterprise; that if psychoanalysis indeed puts rationality as such in question, it also by the same token puts *itself* in question.

Krutch, in other words, reduces not just Poe but analysis itself to an ideologically biased and psychologically opinionated caricature, missing totally (as is most often the case with "Freudian" critics) the *radicality* of Freud's psychoanalytic insights: their self-critical potential, their power to return upon themselves and to unseat the critic from any condescending, guaranteed, authoritative stance of truth. Krutch's approach does not, then, make sophisticated use of psychoanalytic insights, nor does it address the crucial question of "the relationship between psychology and aesthetics," nor does it see that the crux of this question is not so much in the interrogation of whether or not all artists are necessarily pathological, but of what it is that makes of *art*—not of the artist—an object of *desire* for the public; of what it is that makes for art's *effect,* for the compelling power of Poe's poetry over its readers. The question of what makes poetry lies, indeed, not so much in what it was that made Poe write, but in what it is that *makes us read him*[7] and that ceaselessly drives so many people to *write about him.* [Including myself.]

Marie Bonaparte: The Approach of Clinical Diagnosis

In contrast to Krutch's claim that Poe's works, as a literal transcription of his sickness, are meaningful only as the expression of morbidity, bearing "no conceivable relation . . . to the life of any people," Marie Bonaparte, on the contrary, though in turn treating Poe's works as nothing other than the recreations of his neuroses, tries to address the question of his power over his readers through her didactic explanation of the relevancy of Poe's pathology to "normal" people: the pathological tendencies to which Poe's text gives expression are an exaggerated version of drives and instincts universally human, but which "normal" people have simply repressed more successfully in their childhood. What fascinates readers in Poe's texts is precisely the unthinkable and unacknowledged but strongly felt *community* of these human—all too human—sexual drives.

If Marie Bonaparte, unlike Krutch, thus treats Poe with human sympathy, suspending the traditional puritan condemnation and refraining, at least explicitly, from passing judgment on his "sickness," she nonetheless, like Krutch, sets out primarily to diagnose that "sickness" and trace the poetry to it. Like Krutch, she comes up with a clinical "portrait of the artist" that, in claiming to account for the poetry, once again verges on caricature and cannot help but make us smile.

If Poe was fundamentally necrophilist, as we saw, Baudelaire is revealed as a declared sadist; the former preferred dead prey or prey mortally wounded . . . ; the latter preferred live prey and killing. . . .

How was it then, that despite these different sex lives, Baudelaire the sadist recognised a brother in the necrophilist Poe? . . . .

This particular problem raises that of the general relation of sadism to necrophilia and cannot be resolved except by an excursus into the theory of instincts. (1971, 680).

classic!

Can poetry thus be clinically diagnosed? In setting out to expose didactically the methods of psychoanalytic interpretation, Bonaparte's pioneering book at the same time exemplifies the very naiveté of compe-

S.f. is diagnosing/stereotyping

tence, the distinctive *professional* crudity of what has come to be the classical psychoanalytic treatment of literary texts. Eager to point out the *resemblances* between psychoanalysis and literature, Bonaparte, like most psychoanalytic critics, is totally unaware of the *differences* between the two: unaware that the differences are as important and as significant for understanding the meeting ground as are the resemblances, and that those differences also have to be accounted for if poetry is to be understood in its own right. Setting out to study literary texts through the application of psychoanalytic methods, Bonaparte, paradoxically enough, but in a manner symptomatic of the whole tradition of applied psychoanalysis, thus remains entirely blind to the very specificity of the object of her research.

It is not surprising that this blind nondifferentiation or confusion of the poetic and the psychotic has unsettled sensitive readers and that various critics have, in various ways, protested against this all too crude equation of poetry with sickness. The protestations, however, most often fall into the same ideological trap as the psychoanalytical studies they oppose: accepting (taking for granted) the polarity of sickness versus health, of normality versus abnormality, they simply trace Poe's art (in opposition, so they think to the psychoanalytic claim) to normality as opposed to abnormality, to sanity as opposed to insanity, to the history of ideas rather than that of sexual drives, to a conscious project as opposed to an unconscious one. Camille Mauclair (quoted in Poe 1967) insists that Poe's texts are "constructed objectively by a will absolutely in control of itself," and that genius of that kind is "always sane" (24). For Allen Tate,

The actual emphases Poe gives the perversions are richer in philosophical implication than his psychoanalytic critics have been prepared to see. . . . Poe's symbols refer to a known tradition of thought, an intelligible order, apart from what he was as a man, and are not merely the index to a compulsive neurosis . . . the symbols . . . point towards a larger philosophical dimension. (1966, 239)

For Floyd Stovall, the psychoanalytic studies "are not literary critiques at all, but clinical studies of a supposed psychopathic personality":

I believe the critic should look within the poem or tale for its meaning, and that he should not, in any case, suspect the betrayal of the author's unconscious self until he has understood all that his conscious self has contributed. To affirm that a work of imagination is only a report of the unconscious is to degrade the creative artist to the level of an amanuensis.

I am convinced that all of Poe's poems were composed with conscious art. (1969, 183)

"The Raven," and with certain necessary individual differences every other poem Poe wrote, was the product of conscious effort by a healthy and alert intelligence. (1969, 186)

It is obvious that this conception of the mutual exclusiveness, of the clear-cut opposition between "conscious art" and the unconscious, is itself naive and oversimplified. Nonetheless, Stovall's critique of applied psychoanalysis is relevant to the extent that the psychoanalytic explanation, in pointing exclusively to the author's unconscious sexual fantasies, indeed does not account for Poe's outstanding "conscious art," for his unusual poetic mastery and his ingenious technical and structural self-control. As do its opponents, so does applied psychoanalysis itself fail precisely to account for the dynamic *interaction* between the *unconscious* and the *conscious* elements of art.

If the thrust of the discourse of applied psychoanalysis is, indeed, in tracing poetry to a clinical reality, to *reduce* the poetic to a "cause" outside itself, the crucial limitation of this process of reduction is, however, that the cause, while it may be *necessary,* is by no means a *sufficient* one. "Modern psychiatry," judiciously writes David Galloway, "may greatly aid the critic of literature, but . . . it cannot thus far explain why other men, suffering from deprivations or fears or obsessions similar to Poe's, failed to demonstrate his particular creative talent. Though no doubt Marie Bonaparte was correct in seeing Poe's own art as a defense against madness, we must be wary of identifying the *necessity* for this defense, in terms of Poe's own life, with the *success* of this defense, which can only be measured in his art" (1967, 24–25).

That the discourse of applied psychoanalysis is limited precisely in that it does not account for Poe's poetic *genius* is in fact the crucial point made by Freud himself in his prefatory note to Marie Bonaparte's study:

Foreword

In this book my friend and pupil, Marie Bonaparte, has shone the light of psychoanalysis on the life and work of a great writer with pathologic trends.

Thanks to her interpretative effort, we now realize how many of the characteristics of Poe's works were conditioned by his personality, and can see how that personality derived from intense emotional fixations and painful infantile experiences. *Investigations such as this do not claim to explain creative genius,* but they do reveal the factors which awake it and the sort of subject matter it is destined to choose.

Sigm. Freud

No doubt, Freud's remarkable superiority over some (most) of his disciples—including Marie Bonaparte—proceeds from his acute *aware-ness* of the very *limitations* of his method, an awareness that in his followers seems most often not to exist.

I would like here to raise a question that, springing out of this limitation of applied psychoanalysis, has, amazingly enough, never been asked as a serious question: is there a way *around* Freud's perspicacious reservation, warning us that studies like those of Bonaparte "do not claim to explain creative genius"? Is there, in other words, a way—a different way—in which psychoanalysis *can* help us account for poetic genius? Is there an alternative to applied psychoanalysis? An alternative that would be capable of touching, in a psychoanalytic manner, upon the very speci-ficity of that which constitutes the poetic?

Before endeavoring to articulate the way this question might be answered, I would like to examine still another manner in which Poe's text has been psychoanalytically approached: Jacques Lacan's "seminar" on Poe's short story "The Purloined Letter."

Jacques Lacan: The Approach of Textual Problematization

I will not enter here into the complexity of the psychoanalytic issues involved in Lacan's "The Seminar on 'The Purloined Letter'" (1972b), nor will I try to deal exhaustively with the nuanced sophistication of the Seminar's rhetoric and theoretical propositions;[8] I will confine myself to a few specific points that bear upon the methodological issue of Lacan's psychoanalytic treatment of the literary material.

What Lacan is concerned with at this point of his research is the psychoanalytic problematics of the "repetition compulsion," as elabo-rated in Freud's speculative text, *Beyond the Pleasure Principle.* The thrust of Lacan's endeavor, with respect to Poe, is thus to point out—so as to elucidate the nature of Freudian repetition—the way the story's plot, its sequence of events (as, for Freud, the sequence of events in a life story), is entirely contingent on, overdetermined by, a principle of repetition that governs it and inadvertently structures its dramatic and ironic impact. "There are two scenes," remarks Lacan, "the first of which we shall straightway designate the primal scene, . . . since the second may be

considered its repetition in the very sense we are considering today"
(Lacan 1972b, 41). The "primal scene" takes place in the Queen's
boudoir: it is the theft of the letter from the Queen by the Minister; the
second scene—its repetition—is the theft of the letter from the Minister
by Dupin, in the Minister's hotel.

What constitutes repetition for Lacan, however, is not the mere thematic resemblance of the double *theft,* but the whole structural situation
in which the repeated theft takes place: in each case, the theft is the
outcome of an intersubjective relationship between three terms; in the
first scene, the three participants are the King, the Queen, and the
Minister; in the second, the three participants are the police, the Minister, and Dupin. In much the same way as Dupin takes the place of the
Minister in the first scene (the place of the letter's robber), the Minister in
the second scene takes the place of the Queen in the first (the dispossessed
possessor of the letter); whereas the police, for whom the letter remains
invisible, take the place formerly occupied by the King. The two scenes
thus mirror each other, in that they dramatize the repeated exchange of
"three glances, borne by three subjects, incarnated each time by different
characters" (44). What is repeated, in other words, is not a psychological
act committed as a function of the individual psychology of the character,
but three functional *positions in a structure* that, determining three different *viewpoints,* embody three different relations to the act of seeing—of
seeing, specifically, the purloined letter.

The first is a glance that sees nothing: the King and the police.

The second, a glance which sees that the first sees nothing and deludes
itself as to the secrecy of what it hides: the Queen, then the Minister.

The third sees that the first two glances leave what should be hidden
exposed to whomever would seize it: the Minister, and finally Dupin.
(44)

Lacan's analysis can be schematized in the accompanying figures:

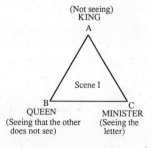

Although Lacan does not elaborate upon the possible further ramifications of the structure above, the diagram is open to a number of illuminating terminological translations, reinterpreting it in the light of Freudian and Lacanian concepts. Below are two such possible translations.

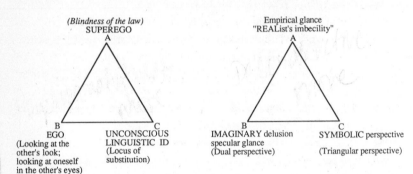

(Blindness of the law)
SUPEREGO
A

B
EGO
(Looking at the
other's look;
looking at oneself
in the other's eyes)

C
UNCONSCIOUS
LINGUISTIC ID
(Locus of
substitution)

Empirical glance
"REAList's imbecility"
A

B
IMAGINARY delusion
specular glance
(Dual perspective)

C
SYMBOLIC perspective

(Triangular perspective)

"What interests us today," insists Lacan,

> is the manner in which the subjects relay each other in their displacement during the intersubjective repetition.
>
> We shall see that their displacement is determined by the place which a pure signifier—the purloined letter—comes to occupy in their trio. And that is what will confirm for us its status as repetition automatism. (45)

The purloined letter, in other words, becomes itself—through its insistence in the structure—a symbol or a signifier of the *unconscious*, to the extent that it "is destined . . . to signify the annulment of what it signifies" (63)—the necessity of its own *repression*, of the repression of its message: "It is not only the meaning but the text of the message which it would be dangerous to place in circulation" (56). But in much the same way as the repressed *returns* in the *symptom*, which is its repetitive symbolic substitute, the purloined letter ceaselessly returns in the tale—as a signifier of the repressed—through its repetitive displacements and replacements. "This is indeed what happens in the repetition compulsion," says Lacan (60). Unconscious desire, once repressed, survives in displaced symbolic media that govern the subject's life and actions without his ever being aware of their meaning or of the repetitive pattern they structure:

If what Freud discovered and rediscovers with a perpetually increasing sense of shock has a meaning, it is that the displacement of the signifier determines the subjects in their acts, in their destiny, in their refusals, in their blindnesses, in their end and in their fate, their innate gifts and social acquisitions notwithstanding, without regard for character or sex, and that, willingly or not, everything that might be considered the stuff of psychology, kit and caboodle, will follow the path of the signifier. (60)

In what sense, then, does the second scene in Poe's tale, while repeating the first scene, nonetheless differ from it? In the sense, precisely, that the second scene, through the repetition, allows for an understanding, for an *analysis* of the first. This analysis through repetition is to become, in Lacan's ingenious reading, no less than an *allegory of psychoanalysis*. The intervention of Dupin, who restores the letter to the Queen, is thus compared, in Lacan's interpretation, to the intervention of the analyst, who rids the patient of the symptom. The analyst's effectiveness, however, does not spring from his intellectual strength but—insists Lacan—from his position in the (repetitive) structure. By virtue of his occupying the third position—that is, the *locus* of the unconscious of the subject as a place of substitution of letter for letter (of signifier for signifier)—the analyst, through transference, allows at once for a repetition of the trauma, and for a symbolic substitution, and thus effects the drama's denouement.

It is instructive to compare Lacan's study of the psychoanalytical repetition compulsion in Poe's text with Marie Bonaparte's study of Poe's repetition compulsion through his text. Although the two analysts study the same author and focus on the same psychoanalytic concept, their approaches are strikingly different. To the extent that Bonaparte's study of Poe has become a classic, a model of applied psychoanalysis that illustrates and embodies the most common understanding of what a psychoanalytic reading of a literary text might be, I would like, in pointing out the differences in Lacan's approach, to suggest the way those differences at once put in question the traditional approach and offer an alternative to it.

1. *What does a repetition compulsion repeat? Interpretation of difference as opposed to interpretation of identity*

For Marie Bonaparte, what is compulsively repeated through the variety of Poe's texts is *the same* unconscious fantasy: Poe's (sadonecrophiliac) desire for his dead mother. For Lacan, what is repeated in the text is not the content of a fantasy but the symbolic displacement of a signifier through the insistence of a signifying chain; repetition is not of *sameness* but of *difference,* not of independent terms or of analogous themes but of a structure of differential interrelationships,[9] in which what *returns* is always *other.* Thus, the triangular structure repeats itself only through the *difference* of the characters who successively come to occupy the three positions; its structural significance is perceived only *through* this difference. Likewise, the significance of the letter is situated in its *displacement,* that is, in its repetitive movements toward a *different* place. And the second scene, being for Lacan an allegory of analysis, is important not just in that it *repeats* the first scene, but in the way this repetition (like the transferential repetition of a psychoanalytical experience) *makes a difference:* brings about a solution to the problem. Thus, whereas Marie Bonaparte analyzes repetition as the insistence of identity, for Lacan, any possible insight into the reality of the unconscious is contingent upon a perception of repetition, not as a confirmation of identity, but as the insistence of the indelibility of a difference.

2.   *An analysis of the signifier as opposed to an analysis of the signified*

In the light of Lacan's reading of Poe's tale as itself an allegory of the psychoanalytic reading, it might be illuminating to define the difference in approach between Lacan and Bonaparte in terms of the story. If the purloined letter can be said to be a sign of the unconscious, for Marie Bonaparte the analyst's task is to uncover the letter's *content,* which she believes—as do the police—to be *hidden* somewhere in the real, in some secret biographical *depth.* For Lacan, on the other hand, the analyst's task is not to read the letter's hidden referential content, but to situate the superficial indication of its textual movement, to analyze the paradoxically invisible symbolic evidence of its displacement, its structural insistence, in a signifying chain. "There is such a thing," writes Poe, "as being too profound. Truth is not always in a well. In fact, as regards the most important knowledge, I do believe she is invariably superficial" (1967, 204). Espousing Poe's insight, Lacan makes the principle of symbolic evidence the guideline for an analysis not of the signified but of the signifier—for an analysis of the unconscious (the repressed) not as hidden, but on the contrary as *exposed*—in language—through a significant (rhetorical) displacement.

This analysis of the signifier, the model of which can be found in Freud's interpretation of dreams, is nonetheless a radical reversal of the traditional expectations and presuppositions involved in the common psychoanalytic approach to literature, and its invariable search for hidden meanings. Indeed, not only is Lacan's reading of "The Purloined Letter" subversive of the traditional model of psychoanalytic reading; it is, in general, a type of reading that is methodologically unprecedented in the whole history of literary criticism. The history of reading has accustomed us to the assumption—usually unquestioned—that reading is finding meaning, that interpretation—of whatever method—can dwell only on the meaningful. Lacan's analysis of the signifier opens up a radically new assumption, an assumption that is nonetheless nothing but an insightful logical and methodological consequence of Freud's discovery: that what *can* be read (and perhaps what *should* be read) is not just meaning, but the lack of meaning; that significance lies not just in consciousness, but, specifically, in its disruption; that the signifier can be analyzed in its effects without its signified being known; that the lack of meaning—the discontinuity in conscious understanding—can and should be interpreted as such, without necessarily being transformed into meaning. "Let's take a look," writes Lacan:

We shall find illumination in what at first seems to obscure matters: the fact that the tale leaves us in virtually total ignorance of the sender, no less than of the contents, of the letter. (1972b, 57)

The signifier is not functional. . . . We might even admit that the letter has an entirely different (if no more urgent) meaning for the Queen than the one understood by the Minister. The sequence of events would not be noticeably affected, not even if it were strictly incomprehensible to an uninformed reader. (56)

But that this is the very effect of the unconscious in the precise sense that we teach that the unconscious means that man is inhabited by the signifier. (66)

Thus, for Lacan, what is analytical par excellence is not (as is the case for Bonaparte) the *readable,* but the *unreadable,* and the *effects* of the unreadable. What calls for analysis is the insistence of the unreadable in the text.

Poe, of course, had said it all in his insightful comment, previously quoted, on the nature of what he too—amazingly enough, before the fact—called "the analytical":

The mental features discoursed of as the analytical are, in themselves, but little susceptible of analysis. We appreciate them only in their effects. (1967, 189)

But, oddly enough, what Poe himself had said so strikingly and so explicitly about "the analytical" had itself remained totally unanalyzed, indeed unnoticed, by psychoanalytic scholars before Lacan, perhaps because it too, according to its own (analytical) logic, had been "a little too self-evident" to be perceived.

3. A textual as opposed to a biographical approach

The analysis of the signifier implies a theory of textuality for which Poe's biography, or his so-called sickness, or his hypothetical personal psychoanalysis, become irrelevant. The presupposition—governing enterprises like that of Marie Bonaparte—that poetry can be interpreted only as autobiography is obviously limiting and limited. Lacan's textual analysis for the first time offers a psychoanalytic alternative to the previously unquestioned and thus seemingly exclusive biographical approach.

4. The analyst/author relation: A subversion of the master/slave pattern and of the doctor/patient opposition

Let us remember how many readers were unsettled by the humiliating and sometimes condescending psychoanalytic emphasis on Poe's "sickness," as well as by an explanation equating the poetic with the psychotic. There seemed to be no doubt in the minds of psychoanalytic readers that if the reading situation could be assimilated to the psychoanalytic situation, the poet was to be equated with the (sick) patient, with the analysand on the couch. Lacan's analysis, however, radically subverts not just this clinical status of the poet, but along with it the "bedside" security of the interpreter. If Lacan is not concerned with Poe's sickness, he is quite concerned, nonetheless, with the *figure of the poet* in the tale, and with the hypotheses made about his specific competence and incompetence. Let us not forget that both the Minister and Dupin are said to be poets, and that it is their *poetic* reasoning that the Prefect fails to understand and which thus enables both to outsmart the police. "D——, I presume, is not altogether a fool," comments Dupin early in the story, to which the Prefect of Police replies:

"Not altogether a fool, . . . but then he's a poet, which I take to be only one remove from a fool."

"True," said Dupin, after a long and thoughtful whiff from his meerschaum, "although I have been guilty of certain doggerel myself." (1967, 334)

A question Lacan does not address could here be raised by emphasizing still another point that would normally tend to pass unnoticed, since, once again, it is at once so explicitly and so ostentatiously insignificant: Why does Dupin say that he too is *guilty* of poetry? In what way does the status of the poet involve guilt? In what sense can we understand *the guilt of poetry?*[10]

Dupin, then, draws our attention to the fact that both he and the Minister are poets, a qualification with respect to which the Prefect feels that he can but be condescending. Later, when Dupin explains to the narrator the Prefect's defeat as opposed to his own success in finding the letter, he again insists upon the Prefect's blindness to a logic or to a "principle of concealment" that has to do with poets and thus (it might be assumed) is specifically *poetic:*

This functionary [the Prefect] has been thoroughly mystified; and the remote source of his defeat lies in the supposition that the Minister is a *fool,* because he has acquired renown as a *poet.* All fools are poets; this the Prefect *feels;* and he is merely guilty of a *non distributio medii* in thence inferring that all poets are fools. (341–42)

In Baudelaire's translation of Poe's tale into French, the word *fool* is rendered, in its strong, archaic sense, as: *fou,* "mad." Here, then, is Lacan's paraphrase of this passage in the story:

After which, a moment of derision [on Dupin's part] at the Prefect's error in deducing that because the Minister is a poet, he is not far from being mad, an error, it is argued, which would consist . . . simply in a false distribution of the middle term, since it is far from following from the fact that all madmen are poets.

Yes indeed. But we ourselves are left in the dark as to the poet's superiority in the art of concealment. (1972b, 52)

Both this passage in the story and this comment by Lacan seem to be marginal, incidental. Yet the hypothetical *relationship between poetry and madness* is significantly relevant to the case of Poe and to the other psychoanalytic approaches we have been considering. Could it not be said that the error of Marie Bonaparte (who, like the Prefect, engages in a search for *hidden* meaning) lies precisely in the fact that, like the Prefect once again, she simplistically *equates* the poetic with the psychotic, and so, blinded by what she takes to be the poetic *incompetence,* fails to see or understand the specificity of poetic *competence?* Many psychoanalytic investigations diagnosing the poet's sickness and looking for his poetic secret on (or in) his person (as do the Prefect's men) are indeed very like police investigations; and like the police in Poe's story, they fail to find the letter, fail to see the textuality of the text.

Lacan, of course, does not say all this—this is not what is at stake in his analysis. All he does is open up still another question where we have believed we have come in possession of some sort of answer:

Yes indeed. But we ourselves are left in the dark as to the poet's superiority in the art of concealment. (52)

This seemingly lateral question, asked in passing and left unanswered, suggests, however, the possibility of a whole different focus or perspective of interpretation in the story. If "The Purloined Letter" is specifically the story of "the poet's superiority in the art of concealment," then it is not just an allegory of psychoanalysis but also, at the same time, an allegory of poetic writing. And Lacan is himself a poet to the extent that a thought about poetry is what is superiorly concealed in his Seminar.

In Lacan's interpretation, however, "the poet's superiority" can be understood only as the structural superiority of the third position with respect to the letter: the Minister in the first scene, Dupin in the second, both, indeed, poets. But the third position is also—this is the main point of Lacan's analysis—the position of the analyst. It follows that, in Lacan's approach, the status of the poet is no longer that of the (sick) patient but, if anything, that of the analyst. If the poet is still the object of the accusation of being a "fool," his folly—if in fact it does exist (which remains an open question)—would at the same time be the folly of the analyst. The clear-cut opposition between madness and health, or between doctor and patient is unsettled by the odd functioning of the purloined letter of the unconscious, which no one can possess or master. "There is no metalanguage," says Lacan: there is no language in which interpretation can itself escape the effects of the unconscious; the interpreter is no more immune than the poet to unconscious delusions and errors.

5.   *Implication, as opposed to application, of psychoanalytic theory*
Lacan's approach no longer falls into the category of what has been called "applied psychoanalysis," since the concept of "application" implies a relation of *exteriority* between the applied science and the field it is supposed, unilaterally, to inform. Since, in Lacan's analysis, Poe's text serves to *reinterpret Freud* just as Freud's text serves to interpret Poe; since psychoanalytic theory and the literary text mutually inform—and displace—each other; since the very position of the interpreter—of the

analyst—turns out to be not *outside,* but *inside* the text, there is no longer a clear-cut opposition or a well-defined border between literature and psychoanalysis: psychoanalysis could be intraliterary just as much as literature is intrapsychoanalytic. The methodological stake is no longer that of the *application* of psychoanalysis *to* literature, but rather, of their *interimplication in* each other.

If I have dealt at length with Lacan's innovative contribution and with the different methodological example of his approach, it is not so much to set up this example as a new model for imitation, but rather to indicate the way it suggestively invites us to go beyond itself (as it takes Freud beyond itself), the way it opens up a whole new range of as yet untried possibilities for the enterprise of reading. Lacan's importance in my eyes does not, in other words, lie specifically in the new dogma his "school" proposes, but lies in his outstanding demonstration that *there is more than one way* to implicate psychoanalysis in literature; that *how to* implicate psychoanalysis in literature is itself a question for interpretation, a challenge to the ingenuity and insight of the interpreter, and not a *given* that can be taken in any way for granted; that what is of analytical relevance in a text is not necessarily and not exclusively "the unconscious of the poet," let alone his sickness or his problems in life; that to situate in a text the analytical as such—to situate the object of analysis or the textual point of its implication—is not necessarily to recognize a *known,* to find an answer, but also, and perhaps more challenging, to locate an *unknown,* to find a question.

THE POE-ETIC ANALYTICAL

Let us now return to the crucial question we left in suspension earlier, after having raised it by reversing Freud's reservation concerning Marie Bonaparte's type of research: *Can* psychoanalysis give us an insight into the specificity of the poetic? We can now supplement this question with a second one: Where can we situate the analytical with respect to Poe's poetry?

The answer to these questions, I suggest, might be sought in two directions. (1) In a direct reading of a poetic text by Poe, trying to locate in the poem itself a signifier of poeticity and to analyze its functioning and its effects; to analyze—in other words—how poetry as such works through signifiers (to the extent that signifiers, as opposed to meanings, are always signifiers of the unconscious). (2) In an analytically informed reading of literary history itself, inasmuch as its treatment of Poe obviously constitutes a (literary) *case history*. Such a reading has never, to my knowledge, been undertaken with respect to any writer: never has literary history itself been viewed as an analytical object, as a subject for a psychoanalytical interpretation.[11] And yet it is overwhelmingly obvious, in a case like Poe's, that the discourse of literary history itself points to some unconscious determinations that structure it but of which it is not aware. What is the unconscious of literary history? Can the question of *the guilt of poetry* be relevant to that unconscious? Could literary history be in any way considered a repetitive unconscious *transference* of the guilt of poetry?

Literary history, or more precisely, the critical discourse surrounding Poe, is indeed one of the most visible ("self-evident") *effects* of Poe's poetic signifier, of his text. Now, how can the question of the peculiar effect of Poe be dealt with analytically? My suggestion is: by locating what seems to be unreadable or incomprehensible in this effect; by situating the most prominent discrepancies or discontinuities in the overall critical discourse concerning Poe, the most puzzling critical contradictions, and by trying to interpret those contradictions as symptomatic of the unsettling specificity of the Poe-etic effect, as well as of the necessary contingence of such an effect on the unconscious.

Before setting out to explore and to illustrate these two directions for research, I would like to recapitulate the primary historical contradictions analyzed at the opening of this study as a first indication of the nature of the poetic. According to its readers' contradictory testimonies, Poe's poetry, let it be recalled, seemed to be at once the most *irresistible* and the most *resisted* poetry in literary history. Poe is felt to be at once the most unequaled master of "conscious art" *and* the most tortuous unconscious case, as such doomed to remain "the perennial victim of the *idée fixe,* and of amateur psychoanalysis."[12] Poetry, I would thus argue, is precisely the effect of a deadly struggle between consciousness and the unconscious; it has to do with resistance and with what can be neither resisted nor escaped. Poe is a symptom of poetry to the extent that poetry is both what most resists a psychoanalytic interpretation and what most depends on psychoanalytic effects.

NOTES

1. "Although Poe was not the social outcast Baudelaire conceived him to be, he was, and still is, perhaps the most thoroughly misunderstood of all American

writers. . . . I have no quarrel with those who dislike Poe's work so long as they understand it. . . . I am persuaded that much of the criticism of Poe in this century, whether favorable or unfavorable, has been done by people who have not taken the trouble to understand his work" (Stovall 1969).

2. T. S. Eliot's famous statement on Poe in his study "From Poe to Valéry," *Hudson Review,* autumn 1949; reprinted in *The Recognition of Edgar Allan Poe: Selected Criticism since 1829,* ed. Eric W. Carlson (Ann Arbor: University of Michigan Press, 1966), 205.

3. Italics mine. As a rule, henceforth, only authors' italics will be indicated; all other italics are mine.

4. "The Murders in the Rue Morgue," in *Edgar Allan Poe: Selected Writings,* ed. David Galloway (New York: Penguin, 1967), 189. Hereafter cited as Poe (1967).

5. Translated by John Rodker. All references to Marie Bonaparte will be to this edition.

6. "Le séminaire sur 'La lettre volée,'" in *Ecrits* (Paris: Seuil, 1966). First translated by Jeffrey Mehlman in *French Freud, Yale French Studies* 48 (1972):38–72. All references here to "The Seminar on 'The Purloined Letter'" are to the *Yale French Studies* translation (Lacan 1972b).

7. Cf. Edmund Wilson: "The recent revival of interest in Poe has brought to light a good deal of new information and supplied us for the first time with a serious interpretation of his personal career, but it has so far entirely neglected to explain why we should still want to read him" (Carlson 1966, 142).

8. For a remarkable analysis of these issues, see Barbara Johnson's essay "The Frame of Reference: Poe, Lacan, Derrida," in *Literature and Psychoanalysis: The Question of Reading—Otherwise, Yale French Studies* 55/56 (1977):457–505. Reprinted Johns Hopkins University Press (1982).

9. Cf. "Need we emphasize the similarity of these two sequences? Yes, for the resemblance we have in mind is *not a simple collection of traits chosen only in order to delete their difference. And it would not be enough to retain those common traits at the expense of the others for the slightest truth to result.* It is rather the intersubjectivity in which the two actions are motivated that we wish to bring into relief, as well as the three terms through which it structures them. The special status of these terms results from their corresponding simultaneously to the three logical moments through which the decision is precipitated and to the three places it assigns to the subjects among whom it constitutes a choice. . . . Thus three moments, structuring three glances, borne by three subjects, incarnated each time by different characters" ("The Seminar on 'The Purloined Letter,'" Lacan 1972b, 43–44).

10. The scope of the present essay does not allow me to pursue this question further, but I intend to return to it in the (forthcoming) extended version of this study.

11. I have attempted, however, an elementary exploration of such an ap-

proach with respect to Henry James in my essay "Turning the Screw of Interpretation," in *Literature and Psychoanalysis: The Question of Reading—Otherwise, Yale French Studies* 55/56 (1977):94–138 (reprinted by Johns Hopkins University Press [1982]).

12. The formula is David Galloway's (Poe 1967, 24).

THREE   *Derrida and Responses*

8 🌿 The Challenge of Deconstruction

Beyond any question, the most serious challenge to Lacan's reading of "The Purloined Letter" comes from his compatriot Jacques Derrida. The challenge is all the more telling because of Derrida's influence upon the contemporary literary scene—at least in Anglo-Saxon countries—by reason of a theory of language and practice of criticism that he proposes under the general rubric "deconstruction." As such it has come to characterize an entire movement that often goes by the name "poststructuralism" or "postmodernism." Since the name of Lacan is often associated with that of Derrida as a leading figure in this movement, the "published debate" between them (Derrida 1984, 10) is significant, partly because it serves to differentiate them, partly because the differentiation itself helps clarify the meaning of deconstruction not only for literary criticism but for psychoanalysis itself. For that reason, Derrida's critique of Lacan's reading of Poe warrants a more elaborate presentation than other essays in this book.

To speak of the exchange between the two men as a "published debate" may be a bit too much, for Lacan never replied to Derrida's attack in any formal way. What we know of his reaction must be gathered indirectly from occasional allusions, some of them in seminars still to be published.

Derrida's critique is sustained in equally indirect though more explicit fashion. What can be said with certainty about the relationship between the two is meager enough.

Derrida was born in Algiers in 1930 when Lacan (born 1901) was already a twenty-nine-year-old resident in psychiatry in Paris. Derrida came to France to do military service and remained to study with Jean Hyppolite, a Hegelian scholar, at the Ecole Normale Supérieur (see Derrida 1974b, ix). After a year on scholarship at Harvard (1956–57) he returned to Paris and began teaching at the Ecole Normale himself, where he continues to lecture. He is currently professor of philosophy at the Ecole des Hauts Etudes. His visits to America are frequent and prolonged.

He was teaching at the Ecole, then, when Lacan was invited to transfer his seminar there (1963–64) from the Saint Anne Hospital where it had taken place weekly for the previous ten years (see Turkle 1978, 114–18). At that time Derrida's familiarity with Lacan's work was limited to an acquaintance with two of the essays that had appeared by then, "The Function and Field of Speech and Language in Psychoanalysis" and "The Agency of the Letter in the Unconscious, or Reason since Freud," but on the basis of these he began to formulate certain critical questions (Derrida 1981b, 108). The *Ecrits* appeared in 1966, and a careful reading of them did not alter his reservations. It was then that he became interested in the "Seminar on 'The Purloined Letter'" (1981b, 112), but he felt that his best contribution to the entire problem at that time was the continued pursuit of his own work, "whether or not this work should encounter Lacan's, and Lacan's—I do not at all reject the idea—more than any other today" (1981b, 111). Derrida's reservations were finally articulated and published in 1975 under the title "Le facteur de la vérité," first translated as "The Purveyor of Truth" (1975a).

During this slow maturation of his critique of Lacan, Derrida's own work was considerable. His first book (1962) was a translation of Husserl's *Origin of Geometry*, with a long (170-page) introduction (Derrida 1977), but his major impact was made in 1967 in the simultaneous publication of three works: *Of Grammatology, Writing and Difference,* and *Speech and Phenomena.* With these, a major statement was made and main lines were drawn. Five years later, in a single year (1972) he brought out simultaneously *Margins of Philosophy, Dissemination,* and *Positions*—and other titles continue to flow. We make no attempt here to resume all the intricacies of Derrida's complex thought. Rather, we endeavor to situate it within its essential parameters, that is, "frame" it in order to help readers appreciate the thrust of his critique of Lacan.[1] First the essentials of the position, then the critique.

But how does one "frame" Derrida? Anyone familiar with his thought will realize that an effort to encapsulate it is bound to betray it—"an essential and ludicrous operation" (Derrida 1981a, 7). Since our purpose is only to make his critique of Lacan accessible to readers, and since he himself sketched the main thrust of that critique in a note appended to the published version of an interview given in 1971 that, together with two other interviews given earlier (1967, 1968), constitutes a presentation of Derrida by himself, we shall take (for purely heuristic purposes) the data offered by these three interviews, published under the title *Positions* (1981b), as the general framework within which to consider his fundamental insight.

Whatever may be his influence in literary circles, Derrida's beginnings were as a philosopher whose primary masters are Nietzsche, Freud, and Heidegger—but "above all" Heidegger (Derrida 1981b, 9).[2] Heidegger's question is about the meaning of Being, where Being is experienced as that which lets a being (Aristotle's *on,* i.e., whatever "is") *be* what and how it is. For Heidegger at the beginning of his quest for its meaning, then, Being is experienced, so to speak, as the "is" of what-is, precisely inasmuch as it is *different* from what-is, the difference being designated the "ontological difference." This question, fundamental though it may be, is for Heidegger not strictly speaking a "metaphysical" question, for metaphysics since Aristotle asks about "beings as beings" (*on hei on*), and this formula in turn came to mean the question either about beings in their most abstract generality (so-called ontology) or about beings in terms of the supreme one among them that founds the rest (so-called theology). By reason of its very structure, then, metaphysics becomes "onto-theo-logy" (see "The Onto-theo-logical Structure of Metaphysics," in *Identity and Difference* [1969]). Heidegger's question is more fundamental still than the metaphysical question. According to an early metaphor, he seeks to "lay the groundwork" for metaphysics, but later on he speaks rather of the "groundlessness" or "abyss" (*Abgrund*) that his question opens up. In any case, the earlier, more flamboyant Heidegger claims that the task involves the "destruction" of the "traditional content of ancient ontology (i.e., onto-theo-logy) until we arrive at those primordial experiences in which we achieved our first ways of determining the nature of Being—the ways which have guided us ever since" (*Being and Time* [1962, 44]). It is the thrust of such an enterprise that Derrida has transformed and made his own.

For "deconstruction," the term that most comprehensively describes Derrida's own effort, is the term by which he very neatly transforms (he would not say "translates") the Heideggerian term "destruction":

I try to respect as rigorously as possible the internal, regulated play of philosophemes or epistimemes by making them slide—without mistreating them—to the point of their nonpertinence, their exhaustion, their closure. To "deconstruct" philosophy, thus, would be to think—in the most faithful, interior way—the structured genealogy of philosophy's concepts, but at the same time to determine—from a certain exterior that is unqualifiable or unnameable by philosophy—what this history has been able to dissimulate or forbid, making itself into a history by means of this somewhere motivated repression. (Derrida 1981b, 6)

The full import of this formulation will appear as we proceed. For the moment let it suffice to remark that the Derridean enterprise, like the Heideggerian one, has a positive as well as a negative component in its movement, operating "at the *limit* of philosophical discourse" (Derrida's emphasis), perhaps, but not on the premise of its "death" (1981b, 6). His use of the word "philosophy," however, warrants pause.

By "philosophy" Derrida understands the metaphysical tradition, to be sure, but in a sense different from Heidegger's. What characterizes metaphysics for Derrida is the emphasis on "presence" (and its correlative negation, "nonpresence"). This lies at the base of all the classic issues of metaphysics: being, unity, truth, the good, reason, identity, continuity, meaning, subjectivity, authenticity, the principle of noncontradiction, and so forth—and their opposites. All these and like notions find their center, he claims, in the notion of presence, which in turn centers the history of metaphysics. The result is a "centrism," which Derrida characterizes, because of the master quality of the name *logos* for Greek thought, as "logocentrism." But the very notion of "center" here is problematic, for in his view there really is no center, and every presumed "center" yields to another that follows as its trace. Derrida's task is to deconstruct logocentrism. [3]

One aspect of logocentric thought that is particularly symptomatic in Derrida's eyes is its perennial tendency to give priority to speech over writing in the functioning of language. This tendency characterizes the tradition from Plato down to Saussure and Husserl in our own day and makes very evident that tradition's fascination with presence. For speech implies a presence of the speaker to himself in consciousness, presence to his own thought in the actual voicing of it, and presence to his dialogue partner in the act of communication (Derrida 1981b, 22–25). By contrast, the written text does not enjoy the same immediacy but takes on a certain exteriority (implicit to "expression"), generality, possible anonymity, and so on. That is why Plato could consider writing an "orphan" by comparison with speech (cited Derrida 1981b, 12), and Saussure could say, "language and writing are two distinct sign systems: the unique *raison d'être* of the second is to *represent* the first" (Derrida's emphasis, cited 1981b, 25). This priority given to speech over writing the author calls "phonologism"—a logocentric fiction, since there is no limit to be drawn between *grammē* and *phonē*. "Phonologism" is to be deconstructed.

What, then, does he propose as an alternative way of conceiving matters? In terms of the contemporary conception of language as fathered by Saussure, Derrida finds no particular fault with the notion of it as a system of signs distinguished from one another always and only by their mutual opposition to—that is, *difference* from—each other. He accepts, as does Lacan, Saussure's distinction between the signifier (speech sound) and signified (mental image) components of such signs. But the latter distinction is for him neither radical nor absolute (1981b, 20). Moreover, he concedes that if we limit our attention to purely phonetic writing, then the secondary role assigned to it vis-à-vis speech by the tradition is justifiable. But if we take account of the fact that our emphasis on phonetic writing is a culturally determined one, and that phonetic writing itself is never completely "pure" (because of the necessary spacing of signs, punctuation, intervals, etc. [1981b, 25]), then the traditional hierarchy becomes problematic. To deal with the issue, Derrida proposes a new concept of writing:

This concept can be called *gram* or *différance*. The play of differences supposes, in effect, syntheses and referrals which forbid at any moment, or in any sense, that a simple element be *present* in and of itself, referring only to itself. Whether in the order of spoken or written discourse, no element can function as a sign without referring to another element which itself is not simply present. This interweaving results in each "element"—phoneme or grapheme—being constituted on the basis of the trace within it of the other elements of the chain or system. This interweaving, this textile, is the *text* produced only in the transformation of another text. Nothing, neither among the elements nor within the system, is anywhere ever simply present or absent. There are only, everywhere, differences and traces of traces. (1981b, 26)

Note here that writing the word *différance* with an *a* rather than an *e* introduces a change in meaning discernible in the writing (or reading) of it but not in the "speech sound" (*phonē*) of it. Derived from the Latin *differre*, *différance* suggests both "differ" and "defer" (in the sense of "displace"). Note too the broadened sense of "text" (and eventually of "textuality") as a weaving that is interwoven with other weavings of displaced/displacing traces. We are well beyond Saussure. Derrida continues:

The gram as *différance*, then, is a structure and a movement no longer conceivable on the basis of the opposition presence/absence. *Différance* is the systematic play of differences, of the traces of differences, of the *spacing* by means of which elements are related to each other. This spacing is the simultaneously active and passive . . . production of the intervals without which the "full" terms would not signify, would not function. (The *a* of *différance* indicates this indecision as concerns activity and passivity, that which cannot be governed by or distributed between the terms of this opposition. [Translator's note: In other words, *différance* combines and confuses "differing" and "deferring" in both their active and passive senses.]) It is also the becoming-space of the spoken chain—which has been called temporal or linear; a becoming-space which makes possible both writing and every correspondence between speech and writing, every passage from one to the other. (1981b, 27)

Note the term "indecision" here. The "undecidability" of terms, based on their essential ambiguity of meaning, is a consequence of *différance* and a recurrent term in Derrida's problematic.

Just how radical this conception is becomes clear when in a kind of summary Derrida makes his position explicit:

Therefore, one has to admit, before any dissociation of language and speech, code and message, etc. (and everything that goes along with such a dissociation), a systematic production of differences, the *production* of a system of differences—a *différance*—within whose effects one eventually, by abstraction and according to determined motivations, will be able to demarcate a linguistics of language and a linguistics of speech, etc. (Author's emphasis; 1981b. 28)

The consequences of all this are far-reaching. The "economy" of *différance* for Derrida is irreducible. It has no center, it has no author. It precedes all subjectivity; that is, the subject is not present, even to itself, except as an effect of it. *Différance* precedes all play of signifiers. As for the signified (i.e., meaning), we can understand now why any conception of stability or identifiable unity in meaning, such as the spiritual ideality that Husserl aspires to (Derrida 1981b, 29–32), is dismissed as the seductive lure of the metaphysics of presence. Hence the perennial hope of such a metaphysics to discern a "transcendental signified," that is, some meaning independent of all function of language, is an impossible—though perhaps inevitable—dream:

In the extent to which what is called "meaning" (to be "expressed") is already, and thoroughly, constituted by a tissue of differences, in the extent to which there is already a *text,* a network of textual referrals to *other* texts, a textual transformation in which each allegedly "simple term" is marked by the trace of another term, the presumed interiority of meaning is already worked upon by its own exteriority. It is always already carried outside itself. It already differs (from itself) before any act of expression. And only on this condition can it constitute a syntagm or text. Only on this condition can it "signify." (1981b, 33)

How this "condition" affects the actual practice of deconstruction we shall see shortly. Before leaving the present context, however, let us add a word (because of its relevance to the essay that follows) about the implication of this conception of *différance* for the notion of truth. In *Of Grammatology,* Derrida is very explicit:

The "rationality" . . . which governs a writing thus enlarged and radicalized, no longer issues from a logos. Further, it inaugurates the destruction, not the demolition but the de-sedimentation, the de-construction, of all the significations that have their source in that of the logos. Particularly the signification of *truth.* All the metaphysical determinations of truth, and even the one beyond metaphysical onto-theology that Heidegger reminds us of, are more or less immediately inseparable from the instance of the logos, or of a reason thought within the lineage of the logos, in whatever sense it is understood. (1974b, 10)

What is left of "truth," then, when deconstruction is over? Derrida admits, after putting in question, the "value of truth" in all its forms (i.e., as conformity, as certitude, as *alētheia,* etc.), that we nonetheless "must have [it]" (1981b, 105). "Paraphrasing Freud, speaking of the present/absent penis (but it is the same thing), we must recognize in truth 'the normal prototype of the fetish.' How can we do without it?" (1981b, 105).

The problem of truth aside, we should add that the economy of *différance* cannot be defined by any specific limit. Derrida insists on the "structural impossibility . . . of putting an edge on its weave, of tracing a margin that would not be a new mark. Since it cannot be elevated into a master-word or master-concept, *différance* finds itself enmeshed in the work that pulls it through a chain of other 'concepts,' other 'words,' other textual configurations" (1981b, 40). And it is a chain that is never static—always in motion. A case in point: the concept of "dissemination" (echoed often in the essays that follow):

A difference: the cause is radically that. . . . Numerical multiplicity does not sneak up like a death threat upon a germ cell previously one with itself. On the contrary, it serves as a pathbreaker for "the" seed, which therefore produces (itself) and advances only in the plural. It is a singular plural, which no single origin will ever have preceded. Germination, dissemination. There is no first insemination. The semen is already swarming. The "primal" insemination is dissemination. A trace, a graft whose traces have been lost. Whether in the case of what is called "language" (discourse, text, etc.) or in the case of some "real" seed-sowing, each term is indeed a germ, and each germ a term. The term, the atomic element, engenders by division, grafting, proliferation. It is a seed and not an absolute term. But each germ *is* its own term, finds its term not outside itself but within itself as its own internal limit. (1981a, 304).

In other words, dissemination is "seminal *différance*" (1981b, 45), based on the "fortuitous resemblance, the purely simulated common parentage of *seme* [i.e., sign, mark] and *semen*" (1981b, 45).

Another concept that germinates from just such dissemination through "playful exploration" is the term *écart* (interval), yielding *carré* (square), *carrure* (stature), *carte* (card), *charte* (chart)—all bearing some affinity to (if not etymological derivation from) the Latin *quartus* (1981b, 42 and n. 10). The importance for us of this little game, played out in conjunction with Derrida's commentary on Sollers's text *Numbers* (where that author speaks, for example, of a quadrangle with one side missing), is that apparently it lies at the base of what Derrida understands by "framing" (see 1981a, 296–300, 312–13). This in turn has its role to play in the polemic against the metaphysics of presence. Thus we are told by a translator:

Through its insistence upon squares, crossroads, and other four-sided figures, "Dissemination" attempts to work a violent but imperceptible displacement of the "triangular"—Dialectical, Trinitarian, Oedipal—foundations of Western thought. This passage from three to four may perhaps be seen as a warning to those who, having understood the necessity for a deconstruction of metaphysical binarity, might be tempted to view the number "three" as a guarantee of liberation from the blindness of logocentrism. (1981a, xxxii)

We should mention, too (because reference will be made to it by one of the commentators), another term that is cognate to the concept of the ineluctable polyvalence of disseminating *différance*—namely, "hymen." Derrida finds the term in Mallarmé's *Mimique,* on which he comments in "The Double Session" (1981a, 173–286). Mallarmé speaks of "a hymen (out of which flows Dream), tainted with vice yet sacred, between desire and fulfillment, perpetration and remembrance: here anticipating, there recalling, in the future, in the past, *under the false appearance of a present"* (cited in 1981a, 175; Mallarmé's emphasis). In his commentary, Derrida observes that the term suggests first of all "the consummation of a marriage, the identification of two beings, the confusion between the two" (1981a, 209). But here is the ambivalence: "*Between* the two, there is no difference but identity" (1981a, 209). But it is precisely the "between" that is problematic, for "between" suggests that difference is maintained between the two partners. Here is the slippage of *différance.* "[Hymen] is an operation that *both* sows confusion *between* opposites *and* stands *between* the opposites 'at once.' What counts here is the *between,* the in-between-ness of the hymen. The hymen 'takes place' in the 'inter-,' in the spacing between desire and fulfillment, between perpetration and its recollection. But this medium of the *entre* has nothing to do with a center" (1981a, 212). When all is said and done, "the word 'between' has no full meaning of its own" (1981a, 221). It simply indicates the movement of *différance.* And:

what holds for "hymen" also holds, *mutatis mutandis,* for all other signs which, like *pharmakon, supplement, différance,* and others have a double, contradictory, undecidable value that always derives from their syntax, whether the latter is in a sense "internal," articulating and combining under the same yoke, *huph'hen,* two incompatible meanings, or "external," dependent on the code in which the word is made to function. (1981a, 221)

Given such a conception of writing as disseminating *différance* that is "no longer conceivable on the basis of the opposition presence/absence" (1981b, 27) and functions also as the "becoming-space of the spoken chain" (1981b, 27), how are we to understand the strategy of deconstruction in terms of a practice of criticism, whether philosophical or literary? Derrida insists that it is not simply a question of "neutralizing" the binary oppositions of metaphysics, leaving them more or less in place.

Rather, the task is to engage in a kind of "double writing": first we must "overturn the hierarchy" that is implicit in these oppositions (e.g., the supposition that presence is superior to absence [1981b, 41]); second, "by means of this double, and precisely stratified, dislodged and dislodging, writing, we must also mark the interval between inversion, which brings low what was high, and the irruptive emergence of a new 'concept,' a concept that can no longer be, and never could be, included in the previous regime" (1981b, 42), that is, engage in the play of displacement.

But this is terribly abstract. Better to watch Derrida himself in action as he pursues the method of deconstruction in engaging the polemic against logocentrism on the most fundamental level—for example (it is but one of many), in analyzing the phonocentrism of Rousseau. This appears in the celebrated analysis of "supplementarity" (1974b, 141–64). According to Rousseau, "languages are made to be spoken, writing serves only as a supplement to speech" (cited 1974b, 144). Here "supplement" is used with a negative valence to indicate an addition to something already complete in itself—hence, superfluous, unnecessary, excessive. But "supplement" has another meaning, namely "replacement" or "substitute" for what is lacking to, or deficient in, the fullness of something else (1974b, 145). The two meanings cannot be separated, and both appear with varying inflections in Rousseau's text. Thus, while eschewing writing as inferior to speech (i.e., only a "supplement" to it), Rousseau tells us in the *Confessions* that he resorted to writing as a compensation for (i.e., "supplement" to) the deficiencies of speech.

[Rousseau] describes the passage to writing as the restoration, by a certain absence and by a sort of calculated effacement, of presence disappointed of itself in speech. To write is indeed the only way of keeping or recapturing speech since speech denies itself as it gives itself. Thus an *economy of signs* is organized. It will be equally disappointing, closer yet to the very essence and to the necessity of disappointment. One cannot help wishing to master absence and yet we must always let go. (1974b, 142; Derrida's emphasis)

The act of writing, then, would be an effort to "reappropriate" a lost presence that speech aspires to but in fact cannot achieve:

Rousseau condemns writing as destruction of presence and as disease of speech. He rehabilitates it to the extent that it promises the reappropriation of that of which speech allowed itself to be dispossessed. But by what, if not already a writing older than speech and already installed in that place? (1974b, 142)

Derrida finds this same torsion in the meaning of "supplement" elsewhere in Rousseau, for example, in the notion of education as a "supplement" to Nature in *Emile* and, curiously, in his account in the *Confessions* of his struggle with masturbation, "that dangerous supplement" to "normal" sexual activity. What is curious is its analogy with writing. "Just as writing opens the crisis of the living speech in terms of its 'image,' its painting or its representation, so onanism announces the ruin of vitality in terms of imaginary seductions" (1974b, 151).

But what is important for our purposes is to recognize that the paradoxical tension interior to the concept of supplement here is due not simply to a subjective failing on the part of Rousseau but rather to the movement of language itself, or rather to the disseminating *différance* that precedes and permeates it. The task of deconstruction is to discern this movement and call attention to the contradictions that permeate a text despite the writer's best intentions. This will involve playing out the polarity of these contradictions in an effort to articulate the self-negating subtext that runs beneath the surface of the author's intention. The result will be the "double writing" that characterizes the method: first the critic reverses the primacy given in the text to the author's intention (here to his conception of "supplement" as "addition"), then by a "dislodged dislodging writing" he explores the "irruptive emergence" of any new concept (here of "supplement" as "substitution" and the "chain of supplements" [1974b, 152–57] that germinates from this disseminating *différance*).

But how does all this affect Derrida's reading of Lacan? In the interview of 1971, he is asked directly about the relation between his thought and that of Lacan, and his improvised answer is emended by a long and very illuminating note. Sketching the evolution of his knowledge of Lacan, Derrida tells us that when "Freud and the Scene of Writing" (1966) and *Of Grammatology* (1967) appeared, he was aware only of Lacan's essays "The Function and Field of Speech and Language in Psychoanalysis" and "The Agency of the Letter, or Reason since Freud." Already he had some reservations:

1. The apparent teleology of "full speech" in terms of its relation to truth was clearly redolent of the whole problem of logocentrism (1981b, 108).

2. Under the guise of a "return to Freud," Lacan's use of Hegelian, Husserlian, and Heideggerian categories without any "theoretical and systematic explanation of the status of these importations" smacked of the "philosophical facileness" that Lacan himself condemned (1981b, 108–9).

3. Lacan's recourse to Saussurian linguistics in its most phonocentric version seemed at best "light-handed" (1981b, 109).

4. Lacan's freewheeling style (ranging from an emphasis on the primacy of the signifier that risked the impression of installing the signifier in a new metaphysics to an echoing of existentialist terminology that seemed to "anchor" it in postwar philosophical thought) seemed to Derrida, in the face of the "theoretical difficulties" that preoccupied him, an exercise—however "remarkable"—in an "art of evasion" (1981b, 109–10).

After Lacan's *Ecrits* appeared (1966), Derrida read, of course, the remaining essays, and his first impressions were "largely confirmed" (1981b, 111). The principal sticking point was the identification of truth (as unveiling) and speech (logos) (e.g., see "Myself, the Truth, I Speak" [Lacan 1966a, 409]). For Derrida, this identification would be a phonologocentrism of the purest sort. It was under these circumstances that he took a special interest in "The Seminar on 'The Purloined Letter' ":

An admirable achievement, and I do not say this conventionally, but one which seems to me, in its flight to find the "illustration" of a "truth" (1981a, 12), to misconstrue the map [*carte*], the functioning or fictioning, of Poe's text, of this text and its links to others, let us say the *squaring* [*carrure*] of a scene of writing played out in it. Lacan's discourse, no more than any other, is not totally closed to this square, or to its figure, which does not equal or unveil any speaking truth. (1981b, 112)

Such then were his initial reactions to this essay. How eventually they came to structure "The Purveyor of Truth," which at the time of this interview was still gestating, is something readers may evaluate in the text below. At any rate, we can see from these remarks why the theme of "framing" becomes of central importance to the commentators.

So much for the "published debate." What was the outcome? There was never any formal response to Derrida's critique from Lacan or, as far as we know, from the Lacanians. Early in their relationship Derrida complains of certain "aggressions" on Lacan's part that nevertheless did not prevent him from "doing what depended on [him]" to prevent the interruption of Lacan's seminars at the Ecole Normale (1981b, 111).

From Lacan's point of view, he reminds his readers (1969) that he had made reference (1957) to "what I properly call the instance of the letter, before any grammatology" (cited by Johnson 1977, 467). Again (1968), in dissociating himself from certain excesses of expression to which his own work had given rise, he says (with customary grace), "my discourse . . . is a different kind of buoy in this rising tide of the signifier, or the signified, of the 'it speaks,' of trace, of *grammē,* of lure, of myth, from the circulation of which I have now withdrawn. Aphrodite of this foam, there has risen from it latterly *différance,* with an *a"* (1968, 47). Derrida, though equally indirect, is much more persistent in sustaining his critique. It seems that all his allusions to castration, lack, talking truth, letters that do not reach their destinations, and so on, are references to Lacan, thus keeping the old fires alive (see 1981a, xvii).

Clearly the two men have much in common, and the tensions that appear in their relations to each other seem to concern issues of originality and priority of discovery more than irreconcilable difference. For the sake of the record, however, it should be noted that, whatever may have been Derrida's familiarity with Lacan before the first publication of his own work (1962), the fact is that Lacan addressed the issue of the priority of writing to speech in his *Seminar IX: L'identification* (1961–62).[4] A serious comparative study of these two thinkers would have to take careful account of that still unpublished text. Be that as it may, two of the crucial issues between them will be the role of truth in language and the nature and function of the signifier. But such matters open up a whole new complex of questions that cannot be adjudicated here.

Notes

1. Derrida has been fortunate in the quality and care of his English translators. Besides the work of translation itself, they have often added very helpful notes, together with essays ("prefaces" of one kind or another) of introduction. Spivak's preface to the translation of *Of Grammatology* (Derrida 1974b), for example, is especially comprehensive. Other specimens of secondary literature that may prove helpful for purposes of general orientation are Jonathan Culler's "Jacques Derrida" (1979), Alan Bass's engaging autobiographical account (1984), and Richard Kearney's perceptive interview (1984).

2. But since Derrida's interest in the philosophers has always been in terms of their writings as *texts,* some literary critics consider him one of their own from the start.

3. The extent to which even Heidegger's text, "which, no more than any other, is not homogeneous, continuous, everywhere equal to the greatest force and to all the consequences of its questions" (Derrida 1981b, 10), must be subjected to the deconstructive fire as a form of logocentrism is a question we cannot pursue here. See, for example, *Positions* (1981b, 54–55) and "Ousia and Grammē" (1982, 29–67).

4. Though the seminar is unpublished, see Allouch (1983), Julien (1983), and Juranville (1984, 285–92).

9   The Purveyor of Truth

JACQUES DERRIDA

Translated by Alan Bass

> *They thank him for the great truths he has*
> *just proclaimed—for they have discovered*
> *(O verifier of that which cannot be*
> *verified!) that everything he has uttered is*
> *absolutely true;—although at first, the*
> *good people confess, they had had the*
> *suspicion that it might indeed be a simple*
> *fiction. Poe answers that, for his part, he*
> *never doubted it.*
>
> —Baudelaire

DIVESTED PRETEXTS

Psychoanalysis, supposedly, is found.

When one believes one finds it, it is psychoanalysis itself, supposedly, that finds itself.

When it finds, supposedly, it finds itself/is found—something.[1]

To be satisfied, here, with deforming the generative, as it is called, grammar of these three or four statements.

Where then? Where does psychoanalysis, always, already refind itself, where is it to be refound?

The article by Derrida, "Le facteur de la vérité," originally appeared in *Poétique* (1975). The English translation is from *The Post Card: From Socrates to Freud and Beyond*, translated, with an introduction and additional notes, by Alan Bass (Chicago: University of Chicago Press, 1987). © 1987 by The University of Chicago. Because of its length, we were allowed to reprint almost half of the original. With the permission of the author, we have omitted long quotations from Lacan, Freud, and Bonaparte, some footnotes, and some of the argument. Readers are encouraged to read the entire piece in *The Post Card*.

TNThe title of this essay, "Le Facteur de la vérité," includes the double meaning of *facteur*: both postman and factor. Thus, the postman/factor of truth, the question of the delivery of truth in psychoanalysis.

That in which, finding itself, it is found, if finding itself it is found, let us call text. And let us do so not only in order to recall that the theoretical and practical inscription of psychoanalysis (in the text as "language," "writing," "culture," "mythology," "the history of religions, of philosophy, of literature, of science, of medicine," etc., in the text as a "historical," "economic," "political," "instinctual," etc., field, in the heterogeneous and conflictual weave of *différance,* which is elsewhere defined as *general text* and without border) must have effects that have to be taken into account. But also in order to demarcate the space of a determined question.

Unless we are concerned, here, with a singular logic: the species including the genus.

For example: What happens in the psychoanalytic deciphering of a text when the latter, the deciphered itself, already explicates itself? When it says more about itself than does the deciphering (a debt acknowledged by Freud more than once)? And especially when the deciphered text inscribes in itself *additionally* the scene of the deciphering? When the deciphered text deploys more force in placing onstage and setting adrift the analytic process itself, up to its very last word, for example, the truth?

For example, the truth. But is truth an example? What happens—and what is dispensed with—when a text, for example a so-called literary fiction—but is this still an example?—puts truth onstage? And when in doing so it delimits the analytic reading, assigns the analyst his position, shows him seeking truth, and even finding it, shows him discoursing on the truth of the text, and then in general proffering the discourse on truth, the truth on truth? What happens in a text capable of such a scene? A text confident, in its program, of situating analytic activity grappling with the truth? . . .

[In the *Traumdeutung,*] examining the history of repression between *Oedipus Rex* and *Hamlet,* demolishing all the differences between (1) the "Oedipus complex," (2) the legend, and (3) Sophocles' tragedy, Freud establishes a rule: everything in a text that does not constitute the semantic core of the two "typical dreams" he has just defined (incest with mother and murder of father), everything that is foreign to the absolute *nudity* of this oneiric content, belongs to the "secondary revision of the material" (*sekundären Bearbeitung des Stoffes*). The formal (textual, in the usual sense) differences that come, as if from the outside, to affect the semantic structure, here the "Oedipus complex," thus constitute secondary revisions. For example, when one views *Oedipus Rex* as a tragedy of destiny, as a conflict between men and the gods, a theological drama, etc., one has taken as essential what actually remains an after-the-fact construction, a garment, a disguise, a material added to the literal *Stoff* precisely in order to mask its nudity.

The denuding of this *Stoff,* the discovery of the semantic material— such would be the end of analytic deciphering. By denuding the meaning behind the formal disguises, by undoing the work, analytic deciphering exhibits the primary content beneath the secondary revisions.

* * * * * * * * *

Exhibiting, denuding, undressing, unveiling: the familiar acrobatics of the metaphor *of* the truth. And one just as well could say the metaphor of metaphor, the truth of truth, the truth of metaphor. When Freud intends to denude the original *Stoff* beneath the disguises of secondary fabrication, he is anticipating the truth of the text. The latter, from its original contention, would be coordinated with its naked truth, but also with truth as nakedness.

The subchapter to which Freud refers us is very short: six pages. It deals with certain dreams of shame or embarrassment (*Verlegensheitstraum*). The dreamer is embarrassed about his nakedness (*Nacktheit*). These six pages contain two to four literary references. Two to four because in question each time is an "initial" text taken up and transformed by a "second" text: Homer by Keller, Andersen by Fulda, which, no more than the *illustrative* recourse to literary material, provokes no question on Freud's part.

Dreams of nakedness, then, provoking a feeling of modesty or shame (*Scham*). They are "typical," precisely, only by virtue of their association with distress, embarrassment, discomfort. This "gist of [their] subject-matter" can then lend itself to all kinds of transformations, elaborations, changes. Nakedness gives rise to substitutes. The lack of clothing, or undress (*Entkleidung, Unbekleidung*), is displaced onto other attributes. The same typical core organizes the dream of the former officer pushed into the street without his saber, without his necktie, or wearing civilian check trousers. All the examples proposed by Freud concern men, and men who exhibit the lack of a phallic attribute, or rather who adopt this exhibitionistic activity. Or, more precisely still: nakedness does not exhibit the penis or the absence of the penis, but the absence of the phallus as an attribute supplementing a possible fault, the absence of the colossal double. Already a certain chain is indicated: truth-unveiled-woman-castration-shame. Schreber: "Besides, we know in our hearts that men's lust is aroused much less, if at all, by the sight of male nudes; yet female nudes arouse *both* sexes to the same degree."

* * * * * * * * * *

homophobic propaganda

THE SURPLUS OF EVIDENCE OR THE LACK IN ITS PLACE*

a little too *self-evident*

. . . In France, the "literary criticism" marked by psychoanalysis had not asked the question of the text. Its interest was elsewhere, as was its wealth. This can be said without injustice, apparently, of Marie Bonaparte's psychobiography, of the psychoanalyses of material imagination, of existential psychoanalysis, or psychocriticism, of the thematist phenomenology tinted with psychoanalysis, etc.

It is entirely otherwise in the "Seminar on 'The Purloined Letter.' " Or so it appears. Although Lacan has never directly and systematically been interested in the so-called literary text, and although the problematic of *Das Unheimliche* ["The Uncanny"] does not intervene in his discourse to my knowledge, the *general* question of the text is at work unceasingly in his writings, where the logic of the signifier disrupts naive semanticism. And Lacan's "style" was constructed so as to check almost permanently any access to an isolatable content, to an unequivocal, determinable meaning beyond writing.

* * * * * * * * * *

If the critique of a certain semanticism constitutes an indispensable phase in the elaboration of a theory of the text, then one may discern in the Seminar a very distinct advance in relation to an entire kind of post-Freudian psychoanalytic criticism. Without precipitation toward the semantic, that is, thematic, content of a text, the organization of the signifier is taken into account. In its materiality as well as its formality.

---

*Editor's note: The French text published in *Poétique* has "Le trop d'évidence—où le manque a sa place," which we translate as "the surplus of evidence—where lack has its place."

* * * * * * * * *

Question of the letter, question of the materiality of the signifier: perhaps
it will suffice to change a letter, perhaps even less than a letter, in the
expression "*manque à sa place*" (Lacan 1972b, 55) [lack in its place,
missing from its place], perhaps it will suffice to introduce into this
expression a written *a*, that is, an *a* without an accent mark, in order to
make apparent that if the lack has its place [*manque a sa place*] in this
atomistic topology of the signifier, if it occupies a determined place with
defined contours, then the existing order will not have been upset: the
letter will always refind its proper place, a circumvented lack (certainly
not an empirical, but a transcendental one, which is better yet, and more
certain), the letter will be where it always will have been, always should
have been, intangible and indestructible via the detour of a *proper,* and
properly *circular,* itinerary. But we are not there yet.

Lacan, then, is attentive to the letter, that is, to the materiality of the
signifier. To its formality also, which determines the subject as much as
does the site of the literal atom: "Subjectivity originally is of no relation
to the real, but of a syntax which engenders in the real the signifying
mark" [Lacan 1966a, 50].

A break with naive semanticism and psychobiographism, an elaboration of a logic of the signifier (in its literal materiality and syntactic
formality), an assumption of the problematic of *Beyond the Pleasure Principle:* such are the most general forms of an advance legible in the Seminar
at first glance. But the excess of evidence always demands the supplement
of inquiry.

Now we must come closer, reread, question.

From the outset, we recognize the classical landscape of applied psychoanalysis. Here applied to literature, Poe's text, whose status is never
examined—Lacan simply calls it "fiction"—finds itself invoked as an
"example." An example destined to "illustrate," in a didactic procedure,
a law and a truth forming the proper object of a seminar. Literary
writing, here, is brought into an *illustrative* position: "to illustrate" here
meaning to read the general law in the example, to make clear the
meaning of a law or of a truth, to bring them to light in striking or
exemplary fashion. The text is in the service of the truth, and of a truth
that is taught, moreover: "Which is why we have decided to illustrate for
you today the truth which may be drawn from that moment in Freud's
thought under study—namely, that it is the symbolic order which is
constitutive for the subject—by demonstrating in a story the decisive
orientation which the subject receives from the itinerary of a signifier.

"It is that truth, let us note, which makes the very existence of fiction possible" (Lacan 1972b, 40).

Again, illustration, and the illustration of instruction, Freud's instruction: "What Freud teaches us in the text that we are commenting on is that the subject must pass through the channels of the symbolic, but what is illustrated here is more gripping still: it is not only the subject, but the subjects, grasped in their intersubjectivity, who line up. . ." (1972b, 60).

The "truth which may be drawn from that moment in Freud's thought under study," the truth with which the most decorative and pedagogical literary illustration is coordinated, is not, as we will see, this or that truth, but is the truth itself, the truth of the truth. It provides the Seminar with its rigorously philosophical import.

One can identify, then, the most classical practice. Not only the practice of philosophical "literary criticism," but also Freud's practice each time that he demands of literature examples, illustrations, testimony, and confirmation in relation to knowledge, truth, and laws that he treats elsewhere in another mode. Moreover, if Lacan's statements on the relation between fiction and truth are less clear and less unequivocal elsewhere, here there is no doubt about the order. "Truth inhabits fiction" cannot be understood in the somewhat perverse sense of a fiction more powerful than the truth which inhabits it, the truth that fiction inscribes within itself. In truth, the truth inhabits fiction as the master of the house, as the law of the house, as the economy of fiction. The truth executes the economy of fiction, directs, organizes, and makes possible fiction: "It is that truth, let us note, which makes the very existence of fiction possible" (1972b, 40).

The issue then is to ground fiction in truth, to guarantee fiction its conditions of possibility in truth, and to do so without even indicating, as does *Das Unheimliche*, literary fiction's eternally renewed resistance to the general law of psychoanalytic knowledge. Additionally, Lacan never asks what distinguishes one literary fiction from another. Even if every fiction were founded in or made possible by the truth, perhaps one would have to ask from what kind of fiction something like literature, here "The Purloined Letter," derives, and what effects this might have on that very thing which appears to make it possible.

This first limit contains the entire Seminar, and it reprints its marks indefinitely on it: what the literary example yields is a *message*. Which will have to be deciphered on the basis of Freud's teaching. Reprint: "The Opening of This Collection" (October 1966, ten years after the Seminar) speaks of "Poe's message deciphered and coming back from him, the reader, in that to read it, it says itself to be no more feigned than the truth when it inhabits fiction" (Lacan 1969, 16).

What Lacan analyzes, decomposing it into its elements, its origin, and its destination, uncovering it in its truth, is a *story* [*histoire*] (1972b, 40–41).

* * * * * * * *

This story is certainly that of a letter, of the theft and displacement of a signifier. But what the Seminar treats is only the content of this story, what is justifiably called its history, what is recounted in the account, the internal and narrated face of the narration. Not the narration itself. The Seminar's interest in the agency of the signifier in its letter seizes upon this agency to the extent that it constitutes, precisely, on the first approach, the exemplary content, the meaning, the written of Poe's fiction, as opposed to its writing, its signifier, and its narrating form. The displacement of the signifier, therefore, is analyzed as a signified, as the recounted object of a short story.

One might be led to believe, at a given moment, that Lacan is preparing to take into account the (narrating) narration, the complex structure of the scene of writing played out within it, the very curious place of the narrator. But once it is glimpsed, the analytic deciphering excludes this place, neutralizes it, or, more precisely, along lines we will follow, allows the narrator to dictate an effect of neutralizing exclusion (the "narration" as "commentary") that transforms the entire Seminar into an analysis fascinated by a content. Which makes it miss a scene. When it sees two ("There are two scenes" [1972b, 41]), there are three. At least. And when it sees one or two "triads," there is always the supplement of a square whose opening complicates the calculations.

* * * * * * * *

To what does this neutralization of the narrator commit the Seminar?

1. The narrator (himself doubled into a narrating narrator and a narrated narrator, not limiting himself to reporting the two dialogues) is evidently neither the author himself (to be called Poe), nor, less evidently, the inscriber of a text which recounts something for us, or rather which makes a narrator speak, who himself, in all kinds of ways, makes many people speak. The inscriber and the inscribing are original functions that are not to be confused with either the author and his actions, or with the narrator and his narration, and even less with the particular object, the narrated content, the so-called real drama which the psychoanalyst hastens to recognize as "Poe's message deciphered." That the inscribing

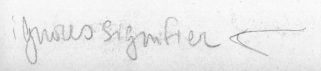

in its entirety—the fiction named "The Purloined Letter"—is covered, over its entire surface, by a narration whose narrator says "I" does not permit us to confuse the fiction with a narration. And even less, of course, with any given narrated section, however lengthy and apparent. There is here a problem of framing, of bordering and delimitation, whose analysis must be very finely detailed if it wishes to ascertain the effects of fiction. Without ever saying a word about it, Lacan excludes the textual fiction from within which he has extracted the so-called general narration. An operation made that much easier, and all too self-evidently easier, by the fact that the narration does not surpass by a word the fiction entitled "The Purloined Letter." But that is the fiction. There is an invisible, but structurally irreducible, frame around the narration. Where does it begin? With the first letter of the title? With the epigraph from Seneca? With "At Paris, just after dark . . ."? The question is even more complicated than that—we will come back to it—and this complication even now suffices to indicate everything about the structure of the text that is misconstrued in overlooking the frame. Within this neutralized or naturalized frame, Lacan takes up the narration without border and operates another extraction, again by dropping the frame. From within the narration he lifts out two dialogues which form the narrated history, that is, the content of a representation, the internal meaning of a story, the all-enframed, which demands all the attention, mobilizes all the psychoanalytic schemas (Oedipal ones here), and pulls toward its center the entire deciphering enterprise. There is missing here an elaboration of the problem of the frame, the signature, and the *parergon*. This lack permits the scene of the signifier to be reconstructed into a signified (a process always inevitable in the logic of the sign), permits writing to be reconstructed into the written, the text into discourse, and more precisely into an "intersubjective" dialogue (and it is not fortuitous that the Seminar's commentary concerns only the two dialogued parts of "The Purloined Letter").

2. There is here, first of all, a *formal* limit of the analysis. The formal structure of the text is overlooked, in very classical fashion, at the very moment when, and perhaps in the extent to which, its "truth," its exemplary message, allegedly is "deciphered." The structure of fiction is reduced at the very moment when it is related to its condition of truth. This leads to poor formalism. Formalism is practiced because one is not interested in the subject-author, something which might, in certain theoretical situations, constitute progress, or even a legitimate demand. But this formalism is rigidly illogical once, on the pretext of excluding

the author, one no longer takes into account either the "scription-fiction" and the "scriptor-fictor," or the narrating narration and the narrator. This formalism guarantees, as always, the surreptitious extraction of a semantic content, within which psychoanalysis applies its entire interpretive work. Formalism and hermeneutic semanticism always support one another: question of the frame.

3. The limit, then, is not only a formal one, and for the moment it does not concern a science of poetic fiction or of narrative structure. The issue here is not—quite to the contrary—one of rescuing something like literature or literary form from the grasp of psychoanalysis. There is a deep historical and theoretical complicity between psychoanalysis *applied* to literature and the formalist withdrawal which would pretend to escape this application. We have just seen how this works in principle. What is important here is that the formal deficiency implies a semantic and psychoanalytic decision. Once the narrator is distinguished from the author and then the "scriptor," he is no longer the formal condition of the narration that might symmetrically be opposed to the content, as the narrating to the narrated, for example. He intervenes in a specific fashion, is simultaneously *too self-evident* and invisible in a triangle, and therefore in a triangle that touches the other triangle at one of its "angles," touching both "intersubjective" triangles. Which singularly complicates the "intersubjective" structure, and this time from within the framed, the twice-framed, scenes, from within the represented content. Not to take into account this complication is not a failure of "formalist" literary criticism; it is an operation of the semanticist psychoanalyst. The narrator is not effaced as the "general narrator," or rather, in effacing himself within the homogeneous generality, he puts himself forward as a very singular character within the narrated narration, within the enframed. He constitutes an agency, a "position" with which the triangle, through the intermediary of Dupin (who in turn himself represents all the positions), maintains a very determined, very invested relation. By framing in this violent way, by cutting the narrated figure itself from a fourth side in order to see only triangles, one evades perhaps a certain complication, perhaps of the Oedipal structure, which is announced in the scene of writing.

* * * * * * * * *

Lacan leads us back to the truth, to a truth which itself cannot be lost. He brings back the letter, shows that the letter brings itself back toward its *proper* place via a *proper* itinerary, and, as he overtly notes, it is this destination which interests him, destiny as destination. The signifier has its place in the letter, and the letter refinds its proper meaning in its proper place. A certain reappropriation and a certain readequation will reconstitute the proper, the place, meaning, and truth that have become distant from themselves for the time of a detour or of a non-delivery. The time of an algorithm. Once more a hole will be stopped: and to do so one does not have to fill it, but only to see and to delimit its contour.

We have read: the signifier (in the letter, in the note) has no place identical to itself, it *is missing from its place*. Its meaning counts for little, it cannot be reduced to its meaning. But what the Seminar insists upon showing, finally, is that there is a single *proper* itinerary of the letter which returns to a determinable place that is always the same and that is *its own;* and that if its meaning (what is written in the note in circulation) is indifferent or unknown for our purposes (according to the hypothesis whose fragility nevertheless supports the entire logic of the Seminar), the meaning of the letter and the sense of its itinerary are necessary, unique, and determinable in truth, that is, as truth.

Certainly the place and meaning of the letter are not at the disposition of the subjects. Certainly the latter are subjected to the movement of the signifier. But when Lacan says that the letter has no proper place, this must be understood henceforth as objective place, a place determinable in an empirical and naive topology. When he says that it has no proper meaning, this must henceforth be understood as the exhaustible content of what is written in the note. For the signifier-letter, in the topology and psychoanalytico-transcendental semantics with which we are dealing, has a proper place and meaning which form the condition, origin, and destination of the entire circulation, as of the entire logic of the signifier.

The proper place, first of all. The letter has a place of emission and of destination. This is not a subject, but a hole, the lack on the basis of which the subject is constituted. The contour of this hole is determinable, and it magnetizes the entire itinerary of the detour which leads from hole to hole, from the hole to itself, and which therefore has a *circular* form. In question is indeed a regulated *circulation* which organizes a return from the detour toward the hole. A transcendental reappropriation and a transcendental readequation fulfilling an authentic contract. That the itinerary is proper and circular is what Lacan literally says [1972b, 59–60].

* * * * * * * * *

The proper meaning, next. The letter having a (single) place of origin and destination, and remaining what it is *en route* (What guarantees this?), it has a proper meaning: the law of its itinerary first of all, if not its content, although the latter gains from the deciphering a minimal determination which says enough about it. The letter must have a relation to whatever constitutes the contract or the "pact," that is, a relation with the subjection of the subject, and therefore somewhere with the hole as the proper place of the letter. Its place has an essential relation with its meaning, and the latter must be such that it makes the letter come back to its place. In fact, we know what is in the note. Lacan indeed is obliged to speak of and hold onto its meaning, at very least as that which threatens the pact which constitutes the letter's meaning: the phallic law represented by the King and guarded by the Queen, the law that she should share with him according to the pact, and that she threatens to divide, to dissociate, and to betray [1972b, 57–60].

* * * * * * * * *

Therefore the letter has a proper meaning, its own proper itinerary and location. What are they? In the triangle, only Dupin seems to know. For the moment, let us set aside the question of this knowing, and let us concern ourselves first with what is known. What does Dupin know? He knows that finally the letter *is found,* and knows where it must *be found* in order to return circularly, adequately to its proper place. This proper place, known to Dupin, and to the psychoanalyst, who in oscillating fashion, as we shall see, occupies Dupin's position, is the place of castration: woman as the unveiled site of the lack of a penis, as the truth of the phallus, that is of castration. The truth of the purloined letter is the truth, its meaning is meaning, its law is the law, the contract of truth with itself in logos. Beneath this notion of the pact (and therefore of adequation), the notion of veiling/unveiling tunes the entire Seminar to the Heideggerian discourse on the truth. Veiling/unveiling here concerns a hole, a non-being: the truth of Being as non-being. The truth is "woman" as veiled/unveiled castration. This is where the signifier (its inadequation with the signified) gets under way, this is the site of the signifier, the letter. But this is also where the trial begins, the promise of reappropriation, of return, of readequation: "the search for and restitution of the object" (1972b, 45). The singular *unity* of the letter is the site of the contract of the truth with itself. This is why the letter *comes back to, amounts to* [*revient à*] woman (at least in the extent to which she wishes to save the pact and, therefore, that which is the King's, the phallus that is in her guardianship); this is why, as Lacan says elsewhere, the letter amounts to, comes back to Being [*la lettre revient à l'être*], that is, to the nothing that would be opening itself as the hole between woman's legs. Such is the proper place in which the letter is found, where its meaning is found, where the Minister believes it to be in the shadows and where it is, in its very hiding place, the most exposed. Possessing the letter in the shadows, the Minister begins to identify himself with the Queen (but must not Dupin, and the psychoanalyst within him, do so in turn? We are not there yet) [1972b, 66].

* * * * * * * * *

The letter—place of the signifier—is found in the place where Dupin and the psychoanalyst expect to find it: on the immense body of a woman, between the "legs" of the fireplace. Such is its proper place, the terminus of its circular itinerary. It is returned to the sender, who is not the signer of the note, but the place where it began to *detach* itself from its possessor or feminine legatee. The Queen, seeking to reappropriate for herself that which, by virtue of the pact which subjects her to the King, that is, by virtue of the Law, guaranteed her the disposition of a phallus of which she would otherwise be deprived, of which she has taken the risk of depriving herself, that she has taken the risk of dividing, that is, of multiplying— the Queen, then, undertakes to reform, to reclose the circle of the restricted economy, the circulatory pact. She wants the letter-fetish brought back to her, and therefore begins by replacing, by exchanging one fetish for another: she emits—without really spending it, since there is an equivalence here—a quantity of money which is exchanged for the letter and assures its circular return. Dupin, as (the) analyst, is found [*se trouve*] on the circuit, in the circle of the restricted economy, in what I call elsewhere the stricture of the ring which the Seminar analyzes as the truth of fiction. We will come back to this problem of economics.

This determination of the proper, of the law of the proper, of *economy,* therefore leads back to castration as truth, to the figure of woman as the figure of castration *and* of truth. Of castration as truth. Which above all does not mean, as one might tend to believe, to truth as essential disloca- tion and irreducible fragmentation. Castration-truth, on the contrary, is that which contracts itself (stricture of the ring) in order to bring the phallus, the signifier, the letter, or the fetish back into their *oikos,*[2] their familiar dwelling, their proper place. In this sense castration-truth is the opposite of fragmentation, the very antidote for fragmentation: that which is missing from its place has in castration a fixed, central place, freed from all substitution. Something is missing from its place, but the lack is never missing from it [*Quelque chose manque à sa place, mais le manque n'y manque jamais*]. The phallus, thanks to castration, always remains in its place, in the transcendental topology of which we were speaking above. In castration, the phallus is indivisible, and therefore indestructible, like the letter which *takes its place*. And this is why the motivated, never demonstrated presupposition of the materiality of the letter as *indivisibility* is indispensable for this restricted economy, this circulation of the proper.

The difference which interests me here is that—a formula to be understood as one will—the lack does not have its place in dissemination.

By determining the place of the lack, the topos of that which is lacking from its place, and in constituting it as a fixed center, Lacan is indeed proposing, at the same time as a truth-discourse, a discourse on the truth of the purloined letter as the truth of "The Purloined Letter." In question is a hermeneutic deciphering, despite any appearances or denegation. The link of Femininity and Truth is the ultimate signified of this deciphering. Fourteen years later, reintroducing the Seminar at the head of the *Ecrits* with an "Unpublished Presentation," Lacan insists above all on this link and this meaning. He gives to Woman or to Femininity a capital letter that elsewhere he often reserves for Truth: "What Poe's tale demonstrates through my efforts is that the signifier's effect of subjection, in this instance the purloined letter's, bears above all on whoever wields it after the theft, and that along its itinerary what it conveys is the very Femininity that it has taken into its shadows . . ." [1969, 1]. Femininity is the Truth (of) castration, is the best figure of castration, because in the logic of the signifier it has always already been castrated; and Femininity "leaves" something in circulation (here the letter), something detached from itself in order to have it brought back to itself, because she has "never had it: whence truth comes out of the well, but only half-way."

This first castration (pre-castration) afterward affects with castration, and with femininity therefore, whoever holds the letter that signifies the phallus and castration: "This is why the Minister comes to be castrated, castrated, the very word of that which he still believes he has: the letter that Dupin was able to pick out between the legs of his very smooth fireplace.

"Here is but completed that which initially feminizes him [the Minister] as in a dream. . . . To which extent our Dupin shows himself equal in his success to the success of the psychoanalyst" [1969, 8].

POINT DE VUE:[3] TRUTH IN (THE) PLACE OF FEMALE SEXUALITY

What about this success? In order to answer, let us await reconsideration, in all its complexity, of the relationship between Dupin's position and the analyst's position, and then the relation between the analyst and he who says Freud and myself in the Seminar and in the introductions to the Seminar. This requires a long detour.

Until now, our questions have led us to suspect that if there is something like a purloined letter, perhaps it has a supplementary trap: it would have no fixed location, not even that of a definable hole or assignable lack. The letter might not be found, or could always possibly not be found, or would be found less in the sealed writing whose "story" is recounted by the narrator and deciphered by the Seminar, less in the content of the story, than "in" the text which escapes, from a fourth side, the eyes of both Dupin and the psychoanalyst. The remainder, what is left unclaimed, would be "The Purloined Letter," that is, the text bearing this title whose location, like the large letters once more become invisible, is not where one would expect to find it, in the framed content of the "real drama" or in the hidden and sealed interior of Poe's tale, but rather in and as the open, the very open, letter that is fiction. The latter, because it is written, at very least implies a self-divesting fourth agency, which at the same time divests the letter of the text from whoever deciphers it, from the *facteur* of truth who puts the letter back into the circle of its own, proper itinerary: which is what the Seminar does in repeating Dupin's operation, for he, in accord with the circularity of the "proper itinerary," "has succeeded in returning the letter to its proper course" (1972b, 69), according to the desire *of* the Queen. To return the letter to its proper course, supposing that its trajectory is a line, is to correct a deviation, to rectify a departure, to recall, for the sake of the rule, that is, the norm, an orientation, an authentic line. Dupin is adroit, knows his address, and knows the law. At the very moment one believes that by drawing triangles and circles, and by wielding the opposition imaginary/symbolic, one grasps "The Purloined Letter," at the very moment one reconstitutes the truth, the proper adequation, "The Purloined Letter" escapes through a too self-evident opening. As Baudelaire bluntly reminds us. The purloined letter is in the text: not only as an object whose proper itinerary is described, contained in the text, a signifier become the theme or signified of the text, but also as the text producing the effects of the frame. At the very moment when Dupin and the Seminar find it, when they determine its proper location and itinerary, when they believe that it is here or there as on a map, a place on a map as on the body of a woman, they no longer see the map itself: not the map that the text describes at one moment or another, but the map [*carte*] that the text "is," that it describes, "itself," as the deviation of the four [*l'écart du quatre*] with no promise of topos or truth. The remaining[4] structure of the letter is that—contrary to what the Seminar says in its last words ("what the 'purloined letter,' that is, the not delivered letter [*lettre en souffrance*] means is that a letter always arrives at its destination" [1972b, 72])—a letter can always not arrive at its destination. Its "materiality" and "topology" are due to its divisibility, its always possible partition. It can always be fragmented without return, and the system of the symbolic, of castration, of the signifier, of the truth, of the contract, etc., always attempt to protect the letter from this fragmentation: this is the point of view of the King or the Queen, which are the same here; they are bound by contract to reappropriate the bit. Not that the letter never arrives at its destination, but that it belongs to the structure of the letter to be capable, always, of not arriving. And without this threat (breach of contract, division or multiplication, the separation without return from the phallus which was begun for a moment by the Queen, that is, by every "subject"), the circuit of the letter would not even have begun. But with this threat, the circuit can always not finish. Here dissemination threatens the law of the signifier and of castration as the contract of truth. It *broaches, breaches* [*entamer*] the unity of the signifier, that is, of the phallus.

At the moment when the Seminar, like Dupin, finds the letter where it is found [*se trouve*], between the legs of woman, the deciphering of the enigma is anchored in truth. The sense of the tale, the meaning of the purloined letter ("what the 'purloined letter,' that is, the not delivered letter [*lettre en souffrance*], means is that a letter always arrives at its destination") is uncovered. The deciphering (Dupin's, the Seminar's), uncovered via a meaning (the truth), as a hermeneutic process, itself arrives at its destination.

Why then does the Seminar refind, along with the truth, the same meaning and the same topos as did Marie Bonaparte when, skipping over the text, she proposed a psychobiographical analysis of "The Purloined Letter" in 1933? Is this a coincidence?

Is it a coincidence if, in allegedly breaking with psychobiographical criticism (see Lacan 1966a, 860), one rejoins it in its ultimate semantic anchorage? And after a perhaps more simplifying textual analysis?

For Bonaparte too, the castration of the woman (of the mother) is the final sense, what "The Purloined Letter" means. And truth means a readequation or reappropriation as the desire to stop up the hole. But Bonaparte does what Lacan does not: she relates "The Purloined Letter" to other texts by Poe. And she analyzes the gesture of doing so. Further on we will comprehend the *internal* necessity of this operation.

For example, "The Black Cat," in which "the castration fear, embodied in the woman as the castrated being, lies at the core of the tale" (Bonaparte 1971, 481). "Nevertheless, all the primitive anxieties of the child, which often remain those of the adult, seem to be gathered here as if by appointment, in this story of extreme anxiety, as if at a crossroads" (481). Within this quadrifurcum, named absentmindedly, omitted like a frame, there is the representation of a circle or a triangle. The Seminar: "Here we are, in fact, yet again at the crossroads at which we had left our drama and its round with the question of the way in which the subjects replace each other in it" (1972b, 60). Bonaparte continues with a page of generalizations about castration anxiety that could be summarized by a statement of Freud's that she does not cite here: the assertion that the mother's lack of a penis is "the greatest trauma"; or of Lacan's: "Division of the subject? This point is a knot.

"Let us recall where Freud spells it out: on the mother's lack of a penis in which the nature of the phallus is revealed" (Lacan 1966a, 877).

After treating the Law and fetishism as a process of rephallicizing the mother (what has been stolen or detached from her is to be returned to her), Bonaparte writes the following, in which the knot of the Lacanian interpretation is to be found, along with several other things:

Finally, with the gallows theme, we see death-anxiety, or fear of death.

All these fears, however, remain subordinate to the main theme of fear of castration, with which all are closely interwoven. The cat with the white breast has also a missing eye; hanging represents not only death, but rephallization; the urge to confess leads to the discovery of a corpse surmounted by an effigy of castration; even the cellar and tomb, and the gaping aperture of the chimney, recall the dread cloaca of the mother. [Bonaparte 1971, 483].

* * * * * * * * *

[Bonaparte's] note [see above, chap. 5, Notes, 48f/36b] is not without importance. First, it shows that Lacan had read Bonaparte, although the Seminar never names her. As an author so scrupulous about debts and priorities, he could have acknowledged an exploration which orients his entire interpretation, to wit the process of rephallization as the proper itinerary of the letter, the "return of the letter" to its "destination" after having been refound between the legs of the fireplace. Or could have silenced it. But since footnotes are, if not the truth, the appendix in which is shown that which must not be said, or that which, as Schelling cited in *Das Unheimliche* says, "should remain hidden," the Seminar lets fall a footnote in response: "Look! between the jambs of the fireplace, there is the object already within reach of the hand the ravisher has but to extend. . . . The question of deciding whether he seizes it above the mantelpiece, as Baudelaire translates, or beneath it, as in the original text, may be abandoned without harm to the inferences of cooking[38]" [Lacan's note reads: "38. And even to the cook herself' (1972b, 67)].

Without harm? On the contrary, the damage would be irreparable, within the Seminar itself: *on* the mantelpiece of the fireplace, the letter could not have been "between the jambs of the fireplace," "between the legs of the fireplace." What is at stake, then, is something major, even if one sets aside, imagining it not relevant, the Seminar's disdainful nervousness as concerns a psychoanalyst and her legacy.[5] Why relegate the question to the kitchen, as if to an outbuilding, and the woman who answers it to the status of cook? Certain "masters of the truth" in Greece knew how to keep the kitchen a place for thinking.

Just before this note, it will be recalled, the Seminar had invoked the "toponymical inscriptions," the "geographical map" of the "immense body," and the location of that which Dupin "expects to find," since he is repeating the gesture of the Minister, who himself is identified with the Queen whose letter still, properly, occupies the same place: the place of detachment and reattachment.

* * * * * * * * *

After [a] brief allusion to the knob [1971, 483] (which the Seminar does not pick up), Bonaparte reattaches her interpretation to an Oedipal typology and clinical practice. Her interest in "the-author's-life" no more simplifies her reading of the text than the Seminar's lack of interest suffices to guarantee a reading. The accent is placed on a "pre-genital, phallic and archaic" Oedipal struggle for the possession of the maternal penis, which is here determined as a part object. Bonaparte is never tempted to grant Dupin the position of the analyst, even if to watch over him with an other kind of mastery. Dupin's lucidity comes to him from the war in which he is engaged, and this has motivated him throughout. As it has situated him on the circuit of the debt, of the phallus, of the signifier in its letter, and of the money which, unlike Lacan, Bonaparte does not consider as neutralizing or as "destructive of" "all signification" [see 484]. . . .

The circle of this restitution indeed forms the "proper course" of the Seminar. What, then, of the Seminar's attempted thrust to identify Dupin's position with the analyst's position? This idea never tempts Bonaparte. And it is strangely divided or suspended in the Seminar.

* * * * * * * * *

In beginning by identifying Dupin with the psychoanalyst, a double profit is prepared: 1. The lucidity of the one who is able to see what no one else has seen: the place of the thing, between the legs (and the author of the Seminar says then: we-psychoanalysts, we withdraw ourselves from the symbolic circuit and we neutralize the scene in which we are not participants). 2. The possibility—by emphasizing that Dupin remains a participant (and how), by maintaining the identification Dupin-psycho-analyst—of denouncing the naïveté of the analytic community, of saying: you-psychoanalysts, you are deluding yourselves at precisely the moment when like Dupin you believe yourselves to be masters.

In effect. After the paragraph whose indecision we have delineated [1972b, 68] ("perhaps," "the signifier the most destructive," etc.), a very clever game is played, but in order to demonstrate how Dupin's ruse— the biggest of all in the Oedipal scene—bears within its own trap a *motivation,* the game will go to the point of getting carried away with itself.

In question are the last pages of the Seminar, pages punctuated by a "But that's not all" (1972b, 68) and an "Is that all . . ." (1972b, 72). As soon as one interprets the retribution demanded by Dupin as an analytic procedure in order to withdraw from the circuit thanks to "the signifier most destructive of all signification, namely: money," it is difficult to account for all the signs of non-neutrality multiplied at the end of "The Purloined Letter." Is this not a shocking paradox? . . . And Dupin's "explosion of feeling at the end of the story" (1972b, 68), his "rage of manifestly feminine nature" (1972b, 71) when he claims to be settling his account with the Minister by signing his own maneuver, must be pointed out. Dupin, then, reproduces the process called feminization: he subjects himself to the (desire of the) Minister, whose place he occupies as soon as he possesses the letter—the place of the signifier—and conforms to the Queen's desire. Here, by virtue of the pact, one can no longer distinguish between the place of the King (which is marked by blindness) and the place of the Queen, the place to which the letter, in its "right

course" and following its "proper itinerary," must return in circular
fashion. As the signifier has but one proper place, fundamentally there is
but one place for the letter, and this place is occupied successively by all
those who possess it. It must be recognized, then, that Dupin, once he
has entered into the circuit, having identified with the Minister in order
to take the letter back from him and to put it back on its "proper course,"
can no longer depart from this course. He must go through it in its
entirety. The Seminar asks a strange question on this topic: "He is thus,
in fact, fully participant in the intersubjective triad, and, as such, in the
median position previously occupied by the Queen and the Minister.
Will he, in showing himself to be above it, reveal to us at the same time
the author's intentions?

"If he has succeeded in returning the letter to its proper course, it
remains for him to make it arrive at its address. And that address is in the
place previously occupied by the King, since it is there that it would reenter the order of the Law.

"As we have seen, neither the King nor the Police who replaced him in
that position were able to read the letter because that *place entailed
blindness*" (1972b, 69).

If Dupin now occupies the "median position," has he not always done
so? And is there any other position in the circuit? Is it only at this
moment of the narrative, when he has the letter in hand, that he once
more finds himself in this position? We cannot stop here: from the outset
Dupin acts with his sights set on the letter, on possessing it in order to
return it to its rightful owner (neither the King, nor the Queen, but the
Law which binds them), and thus finds himself preferable to his (brother)
enemy, his younger or twin brother (Atreus/Thyestes), to the Minister
who fundamentally pursues the same aims, with the same gestures.
Therefore, if he is in a "median position," the differentiation of the three
glances given above is no longer pertinent. There are only ostriches, no
one can avoid being plucked, and the more one is the master, the more
one presents one's rear. Which will be the case for whoever identifies with
Dupin.

Concerning Dupin, a strange question, as we said: "Will he, in
showing himself to be above it, reveal to us at the same time the author's
intentions?"

This is not the only allusion to "the author's intentions" (see also
1972b, 41). Its form implies that the author, in his intention, is in a
situation of general mastery, his *superiority* as concerns the triangles

placed on stage (supposing that he is staging only triangles) being representable only by the superiority of an actor, to wit, Dupin. Let us abandon this implication here: an entire conception of "literature."

* * * * * * * * *

FIRST SECOND: THE TRUTH OF THE LETTER FROM FREUD'S HAND

* * * * * * * * *

What about the truth according to Lacan then? Is there *a* doctrine, a Lacanian *doctrine* of the truth? We might doubt this for two reasons. The first is a general one, and has to do with the terms of the question. That a purely homogeneous system is structurally impossible we have seen elsewhere. The second reason has to do with the mobility of the discourse which concerns us here. In the publications subsequent to the *Ecrits,* in their indications of a continuing oral instruction, one perceives a certain withdrawal [*retrait*] that muffles the incantations on *aletheia, logos,* speech, the word, etc. And one perceives an even more palpable erasure of the postwar existentialist connotations, if not concepts. It remains that a certain type of statement on the truth has been made, and enlarged, at a specific moment, in the form of a system. And it bears all the characteristics necessary for this effect. Since the Seminar belongs to this system (such, at least, is my hypothesis), as do a certain number of other essays to which I will refer (in order not, in turn, to enclose the *Ecrits* in the Seminar), it must be demarcated if one wishes to understand the reading of "The Purloined Letter." One can and must do this, even if after 1966, in a transformed theoretical field, the Lacanian discourse on the truth, the text, and literature lent itself to a certain number of major rearrangements or decisive reworkings, although this is not certain.[6] The chronological and theoretical outline of this system would always be subject to caution, moreover, given the distant aftereffects of publications.

Whatever may have happened after 1965–66, all the texts situated, or more precisely published, between 1953 (the Discourse said to be of Rome) and 1960 appear to belong to the same system of the truth. Or, quantitatively, almost the entirety of the *Ecrits,* including, therefore, the Seminar (1955–57): works of the young Lacan, as will perhaps be said one day, and once more, by the academics who are always in a hurry to cut to the quick that which does not bear partition.

We are not going to give an exposition of this system of the truth, which is the condition for a logic of the signifier. Moreover, it consists of what is *non-exposable* in the exposition. We will only attempt to recognize those characteristics of it which are pertinent to the Seminar, to its possibility and its limits.

First of all, what is at issue is an *emphasis* [*emphase*], as could equally be said in English, on the authentic excellence of the spoken, of speech, and of the word: of *logos* as *phonē*. This emphasis must be explained, and its necessary link to the theory of the signifier, the letter, and the truth must be accounted for. It must be explained why the author of *The Agency of the Letter in the Unconscious* and of the "Seminar on 'The Purloined Letter'" ceaselessly subordinates the letter, writing, and the text. Even when he repeats Freud on rebuses, hieroglyphics, engravings, etc., in the last analysis his recourse is always to a writing spiritualized [*relevé*] by the voice. This would be easy to show. One example, among many others: "A writing, like the dream itself, may be figurative, it is like language always articulated symbolically, that is, it is like language *phonematic,* and in fact phonetic, as soon as it may be read."[7] This *fact* has the stature of a *fact* only within the limits of the so-called phonetic systems of writing. At the very most, for there are non-phonetic elements in such systems. As for the non-phonetic field of writing, its factual enormity no longer has to be demonstrated. But small matter. What does count here, and even more than the relation of the *de facto* to the *de jure,* is the implied equivalence ("that is") between symbolic articulation and phonematicity. The symbolic occurs through the voice, and the law of the signifier takes place only within vocalizable letters. Why? And what relation does this phonematism (which cannot be attributed to Freud, and thus is lost in the unfolding of the return to Freud) maintain with a certain value of truth?

Both imports of the value of truth are represented in the Seminar, as we have seen. 1. *Adequation,* in the circular return and proper course, from the origin to the end, from the signifier's place of detachment to its place of reattachment. This circuit of adequation guards and regards [*garde et regarde*] the circuit of the pact, of the contract, of sworn faith. It restores the pact in the face of what threatens it, as the symbolic order. And it is constituted at the moment when the *guardianship* [*la garde*] of the phallus is confided as guardianship *of the* lack. Confided by the King to the Queen, but thereby in an endless play of alternations. 2. *Veiling-unveiling* as the structure of the lack: castration, the *proper* site of the signifier, origin and destination of its letter, shows nothing in unveiling itself. Therefore, it veils itself in its unveiling. But this operation of the

truth has a proper place: its contours *being* [*étant*] the place of the lack of
Being [*manque à être*] on the basis of which the signifier detaches itself for
its literal circuit. These two values of truth lean on and support each
other [*s'étaient*]. They are indissociable. They need speech or the
phonetization of the letter as soon as the phallus has to be *kept* [*gardé*], has
to return to its point of departure, has not to be disseminated en route.
Now, for the signifier to be kept [*pour que le signifiant se garde*] in its letter
and thus to make its return, it is necessary that in its letter it does not
admit "partition," that one cannot say *some* letter [*de la lettre*], but only a
letter, letters, the letter (1972b, 53–54). If it were divisible, it could
always be lost en route. It is against this possible loss that the statement
of the "materiality of the signifier," that is, about the signifier's indivisible singularity, is constructed. *This "materiality," deduced from an indivisibility found nowhere, in fact corresponds to an idealization.* Only the
ideality of a letter resists destructive division. "Cut a letter in small
pieces, and it remains the letter it is" (1972b, 53): since this cannot be
said of empirical materiality, it must imply an ideality (the intangibility
of a self-identity displacing itself without alteration). This alone permits
the singularity of the letter to be maintained [*se garder*]. If this ideality is
not the content of meaning, it must be either a certain ideality of the
signifier (what is identifiable in its form to the extent that it can be
distinguished from its empirical events and re-editions), or the *"point de
capiton"*[8] which staples the signifier to the signified. The latter hypothesis
conforms more closely to the system. This system is in fact the system of
the ideality of the signifier. The idealism lodged within it is not a
theoretical position of the analyst; it is a structural effect of *signification* in
general, to whatever transformations or adjustments one subjects the
space of *semiosis*. One can understand that Lacan finds this "materiality"
"odd" [*"singulière"*]: he retains only its ideality. He considers the letter
only at the point at which it is determined (no matter what he says) by its
content of meaning, by the ideality of the message that it "vehiculates,"
by the speech whose meaning remains out of the reach of partition, so
that it can circulate, intact, from its place of detachment to its place of
reattachment, that is, to the same place. In fact, this letter does not only
escape partition, it escapes movement, it does not change its place.

Aside from a phonematic limitation of the letter, this supposes an
interpretation of *phonē* which also spares it divisibility. The voice occasions such an interpretation in and of itself: it has the phenomenal
characteristics of spontaneity, of self-presence, of the circular return to
itself. And the voice retains [*garde*] all the more in that one believes one

can retain [*garder*] it without external accessory, without paper and without envelope: it finds itself [*se trouve*], it tells us, always available wherever it is found [*se trouve*]. This is why it is believed that the voice remains more than do writings: "May it but please heaven that writings remain, as is rather the case with spoken words" (1972b, 56). Things would be quite otherwise if one were attentive to the writing within the voice, that is, before the letter. For the same problem is reproduced concerning the voice, concerning what one might still call its "letter," if one wished to conserve the Lacanian definition of this concept (indivisible locality or materiality of the signifier). This vocal "letter" therefore also would be indivisible, always identical to itself, whatever the fragmentations of its body. It can be assured of this integrity only by virtue of its link to the ideality of a meaning, in the unity of a speech. We are always led back, from stage to stage, to the contract of contracts which guarantees the unity of the signifier with the signified through all the "*points de capiton,*" thanks to the "presence" (see below) of the *same* signifier (the phallus), of the "signifier of signifiers" beneath all the effects of the signified. This transcendental signifier is therefore also the signified of all signifieds, and this is what finds itself sheltered within the indivisibility of the (graphic or oral) letter. Sheltered from this threat, but also from the disseminating power that in *Of Grammatology* I proposed to call *Writing before the Letter* (title of the first part): the privilege of "full speech" is examined there. The agency of the Lacanian letter is the *relève* of writing in the system of speech.

"The drama" of the purloined letter begins at the moment—which is not a moment—when the letter *is retained* [*se garde*]. With the movement of the Minister who acts in order to conserve it (for he could have torn it up, and this is indeed an ideality which then would have remained available and effective for a time),9 certainly, but well before this, when the Queen wishes to retain it or refind it [*la garder ou la retrouver*]: as a double of the pact which binds her to the King, a threatening double, but one which in her guardianship [*sous sa garde*] cannot betray the "sworn faith." The Queen wishes to be able to play on two contracts. We cannot develop this analysis here; it is to be read elsewhere.

What counts here is that the indestructibility of the letter has to do with its elevation toward the ideality of a meaning. However little we know of its content, the content must be in relation to the original contract that it simultaneously signifies and subverts. And it is this knowledge, this memory, this (conscious or unconscious) retention which form its properness [*propriété*] and ensure its proper course toward the proper place. Since its ultimate content is that of a pact binding two "singularities," it implies an irreplaceability and excludes, as uncontrollable threat and anxiety, all double simulacra. It is the effect of living and present speech which in the last analysis guarantees the indestructible and unforgettable singularity of the letter, the taking-place of a signifier which never is lost, goes astray, or is divided. The subject is very divided, but the phallus is not to be cut. Fragmentation is an accident which does not concern it. At least according to the certainty constructed by the symbolic. And by a discourse on the assumption of castration which edifies an ideal philosophy against fragmentation. [10]

In principle this is how the logic of the signifier is articulated with a phonocentric interpretation of the letter. The two values of the truth (adequation and movement of the veil) henceforth cannot be dissociated from the word, from present, living, authentic speech. The final word is that when all is said and done, there is, at the origin or the end (proper course, circular destination), a word which is not feigned, a meaning which, through all imaginable fictional complications, does not trick, or which at that point tricks *truly,* again teaching us the truth of the lure. At this point, the truth permits the analyst to treat fictional characters as real, and to resolve, at the depth of the Heideggerian meditation on truth, the problem of the literary text which sometimes led Freud (more naively, but more surely than Heidegger and Lacan) to confess his confusion.

* * * * * * * * *

But once again, why would speech be the privileged element of this truth declared *as* fiction, in the mode of structure of fiction, of verified fiction, of what Gide calls "superior realism"?

As soon as the truth is determined as adequation (with an original contract: the acquitting of a debt) and as unveiling (of the lack on the basis of which the contract is contracted in order to reappropriate symbolically what has been detached), the guiding value is indeed that of propriation, and therefore of proximity, of presence, and of maintaining [*garde*]: the very value procured by the idealizing effect of speech. If one grants this demonstration, it will not be surprising to find it confirmed. If one does not, then how is one to explain the massive co-implication, in Lacanian discourse, of truth and speech, "present," "full," and "authentic" speech? And if it is taken into account, one better understands: 1. That fiction for Lacan is permeated by truth as something spoken, and therefore as something non-real. 2. That this leads to no longer reckoning, in the text, with everything that remains irreducible to speech, the spoken [*le dit*], and meaning [*vouloir-dire*]: that is, irreducible dis-regard, theft without return, destructibility, divisibility, the failure to reach a destination [*le manque à destination*] (which definitively rebels against the destination of the lack [*la destination du manque*]: an unverifiable non-truth).

When Lacan recalls "the passion for unveiling which has one object: the truth"[11] and recalls that the analyst "above all remains the master of the truth" [1977, 98], it is always in order to link the truth to the power of speech. And to the power of communication as a contract (sworn faith) between two present things. Even if communication communicates nothing, it communicates to itself: and in this case better yet as communication, that is, truth. For example: "Even if it communicates nothing, the discourse represents the existence of communication; even if it denies the evidence, it affirms that speech constitutes truth; even if it is intended to deceive, the discourse speculates on faith in testimony."[12]

What is neither true nor false is reality. But as soon as speech is inaugurated, one is in the register of the unveiling of the truth as of its contract of properness [*propriété*]: presence, speech, testimony: "The ambiguity of the hysterical revelation of the past is due not so much to the vacillation of its content between the imaginary and the real, for it is situated in both. Nor is it because it is made up of lies. The reason is that it presents us with the birth of truth in speech, and thereby brings us up against the reality of what is neither true nor false. At any rate, that is the most disquieting aspect of the problem.

"For it is present speech that bears witness to the truth of this revelation in present reality, and which grounds it in the name of that reality. Yet in that reality, only speech bears witness to that portion of the powers of the past that has been thrust aside at each crossroads where the event has made its choice" [1977, 47]. Just before this passage there is a reference to Heidegger, which is not surprising; the reference resituates *Dasein* in the subject, which is more so.

* * * * * * * * *

MEETING PLACE: THE DOUBLE SQUARE OF KINGS

. . . Let us return to "The Purloined Letter" in order "to glimpse" its disseminal structure, that is, the without-possible-return of the letter, the other scene of its remaining [*restance*].

Because there is a narrator on stage, the "general" scene is not ex-

hausted in a narration, a "tale" or a "story." We have already recognized
the effects of invisible framing, of the frame within the frame, *from within
which* the psychoanalytic interpretations (semantico-biographical or tri-
ado-formalist) lifted out their triangles. In missing the position of the
narrator, his engagement in the content of what he seems to recount, one
omits everything in the scene of writing that overflows the two triangles.

For the issue first of all, and with no possible approach or bordering, is
one of a scene of writing with ruined [*abîmé*] limits. Right from the
simulacrum of the opening, from the "first word," the narrator advances
by narrating to himself several propositions which engage the unity of
the "tale" in an interminable drift: a textual drift of which the Seminar
takes not the slightest account. But in taking it into account here, above
all the question is not one of making of this drift the "*real subject* of the
tale." Which therefore would not have one.

I. Everything begins "in" a library: in books, writings, references.
Therefore nothing begins. Only a drifting or disorientation from which
one does not emerge.

II. Additionally, an explicit reference is made in the direction of two
other narratives onto which "this one" is grafted. The "analogy" between
the three accounts is the milieu of "The Purloined Letter." The independence of this tale, as presumed by the Seminar, is therefore the effect of an
ablation, even if one takes the tale in its totality, with its narrator and his
narration. This ablation is all the more absentminded in that the "analogy" is recalled from the very first paragraph. It is true that the word
"analogy," "coincidence" more precisely, authorizes the ablation, invites
it, and therefore acts as a trap. The work of the Seminar begins only after
the entry of the Prefect of the Parisian police. But before this, the title,
the epigraph, the first paragraph gave us to read (silence in silence):

THE PURLOINED LETTER

Nil sapientiae odiosius acumine nimio

Seneca

At Paris, just after dark one gusty evening in the autumn of 18—, I was
enjoying the twofold luxury of meditation and a meerschaum, in company with my friend C. Auguste Dupin, in his little back library, or
book-closet. . . .

Everything "begins," then, by obscuring this beginning in the "silence," "smoke," and "dark" of this library. The casual observer sees only
the smoking meerschaum: a literary decor in sum, the ornamental frame
of a narrative. On this border, which is negligible for the hermeneut

interested in the center of the picture and in what is within the representation, one could already read that all of this was an affair of writing, and
of writing adrift, in a place of writing open without end to its grafting
onto other writings, and that this affair of writing (the third of a series in
which the "coincidence" with the two preceding ones already caused
itself to be remarked upon) suddenly breaks into its first word *"au
troisième, No. 33 Rue Dunôt, Faubourg St. Germain."* In French in the text.

Fortuitous notations, curling eddies of smoke, contingencies of framing? That they go beyond the "author's intention," about which the
Seminar is tempted to question Dupin, that they are even pure accidental
"coincidence," an event of fortune, can only recommend them all the
more to the reading of a text which makes of chance as writing what we
will indeed refrain from calling "the *real subject* of the tale."

Its remarkable ellipsis, rather. In effect, if we do as we are invited, and
go back from the internal bordering of the frame to what is before "The
Purloined Letter," the remarkable insists: scene of writing, library, events
of chance, coincidences. At the beginning of "The Murders in the Rue
Morgue" what might be called the meeting place between the (narrating-
narrated) narrator and Dupin is already an "obscure library," the "accident" (which Baudelaire this time translates as *"coincidence,"* and not as
"analogie")[13] "of our both being in search of the same very rare and
remarkable volume." And the least one might say about the relationship
formed in this meeting place is that it will never leave the so-called
general narrator in the position of a neutral and transparent reporter who
does not intervene in the narration in progress. For example (But this
time the example read on the frame is not at the beginning of the text.
The frame describing the "meeting" cuts through the narration, if you
will. Before the appearance of Dupin in the narrative, the frame is
preceded by a feint in the guise of an abandoned preface, a false short
treatise on analysis: "I am not now writing a treatise, but simply prefac-
ing a somewhat peculiar narrative by observations very much at random."
Not a treatise, a preface [to be dropped[14] as usual], and random observations. At the end of the preface the narrator feigns the Seminar):

The narrative which follows will appear to the reader somewhat in the
light of a commentary upon the propositions just advanced.

Residing in Paris during the spring and part of the summer of 18—, I
there became acquainted with a Monsieur C. Auguste Dupin. This
young gentleman was of an excellent—indeed of an illustrious family,
but, by a variety of untoward events, had been reduced to such poverty
that the energy of his character succumbed beneath it, and he ceased to

bestir himself in the world, or to care for the retrieval of his fortunes. By courtesy of his creditors, there still remained in his possession a small remnant of his patrimony; and, upon the income arising from this, he managed, by means of a rigorous economy, to procure the necessaries of life, without troubling himself about its superfluities. Books, indeed, were his sole luxuries, and in Paris these are easily obtained. (Poe 1956, 142)

By means of a *remnant* of the paternal inheritance, apparently left out of account for the debtor, who by calculating (*rigorous economy*) can draw an *income,* a revenue from it, the surplus-value of a capital which works by itself, Dupin permits himself to pay for a single superfluity, a sole luxury in which the initial remnant is relocated [*se retrouve*] therefore, and which cuts across the space of the restricted economy like a gift without return. This sole luxury (*sole luxuries:* the very word found for the second time on the second line of "The Purloined Letter," but this time as a singular *double luxury, the twofold luxury of meditation and a meerschaum*) is writing: the books which will organize the meeting place and the ruination [*mise en abîme*] of the entire so-called general narration. The meeting place of the meeting between the narrator and Dupin is due to the meeting of their interest in the same book; it is never said whether they find it. Such is the literal accident:

Our first meeting was at an obscure library in the Rue Montmartre, where the accident of our both being in search of the same very rare and very remarkable volume, brought us into closer communion. We saw each other again and again. I was deeply interested in the little family history which he detailed to me with all that candor which a Frenchman indulges whenever mere self is the theme. (1956, 142)

Thus the narrator permits himself to narrate: that he is interested in Dupin's family history ("I was deeply interested in the little family history . . ."), the very history which leaves a remnant of income with which to pay for the luxury of books; and then, as we shall see, that Dupin's capacity for reading astonishes him above all, and that the society of such a man is without a price for him, beyond all evaluation ("a treasure beyond price"). The narrator, therefore, will permit himself to pay for the priceless Dupin, who permits himself to pay for priceless writing, which is without a price for this very reason. For the narrator, in confiding—in yielding [*se livrant*] as Baudelaire says—frankly to Dupin must pay for doing so. He must rent the analyst's office. And provide the economic equivalent of the priceless. The analyst—or his own fortune, more or less equivalent to Dupin's, simply "somewhat less embarrassed"—authorizes him to do so: "I was permitted to be at the expense of renting. . . ." The narrator is therefore the first to pay Dupin in order to be certain of the availability of letters. Let us then follow the movement of this chain. But what he pays for is also the place of the narration, the writing within which the entire story will be recounted and offered to interpretations. And if he is paying in order to write or to speak, he is also making Dupin speak, making him return his letters, and leaving him the last word in the form of a confession. In the economy of this office, as soon as the narrator is placed on stage by a function which is indeed that of a public corporation [société anonyme] of capital and desire, no neutralization is possible, nor is any general point of view, any view from above, any "destruction" of signification by money. It is not only Dupin, but the narrator who is a "participant." As soon as the narrator makes Dupin return his letters, and not only to the Queen (the other Queen), the letter divides itself, is no longer atomistic (atomism, Epicurus's atomism is also one of Dupin's propositions in "The Murders in the Rue Morgue"), and therefore loses any certain destination. The divisibility of the letter— this is why we have insisted on this key or theoretical safety lock of the Seminar—is what chances and sets off course, without guarantee of return, the remaining [restance] of anything whatsoever: a letter does not always arrive at its destination, and from the moment that this possibility belongs to its structure one can say that it never truly arrives, that when it does arrive its capacity not to arrive torments it with an internal drifting.

The divisibility of the letter is also the divisibility of the signifier to which it gives rise, and therefore also of the "subjects," "characters," or "positions" which are subjected to it and which "represent" them. Before showing this in the text, a citation as reminder:

I was astonished, too, at the vast extent of his reading; and above all, I felt my soul enkindled within me by the wild fervor, and the vivid freshness of his imagination. Seeking in Paris the objects I then sought, I felt that the society of such a man would be to me a treasure beyond price; and this feeling I frankly confided to him. It was at length arranged that we should live together during my stay in the city; and as my worldly circumstances were somewhat less embarrassed than his own, I was permitted to be at the expense of renting, and furnishing in a style which suited the rather fantastic gloom of our common temper, a time-eaten and grotesque mansion, long deserted through superstitions into which we did not inquire, and tottering to its fall in a retired and desolate portion of the Faubourg St. Germain. (1956, 142–43)

Thus we have two gloomy (melancholic) fantastics, one of whom does not tell us what objects he previously was seeking in Paris, or who are the "former associates" from whom he now is going to hide the secret of the locality. The entire space is now one of the speculation of these two "madmen":

Had the routine of our life at this place been known to the world, we should have been regarded as madmen—although, perhaps, as madmen of a harmless nature. Our seclusion was perfect. We admitted no visitors. Indeed the locality of our retirement had been carefully kept a secret from my own former associates; and it had been many years since Dupin had ceased to know or be known in Paris. We existed within ourselves alone. (1956, 143)

From here on, the narrator permits himself to narrate his progressive identification with Dupin. And first of all with the love of night, the "sable divinity" whose "presence" they "counterfeit" when she is not there:

It was a freak of fancy in my friend (for what else shall I call it?) to be enamored of the Night for her own sake; and into this *bizarrerie,* as into all his others, I quietly fell; giving myself up to his wild whims with a perfect *abandon.* The sable divinity would not herself dwell with us always; but we could counterfeit her presence. (1956, 143)

Himself doubled in this position, the narrator thus *identifies* with Dupin, whose "peculiar analytic ability" he cannot help "remarking and admiring"; and Dupin gives him multiple proofs of his "intimate knowledge" of his own, the narrator's, personality. But Dupin himself, precisely at these moments, appears double. And this time it is a "fancy" of the narrator, who sees Dupin as double: "his manner at these moments was frigid and abstract; his eyes were vacant in expression; while his voice, usually a rich tenor, rose into a treble which would have sounded petulantly but for the deliberateness and entire distinctness of the enunciation. Observing him in these moods, I often dwelt meditatively upon the old philosophy of the Bi-Part Soul, and amused myself with the fancy of a double Dupin—the creative and the resolvent" (1956, 144).

The fancy of an identification between two doubled doubles, the major investment in a relationship which engages Dupin *outside* of the "intersubjective triads" of the "real drama" and the narrator *inside* what he narrates;[15] the circulation of desires and capital, of signifiers and letters, before and beyond the "two triangles," the "primal" and secondary ones, the consecutive fissioning of the positions, starting with the position of Dupin, who like *all* the characters, inside and outside the narration, successively occupies *all* the places—all of this makes of triangular logic a very limited play within the play. And if the dual relation between two doubles (which Lacan would reduce to the imaginary) includes and envelops the entire space said to be of the symbolic, overflows and simulates it, ceaselessly ruining and disorganizing it, then the opposition of the imaginary and the symbolic, and above all its implicit hierarchy, appears to be of very limited pertinence: that is, if one measures it against the squaring of such a scene of writing.

We have seen that *all* the characters of "The Purloined Letter," and those of the "real drama" in particular, Dupin included, successively and structurally occupied *all* the positions, the position of the dead-blind King (and of the Prefect of Police thereby), then the positions of the Queen and of the Minister. Each position identifies itself with the other and divides itself, even the position of the dummy and of a supplementary fourth. This compromises the distinction of the three glances proposed by the Seminar in order to determine the proper course of the circulation. And above all the (duplicitous and identificatory) opening set off to the side, in the direction of the (narrating-narrated) narrator, brings back one letter only to set another adrift.

And the phenomena of the double, and therefore of *Unheimlichkeit,* do not belong only to the trilogic "context" of "The Purloined Letter." In effect, the question arises, between the narrator and Dupin, of knowing whether the Minister is himself or his brother ("There are two brothers . . . both have attained reputation"; Where? "in letters" [1956 219]). Dupin affirms that the Minister is both "poet and mathematician." The two brothers are almost indistinguishable in him. In rivalry within him, the one playing and checking the other. "You are mistaken," says Dupin, "I know him well; he is both. As poet *and* mathematician, he would reason well; as mere mathematician, he could not have reasoned at all, and thus would have been at the mercy of the Prefect" (1956, 219).

But Dupin strikes a blow against the Minister, who is "well acquainted with my MS.," a blow signed by a brother or confrere, a twin, younger, or elder brother (Atreus/Thyestes). This rivalrous and duplicitous identification of the two brothers, far from entering into the symbolic space of the familial triangle (the first, second, or next triangle), endlessly carries off the triangle into a labyrinth of doubles without originals, of *fac-similes* without an authentic and indivisible letter, of forgeries without something forged, thereby imprinting on the purloined letter an incorrigible indirection.

The text entitled "The Purloined Letter" imprints (itself in) these effects of indirection. I have indicated only the most salient ones in order to begin to unlock a reading: the play of doubles, divisibility without end, textual references from *fac-simile* to *fac-simile,* the framing of the frames, the interminable supplementarity of the quotation marks, the insertion of "The Purloined Letter" into a purloined letter beginning before it, through the narratives of narratives in "The Murders in the Rue Morgue," and the newspaper clippings in "The Mystery of Marie Rogêt (A Sequel to 'The Murders in the Rue Morgue')." The *mise en abîme* of the title above all: "The Purloined Letter" is the text, the text in a text (the purloined letter as a trilogy). The title is the title of the text, it names the text, it names itself, and thus includes itself by pretending to name an object described in the text. "The Purloined Letter" operates as a text which evades every assignable destination, and produces, or rather induces by deducing itself, this unassignableness at the precise moment when it narrates the arrival of a letter. It feigns meaning to say something, and letting one think that "a letter always arrives at its destination," authentic, intact, and undivided, at the moment when and in the place where the feint, written before the letter, by itself separates from itself. In order to take another jump to the side.

Who signs? Dupin absolutely wants to sign. And in fact the narrator, after having made or let him speak, leaves him the last word, [16] the last word of the last of the three stories. It seems. I am not remarking this in order to place the narrator in turn, and even less the author, in the position of the analyst who knows how to keep silent. Measured against the squaring of this scene of writing, perhaps there is here no possible enclosure for an analytic situation. Perhaps there is no possible analyst here, at least in the situation of psychoanalysis in X. . . . Only four kings, and therefore four queens, four prefects of police, four ministers, four analysts-Dupins, four narrators, four readers, four kings, etc., each of them more lucid and more stupid than the others, more powerful and more disarmed.

Yes, without a doubt, Dupin wants to sign the last word of the last message of the purloined letter. First by not being able to prevent himself from leaving his own imprimatur—or at least the seal with which he will have to be identified—beneath the *fac-simile* which he leaves for the minister. He is afraid of the *fac-simile,* and insisting upon his very confraternal vengeance, he absolutely wants the minister to know where it is coming from. Thus he limits the *fac-simile,* the counterfeit, to the outside of the letter. The inside is authentic and properly identifiable. In effect: at the moment when the madman (who is a false madman paid by him: "the pretended lunatic was a man in my own pay") distracts everyone with his "frantic behavior," what does Dupin do? He adds a note. He sets in place the false letter, that is, the one concerning his own interests, the *true one* which is an *ersatz only on its outside.* If there were a man of truth in all this, a lover of the authentic, Dupin would indeed be his model: "In the meantime I stepped to the card-rack, took the letter, put it in my pocket, and replaced it by a *fac-simile* (so far as regards externals), which I had carefully prepared at my lodgings; imitating the D—— cipher, very readily, by means of a seal formed of bread" (1956, 224).

Thus will D. have to decipher, internally, what the decipherer will have meant and from whence and why he has deciphered, with what aim, in the name of whom and of what. The initial—which is the same, D, for the minister and for Dupin—is a *fac-simile* on the outside, but a proper on *the inside.*

But what is this proper on the inside? This signature? This "last word" in a doubly confraternal war?

Again, a citation by means of which the signer is dispossessed, no matter what he says: ". . . I just copied into the middle of the blank sheet the words—

——Un dessein si funeste,
S'il n'est digne d'Atrée, est digne de Thyeste." (1956, 225)

Play of quotation marks. In the French translation, there are no quotation marks—Crébillon's text is in small type. The sentence that follows ("They are to be found in Crébillon's 'Atrée' ") thus can equally be attributed to the author of "The Purloined Letter," to the narrator, to the author of the avenging letter (Dupin). But the American edition[17] that I am using leaves no doubt:

" '. . . He is well acquainted with my MS., and I just copied into the middle of the blank sheet the words—

——Un dessein si funeste,
S'il n'est digne d'Atrée, est digne de Thyeste.

They are to be found in Crébillon's 'Atrée.' "

Thus it is clear that the last sentence is Dupin's, Dupin saying to the Minister: I the undersigned, Dupin, inform you of the fate of the letter, of what it means, with what aim I am filching one from you in order to return it to its addressee, and why I am replacing it with this one, remember.

But this last word, aside from the invisible quotation marks that border the entire story, Dupin is obliged to cite between quotation marks, to recount his signature: this is what I wrote to him and this is how I signed. What is a signature between quotation marks? And then, within these quotation marks, the imprimatur itself is a citation between quotation marks. This remainder is (again) still (from) literature.

Two out of three times, the author of the Seminar will have forced *dessein* (design) into *destin* (destiny), perhaps, thereby, bringing a meaning to its destination: expressly, no doubt, for in any case nothing permits one to exclude a design (*dessein*) somewhere. (This coda dedicates itself to Abbé D. Coppieters de Gibson. The thing in truth—an alteration subtracting one letter and substituting another, in order to achieve its destiny while *en route*—did not escape him.)

"Whatever the case, the Minister, when he tries to make use of it, will be able to read these words, written so that he may recognize Dupin's hand: '. . . *Un dessein si funeste | S'il n'est digne d'Atrée est digne de Thyeste,*' whose source, Dupin tells us, is Crébillon's *Atrée*" (1972b, 43). Then, after a lapse of time: "The commonplace of the quotation is fitting for the oracle that this face bears in its grimace, as is also its source in tragedy: '. . . *Un destin si funeste, | S'il n'est digne d'Atrée, est digne de Thyeste*'" (1972b, 71). And finally, ("Points" [1969, 8]): ". . . and I add (52) that the song with which this Lecoq, in the love note that he destines for him, would like to awaken him ('*un destin si funeste . . .*'), has no chance of being heard by him."

NOTES

1. TN. *La psychanalyse, à supposer, se trouve. Quand on croit la trouver, c'est elle, à supposer, qui se trouve. Quand elle trouve, à supposer, elle se trouve—quelque chose.* The double meaning of reflexive verbs in French is being played on here. *Se trouver* can mean both to find itself and to be found. Thus, these are three or four statements, since the third sentence must be read in two ways. The passage from three to four via irreducible doubleness is a constant theme in Derrida's works. Throughout this essay, I have given *se trouver* in brackets whenever this wordplay occurs.

2. TN. The Greek *oikos* means the house, the dwelling, and is also the root from which the word *economy* is derived.

3. TN. *Point de* means both "point of" and "no, none at all." Thus, point of view/no view, blindness.

4. TN. "*La structure* restante *de la lettre. . . .*" For Derrida, writing is always that which is an excess remainder, *un reste.* Further, in French, mail delivered to a post office box is called *poste restante,* making the dead letter office the ultimate *poste restante,* literally "remaining mail." Thus, Derrida is saying that Lacan's notion that the non-delivered letter, *la lettre en souffrance,* always arrives at its destination overlooks the structural possibility that a letter can always *remain* in the dead letter office, and that without this possibility of deviation and remaining—the entire postal system—there would be no delivery of letters to any address at all.

5. Legacy [*legs*] and rephallization: 1. "Could it be the letter which brings Woman to be that subject, simultaneously all-powerful and enslaved, such that every hand to which Woman leaves the letter, takes back along with it, that which in receiving it, she herself has legated [*fait lais*]? 'Legacy' [*lais*] means that which Woman bequeaths in never having had it: whence truth emerges from the well, but only halfway" (Presentation of the *Ecrits,* "Points," 1969, 7–8). 2. "To the grim irony of rephallizing the castrated mother, by hanging, we must now add the irony that relactifies her dry breasts by the broad spattering of the splotch of milk . . . even though the main resentment comes from the absence of the penis on the woman's body" (Bonaparte 1971, 475).

Further on we will come back to the question of the "part object" that is implied here. As for the well, in "The Murders in the Rue Morgue," Dupin, after the discovery of the "fearfully mutilated" "body of the mother," recalls: " 'He (Vidocq) impaired his vision by holding the object too close. He might see, perhaps, one or two points with unusual clearness, but in so doing he, necessarily, lost sight of the matter as a whole. Thus there is such a thing as being too profound. Truth is not always in a well." *Selected Writings of Edgar Allan Poe,* ed. Edward Davidson (Boston: Houghton Mifflin, 1956), 153. All further references to Poe will be to this edition. Also note that the French for legacy is *legs;* Derrida constantly plays on the *leg* in *leg*acy. Moreover, the older form of *legs* is *lais,* which is the homonym of *lait,* milk. Thus the question of legacy, rephallization, and re*lact*ification.

6. The doctrine of the truth as cause (*Ursache*), as well as the expression "effects of truth," can be aligned with the system we are about to examine. The effects of truth are the effects of the truth, as "The Direction of the Treatment" (in which it is a question of "directing the subject towards 'full' speech," or in any event of leaving him "free to try it," *Ecrits* [1977, 275], has already said: "it is a question of truth, of the only truth, of the truth about the effects of truth" (ibid.). Circulation will always be circulation of the truth: toward the truth. Cause and effect of the circle, *causa sui,* proper course and destiny of the letter.

7. *Situation de la psychanalyse en* 1956 (Lacan 1966a, 470).

8. TN. *Capitonner* means to quilt; *point de capiton* is Lacan's term for the "quilted stitch" that links signifier to signified.

9. For a time only: until the moment when, unable to return a "material," divisible letter, a letter subject to partition, an effectively "odd" letter, he would have to release the hold over the Queen that only a destructible document could have assured him.

10. What we are analyzing here is the most rigorous philosophy of psycho-analysis today, more precisely the most rigorous Freudian philosophy, doubtless more rigorous than Freud's philosophy, and more scrupulous in its exchanges with the history of philosophy.

It would be impossible to exaggerate the import of the proposition about the indivisibility of the letter, or rather about the letter's self-identity that is inaccessible to fragmentation ("Cut a letter in small pieces, it remains the letter it is"), or of the proposition about the so-called materiality of the signifier (the letter) which does not bear partition. Where does this come from? A fragmented letter can purely and simply be destroyed, this happens (and if one considers that the unconscious effect here named letter is never lost, that repression maintains everything and never permits any degradation of insistence, this hypothesis— nothing is ever lost or goes astray—must still be aligned with *Beyond the Pleasure Principle,* or other letters must be produced, whether characters or messages).

11. "You have heard me, in order to situate its place in the investigation, refer with brotherly love to Descartes and to Hegel. These days, it is rather fashionable to 'surpass' the classical philosophers. I equally could have taken the admirable dialogue with Parmenides as my point of departure. For neither Socrates, nor Descartes, nor Marx, nor Freud can be 'surpassed' to the extent that they have conducted their investigations with that passion for unveiling which has a single object: the truth.

"As one of those, princes of the verb, and through whose fingers the strings of the mask of the Ego seem to slip by themselves, has written—I have named Max Jacob, poet, saint, and novelist—yes, as he has written in his *Dice Cup,* if I am not mistaken: the true is always new," *Ecrits* [1966a, 193]. This is true, always. How not to subscribe to it?

12. TN. "Empty and full speech in the psychoanalytic realization of the subject" in the Rome Report (*Function and Field of Speech* . . .), *Ecrits* [1977, 43].

13. Kitchen questions: in translating "coincidence" by "*analogie*" at the beginning of the tale, at the very moment of the reference to the two other "affairs" (the "Rue Morgue" and "Marie Rogêt"), Baudelaire misses not only the insistence of this word but also the fact that "The Purloined Letter" itself is presented in a series of these coincidences, as one of them, the coincidences whose network is elaborated before this third fiction. One detail from among all of those that now can be analyzed in an open reading of the trilogy: the epigraph to the "Mystery of Marie Rogêt," a citation from Novalis both in German and in

English translation, which begins: "There are ideal series of events which run parallel with the real ones. They rarely coincide. . . ." Baudelaire purely and simply omits the last three words. The word *coincidences* then appears three times in two pages, always underlined. And the last time it has to do with the intersection of the three affairs: "The extraordinary details which I am now called upon to make public, will be found to form, as regards sequence of time, the primary branch of a series of scarcely intelligible *coincidences,* whose secondary or concluding branch will be recognized by all readers in the late murder of MARY CECELIA ROGERS at New York." The subtitle of the "Mystery of Marie Rogêt": "A Sequel to 'The Murders in the Rue Morgue.'"

These reminders, which could be multiplied endlessly, are to make us attentive to the effects of the frame and to the paradoxes of parergonal logic. The point is not to show that "The Purloined Letter" functions within a frame (a frame that is omitted by the Seminar which thereby can assure itself of the tale's triangular interior by means of an active and subreptitious limitation on the basis of a metalinguistic overlay), but that the structure of the effects of framing is such that no totalization of the bordering can even occur. The frames are always enframed: and therefore enframed by a given piece of what they contain. Parts without a whole, "partitions" without unification: this is what checks the dream of a letter without partition, a letter allergic to partition. On the basis of which the linguistic unit phallus [*le sème "phallus"*] wanders, begins by disseminating, and not even by disseminating *itself.*

The naturalizing neutralization of the frame permits the Seminar, by virtue of its imposition or importation of an Oedipal contour, finding (itself within) this contour in truth—and, in effect, it is there, but as one part, even if a precisely central part, within the letter—to constitute a metalanguage and to exclude the text in general in all the dimensions that we began here by recalling (return to the "first page"). Without even going further into details, the trap of metalanguage—which in the last analysis is used by no one, is at the disposition of no one, involves no one in the consequences of an error or a weakness—is a trap belonging to writing before the letter, and shows and hides itself in the shown-hidden of the feigned title: "The Purloined Letter" is the title of the text and not only of its object. But a text never entitles itself, never writes: I, the text, write, or write myself. It causes to be said, it lets be said, or rather it leads to being said, "I, the truth, speak." I am always (I am still following) [*Je suis toujours*] the letter that never arrives at itself [*s'arrive*]. And right up to its destination.

14. Before dropping them, as everyone drops a preface, or before exalting them as the properly instructive theoretical concepts, the truth of the story, I will lift out, somewhat at random, several propositions. Which are not necessarily the best ones. One also would have to recall each word of the title, and again the epigraph on the name of Achilles when he hid himself among women. "The mental features discoursed of as the analytical, are, in themselves, but little susceptible of analysis . . . the analyst glories in that moral activity which

disentangles [*dont le fonction est de débrouiller*]. He derives pleasure from even the most trivial occupations bringing his talents into play. He is fond of enigmas, of conundrums, of hieroglyphics. . . . Yet to calculate is not in itself to analyze. A chess-player, for example, does the one without effort at the other. . . . I will, therefore, take occasion to assert that the higher powers of the reflective intellect are more decidedly and more usefully tasked by the unostentatious games of draughts than by all the elaborate frivolity of chess [*la laborieuse futilité des échecs*]. . . . To be less abstract—Let us suppose a game of draughts where the pieces are reduced to four kings ["draughts" in French is *le jeu de dames,* and Baudelaire's translation here speaks of four *"dames,"* not kings], and where, of course, no oversight is to be expected. It is obvious that here the victory can be decided (the players being at all equal) only by some *recherché* movement [*tactique habile*], the result of some strong exertion of the intellect. Deprived of ordinary resources, the analyst throws himself into the spirit of his opponent, identifies himself therewith, and not unfrequently sees thus, at a glance, the sole methods (sometimes indeed absurdly simple ones) by which he may seduce into error or hurry into miscalculation. . . . But it is in matters beyond the limits of mere rule [*les cas situés au-delà de la règle*] that the skill of the analyst is evinced [*se manifeste*]. . . . Our player confines himself not at all; nor, because the game is the object, does he reject deductions from things external to the game . . ." (Poe 1956, 139–41 *passim*). Etc. The entire passage must be read, and in both languages. I have allowed myself to do some cooking based on Baudelaire's translation, which I do not always respect.

Meryon had asked Baudelaire if he believed "in the reality of this Edgar Poe," and had attributed his stories "to a society of very adept, very powerful litterateurs, up to date on everything." This society does not specify, therefore, if the "things external to the game" border a game recounted in the text or constituted by the text, nor whether *the game* which is *the object* is or is not (in) the story. Nor whether seduction seeks its prey among the characters or the readers. The question of the "narratee," and then of the addressee, which is not the same thing, never arrives at itself [*ne s'arrive jamais*].

15. The Seminar never takes into account the very determined involvement of the narrator in the narration. Ten years later, in a 1966 addition, Lacan writes the following: "An effect (of the signifier) so manifest as to be grasped here as it is in the fiction of the purloined letter.

"Whose essence is that the letter could import its effects within: on the actors of the tale, including the narrator, as well as without: on us, readers, and equally on its author, without anyone ever having to be concerned with what it meant. Which of everything that is written is the ordinary fate" (*Ecrits* [1966a, 56–57]).

Although we subscribe to this up to a certain point, we again must specify that the Seminar said nothing about the effects on the narrator, *neither in fact nor in principle.* The structure of the interpretation would exclude it. And as for the nature of these effects, the structure of the narrator's involvement, the repentance still says nothing, limiting itself to the framing operated by the Seminar. As for the allegation that in this affair everything occurs "without anyone ever having to be concerned with what it [the letter] meant," *it is false* for several reasons.

1st: Everyone, as the Prefect of Police reminds us, knows that the letter contains enough to "bring in question the honor of a personage of most exalted station," and therefore also that person's "peace": a solid semantic bond.

2d: This knowledge is repeated by the Seminar, and supports the Seminar, at two levels:

a) As concerns the minimal and active meaning of the letter, the Seminar reports or transcribes the Prefect's information: "But all this tells us nothing of the message it conveys.

"Love letter or conspiratorial letter, letter of betrayal or letter of mission, letter of summons or letter of distress, we are assured of but one thing: the Queen must not bring it to the knowledge of her lord and master" (1972b, 57). This tells us the essentials of the message that the letter vehiculates: and the variations just proposed are not indifferent to this message, no matter what they would have us believe. In each of the possible hypotheses, the letter's message (not only its being-sent, its emission, but the content of what is emitted within it) necessarily implies the betrayal of a pact of a "sworn faith." It was not forbidden for just anyone to send just any kind of letter to the Queen, nor for her to receive it. The Seminar contradicts itself when, several lines later, it radicalizes the logic of the signifier and of its literal place by allegedly neutralizing the "message," and then brings to rest or anchors this logic in its meaning or symbolic truth: ". . . it remains that the letter is the symbol of a pact" (1972b, 58). Contrary to what the Seminar says (an enormous proposition, by virtue of the blindness it could induce, but indispensable to the demonstration), everyone had "to be concerned with what it [the letter] meant." On the subject of this meaning, ignorance or indifference remains minimal and provisional. Everyone is aware of it, everyone is preoccupied with it, starting with the author of the Seminar. And if it did not have a very determined meaning, no one would be so worried about having another one palmed off on him, which happens to the Queen, and then to the Minister. At least. All of them assure themselves, starting with the Minister and including Lacan, passing through Dupin, that it is indeed a question of the letter which indeed says what it says: the betrayal of the pact, and what it says, "the symbol of a pact." Otherwise there would be no "abandoned" letter: whether by the Minister first of all, or then by Dupin, or finally by Lacan. They all verify the contents of the letter, of the "right" letter, and they all do what the Prefect of Police does at the moment when, in exchange for a retribution, he takes the letter from Dupin's hands, and checks its tenor: "This functionary grasped it in a perfect agony of joy, opened it with a trembling hand, cast a rapid glance at its contents, and then, scrambling and struggling to the door, rushed at length unceremoniously from the room . . ." (Poe 1956, 216). The exchange of the check and the letter takes place across an *escritoire* (in French in the text) where Dupin had the document locked up.

b) As for the law of the meaning of the purloined letter in its exemplary generality, such, once again, are the last words of the Seminar. ("Thus it is that what the 'purloined letter,' nay the 'non-delivered letter' means is that a letter always arrives at its destination" [1972b, 72]).

16. One might even consider that he is the only one "to speak" in the tale. His is the dominant discourse which, with a loquacious and didactic braggadocio that is magisterial in truth, dispenses directives, controls directions, redresses wrongs, and gives lessons to everyone. He spends his time, and everyone else's, inflicting punishments and recalling the rules. He posts himself and addresses himself. Only the address counts, the right and authentic one. Which comes back, according to the law, to its rightful owner. Thanks to the man of law, the guide and rector of the proper way. The entire "Purloined Letter" is written in order for him to bring it back, finally, while giving a lecture. And since he shows himself more clever than all the others, the letter plays one more trick on him at the moment when he recognizes its place and true destination. It escapes and entraps him (literature stage-left) at the moment when, at his most authoritatively arrogant, he hears himself say that he entraps while explaining the trap, at the moment when he strikes his blow and returns the letter. Unwittingly he gives in to all the demands, and doubles, that is replaces, the Minister and the police; if there were only one, a hypothesis to be dismissed, he would be the greatest dupe of the "story." It remains to be seen—what about the lady. He addresses-her-the-Queen-the-address-dupes-her. [. . . *s'il n'y en avait qu'une, hypothèse en conge, ce serait la plus belle dupe de l'"histoire." Reste à savoir—quoi de la belle. Il-l'adresse-la-Reine-l'adresse-la-dupe.*]

17. In the first publication of this text, the following remark concerning the quotation marks could be read: "It is incorrect, however, in presenting itself thus, and in leaving the internal quotation marks, the so-called 'English' quotation marks, suspended." I was wrong: the last quotation marks signal the end of Dupin's discourse, which is what was important to me, and there is no error in the edition to which I am referring. The deletion of this phrase (which is inconsequential) is the only modification of this essay since its first publication.

10 ✿ The Frame of Reference: Poe, Lacan, Derrida

BARBARA JOHNSON

THE PURLOINED PREFACE

A literary text that both analyzes itself and shows that it actually has neither a self nor any neutral metalanguage with which to do the analyzing calls out irresistibly for analysis. When that call is answered by two eminent French thinkers whose readings emit their own equally paradoxical call-to-analysis, the resulting triptych, in the context of the question of the act-of-reading(-literature), places its would-be reader in a vertiginously insecure position.

The three texts in question are Edgar Allan Poe's short story "The Purloined Letter," Jacques Lacan's "Seminar on 'The Purloined Letter,'" and Jacques Derrida's reading of Lacan's reading of Poe, "The Purveyor of Truth" ("Le facteur de la vérité"). [1] In all three texts, it is the *act of analysis* which seems to occupy the center of the discursive stage, and the *act of analysis of the act of analysis* which in some way disrupts that centrality. In the resulting asymmetrical, abyssal structure, no analysis—including this one—can intervene without transforming and repeating other ele-

Reprinted by permission from "Literature and Psychoanalysis: The Question of Reading—Otherwise," *Yale French Studies* 55–56 (1977):457–505.

ments in the sequence, which is thus not a stable sequence, but which nevertheless produces certain regular effects. It is the functioning of this regularity, and the structure of these effects, which will provide the basis for the present study.

The subversion of any possibility of a position of analytical mastery occurs in many ways. Here, the very fact that we are dealing with *three* texts is in no way certain. Poe's story not only fits into a triptych of its own, but is riddled with a constant, peculiar kind of intertextuality (the epigraph from Seneca which is not from Seneca, the lines from Crébillon's *Atrée* which serve as Dupin's signature, etc.). Lacan's text not only presents itself backward (its introduction *following* its conclusion), but it never finishes presenting itself ("Ouverture de ce recueil," "Présentation de la suite," "Présentation" to the "Points" edition). And Derrida's text not only is preceded by several years of annunciatory marginalia and footnotes but is itself structured by its own deferment, its *différance* (cf. the repetition of such expressions as "mais nous n'en sommes pas encore là" ["but we are getting ahead of ourselves"], etc.). In addition, an unusually high degree of apparent digressiveness characterizes these texts, to the point of making the reader wonder whether there is really any true subject matter there at all. It is as though any attempt to follow the path of the purloined letter is automatically purloined from itself. Which is, as we shall see, just what the letter has always already been saying.

Any attempt to do "justice" to three such complex texts is obviously out of the question. But in each of these readings of the act of analysis the very question being asked is, What is the nature of such "justice"? It can hardly be an accident that the debate proliferates around a *crime* story—a robbery and its undoing. Somewhere in each of these texts, the economy of justice cannot be avoided. For in spite of the absence of mastery, there is no lack of effects of power.

As the reader goes on with this series of prefatory remarks, he may begin to see how contagious the deferment of the subject of the purloined letter can be. But the problem of how to present these three texts is all the more redoubtable since each of them both presents itself and the others and clearly shows the fallacies inherent in any type of "presentation" of a text. It is small comfort that such fallacies are not only inevitable but also *constitutive* of any act of reading—also demonstrated by each of the texts—since the resulting injustices, however unavoidable in general, always appear corrigible in detail. Which is why the sequence continues.

The question of how to present to the reader a text too extensive to quote in its entirety has long been one of the underlying problems of literary criticism. Since a shorter version of the text must somehow be produced, two solutions constantly recur: paraphrase and quotation. Although these tactics are seldom if ever used in isolation, the specific configuration of their combinations and permutations determines to a large extent the "plot" of the critical narrative to which they give rise. The first act of our own narrative, then, will consist of an analysis of the strategic effects of the use of paraphrase versus quotation in each of the three texts in question.

ROUND ROBBIN'

Round robin: 1) A tournament in which each contestant is matched against every other contestant. 2) A petition or protest on which the signatures are arranged in the form of a circle in order to conceal the order of signing. 3) A letter sent among members of a group, often with comments added by each person in turn. 4) An extended sequence. (*American Heritage Dictionary*)

In 1845, Edgar Allan Poe published the third of his three detective stories, "The Purloined Letter," in a collective volume entitled—ironically, considering all the robberies in the story—*The Gift: A Christmas, New Year, and Birthday Present.* "The Purloined Letter" is a first-person narration of two scenes in which dialogues occur among the narrator, his friend C. Auguste Dupin, and, initially, the prefect of the Parisian police. The two scenes are separated by an indication of the passage of a month's time. In each of the two dialogues, reported to us verbatim by the narrator, one of the other two characters tells the story of a robbery. In the first scene, it is the Prefect of Police who repeats the Queen's eyewitness account of the Minister's theft of a letter addressed to her; in the second scene, it is Dupin who narrates his own theft of the same letter from the Minister, who had meanwhile readdressed it to himself. In a paragraph placed between these two "crime" stories, the narrator himself narrates a wordless scene in which the letter changes hands again before his eyes, passing from Dupin—not without the latter's having addressed not the letter but a check to himself—to the Prefect (who will pocket the remainder of the reward) and thence, presumably, back to the Queen.

By appearing to repeat to us faithfully every word in both dialogues, the narrator would seem to have resorted exclusively to direct quotation in presenting his story. Even when paraphrase could have been expected—in the description of the exact procedures employed by the police in searching unsuccessfully for the letter, for example—we are spared none of the details. Thus it is all the more surprising to find that there *is* one little point at which direct quotation of the Prefect's words gives way to paraphrase. This point, however brief, is of no small importance, as we shall see. It occurs in the concluding paragraph of the first scene:

"I have no better advice to give you," said Dupin. "You have, of course, an accurate description of the letter?"

"Oh, yes!"—And here the Prefect, producing a memorandum-book, proceeded to read aloud a minute account of the internal, and especially of the external, appearance of the missing document. Soon after finishing the perusal of this description, he took his departure, more entirely depressed in spirits than I had ever known the good gentleman before.

What is paraphrased is thus the description of the letter the story is about. And, whereas it is generally supposed that the function of paraphrase is to strip off the form of a speech in order to give us only its contents, here the use of paraphrase does the very opposite: it withholds the contents of the Prefect's remarks, giving us only their form. And what is swallowed up in this ellipsis is nothing less than the contents of the letter itself. The fact that the letter's message is never revealed, which will serve as the basis for Lacan's reading of the story, is thus negatively made explicit by the functioning of Poe's text itself, through what Derrida might have called a repression of the written word (a suppression of what is written in the memorandum book—and in the letter). And the question of the strategic use of paraphrase versus quotation begins to invade the literary text as well as the critical narrative.

Lacan's presentation of Poe's text involves the paraphrase, or plot summary, of the two thefts as they are told to the narrator by the Prefect and by Dupin. Since Derrida, in his critique of Lacan, chooses to quote Lacan's paraphrase, we can combine all the tactics involved by, in our turn, quoting Derrida's quotation of Lacan's paraphrase of Poe's quoted narrations.[2]

There are two scenes, the first of which we shall straightway designate the primal scene, and by no means inadvertently, since the second may be considered its repetition in the very sense we are considering today.

The primal scene is thus performed, we are told [by neither Poe, nor the scriptor, nor the narrator, but by G, the Prefect of Police who is *mis en scène* by all those involved in the dialogues—J. D.[3]] in the royal *boudoir*, so that we suspect that the person of the highest rank, called the "exalted personage," who is alone there when she receives a letter, is the Queen. This feeling is confirmed by the embarrassment into which she is plunged by the entry of the other exalted personage, of whom we have already been told [again by G—J. D.] prior to this account that the knowledge he might have of the letter in question would jeopardize for the lady nothing less than her honor and safety. Any doubt that he is in fact the King is promptly dissipated in the course of the scene which begins with the entry of Minister D. . . . [and so on as in 1975a, 54–55]

Thus, it is neither the character of the individual subjects, nor the contents of the letter, but the position of the letter within the group which decides what each person will do next. Because the letter does not function as a unit of meaning (a *signified*) but as that which produces certain effects (a *signifier*), Lacan reads the story as an illustration of "the truth which may be drawn from that moment in Freud's thought under study—namely, that it is the symbolic order which is constitutive for the subject—by demonstrating . . . the decisive orientation which the subject receives from the itinerary of a signifier" (1972b, 40). The letter acts like a signifier to the extent that its function in the story does not require that its meaning be revealed: "the letter was able to produce its effects *within* the story: on the actors in the tale, including the narrator, as well as *outside* the story: on us, the readers, and also on its author, without anyone's ever bothering to worry about what is *meant*" (not translated in 1972b; 1969, 57, translation and emphasis mine). "The Purloined Letter" thus becomes for Lacan a kind of *allegory of the signifier*.

Derrida's critique of Lacan's reading does not dispute the validity of the allegorical interpretation on its own terms, but questions its implicit presuppositions and its modus operandi. Derrida aims his objections at two kinds of target: (1) what Lacan puts into the letter and (2) what Lacan leaves out of the text.

1. *What Lacan puts into the letter.* While asserting that the letter's meaning is lacking, Lacan, according to Derrida, makes this lack into *the* meaning of the letter. But Derrida does not stop there. He goes on to assert that what Lacan means by that lack is the truth of lack-as-castration-as-truth: "The truth of the purloined letter is the truth itself. . . . What is veiled/unveiled in this case is a hole, a non-being [*non-étant*]; the truth of being [*l'être*], as non-being. Truth is 'woman' as veiled/unveiled castration" (1975a, 60–61). Lacan himself, however, never uses the word *castration* in the text of the original Seminar. That it is suggested is

indisputable, but Derrida, by filling in what *Lacan* left blank is repeating the same gesture of blank-filling for which he criticizes Lacan.

2. *What Lacan leaves out of the text.* This objection is itself double: On the one hand, Derrida criticizes Lacan for neglecting to consider "The Purloined Letter" in connection with the other two stories in what Derrida calls Poe's "Dupin Trilogy." And on the other hand, according to Derrida, at the very moment Lacan is reading the story as an allegory of the signifier, he is being blind to the disseminating power of the signifier in the *text* of the allegory, in what Derrida calls the "scene of writing." To cut out part of a text's frame of reference as though it did not exist and to reduce a complex textual function ng to a single meaning are serious blots indeed in the annals of literary criticism. Therefore it is all the more noticeable that Derrida's own reading of Lacan's text repeats the crimes of which he accuses it: On the one hand, Derrida makes no mention of Lacan's long development on the relation between symbolic determination and random series. And on the other hand, Derrida dismisses Lacan's "style" as a mere ornament, veiling, for a time, an unequivocal message: "Lacan's 'style,' moreover, was such that for a long time it would hinder and delay all access to a *unique* content or a single unequivocal meaning determinable beyond the writing itself" (1975a, 40). Derrida's repetition of the very gestures he is criticizing does not in itself invalidate his criticism of their effects, but it does problematize his statement condemning their existence.

What kind of logic is it that thus seems to turn one-upmanship into inevitable one-downmanship?

It is the very logic of the purloined letter.

ODD COUPLES

Je tiens la reine!
          O sûr châtiment. . . .
                    —Mallarmé, "L'après-midi d'un faune"

L'ascendant que le ministre tire de la situation ne tient donc pas à la lettre, mais, qu'il le sache ou non, au personnage qu'elle lui constitue. (Lacan 1972b)

We have just seen how Derrida, in his effort to right (write) Lacan's wrongs, can, on a certain level, only repeat them, and how the rectification of a previous injustice somehow irresistibly dictates the filling in of a blank which then becomes the new injustice. In fact, the act of clinching one's triumph by filling in a blank is already prescribed in all its details within Poe's story, in Dupin's unwillingness to "leave the interior blank" (Poe 1978, 993) in the facsimile he has left for the Minister, in place of the purloined letter he, Dupin, has just repossessed by means of a precise repetition of the act of robbery he is undoing. What is written in the blank is a quotation-as-signature, which curiously resembles Derrida's initialed interventions in the passages he quotes from Lacan, a resemblance on which Derrida is undoubtedly playing. And the text of the quotation transcribed by Dupin describes the structure of rectification-as-repetition-of-the-crime which has led to its being transcribed in the first place:

> ——Un dessein si funeste,
> S'il n'est digne d'Atrée, est digne de Thyeste.

Atreus, whose wife had long ago been seduced by Thyestes, is about to make Thyestes eat (literally) the fruit of that illicit union, his son Plisthenes. The avenger's plot may not be worthy of him, says Atreus, but his brother Thyestes deserves it. What the addressee of the violence is going to get is simply his own message backward. It is this vengeful anger that, as both Lacan and Derrida show, places Dupin as one of the "ostriches" in the "triad." Not content simply to return the letter to its "rightful" destination, Dupin jumps into the fray as the wronged victim himself, by recalling an "evil turn" the Minister once did him in Vienna and for which he is now, personally, taking his revenge.

Correction must thus posit a previous pretextual, pre-textual crime that will justify its excesses. Any degree of violence is permissible in the act of getting even ("To be *even* with him," says Dupin, "I complained of my weak eyes" [emphasis mine]). And Dupin's backward revision of the story repeats itself in his readers as well. The existence of the same kind of prior aggression on Lacan's part is posited by Derrida in a long footnote in his book *Positions,* in which he outlines what will later develop into *Le facteur de la vérité:* "In the texts I have published up to now, the absence of reference to Lacan is indeed almost total. That is *justified* not only by the *acts of aggression* in the form of, or with the intention of, reappropriation which, ever since *De la grammatologie* appeared in *Critique* (1965) (and even earlier, I am told) Lacan has multiplied" (emphasis mine). The priority of aggression is doubled by the aggressiveness of priority: "At the time of my first publications, Lacan's *Ecrits* had not yet been collected and published.[4] And Lacan, in turn, mentions in his "Presentation" to the "Points" edition of his *Ecrits:* "what I properly call the instance of the letter *before any grammatology*"[5] (emphasis mine). The rivalry over something neither man will credit the other with possessing, the retrospective revision of the origins of both their resemblances and their differences, thus spirals backward and forward in an indeterminable pattern of cancellation and duplication. If it thus becomes impossible to determine "who started it" (or even whether "it" was started by either one of them), it is also impossible to know who is ahead or even whose "turn" it is—which is what makes the business of getting even so *odd.*

This type of oscillation between two items, considered as totalities in binary opposition, is studied by Lacan in connection with Poe's story of the eight-year-old prodigy who succeeded in winning, far beyond his due, at the game of even and odd. The game consists of guessing whether the number of marbles an opponent is holding is even or odd. The schoolboy explains his success by his identification with the physical characteristics of his opponent, from which he deduces the opponent's degree of intelligence and its corresponding line of reasoning. What Lacan shows, in the part of his Seminar which Derrida neglects, is that the mere identification with the opponent as an image of totality is not sufficient to ensure success—and in no way explains Dupin's actual strategy—since, from the moment the opponent becomes aware of it, he can then play on his own appearance and dissociate it from the reasoning that is presumed to go with it. (This is, indeed, what occurs in the encounter between Dupin and the Minister: the Minister's feigned nonchalance is a true vigilance but a blinded vision, whereas Dupin's feigned blindness ["weak eyes"] is a vigilant act of lucidity, later to succumb to its own form of blindness.) From then on, says Lacan, the reasoning "can only repeat itself in an indefinite oscillation" (1969, 58; translation mine). And Lacan reports that, in his own classroom tests of the schoolboy's technique, it was almost inevitable that each player begin to feel he was losing his marbles.[6]

But if the complexities of these texts could be reduced to a mere combat between ostriches, a mere game of heads and tails played out in order to determine a "winner," they would have very little theoretical interest. It is, on the contrary, the way in which each mastermind avoids simply becoming the butt of his own joke that displaces the opposition in unpredictable ways and transforms the textual encounter into a source of insight. For if the very possibility of meeting the opponent on a common ground, without which no contact is possible, implies a certain symmetry, a sameness, a repetition of the error that the encounter is designed to correct, any true avoidance of that error entails a nonmeeting or incompatibility between the two forces. If to hit the target is in a way to become the target, then to miss the target is perhaps to hit it elsewhere. It is not how Lacan and Derrida meet each other but how they miss each other that opens up a space for interpretation.

Clearly, what is at stake here has something to do with the status of the number 2. If the face-off between two opponents or polar opposites always simultaneously backfires and misfires, it can only be because 2 is an extremely "odd" number. On the one hand, as a specular illusion of symmetry or metaphor, it can be either narcissistically reassuring (the image of the other as a reinforcement of my identity) or absolutely devastating (the other whose existence can totally cancel me out). This is what Lacan calls the "*imaginary* duality." It is characterized by its absoluteness, its independence from any accident or contingency that might subvert the unity of the terms in question, whether in their opposition or in their fusion. To this, Lacan opposes the *symbolic,* which is the entrance of difference or otherness or temporality into the idea of identity—it is not something that befalls the imaginary duality, but something that has always already inhabited it, something that subverts not the symmetry of the imaginary couple, but the possibility of the independent unity of any one term whatsoever. It is the impossibility not of the number 2 but of the number *1*—which, paradoxically enough, turns out to lead to the number 3.

If 3 is what makes 2 into the impossibility of 1, is there any inherent increase in lucidity in passing from a couple to a triangle? Is a triangle in any way more "true" than a couple?

It is Derrida's contention that, for psychoanalysis, the answer to that question is yes. The triangle becomes the magical, Oedipal figure that explains the functioning of human desire. The child's original imaginary dual unity with the mother is subverted by the law of the father as that which prohibits incest under threat of castration. The child has "simply" to "assume castration" as the necessity of substitution in the object of his desire (the object of desire becoming the locus of substitution and the focus of repetition), after which the child's desire becomes "normalized." Derrida's criticism of the "triangles" or "triads" in Lacan's reading of Poe is based on the assumption that Lacan's use of triangularity stems from this psychoanalytical myth.

Derrida's criticism takes two routes, both of them numerical:

1. The structure of "The Purloined Letter" cannot be reduced to a

triangle unless the narrator is eliminated. The elimination of the narrator is a blatant and highly revealing result of the way "psychoanalysis" does violence to literature in order to find its own schemes. What psychoanalysis sees as a triangle is therefore really a quadrangle, and that fourth side is the point from which literature problematizes the very possibility of a triangle. Therefore: $3 = 4$.

2. Duality as such cannot be dismissed or simply absorbed into a triangular structure. "The Purloined Letter" is traversed by an uncanny capacity for doubling and subdividing. The narrator and Dupin are doubles of each other, and Dupin himself is first introduced as a "Bi-Part Soul" (Mabbott 1978, 2:533), a sort of Dupin Duplex, "the creative and the resolvent." The Minister, D——, has a brother for whom it is possible to mistake him, and from whom he is to be distinguished because of his doubleness (poet and mathematician). Thus the Minister and Dupin become doubles of each other through the fact of their both being already double, in addition to their other points of resemblance, including their names. "The 'Seminar,'" writes Derrida,

mercilessly forecloses this problematic of the double and of *Unheimlichkeit*—no doubt considering that it is confined to the imaginary, to the dual relationship which must be kept rigorously separate from the symbolic and the triangular. . . . All the "uncanny" relations of duplicity, limitlessly deployed in a dual structure, find themselves omitted or marginalized [in the Seminar]. . . . What is thus kept under surveillance and control is the Uncanny itself, and the frantic anxiety which can be provoked, with no hope of reappropriation, enclosure, or truth, by the infinite play from simulacrum to simulacrum, from double to double. (Derrida 1975b, 124, translation mine; omitted in 1975a)

Thus the triangle's angles are always already bisected, and $3 = $ (a factor of) 2.

In the game of odd versus even, then, it would seem that Derrida is playing evens (4 or 2) against Lacan's odds (3). But somehow the numbers 2 and 4 have become uncannily odd, while the number 3 has been evened off into a reassuring symmetry. How did this happen, and what are the consequences for an interpretation of "The Purloined Letter"?

Before any answer to this question can be envisaged, several remarks should be made here to problematize the terms of Derrida's critique:

1. If the narrator and Dupin are a strictly dual pair whose relationship is in no way mediated by a third term in any Oedipal sense, how is one to explain the fact that their original meeting was brought about by their

potential rivalry over the same object: "the accident of our both being in search of the *same* very rare and very remarkable volume" (emphasis mine)? Whether or not they ever found it, or can share it, is this not a triangular relationship?

2. Although Lacan's reading of "The Purloined Letter" divides the story into triadic structures, his model for (inter-)subjectivity, the so-called schema L, which is developed in that part of the Seminar's introduction glossed over by Derrida, is indisputably quadrangular. In order to read Lacan's repeating triads as a triangular, Oedipal model of the subject instead of as a mere structure of repetition, Derrida must therefore lop off one corner of the schema L in the same way as he accuses Lacan of lopping off a corner of Poe's text—and Derrida does this by lopping off that corner of Lacan's text in which the quadrangular schema L is developed.

But can what is at stake here really be reduced to a mere numbers game?

Let us approach the problem from another angle, by asking two more questions:

1. What is the relation between a divided unity and a duality? Are the two 2's synonymous? Is a "Bi-Part Soul," for example, actually composed of two wholes? Or is it possible to conceive of a division which would not lead to two separate parts, but only to a problematization of the idea of unity? This would class what Derrida calls "duality" not in Lacan's "imaginary," but in Lacan's "symbolic."

2. If the doubles are forever redividing or multiplying, does the number 2 really apply? If $1 = 2$, how can $2 = 1 + 1$? If what is uncanny about the doubles is that they never stop doubling up, would the number 2 still be uncanny if it did stop at a truly dual symmetry? Is it not the very limitlessness of the process of the dissemination of unity, rather than the existence of any one duality, which Derrida is talking about here?

Clearly, in these questions, the very notion of a number becomes problematic, and the argument on the basis of numbers can no longer be read literally. If Derrida opposes doubled quadrangles to Lacan's triangles, it is not because he wants to turn Oedipus into an octopus.

To what, then, does the critique of triangularity apply?

The problem with psychoanalytical triangularity, in Derrida's eyes, is not that it contains the wrong number of terms, but that it presupposes the possibility of a successful dialectical mediation and harmonious normalization, or *Aufhebung,* of desire. The three terms in the Oedipal triad enter into an opposition whose resolution resembles the synthetic moment of a Hegelian dialectic. The process centers on the phallus as the locus of the question of sexual difference; when the observation of the mother's lack of a penis is joined with the father's threat of castration as the punishment for incest, the child passes from the alternative (thesis vs. antithesis; presence vs. absence of penis) to the synthesis (the phallus as a sign of the fact that the child can only enter into the circuit of desire by assuming castration as the phallus's simultaneous presence and absence; that is, by assuming the fact that both the subject and the object of desire will always be substitutes for something that was never really present). In Lacan's article "La signification du phallus," which Derrida quotes, this process is evoked in specifically Hegelian terms:

All these remarks still do nothing but veil the fact that it [the phallus] cannot play its role except veiled, that is to say as itself sign of the latency with which anything signifiable is stricken as soon as it is raised (*aufgehoben*) to the function of signifier.

The phallus is the signifier of this *Aufhebung* itself which it inaugurates (initiates) by its disappearance. (Lacan 1969, 692; Derrida 1972b, 98)

"It would appear," comments Derrida, "that the Hegelian movement of *Aufhebung* is here reversed since the latter sublates [*relève*] the sensory signifier in the ideal signified" (1975a, 98). But then, according to Derrida, Lacan's privileging of the spoken over the written word annuls this reversal, reappropriates all possibility of uncontainable otherness, and brings the whole thing back within the bounds of the type of "logocentrism" that has been the focus of Derrida's entire deconstructive enterprise.

The question of whether or not Lacan's privileging of the voice is strictly logocentric in Derrida's sense is an extremely complex one with which we cannot hope to deal adequately here.[7] But what does all this have to do with "The Purloined Letter"?

In an attempt to answer this question, let us examine how Derrida deduces from Lacan's text that, for Lacan, the letter is a symbol of the (mother's) phallus. Since Lacan never uses the word *phallus* in the Seminar, this is already an interpretation on Derrida's part, and quite an astute one at that, with which Lacan, as a later reader of his own Seminar, implicitly agrees by placing the word *castrated*—which had not been used in the original text—in his "Points" "Presentation." The disagreement between Derrida and Lacan thus arises not over the *validity* of the equation "letter = phallus," but over its *meaning*.

How, then, does Derrida derive this equation from Lacan's text? The deduction follows four basic lines of reasoning, all of which will be dealt with in greater detail later in the present essay:

1. The letter "belongs" to the Queen as a substitute for the phallus she does not have. It feminizes (castrates) each of its successive holders and is eventually returned to her as its rightful owner.

2. Poe's description of the position of the letter in the Minister's apartment, expanded upon by the figurative dimensions of Lacan's text, suggests an analogy between the shape of the fireplace from the center of whose mantelpiece the letter is found hanging and that point on a woman's anatomy from which the phallus is missing.

3. The letter, says Lacan, cannot be divided: "But if it is first of all on the materiality of the signifier that we have insisted, that materiality is *odd* [singulière] in many ways, the first of which is not to admit partition" (1972b, 53). This indivisibility, says Derrida, is odd indeed, but becomes comprehensible if it is seen as an *idealization* of the phallus, whose integrity is necessary for the edification of the entire psychoanalytical system. With the phallus safely idealized and located in the voice, the so-called signifier acquires the "unique, living, non-mutilable integrity" of the self-present spoken word, unequivocally pinned down to and by the *signified*. "Had the phallus been per(mal)-chance divisible or reduced to the status of a partial object, the whole edification would have crumbled down, and this is what has to be avoided at all cost" (1975a, 96–97).

4. And finally, if Poe's story "illustrates" the "truth," the last words of the Seminar proper seem to reaffirm that truth in no uncertain terms: "Thus it is that what the 'purloined letter,' nay, the 'letter in sufferance' means is that *a letter always arrives at its destination*" (1972b, 72; emphasis mine). Now, since it is unlikely that Lacan is talking about the efficiency of the postal service, he must, according to Derrida, be affirming the possibility of unequivocal meaning, the eventual reappropriation of the message, its total equivalence with itself. And since the "truth" Poe's story illustrates is, in Derrida's eyes, the truth of veiled/unveiled castration and of the transcendental identity of the phallus as the lack that makes the system work, this final sentence in Lacan's Seminar seems to affirm both the absolute truth of psychoanalytical theories and the absolute decipherability of the literary text. Poe's message will have been totally, unequivocally understood and explained by the psychoanalytical myth. "The hermeneutic discovery of meaning (truth), the deciphering (that of Dupin and that of the Seminar), arrives itself at its destination" (1975a, 66).

Thus, the law of the phallus seems to imply a reappropriating return to the place of true ownership, an indivisible identity functioning beyond the possibility of disintegration or unrecoverable loss, and a totally self-present, unequivocal meaning or truth.

The problem with this type of system, counters Derrida, is that it cannot account for the possibility of sheer accident, irreversible loss, unreappropriable residues, and infinite divisibility, which are necessary and inevitable in the system's very elaboration. In order for the circuit of the letter to end up confirming the law of the phallus, it must begin by transgressing it; the letter is a sign of high treason. Phallogocentrism mercilessly represses the uncontrollable multiplicity of ambiguities, the disseminating play of *writing*, which irreducibly transgresses any un-equivocal meaning. "Not that the letter never arrives at its destination, but part of its structure is that it is always capable of not arriving there. . . . Here dissemination threatens the law of the signifier and of castration as a contract of truth. Dissemination mutilates the unity of the signifier, that is, of the phallus" (1975a, 66).

In contrast to Lacan's Seminar, then, Derrida's text would seem to be setting itself up as a "Disseminar."

From the foregoing remarks, it can easily be seen that the disseminal criticism of Lacan's apparent reduction of the literary text to an unequivo-cal message depends for its force upon the presupposition of unam-biguousness in Lacan's text. And indeed, the statement that a letter always reaches its destination seems straightforward enough. But when the statement is reinserted into its context, things become palpably less certain:

Is that all, and shall we believe we have deciphered Dupin's real strategy above and beyond the imaginary tricks upon which he was obliged to deceive us? No doubt, yes, for if "any point requiring reflection," as Dupin states at the start, is "examined to best purpose in the dark," we may now easily read its solution in broad daylight. It was already implicit and easy to derive from the title of our tale, according to the very formula we have long submitted to your discretion: in which the sender, we tell you, receives from the receiver his own message in reverse form. Thus it is that what the "purloined letter," nay, the "letter in sufferance," means is that a letter always arrives at its destination. (1972b, 72)

The meaning of this last sentence is problematized not so much by its own ambiguity as by a series of reversals in the preceding sentences. If the "best" examination takes place in darkness, what does "reading in broad daylight" imply? Could it not be taken as an affirmation not of actual lucidity but of delusions of lucidity? Could it not then move the "yes, no doubt" as an answer, not to the question, Have we deciphered? but to the question, Shall we *believe* we have deciphered? And if this is possible, does it not empty the final affirmation of all unequivocality, leaving it to stand with the *force* of an assertion, without any definite content? And if the sender receives from the receiver his own message backward, who is the sender here, who the receiver, and what is the message? It is not even clear what the expression "the purloined letter" refers to: Poe's text? The letter it talks about? Or simply the expression "the purloined letter"?

We will take another look at this passage later, but for the moment its ambiguities seem sufficient to problematize, if not subvert, the presupposition of univocality that is the very foundation on which Derrida has edified his interpretation.

But surely such an oversimplification on Derrida's part does not result from mere blindness, oversight, or error. As Paul deMan (1983) says of Derrida's similar treatment of Rousseau, "the pattern is too interesting not to be deliberate." Derrida being the sharp-eyed reader that he is, his consistent forcing of Lacan's statements into systems and patterns from which they are actually trying to escape must correspond to some strategic necessity different from the attentiveness to the letter of the text which characterizes Derrida's way of reading Poe. And in fact, the more one works with Derrida's analysis, the more convinced one becomes that although the critique of what Derrida calls psychoanalysis is entirely justified, it does not quite apply to what Lacan's text is actually saying. Derrida argues, in effect, not against Lacan's *text* but against Lacan's *power*—or rather, against "Lacan" as the apparent cause of certain effects of power in French discourse today. Whatever Lacan's text may *say,* it functions, according to Derrida, as if it said what *he* says it says. The statement that a letter always reaches its destination may be totally undecipherable, but its assertive force is taken all the more seriously as a sign that Lacan himself has everything all figured out. Such an assertion, in fact, gives him an appearance of mastery like that of the Minister in the eyes of the letterless Queen. "The ascendancy which the Minister derives from the situation," explains Lacan, "is attached not to the letter but to the character it makes him into."

Thus Derrida's seemingly "blind" reading, whose vagaries we shall be following here, is not a mistake, but the positioning of what can be called the "average reading" of Lacan's text—the true object of Derrida's deconstruction. Since Lacan's text is read as if it said what Derrida says it says, its actual textual functioning is irrelevant to the agonistic arena in which Derrida's analysis takes place and which is suggested by the very first word of the epigraph: *ils* (they):

They thank him for the grand truths he has just proclaimed—for they have discovered (O verifier of what cannot be verified) that everything he said was absolutely true; even though, at first, these honest souls admit, they might have suspected that it could have been a simple fiction. (1975a, 31; translation mine)

The fact that this quotation from Baudelaire refers to Poe and not Lacan does not completely erase the impression that the unidentified "him" in its first sentence is the "Purveyor of Truth" of the title. The evils of Lacan's analysis of Poe are thus located less in the letter of the text than in the gullible readers, the "*brave gens*" who are taken in by it. Lacan's ills are really *ils*.

If Derrida's reading of Lacan's reading of Poe is actually the deconstruction of a reading whose status is difficult to determine, does this mean that Lacan's text is completely innocent of the misdemeanors of which it is accused? If Lacan can be shown to be opposed to the same kind of logocentric error that Derrida opposes, does that mean that they are both really saying the same thing? These are questions that must be left, at least for the moment, hanging.

But the structure of Derrida's transference of guilt from a certain reading of Lacan onto Lacan's text is not indifferent in itself, in the context of what, after all, started out as a relatively simple crime story. For what it amounts to is nothing less than a *frame*.

THE FRAME OF REFERENCE

> Elle, défunte *nue* en le miroir, encor
> Que, *dans l'oubli fermé par le cadre,*
> se fixe
> De scintillations sitôt le septuor.
>
> —Mallarmé, "Sonnet en X"

If Derrida is thus framing Lacan for an interpretative malpractice of which he himself is, at least in part, the author, what can this frame teach us about the nature of the act of reading, in the context of the question of literature and psychoanalysis?

Interestingly enough, one of the major crimes for which Derrida frames Lacan is the psychoanalytical reading's elimination of the literary text's *frame*. That frame here consists not only of the two stories that precede "The Purloined Letter" but also of the stratum of narration through which the stories are told, and, "beyond" it, of the text's entire functioning as *écriture:*

Without breathing a word about it, Lacan excludes the textual fiction within which he isolates the so-called general narration. Such an operation is facilitated, too obviously facilitated, by the fact that the narration covers the entire surface of the fiction entitled "The Purloined Letter." But *that* is the fiction. There is an invisible but structurally irreducible frame around the narration. Where does it begin? With the first letter of the title? With the epigraph from Seneca? With the words, "At Paris, just after dark . . ."? It is more complicated than that and will require reconsideration. Such complication suffices to point out everything that is misunderstood about the structure of the text once the frame is ignored. Within this invisible or neutralized frame, Lacan takes the borderless narration and makes another subdivision, once again leaving aside the frame. He cuts out two dialogues from within the frame of the narration itself, which form the narrated history, i.e., the content of a representation, the internal meaning of a story, the all-enframed which demands our complete attention, mobilizes all the psychoanalytical schemes—Oedipal, as it happens—and draws all the effort of decipherment toward its center. What is missing here is an elaboration of the problem of the frame, the signature and the *parergon.* This lack allows us to reconstruct the scene of the signifier as a signified (an ever inevitable process in the logic of the sign), writing as the written, the text as discourse or more precisely as an "intersubjective" dialogue (there is nothing fortuitous in the fact that the Seminar discusses only the two *dialogues* in "The Purloined Letter"). (1975a, 52–53; translation modified)

It is well known that "The Purloined Letter" belongs to what Baudelaire called a "kind of trilogy," along with "The Murders in the Rue Morgue" and "The Mystery of Marie Rogêt." About this Dupin trilogy, the "Seminar" does not breathe a word; not only does Lacan lift out the narrated triangles (the "real drama") in order to center the narration around them and make them carry the weight of the interpretation (the letter's destination), but he also lifts one-third of the Dupin cycle out of an ensemble discarded as if it were a natural, invisible frame. (Derrida 1975b, 123, translation mine; not translated in 1975a)

In framing with such violence, in cutting a fourth side out of the narrated figure itself in order to see only triangles, a certain complication, perhaps a complication of the Oedipal structure, is eluded, a complication which makes itself felt in the scene of writing. (1975a, 54; translation entirely modified)

It would seem, then, that Lacan is guilty of several sins of omission: the omission of the narrator, the nondialogue parts of the story, the other stories in the trilogy. But does this criticism amount to a mere plea for the inclusion of what has been excluded? No; the problem is not simply quantitative. What has been excluded is not homogeneous to what has been included. Lacan, says Derrida, misses the specifically literary dimension of Poe's text by treating it as a "real drama," a story like the stories a psychoanalyst hears every day from his patients. What has been left out is literature itself.

Does this mean that the frame is what makes a text literary? In an issue of *New Literary History* devoted to the question "What is literature?" (and totally unrelated to the debate concerning the purloined letter) one of the contributors comes to this very conclusion: "Literature is language . . . but it is language around which we have drawn a *frame,* a frame that indicates a decision to regard with a particular self-consciousness the resources language has always possessed" (Fish 1973, 52; emphasis mine).

Such a view of literature, however, implies that a text is literary because it remains inside certain definite borders; it is a many-faceted object, perhaps, but still, it is an object. That this is not quite what Derrida has in mind becomes clear from the following remarks:

By overlooking the narrator's position, the narrator's involvement in the content of what he seems to be recounting, one omits from the scene of writing anything going beyond the two triangular scenes.

And first of all one omits that what is in question—with no possible access route or border—is a scene of writing whose boundaries crumble off into an abyss. From the simulacrum of an overture, of a "first word," the narrator, in narrating himself, advances a few propositions which carry the unity of the "tale" into an endless drifting-off course: a textual drifting not at all taken into account in the Seminar. (1975a, 100–101; translation modified)

These reminders, of which countless other examples could be given, alert us to the effects of the frame, and of the paradoxes in the parergonal logic. Our purpose is not to prove that "The Purloined Letter" functions within a frame (omitted by the Seminar, which can thus be assured of its triangular interior by an active, surreptitious limitation starting from a metalinguistic overview), but to prove that the structure of the framing effects is such that no totalization of the border is even possible. Frames are always framed: thus, by part of their content. Pieces without a whole, "divisions" without a totality—this is what thwarts the dream of a letter without division, allergic to division. (1975a, 99; translation slightly modified)

Here the argument seems to reverse the previous objection; Lacan has eliminated not the frame but the unframability of the literary text. But what Derrida calls "parergonal logic" is paradoxical precisely because both of these incompatible (but not totally contradictory) arguments are equally valid. The total inclusion of the frame is both mandatory and impossible. The frame thus becomes not the borderline between the inside and the outside, but precisely what subverts the applicability of the inside/outside polarity to the act of interpretation.

The frame is, in fact, one of a series of paradoxical "borderline cases"— along with the tympanum and the hymen—through which Derrida has recently been studying the limits of spatial logic as it relates to intelligibility. Lacan, too, has been seeking to displace the Euclidean model of understanding (comprehension, for example, means spatial inclusion) by inventing a "new geometry" by means of the logic of knots. The relation between these two attempts to break out of spatial logic has yet to be articulated, but some measure of the difficulties involved may be derived from the fact that *to break out of* is still a spatial metaphor. The urgency of these undertakings cannot, however, be overestimated, since the logic of metaphysics, of politics, of belief, and of knowledge itself is based on the imposition of definable objective frontiers and outlines whose possibility and/or justifiability are here being put in question. If "comprehension" is the framing of something whose limits are undeterminable, how can we know what we are comprehending? The play on the spatial and the criminal senses of the word *frame* with which we began this section may thus not be as gratuitous as it seemed. And indeed, the question of the fallacies inherent in a Euclidean model of intelligibility, far from being a tangential theoretical consideration here, is central to the very plot of "The Purloined Letter" itself. For it is precisely the notion of space as finite and homogeneous that underlies the Prefect's method of investigation: "I presume you know," he explains, "that, to a properly trained police-agent, such a thing as a 'secret' drawer is impossible. Any man is a dolt who permits a 'secret' drawer to escape him in a search of this kind. The thing is *so* plain. There is a certain amount of bulk—of space—to be accounted for in every cabinet. Then we have accurate rules. The fiftieth part of a line could not escape us." The assumption that what is not seen must be hidden—an assumption Lacan calls the "realist's imbecility"— is based on a falsely objective notion of the act of *seeing*. The polarity "hidden/exposed" cannot alone account for the police's *not* finding the letter—which was entirely exposed, inside out—let alone for Dupin's finding it. A "subjective" element must be added, which subverts the geometrical model of understanding through the interference of the polarity "blindness/sight" with the polarity "hidden/exposed." The same problematic is raised by the story "The Emperor's New Clothes," which Derrida cites as an example of psychoanalysis's failure to go beyond the polarity "hidden/exposed" (in Freud's account). We will return to the letter's "place" later on in this essay, but it is already clear that the "range" of any investigation is located not in geometrical space, but in its implicit notion of what "seeing" is.

What enables Derrida to problematize the literary text's frame is, as we have seen, what he calls "the scene of writing." By this he means two things.

1. *The textual signifier's resistance to being totally transformed into a signified.* In spite of Lacan's attentiveness to the path of the letter in Poe's story as an illustration of the functioning of a signifier, says Derrida, the psychoanalytical reading is still blind to the functioning of the signifier in the narration itself. In reading "The Purloined Letter" as an allegory of the signifier, Lacan, according to Derrida, has made the "signifier" into the story's truth: "The displacement of the signifier is analyzed as a signified, as the recounted object in a short story" (1975a, 48). Whereas, counters Derrida, it is precisely the textual signifier that resists being thus totalized into meaning, leaving an irreducible residue: "The rest, the remnant, would be 'The Purloined Letter,' the text that bears this title, and whose place, like the once more invisible large letters on the map, is not where one was expecting to find it, in the enclosed content of the 'real drama' or in the hidden and sealed interior of Poe's story, but in and as the open letter, the very open letter which fiction is" (1975a, 64).

2. *The actual writings*—the books, libraries, quotations, and previous tales that surround "The Purloined Letter" with a frame of (literary) references. The story begins in "a little back library, or book-closet,"

where the narrator is mulling over a previous conversation on the subject of the two previous instances of Dupin's detective work as told in Poe's two previous tales, the first of which recounted the original meeting between Dupin and the narrator—in a library, of course, where both were in search of the same rare book. The story's beginning is thus an infinitely regressing reference to previous writings. And therefore, says Derrida, "nothing begins. Simply a drifting or a disorientation from which one never moves away" (1975a, 101). Dupin, himself, is in fact a walking library; books are his "sole luxuries," and the narrator is "astonished" at "the vast extent of his reading." Even Dupin's last, most seemingly personal words—the venomous lines he leaves in his substitute letter to the Minister—are a quotation, whose transcription and proper authorship are the last things the story tells us. "But," concludes Derrida, "beyond the quotation marks that surround the entire story, Dupin is obliged to quote this last word in quotation marks, to recount his signature: that is what I wrote to him and how I signed it. What is a signature within quotation marks? Then, within these quotation marks, the seal itself is a quotation within quotation marks. This remnant is still literature" (1975a, 112–13).

It is by means of these two extra dimensions that Derrida intends to show the crumbling, abyssal, nontotalizable edges of the story's frame. Both of these objections, however, are in themselves more problematic and double-edged than they appear. Let us begin with the second. "Literature" in Derrida's demonstration is indeed clearly the beginning, middle, and end—and even the interior—of the purloined letter. But how was this conclusion reached? To a large extent, by listing the books, libraries, and other writings recounted in the story. That is, by following the theme—and not the functioning—of "writing" within "the content of a representation." But if Dupin's signing with a quotation, for example, is for Derrida a sign that "this remnant is still literature," does this not indicate that "literature" has become not the signifier but the signified in the story? If the play of the signifier is really to be followed, does it not play beyond the range of the *seme* "writing"? And if Derrida criticizes Lacan for making the "signifier" into the story's signified, is Derrida not here transforming "writing" into "the written" in much the same way? What Derrida calls "the reconstruction of the scene of the signifier as a signified" seems indeed to be "an inevitable process" in the logic of reading the purloined letter.

Derrida, of course, implicitly counters this objection by protesting—twice—that the textual drifting for which Lacan does not account should not be considered "the *real subject* of the tale," but rather the "remarkable ellipsis" of any subject (1975a, 102). But the question of the seemingly inevitable slipping from the signifier to the signified still remains, and not as an objection to the logic of the frame, but as its fundamental question. For if the "paradoxes and parergonal logic" are such that the frame is always being framed by part of its contents, it is this very slippage between signifier and signified, *acted out* by both Derrida and Lacan against their intentions, which best illustrates those paradoxes. Derrida's justification of his framing of the "Lacan" he is reading as neither being limited to the Seminar nor including Lacan's later work, itself obeys the contradictory logic of the frame. On the one hand, Derrida will study that part of Lacan's work which seems to embody a system of truth even though other writings might put that system in question, and on the other hand this same part of Lacan's work, says Derrida, will probably someday be called the work of the "young Lacan" by "academics eager to divide up *what cannot be divided*" (1975a, 82; translation modified). Whatever Derrida actually thinks he is doing here, his contradictory way of explaining it obeys the paradoxes of parergonal logic so perfectly that this self-subversion may have even been deliberate.

If the question of the frame thus problematizes the object of any interpretation by setting it at an angle or fold (*pli*) with itself, then Derrida's analysis errs not in opposing this paradoxical functioning to Lacan's allegorical reading, but in not following the consequences of its own insight far enough. For example, if it is the frame that makes it impossible for us to know where to begin and when to stop, why does Derrida stop within the limits of the Dupin trilogy? And if the purpose of studying "writing" is to sow an uncanny uncertainty about our position in the abyss, is not the disseminal library Derrida describes still in a way just a bit too comfortable?

"The Purloined Letter," says Derrida, is signed "literature." What does this mean, if not that the letter's contents—the only ones we are allowed to see—are in another text? That the locus of the letter's meaning is not in the letter, but somewhere else? That the context of that meaning is the way in which its context is lacking, both through the explicit designation of a proper origin (Crébillon's *Atrée*) *outside* the text and through a substitute structure from letter to letter, from text to text, and from brother to brother, *within* the text, such that the expressions *outside* and *within* have ceased to be clearly definable? But until we have actually opened that other text, we cannot know the modality of the precise otherness of the abyss to itself, the way in which the story's edges do not simply crumble away.

In order to escape the reduction of the "library" to its thematic presence as a *sign* of writing, let us therefore pull some of the books off the shelves and see what they contain. This is a track neither Lacan nor Derrida has taken, but we will soon see how it in some way enfolds them both.

First of all, the name *Dupin* itself, according to Poe scholars, comes out of Poe's interior library: from the pages of a volume called *Sketches of Conspicuous Living Characters of France* (Philadelphia: Lea and Blanchard, 1841), which Poe reviewed for *Graham's Magazine* during the same month his first Dupin story appeared. André-Marie-Jean-Jacques Dupin, a minor French statesman, is there described as himself a walking library: "To judge from his writings, Dupin must be a perfect living encyclopedia. From Homer to Rousseau, from the Bible to the civil code, from the laws of the twelve tables to the Koran, he has read every thing, retained every thing" (224). Detective Dupin's "origin" is thus multiply bookish. He is a reader whose writer read his name in a book describing a writer as a reader—a reader whose nature can only be described in writing, in fact, as irreducibly double: "He is the personage for whom the painters of political portraits, make the most enormous consumption of antithesis. In the same picture, he will be drawn as both great and little, courageous and timid, trivial and dignified, disinterested and mercenary, restive and pliable, obstinate and fickle, white and black; there is no understanding it" (210). And the writing that serves as the vehicle of this description of written descriptions of double Dupin is itself double: a translation, by a Mr. Walsh, of a series of articles by a Frenchman whose name is not even known to the translator but who is said to call himself "an *homme de rien,* a nobody" (2). "Nobody" thus becomes the proper name of the original author in the series.[8]

But the author of the last word in "The Purloined Letter" is clearly *not* nobody. It is not even Poe; it is Crébillon. When read as the context from which Dupin's letter to the Minister has been purloined, Crébillon's *Atrée* is remarkable not simply because it tells the story of revenge as a symmetrical repetition of the original crime, but because it does so precisely by means of a purloined letter. A *letter* informs King Atreus of the extent of his betrayal and serves as an instrument of his revenge; the King himself has purloined the letter—written by the Queen to her lover, Thyestes, just before her death. The letter reveals that Plisthenes, whom

everyone believes to be Atreus's son, is really the son of his brother
Thyestes. Having kept the letter and its message secret for twenty years,
Atreus plans to force Plisthenes, unaware of his true parentage, to commit patricide. Thwarted in this plan by Plisthenes' refusal to kill the
father of his beloved, Theodamia, who is, unknown to him, his sister,
Atreus is forced to produce the letter, reunite the illicit family, and
transfer his revenge from Plisthenes' patricide to Thyestes' infantophagy.
A queen betraying a king, a letter representing that betrayal being
purloined for purposes of power, an eventual return of that letter to its
addressee, accompanied by an act of revenge which duplicates the original crime—"The Purloined Letter" as a story of repetition is itself a
repetition of the story from which it purloins its last words. The Freudian
"truth" of the repetition compulsion is not simply illustrated *in* the story;
it is illustrated *by* the story. The story obeys the very law it conveys; it is
framed by its own content. And thus "The Purloined Letter" no longer
simply repeats its own "primal scene": what it repeats is nothing less than
a previous story of repetition. The "last word" names the place where the
"nonfirstness" of the "first word" repeats itself.

This is not the only instance of the folding-in of the frame of reference
upon the purloined letter's interior. Another allusion, somewhat more
hidden, is contained in the description of the Minister as someone "who
dares all things, those unbecoming as well as those becoming a man."
These words echo Macbeth's protestation to his ambitious wife: "I dare
do all that may become a man / Who dares do more is none" (1.7). The
reference to *Macbeth* substantiates Lacan's reading of the description of
the Minister as pointing toward femininity; it is indeed Lady Macbeth
who dares to do what is unbecoming a man. And what is Lady Macbeth
doing when we first catch sight of her? She is reading a letter. Not a
purloined letter, perhaps, but one that contains the ambiguous letter of
destiny, committing Macbeth to the murder of the King, whose place
Macbeth will take and whose fate he will inevitably share. Kings seem to
be unable to remain unscathed in the face of a letter—Atreus betrayed by
his wife's letter to his brother; Duncan betrayed by Macbeth's letter to
Lady Macbeth; Macbeth himself betrayed by his own confidence in his
ability to read the letter of his Fate; and of course, the King in "The
Purloined Letter," whose power is betrayed by his not even knowing
about the existence of the letter that betrays him.

The questions raised by all these texts together are legion. What is a
man? Who is the child's father? What is the relation between incest,
murder, and the death of a child? What is a king? How can we read the

letter of our destiny? What is seeing? The crossroads where these stories come together seems to point to the story of what occurred at another crossroads: the tragedy of Oedipus the King. We seem to have returned to our starting point, then, except for one thing: it is no longer "The Purloined Letter" that repeats the story of Oedipus, but the story of Oedipus that repeats all the letters purloined from "The Purloined Letter's" abyssal interior.

But the letter does not stop there. For the very Oedipal reading that Derrida attributes to Lacan is itself, according to Derrida, a purloined letter—purloined by Lacan from Marie Bonaparte's psychobiographical study of the life and works of Edgar Allan Poe: "At the moment when the Seminar, like Dupin, finds the letter where it is to be found, between the legs of the woman, the deciphering of the enigma is anchored in truth. . . . Why then does it find, at the same time that it finds truth, the same meaning and the same topos as Bonaparte when, leaping over the text, she proposes a psychobiographical analysis of 'The Purloined Letter'?" (1975a, 66). In that analysis, Bonaparte sees Dupin's restitution of the letter to the Queen as the return of the missing maternal penis to the mother. The letter's hiding place in the Minister's apartment, moreover, is "almost an anatomical chart" of the female body—which leads Bonaparte to note that Baudelaire's translation of "hung from a little brass knob just beneath the middle of the mantelpiece" as "suspendu à un petit bouton de cuivre—au dessus du manteau de la cheminée" ("*above* the mantelpiece") is "completely wrong" (quoted in 1975a, 68). Bonaparte's frame of reference—the female body—cannot tolerate this error of translation.

A note that Lacan drops on the subject of the letter's position enables Derrida to frame Lacan for neglecting to mention his references: "The question of deciding," says Lacan, "whether he [Dupin] seizes it [the letter] above the mantelpiece as Baudelaire translates, or beneath it, as in the original text, may be abandoned without harm to the inferences of those whose profession is grilling [*aux inférences de la cuisine*]." Lacan's note: "And even to the cook herself" (1972b, 66–67). In this cavalier treatment of Bonaparte as the "cook," Lacan thus "makes clear" to Derrida "that Lacan had read Bonaparte, although the Seminar never alludes to her. As an author so careful about debts and priorities, he could have acknowledged an irruption that orients his entire interpretation, namely, the process of rephallization as the proper course of the letter, the 'return of the letter' restored to its 'destination' after having been found between the legs of the mantelpiece" (1975a, 68). The interpretation of the letter (as the phallus that must be returned to the mother) must itself be returned to the "mother" from whom it has been purloined—Marie Bonaparte. Derrida thus follows precisely the logic he objects to in Lacan, the logic of rectification and correction: "to return the letter to its proper course, supposing that its trajectory is a line, is to correct a deviation, to rectify a divergence, to recall a direction, an authentic line" (1975a, 65). But the mere fact that Derrida's critique repeats the same logic he denounces is in itself less interesting than the fact that this rectification presupposes another, which puts its very foundations in question. For when Lacan says that the question of the exact position of the letter "may be abandoned without harm" to the grillers, Derrida protests, "Without harm? On the contrary, the harm would be decisive, within the Seminar itself: *on* the mantelpiece, the letter could not have been 'between the cheeks of the fireplace,' 'between the legs of the fireplace'" (1975a, 69). Derrida must thus correct Lacan's text, eliminate its apparent contradiction, in order to return the letter of interpretation to its rightful owner. And all this in order to criticize Lacan's enterprise as one of rectification and circular return. If "rectification" as such is to be criticized, it is difficult to determine where it begins and where it ends. In rectifying Lacan's text in order to make it fit into the logic of rectification, Derrida thus problematizes the very status of the object of his criticism.

But if the correction of Lacan's text is itself a mutilation that requires correction, how *are* we to interpret the contradiction between Lacan's description of the Minister's apartment as "an immense female body" (1972b, 66) and his statement that the letter's exact location does not matter? This, it seems to me, is the crux of the divergence between Derrida's and Lacan's interpretation of what the equation "letter = phallus" means.

For Bonaparte, it was precisely the analogy between the fireplace and the female body which led to the letter's phallic function. The phallus was considered as a real, anatomical referent serving as the model for a figurative representation. Bonaparte's frame of reference was thus *reference* itself.

For Derrida, on the other hand, the phallus's frame of reference is "psychoanalytical theory's" way of preserving the phallus's referential status in the act of negating it. In commenting on Lacan's discussion "The Meaning of the Phallus," Derrida writes:

Phallogocentrism is one thing. And what is called man and what is called woman might be subject to it. The more so, we are reminded, since the phallus is neither a phantasy ("imaginary effect") nor an object ("partial, internal, good, bad"), even less the organ, penis or clitoris, which it symbolizes [Lacan 1969, 690]. Androcentrism ought therefore to be something else.

Yet what is going on? The entire phallogocentrism is articulated from the starting-point of a determinate *situation* (let us give this word its full impact) in which the phallus *is* the mother's desire inasmuch as she does not have it. An (individual, perceptual, local, cultural, historical, etc.) situation on the basis of which is developed something called a "sexual theory": in it the phallus is not the organ, penis or clitoris, which it symbolizes; but it does to a larger extent and in the first place symbolize the penis. . . . This consequence had to be traced in order to recognize the meaning [the direction, *sens*] of the purloined letter in the "course *which is proper to it.*" (1975a, 98–99)

Thus, says Derrida, the very nonreferentiality of the phallus, in the final analysis, ensures that the penis is its referent.

Before trying to determine the applicability of this summary to Lacan's actual statements in "The Meaning of the Phallus"—not to mention in the Seminar—let us follow its consequences further in Derrida's critique. From the very first words of "The Purveyor of Truth," psychoanalysis is implicitly being criticized for being capable of finding only itself wherever it looks: "Psychoanalysis, supposing, finds itself" (1975a, 31; translation mine). In whatever it turns its attention to, psychoanalysis seems to recognize nothing but its own (Oedipal) schemes. Dupin finds the letter because "he knows that the letter finally *finds itself* where it must *be found* in order to return circularly and adequately to its proper place. This proper place, known to Dupin and to the psychoanalyst who intermittently takes his place, is the place of castration" (1975a, 60; translation modified). The psychoanalyst's act, then, is one of mere *recognition* of the expected, a recognition that Derrida finds explicitly stated as such by Lacan in the underlined words he quotes from the Seminar: "Just so does the purloined letter, like an immense female body, stretch out across the Minister's office when Dupin enters. But just so does he already *expect to find it* [emphasis mine—J. D.] and has only, with his eyes veiled by green lenses, to undress that huge body" (1975a, 61–62; emphasis and brackets in original).

But if recognition is a form of blindness, a form of violence to the otherness of the object, it would seem that, by eliminating Lacan's suggestion of a possible complication of the phallic scheme, and by lying in wait between the brackets of the fireplace to catch the psychoanalyst at his own game, Derrida, too, is "recognizing" rather than reading. He recognizes, as he himself says, a certain classical conception of psycho-analysis: "From the beginning," writes Derrida early in his study, "*we recognize* the classical landscape of applied psychoanalysis" (1975a, 45; emphasis mine). It would seem that the theoretical frame of reference which governs recognition is a constitutive element in the blindness of any interpretative insight. That frame of reference allows the analyst to frame the author of the text he is reading for practices whose locus is simultaneously beyond the letter of the text and behind the vision of its reader. The reader is framed by his own frame, but he is not even in possession of his own guilt, since it is that which prevents his vision from coinciding with itself. Just as the author of a criminal frame transfers guilt from himself to another by leaving *signs* that he hopes will be read as insufficiently erased traces or referents left by the other, the author of any critique is himself framed by his own frame of the other, no matter how guilty or innocent the other may be.

What is at stake here is therefore the question of the relation between referentiality and interpretation. And here we find an interesting twist: while criticizing Lacan's notion of the phallus as being too referential, Derrida goes on to use referential logic against it. This comes up in connection with the letter's famous "materiality," which Derrida finds so odd. "It would be hard to exaggerate here the scope of this proposition on the indivisibility of the letter, or rather on its identity to itself inaccessi-ble to dismemberment . . . as well as on the so-called materiality of the signifier (the letter) intolerant to partition. But where does this idea come from? A torn-up letter may be purely and simply destroyed, it happens" (1975a, 86–87; translation modified). The so-called mate-riality of the signifier, says Derrida, is nothing but an *idealization*.

But what if the signifier were precisely what put the polarity "mate-riality/ideality" in question? Has it not become obvious that neither Lacan's description ("Tear a letter into little pieces, it remains the letter that it is") nor Derrida's description ("A torn-up letter may be purely and simply destroyed, it happens") can be read literally? Somehow, a rhetor-ical fold (*pli*) in the text is there to trip us up whichever way we turn. Especially since the expression "it happens" (*ça arrive*) uses the very word on which the controversy over the letter's *arrival* at its destination turns.

Our study of the readings of "The Purloined Letter" has thus brought us to the point where the word *letter* no longer has any literality.

But what is a letter that has no literality?

A "Pli" for Understanding

> *I pull in resolution, and begin*
> *To doubt the equivocation of the fiend*
> *That lies like truth.*
>
> *—Macbeth*
>
> *"Why do you lie to me saying you're going*
> *to Cracow so I should believe you're going*
> *to Lemberg, when in reality you* are *going*
> *to Cracow?"*
>
> —Joke quoted by Lacan after Freud

The letter, then, poses the question of its own rhetorical status. It moves rhetorically through the two long, minute studies in which it is presumed to be the literal object of analysis, without having any literality. Instead of simply being explained by those analyses, the rhetoric of the letter problematizes the very rhetorical mode of analytical discourse. And if *literal* means "to the letter," the literal becomes the most problematically figurative mode of all.

As the locus of rhetorical displacement, the letter made its very entrance into Poe's story by "traumatizing" the Prefect's discourse about it. After a series of paradoxes and pleas for absolute secrecy, the Prefect describes the problem created by the letter with a proliferation of *periphrases* which the narrator dubs "the cant of diplomacy":

"Well, then; I have received personal information, from a very high quarter, that a certain document of the last importance has been purloined from the royal apartments. The individual who purloined it is known; this beyond a doubt; he was seen to take it. It is known, also, that it still remains in his possession."

"How is this known?" asked Dupin.

"It is clearly inferred," replied the Prefect, "from the nature of the document, and from the non-appearance of certain results which would at once arise from its passing *out* of the robber's possession—that is to say, from his employing it as he must design in the end to employ it."

"Be a little more explicit," I said.

"Well, I may venture so far as to say that the paper gives its holder a certain power in a certain quarter where such power is immensely valuable." The Prefect was fond of the cant of diplomacy. (Poe 1978, 976)

The letter thus enters the discourse of Poe's story as a rhetorical fold that actually hides nothing, since, although *we* never find out what was written in the letter, presumably the Queen, the Minister, Dupin, the Prefect—who all held the letter in their hands—and even the narrator, who heard what the Prefect read from his memorandum book, *did*. The way in which the letter dictates a series of circumlocutions, then, resembles the way in which the path of the letter dictates the characters' circumvolutions—not that the letter's contents *must* remain hidden, but that the question of whether or not they are revealed is immaterial to the displacement the letter governs. The character and actions of each of the letter's holders are determined by the rhetorical spot it puts them in *whether or not* that spot can be read by the subjects it displaces.

The letter, then, acts as a signifier *not* because its contents are lacking, but because its function is not dependent on the knowledge or non-knowledge of those contents. Therefore, by saying that the letter cannot be divided Lacan does not mean that the phallus must remain intact, but that the phallus, the letter, and the signifier *are not substances*. The letter cannot be divided because it only functions as a division. It is not something with "an *identity* to itself inaccessible to dismemberment" (1975a, 86–87; emphasis mine) as Derrida interprets it; it is a *difference*. It is known only in its effects. The signifier is an articulation in a chain, not an identifiable unit. It cannot be known in itself because it is capable of "sustaining itself *only* in a displacement" (1972b, 59; emphasis mine). It is localized, but only as the nongeneralizable locus of a differential relationship. Derrida, in fact, enacts this law of the signifier in the very act of opposing it:

Perhaps only one letter need be changed, maybe even less than a letter in the expression: "missing from its place" [*manque à sa place*]. Perhaps we need only introduce a written *a*, i.e., without accent, in order to bring out that if the lack *has* its place [*le manque a sa place*] in this atomistic topology of the signifier, that is, if it occupies therein a specific place of definite contours, the order would remain undisturbed. (1975a, 45)

While thus criticizing the hypostasis of a lack—the letter as the substance of an absence (which is not what Lacan is saying)—Derrida is
illustrating what Lacan *is* saying about both the materiality and the
localizability of the signifier as the mark of difference by operating on the
letter as a material locus of differentiation: by removing the little signifier
" ` ," an accent mark which has no meaning in itself.[9]

The question of the nature of the "lack," however, brings us back to
the complexities of the meaning and place of the "phallus." For while it is
quite easy to show the signifier as a "difference" rather than a "lack," the
question becomes much trickier in relation to the phallus. There would
seem to be no ambiguity in Lacan's statement that "clinical observation
shows us that this test through the desire of the Other is not decisive
insofar as the subject thereby learns whether or not he himself has a real
phallus, but insofar as he learns *that the mother does not*" (1966, 693;
translation and emphasis mine). The theory seems to imply that at some
point in human sexuality, a referential moment is unbypassable: the
observation that the mother does not have a penis is necessary. And
therefore it would seem that the "lack" is localizable as the substance of
an absence or a hole. To borrow a joke from Geoffrey Hartman's discussion of certain solutionless detective stories, if the purloined letter is the
mother's phallus, "instead of a whodunit we get a whodonut, a story with
a hole in it" (1975, 206).

rubbing donuts!

But even on this referential level, is the object of observation really a
lack? Is it not instead an interpretation—an interpretation ("castration")
not of a lack but of a *difference?* If what is observed is irreducibly anatomical, what is anatomy here but the irreducibility of difference? Even on
the most elementary level, the phallus is a sign of sexuality as difference,
and not as the presence or absence of this or that organ.

But Lacan defines the phallus in a much more complicated way. For if
the woman is defined as "giving in a love-relation that which she does not
have," the definition of what the woman does not have is not limited to
the penis. At another point in the discussion, Lacan refers to "the gift of
what one does not have" as "love" (1966a, 691/1977, 286). Is "love" here
a mere synonym for the phallus? Perhaps; but only if we modify the
definition of the phallus. Love, in Lacan's terminology, is what is in
question in the "request for love" (*demande d'amour*), which is "unconditional," the "demand for a presence or an absence" (1966a, 691/1977,
286). This *demande* is not only a reference to "what the Other doesn't
have," however. It is also language. And language is what alienates
human desire such that "it is from the place of the Other that the subject's

message is emitted" (1966a, 690/1977, 286). The *demande* is thus a request for the unconditional presence or absence not of an organ but of the Other in answer to the question asked by the subject from the place of the Other. But this *demande* is not yet the definition of "desire." Desire is what is left of the *demande* when all possible satisfaction of "real" needs has been subtracted from it. "Desire is neither the appetite for satisfaction, nor the demand for love, but the difference which results from the subtraction of the first from the second, the very phenomenon of their split [*Spaltung*]" (1966a, 691/1977, 287). And if the phallus as a signifier, according to Lacan, "gives the *ratio* of desire," the definition of the phallus can no longer bear a simple relation either to the body or to language, because it is that which prevents both the body and language from being simple: "The phallus is the privileged signifier of that mark where logos is joined together with the advent of desire" (1966a, 692/1977, 287; all translations in this paragraph mine).

The important word in this definition is *joined*. For if language (alienation of needs through the place of the Other) and desire (the remainder that is left after the subtraction of the satisfaction of real needs from absolute demand) are neither totally separable from each other nor related in the same way to their own division, the phallus is the signifier of the articulation between two very problematic chains. But what is a signifier in this context? "A signifier," says Lacan, "is what represents a subject for another signifier." A signifier represents, then, and what it represents is a subject. But it only does so for another signifier. What does the expression "for another signifier" mean, if not that the distinction between subject and signifier posed in the first part of the definition is being subverted in the second? "Subject" and "signifier" are coimplicated in a definition that is unable either to separate them totally or to fuse them completely. There are three positions in the definition, two of which are occupied by the same word, but that word is differentiated from itself in the course of the definition—because it begins to take the place of the *other* word. The signifier for which the other signifier represents a subject thus acts like a subject because it is the place where the representation is "understood." The signifier, then, situates the place of something like a reader. And the reader becomes the place where representation would be understood if there were any such thing as a place beyond representation; the place where representation is inscribed as an infinite chain of substitutions whether or not there is any place from which it can be understood.

The letter as a signifier is thus not a thing or the absence of a thing, not a word or the absence of a word, not an organ or the absence of an organ, but a *knot* in a structure where words, things, and organs can neither be definably separated nor compatibly combined. This is why the exact representational position of the letter in the Minister's apartment both matters and does not matter. It matters to the extent that sexual anatomical difference creates an irreducible dissymmetry to be accounted for in every human subject. But it does not matter to the extent that the letter is not hidden in geometrical space, where the police are looking for it, or in anatomical space, where a literal understanding of psychoanalysis might look for it. It is located "in" a *symbolic* structure, a structure that can only be perceived in its effects, and whose effects are perceived as repetition. Dupin finds the letter "in" the symbolic order not because he knows where to look, but because he knows *what to repeat*. Dupin's "analysis" is the repetition of the scene that led to the necessity of analysis. It is not an interpretation or an insight, but an act—an act of untying the knot in the structure by the repetition of the act of tying it. The word *analyze,* in fact, etymologically means "untie," a meaning on which Poe plays in his prefatory remarks on the nature of analysis as "that moral activity which *disentangles*." The analyst does not intervene by giving meaning, but by effecting a *dénouement.*

But if the act of (psycho-)analysis has no identity apart from its status as a repetition of the structure it seeks to analyze (to untie), then Derrida's remarks against psychoanalysis as being always ready *mise en abyme* in the text it studies and as being only capable of finding *itself,* are not objections to psychoanalysis but a profound insight into its very essence. Psychoanalysis is, in fact, itself the primal scene it seeks: it is the first occurrence of what has been repeating itself in the patient without ever having occurred. Psychoanalysis is not the interpretation of repetition; it is the repetition of a *trauma of interpretation*—called "castration" or "parental coitus" or "the Oedipus complex" or even "sexuality"—the traumatic deferred interpretation not *of* an event, but *as* an event that never took place as such. The "primal scene" is not a scene but an interpretative infelicity whose result was to situate the interpreter in an intolerable position. And psychoanalysis is the reconstruction of that interpretative infelicity not as its interpretation, but as its first and last act. Psychoanalysis has content only insofar as it repeats the dis-content of what never took place.

But, as Dupin reminds us, "there is such a thing as being too profound. Truth is not always in a well. In fact, as regards the more important knowledge, I do believe that she is invariably superficial" (Mabbot

1978, 2:545). Have we not here been looking beyond Lacan's signifier instead of *at* it? When Lacan insists on the "materiality of the signifier" that does not "admit partition," what is *his* way of explaining it? Simply that the word *letter* is never used with a partitive article: you can have "some mail" but not "some letter."

Language delivers its judgment to whoever knows how to hear it: through the usage of the article as partitive particle. It is there that the spirit—if spirit be living meaning—appears, no less oddly, as more available for quantification than the letter. To begin with meaning itself, which bears our saying: a speech rich with meaning [*plein de signification*], just as we recognize a measure of intention [*de l'intention*] in an act, or deplore that there is no more love [*plus d'amour*]; or store up hatred [*de la haine*] and expend devotion [*du dévouement*], and so much infatuation [*taut d'infatuation*] is easily reconciled to the fact that there will always be ass [*de la cuisse*] for sale and brawling [*du rififi*] among men.

But as for the letter—be it taken as typographical character, epistle, or what makes a man of letters—we will say that what is said is to be understood *to the letter* [*à la lettre*], that *a letter* [*une lettre*] awaits you at the post office, or even that you are acquainted with *letters* [*que vous avez des lettres*]—never that there is *letter* [*de la lettre*] anywhere, whatever the context, even to designate overdue mail. (1972b, 53–54)

If this passage is particularly resistant to translation, that is because its message is in the "superficial" play of the signifier. Like the large letters on the map which are so obvious as to be invisible, Lacan's textual signifier has gone unnoticed in the search for the signified, "signifier."

But the question of translation in connection with a message so obvious that it goes unseen is not an accident here. For in his discussion of Dupin's statement that " 'analysis' conveys 'algebra' about as much as, in Latin, '*ambitus*' implies 'ambition,' '*religio*,' religion, or '*homines honesti*' a set of '*honorable*' men,' " Lacan asks:

Might not this parade of erudition be destined to reveal to us the key words of our drama?[10] Is not the magician repeating his trick before our eyes, without deceiving us this time about divulging his secret, but pressing his wager to the point of really explaining it to us without us seeing a thing. *That* would be the summit of the illusionist's art: through one of his fictive creations to *truly delude us*. (1972b, 50–51)

But the trick does not end here. For has Lacan himself not slipped into the paragraph on the quantification of the letter a parade of "key words" for his reading of the situation? "Full of meaning," "intention," "hatred," "love," "infatuation," "devotion," "ass for sale," and "brawling among men"—all of these words occur as the possible "signifieds" of "The Purloined Letter" in the Seminar. But if the key words of a reading of the story thus occur only in the mode of a play of the signifier, the *difference* between "signifier" and "signified" in Lacan's text, as well as in Poe's, has been effectively subverted. What the reader finally reads when he deciphers the signifying surface of the map of his misreading is: "You have been fooled." And in this discussion of "being fooled" Lacan, far from excluding the narrator, situates him in the dynamic functioning of the text, as a reader *en abyme* duped by Dupin's trick explanations of his technique; a reader who, however, unconscious of the nonsequiturs he is repeating, is so much in awe of his subject that his admiration blinds *us* to the tricky functioning of what he so faithfully transmits.

To be fooled by a text implies that the text is not constative but performative, and that the reader is in fact one of its effects. The text's "truth" puts the status of the reader in question, "performs" him as its "address." Thus "truth" is not what the fiction reveals as a nudity behind a veil. When Derrida calls Lacan's statement that "truth inhabits fiction" an unequivocal expression or revelation of the truth of truth (1975a, 46), he is simply not seeing the performative perversity of the rest of the sentence in which that "statement" occurs: "It is up to the reader to give the letter . . . what he will find as its last word: its destination. That is, Poe's message deciphered and coming back from him, the reader, from the fact that, in reading it, he is able to say of himself that he is not more feigned than truth when it inhabits fiction" (1969, 10; translation mine). The play between truth and fiction, reader and text, message and feint, has become impossible to unravel into an "unequivocal" meaning.

We have thus come back to the question of the letter's destination and of the meaning of the enigmatic "last words" of Lacan's Seminar. "The sender," writes Lacan, "receives from the receiver his own message in reverse form. Thus it is that what the 'purloined letter,' nay, the 'letter in sufferance' means is that a letter always arrives at its destination" (1972b, 72). The reversibility of the direction of the letter's movement between sender and receiver has now come to stand for the fact, underlined by Derrida as if it were an *objection* to Lacan, that there is no position from which the letter's message can be read as an object: "no neutralization is possible, no general point of view" (1975a, 106). This is the same "discovery" that psychoanalysis makes—that the analyst is involved (through transference) in the very "object" of his analysis.

Everyone who has held the letter—or even beheld it—including the

narrator, has ended up having the letter addressed to him as its destination. The reader is comprehended by the letter; there is no place from
which he can stand back and observe it. Not that the letter's meaning is
subjective rather than objective, but that the letter is precisely that
which subverts the polarity "subjective/objective," that which makes
subjectivity into something whose position in a structure is situated by
an object's passage through it. The letter's destination is thus *wherever it is
read:* the place it assigns to its reader as his own partiality. Its destination
is not a place, decided a priori by the sender, because the receiver is the
sender, and the receiver is whoever receives the letter, including nobody.
When Derrida says that a letter can miss its destination and be disseminated, he reads "destination" as a place that preexists the letter's movement. But if, as Lacan shows, the letter's destination is not its literal
addressee, nor even whoever possesses it, but whoever is possessed by it,
then the very disagreement over the meaning of "reaching the destination" is an *illustration* of the nonobjective nature of that "destination."
The rhetoric of Derrida's differentiation of his own point of view from
Lacan's enacts that law:

Thanks to castration, the phallus always stays in its place in the transcendental topology we spoke of earlier. It is indivisible and indestructible
there, like the letter which takes its place. And that is why the *interested*
presupposition, never proved, of the letter's materiality as indivisibility
was indispensable to this restricted economy, this circulation of property.

The difference I am *interested* in here is that, a formula to be read
however one wishes, the lack has no place of its own in dissemination.
(1975a, 63; translation modified, emphasis mine)

The play of "interest" in this expression of difference is too interesting
not to be deliberate. The opposition between the "phallus" and "dissemination" is not between two theoretical objects but between two
interested positions. And if sender and receiver are merely the two poles
of a reversible message, then Lacan's very substitution of *destin* for *dessein*
in the Crébillon quotation—a misquotation that Derrida finds revealing
enough to end his analysis upon—*is,* in fact, the quotation's message.
The sender (*dessein*) and the receiver (*destin*) of the violence which passes
between Atreus and Thyestes are equally subject to the violence the letter
is.

The reflexivity between receiver and sender is, however, not an expression of symmetry in itself, but only an evocation of the interdepen-
dence of the two terms, of the *question* of symmetry as a *problem* in the

transferential structure of all reading. As soon as accident or exteriority or time or repetition enters into that reflexivity—that is to say, from the beginning—"Otherness" becomes in a way the letter's sender. The message I am reading may be either my own (narcissistic) message backward or the way in which that message is always traversed by its own otherness to itself or by the narcissistic message of the other. In any case, the letter is in a way the materialization of my death. And once these various possibilities are granted, none of them can function in isolation. The question of the letter's origin and destination can no longer be asked as such. And whether this is because it involves two, three, or four terms must remain undecidable.

The sentence "a letter always arrives at its destination" can thus either be simply pleonastic or variously paradoxical; it can mean "the only message I can read is the one I send," "wherever the letter is, is its destination," "when a letter is read, it reads the reader," "the repressed always returns," "I exist only as a reader of the other," "the letter has no destination," and "we all die." It is not any one of these readings, but all of them and others in their incompatibility, which repeat the letter in its way of reading the act of reading. Far from giving us the Seminar's final truth, these last words enact the impossibility of any ultimate analytical metalanguage.

If it at first seemed possible to say that Derrida was opposing the unsystematizable to the systematized, "chance" to psychoanalytical "determinism," or the "undecidable" to the "destination," the positions of these oppositions seem now to be reversed; Lacan's apparently unequivocal ending says only its own dissemination, while "dissemination" has erected itself into a kind of "last word." But these oppositions are themselves misreadings of the dynamic functioning of what is at stake here. For if the letter is what dictates the rhetorical indetermination of any theoretical discourse about it, then the oscillation between unequivocal statements of undecidability and ambiguous assertions of decidability is one of the letter's inevitable effects. For example, the "indestructibility of desire," which could be considered a psychoanalytical belief in the return of the *same,* turns out to name repetition as the repetition not of sameness but of *otherness,* resulting in the dissemination of the subject. And "symbolic determination" is not opposed to "chance": it is what emerges as the *syntax* of chance. [11] But "chance," out of which springs that which repeats, cannot in any way be "known," since "knowing" is one of its effects. We can therefore never be sure whether or not "chance" itself exists at all. "Undecidability" can no more be used as a last word than "destination." "Car," said Mallarmé, "il y a et il n'y a pas de hasard." The "undeterminable" is not opposed to the determinable; "dissemination" is not opposed to repetition. If we could be sure of the difference between the determinable and the undeterminable, the undeterminable would be comprehended within the determinable. What is undecidable is whether a thing is decidable or not.

As a final fold in the letter's performance of its reader, it should perhaps be noted that, in this discussion of the letter as what prevents me from knowing whether Lacan and Derrid are really saying the same thing or only enacting their own differences from themselves, my own theoretical "frame of reference" is precisely, to a very large extent, the writings of Lacan and Derrida. The frame is thus framed again by part of its content; the sender again receives his own message backward from the receiver. And the true otherness of the purloined letter of literature has perhaps still in no way been accounted for.

NOTES

1. Jacques Derrida, published in French in *Poétique* 21 (1975b) and somewhat reduced in *Yale French Studies* 52; unless otherwise indicated, references are to the English version (1975a). Lacan quotations in English are taken, unless otherwise indicated, from the partial translation in *Yale French Studies* 48 (1972b).

2. Such a concatenation could jokingly be called, after the nursery rhyme, "This is the text that Jacques built." But in fact, it is precisely this kind of sequence or chain that is in question here.

3. We will speak about this bracketed signature later; for the time being, it stands as a sign that Derrida's signature has indeed been added to our round robin.

4. Jacques Derrida, *Positions* (1972, 112–13; translation is my own); ibid., 113.

5. Jacques Lacan, *Ecrits* ("Points", 1969, 11; translation is my own).

6. Cf. Lacan's description in *Ecrits* (1966a, 60), of the "effect of disorientation, or even of great anxiety," provoked by these exercises.

7. Some idea of the possibilities for misunderstanding inherent in this question can be gathered from the following: In order to show that psychoanalysis *represses* "writing" in a logocentric way, Derrida quotes Lacan's statement against tape recorders: "But precisely because it comes to him through an alienated form, even a retransmission of his own recorded discourse, be it from the mouth of his

own doctor, cannot have the same effects as psychoanalytical interlocution." This Derrida regards as a *condemnation* of the "simulacrum," a "disqualification of recording or of repetition in the name of the living and present word." But what does Lacan actually *say?* Simply that a tape recording *does not have the same effects* as psychoanalytical interlocution. Does the fact that psychoanalysis is a technique based on verbal interlocution automatically reduce it to a logocentric error? Is it not equally possible to regard what Lacan calls "full speech" as being *full* of precisely what Derrida calls *"writing"*?

8. In a final twist to this *mise en abyme* of writing, the words "by L. L. de Loménie" have been penciled into the Yale library's copy of this book under the title in a meticulous nineteenth-century hand, as the book's *"supplément d'origine."*

9. It is perhaps not by chance that the question here arises of whether or not to put the accent on the letter *a*. The letter *a* is perhaps the purloined letter par excellence in the writings of all three authors: Lacan's "objet *a*," Derrida's *différance,* and Edgar Poe's middle initial, *A,* taken from his foster father, John Allan.

10. *Ambitus* means "detour"; *religio,* "sacred bond"; *homines honesti,* "decent men." Lacan expands upon these words as the "key words" of the story by saying: "All of this . . . does not imply that because the letter's secrecy is indefensible, the betrayal of that secret would in any sense be honorable. The *honesti homines,* decent people, will not get off so easily. There is more than one *religio,* and it is not slated for tomorrow that sacred ties shall cease to rend us in two. As for *ambitus:* a detour, we see, is not always inspired by ambition" (1972b, 58).

11. This is what the mathematical model in the "Introduction" of the Seminar clearly shows; beginning with a totally arbitrary binary series, a syntax of regularity emerges from the simple application of a law of combination to the series. When it is objected that that syntax *is not,* unless the subject *remembers* the series, Lacan responds in *Ecrits* (1966a, 43): "That is just what is in question here: it is less out of anything real . . . than precisely out of *what never was,* that what repeats itself springs"; translation mine. Memory could thus be considered not as a *condition* of repetition, but as one of its syntactic effects. What we call a random series is, in fact, already an *interpretation,* not a given; it is not a materialization of chance itself, but only of something which obeys our conception of the laws of probability.

11 ❧ Structures of Exemplarity in Poe, Freud, Lacan, and Derrida

IRENE HARVEY

Jacques Lacan (1966a) claimed that Edgar Allan Poe's story "The Purloined Letter" could *exemplify* a truth found by Freud that came to be known as "repetition automatism."[1] Jacques Derrida (1980) insists, however, that within Lacan's reading of Freud in general (as *exemplified* by Lacan's analysis of Poe) there lurks an array of traditional Western metaphysical assumptions that Lacan's text thus exemplifies concerning the nature of the sign, the privilege of the phone or voice over writing, and the meaning of Being as presence, to name only a few.[2] Johnson's analysis (1977) of the differences between Derrida and Lacan, as exemplified in their differences over Poe, in turn concludes that both Derrida and Lacan exemplify an essential structure of textuality called by deMan "undecidability" or the self-deconstructive nature of texts.[3] Hence her analysis finds that "Derrida's own reading of Lacan's text repeats precisely the crimes of which he accuses it." Further, she claims that "Derrida dismisses Lacan's 'style.'" Finally, she states: "The fact that Derrida repeats the very gestures he is criticizing does not in itself invalidate his criticism of their *effects,* but it does problematize his statement condemning their *existence*" (1977, 465).

My analysis will take issue with Johnson's, Derrida's, and Lacan's notions of exemplarity, which inhabit, orient, and structure all three analyses. Although a theory of exemplarity is employed in these analyses, this theory is itself never thematized or articulated. I will thus begin with Derrida's objections to Lacan's reading of Poe and with Derrida's use of Lacan's text as an *example*. I should add that to me exemplarity in this case signifies a structure of representation, signification, and transference. Transforming something into an example of something else can be seen as on the one hand, making it into a *sign* for something else and, on the other, making it into a *case* or a particular instance of something more general for which it stands and which, as an example or illustration, it concretizes.

Derrida suggests that Lacan's reading of Poe suffers from three reductions: of the function of the narrator; of fiction to truth; and of the signifier to the signified. Although Lacan does not explicitly thematize them, his reasons for making these reductions are a function of his entrapment within a finite system of conceptuality that organizes his discourse. The finite system that organizes all interpretation, understanding, and analysis in the West is what Derrida, following Heidegger, calls "metaphysics" (see Harvey 1983).

There are two ways, Derrida argues, that Lacan has "reduced the narrator" in the Poe story. First, his function has been reduced to "merely doubling commentator" (1980, 456; my translation). The narrator, Derrida argues, does not play a constitutive role in the drama in Lacan's reading, but rather simply represents, retells, reproduces a series of events that have already occurred. This structure is, not by chance, precisely that of Western metaphysics' notion of the sign and, in turn, of its concept of writing as merely a sign for speech. Derrida's early work, in particular, is focused on the target of changing the concept of the sign, of representation and of writing. He insists that the definition of the sign as merely a sign for something else does not adequately represent or illustrate what a sign actually is and does. The traditional meaning also entails an extrinsic or external relation between a sign and what it stands for; it entails a priority of value to the origin/telos of that sign and in turn a reducibility of the sign with respect to that origin/telos, such that once reached via the sign, this "supplement" can in turn be dispensed with. Further, he claims: "The notion of the sign always implies within itself the distinction between signifier [sound-image] and signified [concept], even if, as Saussure argues, they are distinguished simply as the two faces of one and the same leaf" (1974b, 11).

Returning to Derrida's localization of this issue within Lacan's reading of Poe, we find that Lacan's treatment of the narrator and the narration, or the narrated, is mediated precisely by this concept of the sign. That is, in short, the narrator relates externally to the narrated and does not play a part in the constitution of events that have already occurred, which he is retelling or recounting. He is instead a transparent medium through which these events are presented to us, the readers. As Derrida says: "One might have thought, at a given moment, that Lacan was prepared to take account of the narration (narrating) of the complex structure of the scene of writing which is in play there, of the curious place of the narrator. But once this moment has intervened, the analytic deciphering excludes it, neutralizes it or more precisely . . . an effect of neutralizing exclusion is dictated by the narrator (narration as 'commentary')" (1980, 456; my translation). Hence, as Johnson has pointed out, Derrida seems to be accusing Lacan of having reduced the signifier to the signified by an act of neutralization or exclusion.

In response to this analysis of Lacan, I suggest that, on the contrary, Lacan does *not* exclude the narrator or the act of narration itself; nor does he instill, albeit implicitly, his analysis within the classical Western metaphysical tradition. Let us begin with an assumption made by Derrida. He concludes the quotation above with a parallel between Lacan's narrator (in Poe's story) and mere commentary or the narrator playing the role of commentator. What Derrida means by "commentary," however, is not the same as what Lacan actually does with Poe's narrator. First, let us consider Derrida's sense of "commentator." In the work of deconstruction, Derrida insists there are two moments or stages. One entails a more traditional reading of the text such that the author's intention—the *declared* and stated argument—is brought to light (1974b, 158). The second stage entails an analysis of the *way* this claim is made in and by the text and hence focuses more on the *described* level—what is uncontrolled by the author and in turn has been shown to belie those same explicitly stated claims elaborated at step one. This first stage of the deconstructive project Derrida likens to "doubling commentary," as in the following statement concerning his strategy:

This question is therefore not only of Rousseau's writing but also of our reading. We should begin by taking rigorous account of this *being held within [prise]* or this *surprise:* the writer writes *in* a language and *in* a logic whose proper system, laws, and life his discourse by definition cannot dominate absolutely. He uses them only by letting himself, after a fashion and up to a point, be governed by the system. And the reading must always aim at a certain relationship, unperceived by the writer, between what he commands and what he does not command of the patterns of language that he uses. This relationship is . . . a signifying structure that critical reading should *produce*. (1974b, 158)

On method:

To produce this signifying structure obviously cannot consist of re-producing, by the effaced and respectful doubling of commentary, the conscious, voluntary, intentional relationship that the writer institutes in his exchanges with the history to which he belongs thanks to the element of language. This moment of doubling commentary should no doubt have its place in a critical reading. To recognize and respect all its classical exigencies is not easy and requires all the instruments of traditional criticism. Without this recognition and this respect, critical production would risk developing in any direction at all and authorize itself to say almost anything. But this indispensable guardrail has always only protected, it has never *opened*, a reading. (1974b, 158)

Thus it is clear that the "moment of doubling commentary" for Derrida takes us back to a classical tradition of reading and, indeed, one could find a certain brand of hermeneutics situated precisely here: a reading guided by authorial intent, the voluntary, willful, and conscious relation an author has with his or her text and tradition of signifiers and signifieds. It is this structure as a whole that Derrida labels "commentary" and that he attributes to Lacan's treatment of the narrator as "respectful doubling" of that which has already been said, done, or intended. Let us now consider what Lacan says concerning the narrator and his delineation of this function in terms other than those suggested by Derrida.

Lacan begins by speaking of the narration as that which "doubles the drama with a commentary without which no *mis en scène* would be possible" (1972b, 41). But he continues to articulate more precisely what "doubling commentary" means for him in the following way:

Let us say that [without the narration] the action would remain, properly speaking, invisible from the pit—aside from the fact that the dialogue would be expressly and by dramatic necessity devoid of whatever meaning it might have for an audience: in other words, nothing of the drama could be grasped, neither seen nor heard, without, dare we say, the twilighting which the narration, in each scene, casts on the point of view that one of the actors had while performing it. (1972b, 41)

The functions of the narrator, not simply the narrated, for Lacan thus include the following: making visible what otherwise would remain invisible; giving meaning to the dialogue; and the "twilighting" that is cast on the point of view that one of the actors had while performing the action. In short, commentary or narration for Lacan is far from simply reproductive, representative, or external to what it "signifies," reproduces, or represents. Rather, the narrator plays a *constitutive* and *transformative* role disclosing what is, giving it meaning for the first time, and instituting an ambiguity in the "point of view" of the actors that enriches its meaning possibilities and casts a shadow upon the "pure presence" of the event. In addition, rather than falling into the "metaphysics of presence" or using and being used by the traditional concept of the sign in his "reduction of the narrator," it seems to me that Lacan has precisely avoided such "traps." I might add that Johnson's view supports Derrida's reading though she finds him "equally guilty," which to me seems incorrect on both counts.

Derrida's second objection to Lacan's reading of Poe—also concerning the narrator—focuses on the transformation of the particular narrator into a "general narrator." Thus we have Lacan accused of making the narrator into a concept that neutralizes once again the constitutive roles he plays and also invokes a metaphysics of presence behind the scenes. Derrida's claim runs as follows: "First time. The exclusion is very clear, facilitated by the text of Poe. . . . It is the moment of that which Lacan calls *exactitude.* The narrator is named "general narrator," he is like the neutral, homogeneous transparent element of the story" (1980, 457; my translation). Hence the structure of the narrative function is once again reduced to that of an extrinsic and external sign that effaces itself, becomes transparent and neutral, in the very act of representation or signification. The metaphysics of presence is illustrated here, since "presence," according to Derrida (1974a, 49–53), has always been the meaning of Being, the structure of truth and the distance as no distance at all between logos and truth, mind and being, meaning and truth. The realm of meaning, intelligibility, of the signified, of the concept, never depends on the signifier, the word writing, the sign or materiality according to Derrida's metaphysics. Rather, the means of representing this *signified* can always be discarded and disqualified, neutralized. Hence Lacan's transformation of the narrator into a "general narrator" with its neutralizing ramifications performs an *exemplary* illustration of this same reductive structure that characterizes Western metaphysics. I also disagree with this rendition of Lacan and will suggest that far from constructing such a metaphysical concept of the general narrator, Lacan sustains multiple narrators, each of whom adds something to the "story" narrated, rather than simply reproducing the same.

First, Lacan himself says that our story is multiply narrated in the following ways: the narrative *by the Queen* to the Prefect of Police; the narrative *by the Prefect* to Detective Dupin; and the narrative *by Dupin's friend* and associate. This latter is the one that indeed Lacan chooses to call the "general narrator," and he articulates this one as "the double and even triple subjective filter through which that scene comes to us" (1972b, 47). This narration of a narration of a narration of an event is testament for Lacan that: "The fact that the message is thus *re*transmitted assures us of what may by no means be taken for granted: that it *belongs* to the *dimension of language*" (1972b, 48; my emphasis). This "dimension of language" means much more than the traditional metaphysical concept of the sign, and hence also much more than a reduction of narration to what is narrated. It is perhaps true that the narrator as the speaking subject in these situations is not the focus of Lacan's inquiry per se, but this is not to say that the structure of narration and its essential relation to language—the constitutive role narration plays in the "presentation" of meanings—are not his concern or that he has reduced them. On the contrary, he continues his articulation of the significance of the message belonging to the dimension of language with what appears to be a digression on the nature of the language of the bees. The common referent for two subjects engaged in communication can be established with respect to a mere "pointing" to an object naturally given for both of them. This "communion" with respect to the "common object" of the "talk" (language of bees) is no longer possible once communication has reached the level of the symbolic, Lacan insists. As he says:

But such communication is not transmissible in symbolic form. It may be maintained only in relation with the object. In such a manner it may bring together an indefinite number of subjects in a common "ideal": the communication of one subject with another within the crowd thus constituted will nonetheless remain irreducibly mediated by an ineffable relation.

This digression is not only a recollection of principles . . . in determining the scope of *what speech repeats,* it prepares the question of what symptoms repeat. (1972b, 48; my emphasis)

Thus pure repetition of the same message about the same object or what requires an external relation of the sign to thing signified is not Lacan's claim here. Quite the reverse, contrary to Derrida's interpretation.

The "general narrator" also brings in another dimension, Lacan claims, and this is concerned with the *indirect telling of events,* or the structure of narration itself. This structure, he says, "sifts out the linguistic dimension and the general narrator, by duplicating it, *'hypothetically'* adds nothing to it. But its role in the second dialogue is entirely different" (1972b, 48; my emphasis). It is clear by now that the "hypothetically" means precisely the reverse, in fact. In addition, the general narrator's role is even more constitutive in the second dialogue of the story, Lacan will claim. The details of this claim need not concern us here, since our focus is rather the question of the exemplarity of the narrator in general that in Lacan's reading, from Derrida's point of view, does not seem to be justified. If anything, what this structure of narration exemplifies is an escape from those classical Western metaphysical dictates that Derrida is concerned to deconstruct. It may well be that Lacan and Derrida are closer theoretically than either would admit—and especially than Derrida's analysis might seem to indicate, as Johnson has claimed—but, I would add, not for the reasons she gives. It is not that Derrida falls into the same metaphysical "trap" that Lacan was thought to fall into, but rather that both are articulating, in different ways and different contexts, a new relation of the subject to the sign, of the signified to the signifier, and of the text to truth. But the structure of these relations may, as I shall attempt to show later, not be so homogeneous either.

Derrida (1980, 442–47) also objects to Lacan's use of fiction to *exemplify* a truth in general and, in particular, for the field of psychoanalysis. It is a charge that Derrida equally levels at Freud and *his* transformation of fiction or literature into a sign or example, indeed an "illustrative example" of a truth that: inhabits that same fiction; yet transcends it and stands apart from it as a more general conceptual and abstract essence; and is in turn considered as the condition of possibility of that same fiction. I shall once again consider Derrida's claims and then suggest another possible reading of Lacan's text in particular.

To set the stage for his attack on Lacan's use of fiction, Derrida illustrates a parody of the use of fiction by Freud himself. This example concerns the story by Hans Christian Andersen entitled "The Emperor's New Clothes." In the section "Typical Dreams," in *The Interpretation of*

Dreams, Freud introduces this story as a parallel to dreams of nakedness and embarrassment in the following way:

The embarrassment of the dreamer and the indifference of the onlookers offer us, when taken together, a contradiction of the kind that is so common in dreams. It would after all be more in keeping with the dreamer's feelings if strangers looked at him in astonishment and derision or with indignation. But this objectionable feature of the situation has, I believe, been got rid of by wish-fulfillment. . . . We possess an interesting piece of evidence that the dream in the form in which it appears—partly distorted by wish-fulfillment—has not been rightly understood. For it has become the basis [*die Grundlage*] of a fairy tale which is familiar to us all in Hans Andersen's version, *The Emperor's New Clothes.* . . . [This] fairy tale tells us how two imposters weave the Emperor a costly garment which, they say, will be visible only to persons of virtue and loyalty. The Emperor walks out in this invisible garment, and all the spectators, intimidated by the fabric's power to act as a touchstone, pretend not to notice the Emperor's nakedness.

    This is just the situation in our dream. (1953b, 243)

    Freud goes on to discuss origins of neurotic exhibitionism in children, obsessions, and phobias. Derrida, however, suggests that Freud has, unbeknown to himself, revealed the very structure of his concept of truth here—one that also typifies Western metaphysics, I might add. This notion of truth—as exhibitionism, making nude, unveiling, uncovering, revealing, disclosing—is itself problematized by Freud's own analysis of exhibitionism. Derrida's claim runs thus: "Exhibitionism, making nude, undressing, unveiling, one is familiar with the gymnastics: it is the metaphor of truth. One could equally well say the metaphor of metaphor, the truth of truth, the truth of metaphor. When Freud understands, 'to denude'—he foresees *the truth of the text.* This will be arranged from its original contents to its *naked* truth, but also to the truth as nudity" (1980, 443; my translation). Thus Freud's own exemplary structure reveals, Derrida claims, a parody of the metaphysical notion of truth as "making nude." Freud does this, in fact, while using a vehicle that is itself called *fiction.* The condition of the possibility of the use of fiction to illustrate a truth, for Freud, is that the truth exhibited therein exists apart from and prior to that same fictive example, be that *Hamlet, Oedipus,* or "The Emperor's New Clothes." Thus the role of fiction for Freud is structurally the same as that of the sign (and writing) for the tradition of metaphysics: fiction is not constitutive but only representative, a mere signifier of a signified that exists *independent* of that same signifier.

With respect to Lacan's use of the Poe story, Derrida finds the same structural reduction in the name of exemplarity in operation. Lacan does explicitly claim the following, and Derrida makes much of this: "We have decided *to illustrate* [*à illustrer*] for you today *the truth* which may be drawn from that moment in Freud's thought under study—namely, that it is the symbolic order which is constitutive for the subject—by *demonstrating* [*demontrant*] in a story the decisive orientation which the subject receives from the itinerary of a signifier" (1972b, 40; my emphasis). Thus we have a *truth* already in existence (revealed in advance) and an *example* of that truth in the form of a "fictive" story that will in turn be used to *illustrate* that same truth. In short, we have the abstract idea, its fall into materiality, specificity, and particularity, and the return to the idea as a concrete universal: a typical Hegelian strategy and one Derrida will take exception to.[4] The issue, as Johnson has described it (1977, 464–65, 480–81), is not only the *frame* or framing of the problem as a choice between the priority of truth or fiction, but rather, it seems to me, that Derrida aims to place this choice in question by insisting that the fictive is not reducible to a truth for which it stands (Derrida 1980, 442, 447, 449, 453–55). Fiction (and here we might say literature, since Derrida uses them interchangeably) is not a mere sign, just as writing is not a mere medium for a message it carries from one place (or person) to another and delivers (free of charge). Rather, Derrida claims that the "scene of writing," here fiction, is reduced by Lacan in his teleological trajectory (in order to illustrate a truth) organized by a structure of exemplarity. Thus it is in this context, as Johnson has pointed out, that Derrida accuses Lacan of having "reduced the signifier to a signified" and hence of betraying his own claim that the place of the subject is governed by that of the signifier (Derrida 1980, 446, 468–69). We shall return to this, but first let us turn to Poe's text to investigate the relation of fiction to truth for him.

"The Purloined Letter" should first of all be situated in its context (as Derrida suggests [1980, 487, 489] but does not do) as the third in a sequence or trilogy of stories. The first story begins with a discourse concerning the differences between analysis and calculation as methods of investigation.[5] Two and a half pages later, Poe introduces a "narration" that, he says, will serve as a "commentary" in order to illustrate and exemplify the theoretical discourse with which he has hitherto been preoccupied.[6] Regardless of this structure as a "literary technique," it is clear that one could read Poe's "story" as itself exemplifying this structure of exemplification that Derrida is criticizing in Freud and Lacan and that I am aiming to articulate here.

In the second story, we once again have a reference to another discourse that seems to parallel the "main story." This time Poe refers us to a "real event" that occurred in New York and that serves as "the basis for his tale." As he says: "Herein, under *pretence* of relating the fate of a Parisian *grisette,* the author has *followed,* in minute detail, the essential, while merely paralleling the inessential facts of the *real* murder of Mary Rogers. *Thus all argument founded upon the fiction is applicable to the truth:* and the investigation of the truth was the object" (Mabbott 1978, 3:723; my emphasis). Thus Poe, on the one hand, bases his story on a true account of a murder and follows the details (the essential ones) exactly, yet he also goes beyond the facts (to fiction) and solves the case that in "real life" had never been solved. In turn he suggests that in the end the *fiction* can return to be *applied* to the *true* situation and perhaps indeed *reveal* what had hitherto been concealed and remained a secret. It is thus not clear that one could say univocally that Poe's story is *either* truth or fiction, either the model or the modeled, either the frame or the framed, as Derrida would put it.

Finally, in our third story, the direct focus of Derrida's and Lacan's controversy, Poe continues his project, which he says he had begun in the first story and indeed had already given birth to in the second story. This project is the depicting of the character and idiosyncratic talents of Dupin, the detective.

When, in an article entitled, "The Murders in the Rue Morgue," I *endeavored,* about a year ago, *to depict* some very remarkable features in the mental character of my friend, the Chevalier C. Auguste Dupin, it did not occur to me that I should ever resume the subject. This *depicting of character constituted my design;* and this design was fulfilled in the train of circumstances brought to instance Dupin's idiosyncrasy. I might have adduced *other examples,* but I should have proven no more. (Mabbott 1978, 3:724; my emphasis)

And Poe continues, giving a rationale, as we have discussed, for his second story beyond his claim here. All of this is intended to show that, for our purposes, the third story must be understood within this more general context (Poe's own). What this more general context (or frame) shows, however, is not, as Derrida has insisted, that fiction necessarily forms the framework or context in which the truth is found and must necessarily be situated. Rather, I suggest that Poe's own stories problematize the distinction Derrida needs in order to launch his objection at Lacan—of reducing fiction to truth and, in turn, the signifier to the signified. Instead of the situation being "undecidable" (between Derrida's Poe and Lacan's, as Johnson suggests), I consider Poe himself and the structure of his stories to be *illustrating* exactly what Derrida is arguing for, and arguing against with respect to Lacan. That is, fiction and truth relate reciprocally as example/exemplified in such a way that neither is in the end decipherable as the origin or source of the other. The possible objection—that Poe is playing with a semblance of truth—can be overruled here, since nonetheless this "play" as a whole illustrates, or exemplifies, precisely this reciprocity or cybernetic relation between truth and fiction.

Derrida's final objection and most general claim concerning Lacan's text is, as I mentioned above, the reduction of the signifier to the signified (1980, 455). This reduction, as I have shown, characterizes the tradition of Western metaphysics, and thus Lacan's work can be used (and indeed is, by Derrida) as an illustration of how even he (Lacan) is controlled by a structure of which he is unaware (apparently).

To substantiate his claim, Derrida uses the case of the missing narrator, the general narrator, and the reduction of fiction to truth, all of which I have objected to above. Let me add one final note, though, at a more general level, where I feel Derrida has omitted a crucial point in his analysis of Lacan. The level of the signifier (the form, the sound image, the structure) of Lacan's text is traversed, as Derrida himself has shown, by a structure of *exemplarity* that I insist is never problematized by either Derrida or Lacan (or Johnson). I have shown that Poe's text, the trilogy as a whole, is also suspiciously characterized by a similar if not identical structure of *exemplarity.* The particular case, details, and examples are always invoked as illustrations of some more general trait, characteristic, or theory, and hence Poe too uses *exemplarity* as a method that organizes his "fiction." The reduction Derrida is concerned with at this level is of writing—indeed, what he calls the "scene of writing"—of the signifier and hence of the form and frame of the argument, not its content or semantic intent. Now if the form of Lacan's text (his writing) is itself homologous with that of Poe, how then can one claim that Lacan has reduced Poe's text? Or that Lacan has transformed the signifier into a signified? Or a sound image into a concept? Have I not shown that the structure of exemplarity inhabits both Poe's and Lacan's texts (with respect to the relations of fiction to truth, in particular) as a constitutive feature and thus that they are indeed homologous in the most general terms?

Thus it appears that Johnson's claim might be substantiated, that "Derrida's own reading of Lacan's text repeats precisely the crimes of which he accuses it," and that "Derrida dismisses Lacan's 'style'" (1977, 465). I suggest, however, that it is not Lacan's "style" that Derrida *misses* here, nor does Derrida reduce the signifier to signified in his reading of Lacan; rather, Derrida's frame of analysis is restricted to the third story alone, though it is he himself who suggests that we must take the entire trilogy into account. Although he suggests it, he does not in fact do it, as I mentioned above. The problem then, as I shall proceed to demonstrate, is that Derrida's analysis does not adhere to his own principles for that analysis. It is this irony or paradox that I shall address now.

Deconstruction, or Derrida's strategy of analysis, though indeed different each time he performs it, nonetheless sustains a certain pattern and adheres to a general set of principles.[7] The pattern includes a search for metaphysical presuppositions in the text, an analysis of what is explicitly *excluded* (and stated as such in the text) and its relation to what is included, and a study of the strategy the author adopts in order to make his or her claims. Last, the implicit and unthematized level of the text is thematized or made explicit, or both. The principles take on a form of directives or guidelines for deconstruction, and they include the following, as Derrida himself has articulated them:

(i) to reveal the economy of the written text;
(ii) to show the relationship between metaphysics and non-metaphysics;
(iii) to reveal the relationship between what a writer commands and does not command of the patterns of language that he/she uses;
(iv) to show the relation between the declared (thematized) and the described (unthematized) levels of the text. (1974b, 149, 158)

This last injunction, used explicitly in Derrida's deconstruction of Rousseau, is particularly relevant in this context. The *declared* level is the one that can be revealed by "doubling commentary" via the "classical and traditional modes of criticism." It is also the level of the text that coincides with the intended, voluntary, explicit, and thematized claims made by the author. It is the level of the content, of the semantic dimension of the text, of the "concept" or meaning. The second step in the deconstructive analysis reveals the *way* this content is expressed; it reveals the "style" of the author and what is not under his or her control. It is, in short, the level of analysis that treats the patterns made by the *signifier* apart from the signified. One could (using outdated terminology) call this level the *structure* of the text. Further, deconstruction is concerned with the *relation* between these levels—*between* what is controlled and what is not controlled by the author as exhibited in the text. For Derrida this relation is not one of determination, not one of a dialectical arrangement whereby one could articulate a synthesis, and not one of coherence or parallelism. Rather, first of all, the relation is characterized by disjunction and incoherence. The first level articulated is *not the same as,* or coherent with, the second. More precisely, this relation is, according to deMan's interpretation, one of *undecidability* between these two levels.

The referential mode (Derrida's first level) betrays the rhetorical mode (Derrida's second level), and there is an incessant oscillation for the reader. No absolute choice of priority is possible, yet no coherent and univocal message can be discerned except by effacing one of the two sides (which contemporary hermeneutics of any stripe manages to do quite successfully). It is for these reasons that deMan claimed that a text is "self-deconstructive"; it does not cohere or form an identity.[8] No unified totality is possible (if one analyzes both these levels and does not reduce the rhetorical to the referential, the syntactic to the signifier to the signified, or the sign to what it signifies). There is always, deMan claims with Derrida, a discrepancy between the declared and the described or, to use deMan's terminology, between the referential and the rhetorical. Johnson's concluding remarks take us back to deMan, since she says: "For if the *letter* is precisely that which *dictates* the *rhetorical* indetermination of *any* theoretical discourse about it, then the *oscillation* between unequivocal statements of *undecidability* and ambiguous assertions of decidability is precisely one of the letter's *inevitable* effects." Further: "What is *undecidable* is precisely whether a thing is decidable or not" (1977, 504; my emphasis).

It is no accident that Johnson resigns her analysis to what must be understood as a metaphysical claim: "any theoretical discourse," "inevitable effects," and of course the final quotation above, establishing no limits to its own applicability. I will not undertake a deconstruction of Johnson or deMan here; I wish only to point out the legacy invoked here in how Johnson finally frames the issue at hand itself as "undecidable" and necessarily so. I suggest, however, that this could be otherwise, since the "evidence" upon which she bases her conclusion does not seem to me to be correct. Her accusation that Derrida committed the "crime" of the reduction of the signifier to a signified seems to me to be simply untenable. As I have shown above, it is Derrida that *needs* the distinction between and the maintenance of both the *signifier* and *signified* (sound image and concept literally, and metaphorically or structurally both form and content or described and declared levels of the text) in order to even begin the work of deconstruction. It also seems clear that in practice, in this particular case, Derrida has paid scrupulous attention to the *way* Lacan has done what he has done in his reading of Poe. For instance, Derrida's concern with the role and function of the narrator, the role and function of fiction in relation to truth, is clearly an instance of his attention to the *signifier* (the level of frame, form, sound image) of Lacan's discourse. It is not that Derrida has left out the signified and privileged only the signifier—in antithesis to Johnson, which in the end I am not saying—but rather that the relation of the signified to signifier has been Derrida's constant focus in his analysis. In this sense his reading of Lacan is a typical deconstruction (although Derrida would reject such an adjective, since according to him deconstruction has no method).[9]

My objections to Derrida's reading, therefore, are based not on his having forgotten the signifier, but rather on the way he interprets the signifier in Lacan's text. I also object to the way he superimposes his assumptions concerning "commentary" in his own system of thought on Lacan's use of the same term. Finally, I object to Derrida's framing the issue in his analysis within the one Poe story (the third in the trilogy) rather than—as he himself suggested was necessary but did not do—locating the problem in terms of the trilogy as a whole.

With reference to our original problematic or frame of these issues as a whole, I wish to note the structure of exemplarity required by all the thinkers mentioned above, which they rely on without thematizing it and without providing any justification of its apparent necessity. *Exemplarity,* as the transformation of the given into a sign for something else (either not present now but with the capacity to be made present, or never present intrinsically) or as the transformation of the given into a case, a particular that illustrates or represents a universal, always invokes the same metaphysical assumption. This assumption is the supposedly valid structure of the sign as determined by Plato and Aristotle.[10] I shall not reiterate Derrida's deconstruction of this notion here, but I wish to point out that *exemplarity,* by using that notion of representation, thereby establishes a particular theory of meaning. This "given" is meaningful only insofar as it becomes or can become an *example* of something else. I have shown this structure throughout the texts of Derrida, Lacan, Poe, and Freud, and perhaps it is time to question its legitimacy. Such a notion of meaning sweeps up all particularity, all givens, into a metaphysical frame of reference in order to have meaning. Hence Derrida's earlier claim that all methods of analysis, interpretation, and understanding in the West are governed by metaphysics seems indeed to be vindicated in this case as well. In turn, it seems to me that the notion of *exemplarity* is itself ripe for deconstruction.

NOTES

1. With reference to this particular claim concerning exemplification, Lacan (1972b, 40) says: "We have decided to illustrate for you today the truth which may be drawn from that moment in Freud's thought under study—namely, that it is the symbolic order which is constitutive for the subject." Further (45), he says: "What interests us today is the manner in which the subjects relay each other in their displacement during the intersubjective repetition. We shall see that their displacement is determined by the place which a pure signifier—the purloined letter—comes to occupy in their trio. And that is what will confirm for us its status as *repetition automatism*" (my emphasis).

2. In particular, see Derrida (1980, 491–510), concerning Lacan's connection to the tradition of logocentrism, phonocentrism, and phallocentrism, or what Derrida calls traditional Western metaphysics.

3. For this particular claim see Johnson (1977, 502–5; reprinted here as chap. 10). For instance (502): "The very rhetoric of Derrida's differentiation of his own point of view from Lacan's *enacts* that law."

4. For more on this see Hegel's *Science of Logic* (1969). For more on Derrida's reading of Hegel, see Derrida, *Margins of Philosophy* (1982, 69–109); and also see Derrida, *Writing and Difference* (1978c, 251–73).

5. Poe (Mabbott 1978) writes: "The mental features discoursed of as the analytical, are, in themselves but little susceptible of analysis. We appreciate them only in their effects." And further, "to calculate is not in itself to analyze" (2:527–28).

6. Poe (Mabbott 1978) writes: "The narrative which follows will appear to the reader somewhat in the light of a *commentary* upon the propositions just advanced" (2:531).

7. See chapters 2 and 3 in section 1, "The Principles and Practice of Deconstruction," in my book *Derrida and the Economy of Différance* (1985).

8. See Paul deMan, *Allegories of Reading* (1979, 270–71). See also my forthcoming article in the International Association for Philosophy and Literature Proceedings from the 1982 Conference on "Alternatives to Deconstruction," concerning the differences between Derrida and deMan on this issue. Suffice it to

say that *différance* is included within what deMan calls the "self-deconstructive" nature of textuality, whereas for Derrida *différance* and deconstruction are separable issues, the first of which he aims to reveal by the strategy of textual analysis that he calls "deconstruction."

9. For more on what deconstruction is *not*, see the collection of interviews with him in *Positions* (1981b).

10. For Plato's most significant reference to the sign and to writing see the *Phaedrus*, and for Aristotle's notion of the sign, see his *De interpretatione*.

JANE GALLOP

Jacques Lacan has been the leading psychoanalyst in France since World War II. Beyond the field of psychoanalysis, Lacan has had tremendous influence on contemporary European thought, in realms as diverse as semiotics and feminism. Yet Lacan is still little more than a name to intellectuals in this country. Seldom read, even less understood.

The problem, it would seem, has been one of translation. Until recently Lacan has rarely been translated into English. In 1976, Norton published Alan Sheridan's translation of *The Four Fundamental Concepts of Psycho-analysis,* and a year later Sheridan's translation of a selection of Lacan's *Ecrits* appeared. Yet the problem remains one of translation, in a wider or more etymological sense. "Translate" is from the Latin *translatus,* "carried across." Lacan has yet to be carried across the Atlantic. My project, then, is to attempt to "translate" a translation. It is not simply that Lacan resists "translation," one might also say that America "resists" Lacan. Yet if America has resisted Lacan, then it is quite possible that Lacan is asking for it. Particularly in his writings of the fifties, that is, in those that make up the bulk of the *Ecrits,* Lacan attacks America.

Reprinted from Jane Gallop, *Reading Lacan.* Copyright © 1985 by Cornell University Press. Used by permission of the publisher.

Lacan's main "adversary" in the *Ecrits* is generally understood to be ego psychology, that offshoot of psychoanalysis whose home ground is the United States. Lacan considers ego psychology a betrayal of psychoanalysis, a repression of the unconscious, and a self-righteous manipulation of patients. But he does not limit his attacks to American psychoanalysis. There is a more general campaign against the "American way of life." Ego psychology is seen to be a deformation of psychoanalysis peculiarly suited to American values, giving the American people what they want. In fact, although the founders of ego psychology—Heinz Hartmann, Ernst Kris, and Rudolf Loewenstein—are all immigrants to the United States, Lacan emphasizes the association between the evil and America.

In the index of concepts at the back of *Ecrits,* the last category is "L'idéologie de la libre-entreprise" (the ideology of free enterprise). This category is explained and amplified by the following list: "American way of life, human relations, human engeneering [*sic*], braintrust, success, happiness, happy end, basic personality, pattern, etc."[1] Unlike the rest of the index in the original French text, the elements in this list are all in English. A glance at any of the pages represented by the numbers that follow quickly ascertains that these terms are all objects of derision, sarcasm, or outright attack. The problem of translating or transferring the *Ecrits* into the American scene is not simply to get the *Ecrits* into America, but what to do about the America that is already in the *Ecrits*. That internal America remains so alien that Lacan continually refers to it in English (in American words). His refusal to accept America, to have any exchange with it, to assimilate it, is marked by his refusal to translate the words.

Lacan will not assimilate America. And vice versa. The most common reaction to Lacan here has been rejection. This may actually be fortunate. The American ease of assimilation, the American power of co-optation, can serve to cover over America's ideology, investments, and identity. If Lacan can provoke a resistance, then it may be that Lacan offers America the possibility of understanding itself better.

Not just fortunate for America, but also for Lacan. Lacan has many followers in France and elsewhere in Europe. Such a following is not an unmixed blessing. The refusal to translate, although an act of rejection, also has the effect of keeping the signifier (the material specificity of the sign) and not trying to reduce it to signified (a meaning) that another signifier could represent just as well. For Lacan, the truth is to be found in the signifier—in the letter, not the spirit. The refusal to translate,

Lacan's and America's refusal to translate each other, may have the happy result that the evidence of the truth, the materiality of the signifier, has not yet been covered over. It is still there to be read.

America has not been so unwilling to assimilate Freud. In "La chose freudienne," Lacan recalls that as Freud and Jung arrived in the port of New York in view of the Statue of Liberty, Freud said, "They don't realize we're bringing them the plague." Lacan says that this remark "is sent back to [Freud] as a penalty for hubris" (1966a, 403; 1977, 116). The Statue of Liberty provides an illuminating background for the remark; its inscription, "Give me your tired, your poor," announces America's project to assimilate everything, including that rejected by the rest of the world. It is worth noting that the statue is a gift from France, that there is a smaller replica of it in Paris, that this image of America as melting pot may in some way already be coming from Paris.

Freud's hubris, his pride, prevented him from recognizing the power of America, of his supposed "victim." The penalty for this hubris is that the remark "is sent back to him {*lui est renvoyé*}," like an unopened letter. Return to sender. If, as Lacan emphasized in "La chose freudienne," Freud's truth is in the letter, this one is not read. As Lacan goes on to say, "Nemesis has only to take him at his word." Freud's hubris receives its just punishment. As he predicted, America does not realize, does not *ever* realize he has brought the plague. Our best defense against this "plague" is our lack of recognition, lack of resistance. We assimilate Freud, make psychoanalysis American.

In our attempt to read Lacan here, we must cope not only with the America that is in Lacan's France (the replica of the Statue of Liberty) but also with the France that is already in America. Lacan's marginal acceptance in this country has been, on the whole, strongest in academic French departments whose approval of him may represent identification with his anti-American stance. The American words (success, happiness, etc.) that constitute an unassimilated, internal colony in Lacan's French text may find their mirror image in the status of American French departments that speak and think in French, that refuse to translate French into American.

Yet if one's project is to carry Lacan across, it cannot be accomplished within the confines of a francophile colony internal to America; having arrived here, he would still be there. If my ultimate project is to foster some sort of dialogue between Lacan and America, then the dialogue cannot be a play of mirrors. A mirror image can be understood either as a specular opposite (right versus left) or as something identical. Lacan in fact situates opposites, rivalry, and aggressivity in identification; the adversary is simply one version of the alter ego. He terms the type of relation between the self and its mirror image (either as adversary or as identity) "imaginary." "The imaginary" (a noun for Lacan) is the realm where intersubjective structures are covered over by mirroring. Lacan's writings contain an implicit ethical imperative to break the mirror, an imperative to disrupt the imaginary in order to reach "the symbolic." One might say that "the symbolic"—which for Lacan is the register of language, social exchange, and radical intersubjectivity—would be the locus of dialogue. My project to provoke a dialogue between these two adversaries might be understood as an attempt to break out of an imaginary reading of Lacan and reach the symbolic.

But the imaginary and the symbolic themselves tend to become adversarial terms in a systematic reading of Lacan. Inasmuch as anyone would be "for" the symbolic and "against" the imaginary, he would be operating in the imaginary. Ironically, the ethical imperative to accede to the symbolic and vigilantly to resist the imaginary is itself mired in the imaginary.[2] Which is not to dismiss the value of the ethic. To give a reading of Lacan that is faithful to this ethic means that the reading must not always side "with" Lacan, that it must be suspicious of the imaginary (egotistical or adversarial) dimension of his work.

The difference between an imaginary reading and a symbolic reading is subtle indeed. Before I can attempt to set forth the possibilities for a symbolic reading of *Ecrits* in America, I would like to examine the relationship between the imaginary and the symbolic, the double and the mirror, as they operate in Lacan.

If the difference between the imaginary and the symbolic is understood as an opposition between two identities, we can be sure we have given an imaginary reading of the terms. It could be said that the symbolic can be encountered only as a tear in the fabric of the imaginary, a revealing interruption. The paths to the symbolic are thus *in* the imaginary. The symbolic can be reached only by not trying to avoid the imaginary, by knowingly being *in* the imaginary. Likewise, mastery of the illusions that psychoanalysis calls transference can be attained only by falling prey to those illusions, by losing one's position of objectivity, control, or mastery in relation to them.

The imaginary is made up of *imagoes*. An imago is an unconscious image or cliché "which preferentially orients the way in which the subject apprehends other people."[3] In the imaginary mode, one's understanding of other people is shaped by one's own imagoes. The perceived other is actually, at least in part, a projection. Psychoanalysis is an attempt to recognize the subject's imagoes in order to ascertain their deforming effect upon the subject's understanding of her relationships. The point is not to give up the imagoes (an impossible task) or to create better ones (any static image will deform the perception of the dynamics of intersubjectivity). But, in the symbolic register, the subject understands these imagoes as structuring projections.

Lacan condemns ego psychology as hopelessly mired in the imaginary because it promotes an identification between the analysand's ego and the analyst's. The ego, for Lacan, is an imago. The enterprise of ego psychology reshapes the analysand's imagoes into ones that better correspond to "reality"—that is, to the analyst's reality, which can only mean to the analyst's imagoes. The analysand has no way of grasping the working of his imagoes. He has simply substituted the analyst's imaginary for his own. But this imaginary is now certified by the analyst as "real." The successful mirroring that goes on in ego psychology constitutes a failure to reach the symbolic.

Yet the difference between a "good" analysis and an "imaginary" one is extremely subtle. A "good" analysis does not avoid the imaginary or condemn the mirror. On the contrary.

In "Aggressivity in Psychoanalysis," Lacan insists that the "imago is revealed only insofar as our attitude offers the subject the pure mirror of an unruffled surface" (1966a, 109; 1977, 15). The analyst should be a mirror for the analysand. A mirror but not a mirror image. "Unruffled surface" translates "surface sans accidents." "Accidents" in French means, according to *Le petit Robert,* "that which breaks uniformity," in a terrain, for example. But it also means, philosophically, "that which 'is added' to the essence, can be modified or suppressed without altering its nature. An accessory, as secondary fact." To be a "surface sans accidents" is to be a surface without attributes, without any characteristic except the pure fact of surface. This is the analyst's neutrality. Insofar as she is an unruffled surface, she can serve as a screen for the analysand's personality or values or knowledge. It is not the analyst's ego but her neutrality that should mirror the analysand. Psychoanalysis should be an encounter not with a likeness or a double, but with a mirror.

Yet how does one distinguish a mirror from a mirror image? The mirror itself, devoid of any content, cannot be perceived but is simply that which structures the image, makes it possible. In the ethical imperative to be in the symbolic, the charge is to look into the mirror and see not the image but the mirror itself.

Beginning a new paragraph, Lacan goes on to say, "But imagine what would take place in a patient who saw in his analyst an exact replica of himself." In this case the analyst is not mirror but likeness. "Everyone feels," Lacan continues, "that the excess of aggressive tension would set up such an obstacle to the manifestation of transference that its useful effect could be produced only with extreme sluggishness." For Lacan, aggression is produced in response to the mirror image. There is a rivalry over which is the self and which the other, which the ego and which the replica. This relation of ego and alter ego would block the *manifestation* of the transference, that is, it would obstruct the revelation of the imagoes. Transference would be going on but could not be recognized as such because what is projected would appear to be actually "out there." The imaginary would seem real. It is the imaginary as imaginary which constitutes the symbolic.[4] In this case the analyst would approximate to what he is "presumed" to be, and thus the action of presumption or projection would pass unnoticed.

Lacan continues: "If we will imagine it, as an extreme case, lived in the mode of strangeness proper to apprehensions of the *double,* this situation would set off an uncontrollable anxiety." Sheridan translates the end of this sentence as "an uncontrollable anxiety on the part of the analysand." "On the part of the analysand" is his addition (projection?). Nothing in Lacan's text identifies whose anxiety it is. Sheridan's specification has the effect of controlling the anxiety. The anxiety produced by the "double" is precisely the question of whose anxiety it is. Sheridan would avoid the mirroring of the double, would never fall for the illusion of identity between analyst and analysand. But at the price of maintaining another illusion. In believing the analyst immune from anxiety, in believing the analyst "in control," he is presuming the analyst "to know."

Lacan uses the word "imagine" twice in this paragraph: "But imagine what would take place in a patient who saw in his analyst an exact replica of himself. If we will imagine it, as an extreme case, . . . this situation would set off an uncontrollable anxiety." These "imagines" recall the imago of the preceding sentence. "Our" imagining would appear to be merely the rhetorical frame for the content of what Lacan is talking about. We are imagining what might happen within the analytic situation. But the repetition of the word "imagine" creates an insistence that recalls "imago," that calls attention to an echo between the frame and the image, between our imagining and what we are imagining. How can we tell the frame from the image? How can we tell the mirror from the likeness?

"If we will imagine it, . . . this situation would set off an uncontrollable anxiety." "Our" imagining might itself lead to the anxiety. If the analysand could be sure that the analyst was not anxious, or was at least in control of the anxiety, then the analysand would not experience the analyst as a double, would be able to distinguish between the anxious one and the not-anxious one. What is "uncontrollable" about the anxiety is that it "belongs" to no one, is in no one's possession.

Sheridan's presumption that the anxiety must be the analysand's finds an interesting echo in a scathing critique of Lacan, made by Jacques Derrida, who accuses him of avoiding and repressing manifestations of the double. "By neutralizing the double," writes Derrida (1980, 489), "[Lacan] does everything necessary to avoid what *Aggressivity in Psychoanalysis* calls 'uncontrollable anxiety.' That of the analysand, of course."

Although when Derrida writes "that of the analysand," he is not quoting Lacan, he seems to believe he is bringing out an implicit assumption of Lacan's text. His "of course" marks that he is being ironic. Derrida presumes not that the analyst/Lacan is immune from anxiety, but that Lacan presumes that the analyst/Lacan is immune from anxiety. Nonetheless, the difference between Derrida's ironic comment on the analyst's self-delusion of mastery and Sheridan's apparently more naive illusion of the analyst's mastery is not so very great. It may merely be the difference between a negative and a positive transference. After all, they both project the same thought into Lacan's text, a thought which "preferentially orients apprehension" of the text. As I have tried to show, the Lacan paragraph in question, with its "imagines," can provide a kind of anxious uncertainty about whose anxieties and whose imagoes are in question. Derrida says that Lacan is avoiding the double. But one could likewise say that Derrida and Sheridan are avoiding some anxiety-producing double by attributing a certainty and a distinction between analyst and analysand that is not there in Lacan's paragraph, which is precisely about a confusion between analyst and analysand.

Lacan's paragraph begins "mais qu'on imagine," which I have translated "but imagine." Literally, however, in the French, the imagining is being done by neither interlocutor nor speaker, by neither analyst nor analysand, but by the impersonal pronoun "on." The imagining is done by a subject with no particular attributes. The impersonality of "on" recalls the analyst's neutrality, while the verb "imagine" recalls the analysand projecting imagoes. Thus both subject and verb are elements of the sentence immediately preceding ("the imago is revealed only insofar as our attitude offers the subject the pure mirror of an unruffled surface").

"On imagine" condenses these two terms, condensing the projector and the screen. It may be that the success of Lacan's paragraph is that, in its neutral refusal to decide to whom Lacan attributes the anxiety, it serves as a surface for the *reader's* projections. The text would thus produce manifestations of transference.

Now I am presuming Lacan "knows," presuming that he is controlling the transference, manipulating it, that he is master of its illusions. But even if I were wrong, I would, in some way, be right. Which is to say that even if he were not in control, even if he had no idea of this potential effect of his words, the effect of those words would have nonetheless made me project his knowledge and thus indeed provoked a transference, and at the very moment he is speaking of transference. Whether he knows or not, the very undecidability of the question of whether or not he knows corresponds to the analytic technique of neutrality. Analytic neutrality cannot be actual impartiality. The analyst is a subject and thus cannot avoid having values, prejudices, and opinions. Analytic neutrality is rather a technique that prevents the analysand from determining what those opinions are. Therefore whatever opinion the analysand attributes to the analyst is likely to betray the analysand's imagoes.

The coincidence of Sheridan's and Derrida's interpretations of Lacan is quite apt for a return to the problem of an American "translation" of Lacan.

Sheridan's translation is available for the American who does not read French. Yet from this example, it is clear that the translation is prey to distortion, is unwittingly, unreflectedly, deformed by the translator's imaginary. Perhaps the problem is that any translator, any person who devotes great time and effort to conveying someone else's words, is already operating with a strong identification, already wishing to operate as a double. A translation that presents itself as a faithful rendering of the original operates like the imaginary, which presents itself as an apprehension of the real. If the symbolic is a glimpse of the imaginary as imaginary, then a "translation" of a translation may offer some grasp on the translation, some possibility of going beyond the translation's "imaginary."

The relationship between Derrida and an American "translation" of Lacan is less direct, but perhaps ultimately more illuminating. Derrida is neither translating Lacan nor writing in English or directly for an American audience. But a certain Franco-American exchange is already operating as a background for the confrontation between Derrida and Lacan. Derrida's critique is a reading of Lacan's reading of Edgar Allan Poe's story "The Purloined Letter." Derrida accuses Lacan not only of avoiding doubles in that story, but also of ignoring the persona Lacan calls the "general narrator." These two avoidances may actually be one, since, as Derrida shows (1980, 518), the general narrator and the hero, Dupin, are doubles of each other. But what is perhaps most interesting, in our context, is that this is a relation of identification between a Frenchman and an American.

Thus, with the help of Derrida's reading, we see that Lacan is ignoring some Franco-American imaginary operating in the Poe story between Dupin and the narrator. But there is another Franco-American relation that Lacan does bring out in his text. In the "Seminar on 'The Purloined Letter'" Lacan introduces his subject as "the tale which Baudelaire translated under the title *La lettre volée.*" Lacan explicitly introduces his subject as a translation. Baudelaire is mentioned a full page before Poe. In the American translation of Lacan's text, this oddness is further emphasized, since "la lettre volée" are the first French words that the reader encounters in the text. In a translation, words left in the original language usually represent something so particular to the original context that they cannot be assimilated into the new language. But in this case what resists the "melting pot" of the American text is the French title for an American story. What cannot be translated into American is some America that is already in French.

The appearance of these French words in the American text is mirrored by an appearance of the American title untranslated in the French text. Lacan writes, "it remains, nevertheless, that Baudelaire, despite his devotion, betrayed Poe by translating as 'la lettre volée' his title: *the purloined letter*" (1966a, 29; 1972b, 59). Lacan then goes on to discuss the Anglo-French etymology of the word "purloined." If Lacan begins by introducing the story as Baudelaire's translation only to later accuse Baudelaire of traducement in his *traduction,* we are perhaps brought to the realization that we must inevitably deal with "bad translations." In other words, the imaginary will always block us from apprehending the real (the original text). But at least we can try to catch the functioning distortions of translation as translation (not the real, but the symbolic).

The "Seminar on 'The Purloined Letter'" is the opening essay of *Ecrits.* When a short collection of *Ecrits* is later published in pocketbook format, it is explicitly retained as the opening essay. Thus a potential translator of *Ecrits* into English immediately meets his mirror image in Baudelaire, translator/betrayer of Poe. This encounter entails a danger of narcissistic miring in the imaginary, but by knowingly falling into that imaginary one has the chance of glimpsing the symbolic, of taking cognizance of translation as translation, of the mirror as mirror. Unfortunately this Franco-American seminar that would be a "natural" opener for a translation of *Ecrits* is not translated by Sheridan. As already noted, on at least one occasion Sheridan's translation works to control the anxiety produced by the double. The Seminar lies in wait as a mirror image for Lacan's English translator. By not translating it, Sheridan misses a chance to confront his translating as translation. He misses the chance to do a Lacanian translation and settles for merely a translation of Lacan.

The Seminar is translated by an American, Jeffrey Mehlman, who seems to have benefited from his encounter with this mirror and thus come to articulate his understanding of a certain Franco-American imaginary. In an article called "Poe Pourri," he writes: "One begins wondering then to what extent the French in idealizing Poe, have not quite simply fallen for Poe's deluded idealization of Gallic genius. More specifically and worse yet . . . in taking Lacan's text seriously . . . might we not *at best* be lapsing into Poe's delusion?" (1975, 52). Mehlman then refers to this all as a "proliferating play of mirrors." Lacan is in a long tradition of French men who have celebrated Poe's genius. Poe idealized French genius (in the person of Dupin, hero of "The Purloined Letter"). The French love the American writer because he gives them a flattering image of themselves. But this is a two-way mirror. Psychoanalytically, "idealization" always betrays a marked component of narcissism; one idealizes an object with which one identifies. If Poe creates a mirror for the French, it is not the "pure mirror" of analytic neutrality, but an imaginary likeness. Poe does not reflect French imagoes, he projects his own imagoes onto the French, who accept them. Several times throughout this article Mehlman refers to Lacan's opposition to "American ego psychology"; however, he never connects that adversarial Franco-American relation to the positive idealized Franco-American identification that introduces and situates his article. In the Laplanche and Pontalis article "Idealization," we read that, for Melanie Klein, "the idealization of the object would be essentially a defense against the destructive drives; in this sense, it would be a correlative of an extreme case of *splitting* between a 'good' object, idealized and endowed with all the virtues . . . and a bad object whose persecuting character is equally carried to the limit" (1973, 186–87). Has America thus been "split" into Poe (good object) and the ego psychologists (bad object)? Is not Poe's relation to the French in some way analogous to the ego psychologist's relation to his patients? Poe offers the French a good, strong ego image. What begins as Poe's imago, the French (including Lacan) take on as their own.

Mehlman is promoting the new French genius Lacan and is thus undoubtedly repeating Poe's francophilia. But he is aware of his repetition of Poe; he does not pretend to be immune to delusion, but rather emphasizes his own implication in the dizzying structures he is describing. Mehlman also points to a way out— "a reading of Lacan on Poe may be our best guide in avoiding the pitfalls entailed by a reading of Lacan on Poe" (1975, 52). Lacan's American reader runs the risk of belief in Lacan's "Gallic genius." In other words, the danger is that one might presume Lacan "knows," might produce a transference onto Lacan. But as we have seen before, that transference is best understood through Lacan's explanation of it. But then that means Lacan *does* "know."

How can one distinguish between these two kinds of "knowledge," between the idealized genius product of an identificatory francophilia and the lucid, technical knowledge of precisely such structures of transference? How, in Mehlman's terms, can one distinguish between two different "reading(s) of Lacan on Poe," between the "pitfalls" and the "guide"? Mehlman makes such a distinction in relation to the Poe tale: "It should, moreover, be clear that to the extent that there is a locus of power in Lacan's version of the tale, it is not in the intellectual strength of the master-analyst Dupin, but rather in the persistence of a structure whose mode of existence is the erosion of just such an imaginary autonomy. We are far from Poe as adolescent idealizer of otherworldly genius in the Frenchman's reading" (1975, 55–56). Mehlman accepts Lacan's distinction between Dupin's mastery (merely an illusion) and the sovereignty of a structure. In other words, it is the structure that creates the illusion of mastery; the symbolic makes the imaginary possible. With Lacan we are "far from Poe as adolescent idealizer." But, whereas at the beginning of Mehlman's article Poe worships "Gallic genius," now three pages later he idealizes "otherworldly genius." This shift makes possible the nonrecognition of a certain "play of mirrors" when Mehlman writes, "We are far from Poe as adolescent idealizer of *otherworldly genius* in *the Frenchman's* reading." Yet, if at this moment Lacan is called "the Frenchman," it serves only to remind us that the other occasion of such an appellation immediately follows the statement "A reading of Lacan on Poe may be our best guide in avoiding the pitfalls entailed by a reading of Lacan on Poe" (52). I can only agree and ironically add that a reading of Mehlman on Lacan may be our best guide in avoiding the pitfalls entailed by a reading of Mehlman on Lacan. After all, when Mehlman writes that with the Frenchman "we are *far* from Poe," does not "far" belie the same imaginary belief in "otherworldly" superiority?

Mehlman's situation begins to resemble the uncanny effect Poe can produce—for example, in the story "The Black Cat," when a narrator lucidly describes his own delusion without being any less prey to that delusion. Mehlman himself asks, "Might we not *at best* be lapsing into Poe's delusion?" What is the sense of the italicized "at best"? What could be worse than this lapse? It would be worse *not* to lapse into Poe's delusion. Avoiding delusion altogether is not a possible alternative. There is no direct apprehension of the real, no possible liberation from imagoes, no unmediated reading of a text. The alternative to lapsing into Poe's delusion is lapsing into another delusion, one not shared with Poe, a delusion which is particular, idiosyncratic, and does not already have a place in Lacan's text. To the extent that we can already delineate the structure of Poe's delusion, if *that* is our delusion, we can understand it *as* delusion. Any other delusion is likely to pass as "real."

Mehlman's "lapse" sets up an identification between Lacan and Dupin, the two French geniuses admired by American idealizers. But the identification has even more substance to it. As Mehlman reminds us, Dupin is a "master analyst." "The Purloined Letter" is the third of a trilogy of Dupin stories. "The Murders in the Rue Morgue," the first Dupin story, begins with preliminary remarks on "the mental features discoursed of as the analytical" and on the behavior of "the analyst." At the end of this prologue on "analysis," we read: "The narrative which follows will appear to the reader somewhat in the light of commentary upon the propositions just advanced. Residing in Paris during the spring and part of the summer of 18—, I there became acquainted with a Monsieur C. August Dupin." Dupin is introduced immediately after the discourse on "the analyst," and the reader can only assume that Dupin is "the analyst." The prologue has described "the analyst" as "fond of enigmas, of conundrums, of hieroglyphics; exhibiting in his solutions of each a degree of *acumen* which appears to the ordinary apprehension preternatural" (Mabbott 1978, 2:527–31). Dupin certainly fits this description.

Dupin also fits the popular image of the psychoanalyst. He is clever at interpreting, at guessing what goes on inside other people's minds ("He boasted to me . . . that most men, in respect to himself, wore windows in their bosoms," the narrator says of Dupin). This Dupin bears a striking resemblance to Lacan. Both love riddles and plays on words, both display a biting contempt for the stupidity of all those positivists around them who are mired in naive delusions and incapable of seeing the "truth." In Dupin, we can recognize Lacan's flamboyant style and extreme conceit. Yet let us beware this obvious identification of Dupin with the analyst. "A little *too* self-evident," Dupin says in "The Purloined Letter," and Lacan repeats (1966a, 23; 1972b, 50). "A little *too* self-evident," Lacan says, in English, explicitly repeating Dupin's very words, broadly playing his identification with Dupin, which, the reader should be alerted, is itself a little *too* self-evident.

Dupin is not just too obvious a choice for the "analyst," but he is too "self-evident." His "self" is too evident to be the pure surface of analytic neutrality as Lacan has formulated it. On the other hand, there is the narrator whose "self" is barely evident at all. Derrida, in criticizing Lacan's lack of concern with the narrator, writes: "The narrator . . . is like the neutral, homogeneous, transparent element of the tale. He 'adds nothing,' says Lacan. As if one had to add something to intervene in a scene" (1980, 457). Derrida seems to imply ("as if . . . ") that Lacan considers the narrator unimportant because Lacan says he "adds nothing." However, if anyone has formulated the effect, the "intervention" of someone who is "neutral," it is Lacan who thus describes the structure of the analyst's intervention in the transference. Through Derrida's description of the narrator as homogeneous and transparent, we can see him as "the pure mirror of an unruffled surface."

If "The Purloined Letter" functions as a parable of psychoanalysis, we must ask carefully: Who is the analyst? Dupin is the "too self-evident" answer. Dupin fits the popular image of the analyst; he is the imaginary version of the analyst. But it is the neutral, nearly selfless American narrator who comes closer to functioning as an analyst.

"The Murders in the Rue Morgue" begins thus: "The mental features discoursed of as the analytical are, in themselves, but little susceptible of analysis. We appreciate them only in their effects." The narrator's problem is how to analyze analysis, how to analyze the analyst rather than be taken in by his "effects." (Psycho-)analysis, according to Lacan, is the move from the imaginary to the symbolic. Analysis produces imaginary effects (transference, projection of imagoes), but its goal is to understand what structures those effects. Is not the narrator's difficulty (analyze the analytical) our very problem in trying to give a symbolic reading of Lacan?

A reader opens Lacan's *Ecrits,* presumably in order to learn what the "master analyst" has to say. But thanks to Derrida's delineation of the

structure of the double in "The Purloined Letter," we see that she immediately encounters the question of who is the analyst. The "too self-
evident" answer is Lacan. Lacan plays a certain imaginary of the analyst to
the hilt; he plays the "subject presumed to know," the great oracle,
interpreter of enigmas. To fall for the illusion of Lacan's mastery is to be
trapped in the imaginary of the text. In the same opening essay we are
given an alternative version of the analyst in the "neutral, homogeneous,
transparent" narrator. It would seem, then, that here we might find the
symbolic, here we might have a chance to analyze the analytical rather
than be dazzled by the "master analyst's" flamboyant effects.

So as reader of Lacan, in my attempt to delineate the symbolic in the
Ecrits, I find myself identifying with Poe's narrator. It is certainly to the
point that in situating my reading I choose to identify with the American, not the Frenchman in the story. But more startling, and more
suspect, I choose to locate "the analyst" in the American who is my
double, rather than in the Gallic genius. Rather than simply presuming
Lacan to know, I am presuming he presumes me to know. Might I not *at
best* be lapsing into Lacan's delusion? Although I have identified the
narrator with the symbolic, the fact that he is, after all, a double of Dupin
and the fact that I "identify" with him (her? no real evidence to the
contrary) serve as clues that this identification is an imaginary version of
the symbolic.

Yet if we are to analyze the analytical, we must risk the anxiety of the
double. And if there is a dialogue possible between Lacan and America,
perhaps the only chance is for someone to assume the place where that
dialogue is already going on, the dialogue between Dupin and his American friend. And the best that I could presume to hope for is that I might
"add nothing."

NOTES

1. Lacan (1966a, 902; 1977, 331); the index is compiled by Jacques-Alain
Miller.

2. Fredric Jameson (1977, 350, 378) makes a similar point, in a different
context.

3. Psychoanalytic definitions are taken from Laplanche and Pontalis (1973,
196).

4. I presented this chapter to a seminar taught by John Muller and William
Richardson at the University of Massachusetts, three years after the chapter was

drafted. Richardson asked about this sentence—"It is the imaginary as imaginary which constitutes the symbolic." He was not convinced. Although three years earlier I had been convinced that this was a new and illuminating understanding of the relationship of the imaginary and the symbolic, I no longer had the conviction, only the memory of the conviction. A day later Muller pointed out to me that, in his epilogue to *Interpreting Lacan,* Joseph H. Smith says something quite similar: "It is in the light of the Symbolic order that the Imaginary is situated *as* Imaginary" (1983, 268).

FOUR   *Other Readings*

13 ✿ Narratorial Authority and *"The Purloined Letter"*

NARRATIVE AND NARRATORIAL AUTHORITY

To tell a story is to exercise power (it is even called the power of narration), and "authorship" is cognate with "authority." But, in this instance as in all others, authority is not an absolute, something inherent in a specific individual or in that individual's discourse; it is relational, the result of an act of authorization on the part of those subject to the power, and hence something to be earned. Thus, in conversation, I may be willing to give up my prerogative of turn taking (Grice 1975) in order to listen to a particularly interesting, or useful, or funny report; and in literature, if Mary Louise Pratt's analysis (1977) is accurate, I am prepared to divert my attention away from the various possible objects that might engage it and toward a particular text, in the expectation of some intellectual or aesthetic gain from that text. Etymology tells us that the narrator is one who *knows;*[1] one might infer that the narratee's motivation in authorizing the act of narration lies in the prospect of acquiring "information." The storyteller, as Walter Benjamin (1969) insists—although he distinguishes in this respect between storyteller and novelist—is one who has "experience" to impart.

However, imparting one's experience incorporates a problem; for to the extent that the act of narration is a process of disclosure, in which the information that forms the source of narrative authority is transmitted to the narratee, the narrator gives up the basis of his or her authority in the very act of exercising it. This is not unlike the well-known paradox of the teacher, who, to the extent that he or she is successful in educating the young, thereby renders them independent of the need for education and hence less likely to accord their educator the authorization to teach. There is no need to insist on the various well-known "tricks of the trade" used by teacher and by narrator to "maintain interest," as it is called: divulgence is never complete, the telling of the ultimate secret is indefinitely deferred—and it most often transpires, in art as in education, that there is no ultimate secret. The fact does remain, however, that at the end of a "successful" narration, the interest that authorized the act of narration has been destroyed. It is plausible to assume, then, that at bottom the narrator's motivation is like that of the narratee and rests on the assumption of exchanging a gain for a loss. Where the narratee offers attention in exchange for information, the narrator sacrifices the information for some form of attention. Consequently, there is a sense in which the maintenance of narrative authority implies an act of seduction, and a certain transfer of interest (on the narratee's part) from the information content to the narrating instance itself (be it the person of the narrator, as in "real-life" situations, or, as in the reading situation, the narrative discourse itself). This is never more the case than when the narrative content is acknowledged to be fictional, that is, noninformative (in the conventional sense of the term): the "point" of the narration can only lie then in its obtaining from the narratee a specific type of attention (to which the information divulged may certainly be germane but cannot be essential). It will be my assumption that in the type of narrative with which I am concerned (let us call it, on the analogy of the term "art song," the modern "art story") the production of art is what compensates for the divulgence of (fictional) information and that the texts' production of themselves as "art" has as its object the gaining of a new kind of authority (in the form of the reader's attention, respect, and indeed fascination) in exchange for the purely narrative authority being progressively lost. For the sake of clarity, I will refer to this new kind of authority as "narratorial" (versus "narrative") authority: it is the "art" of seduction.

Texts such as "Sarrasine" and "Sylvie" specifically thematize narration as a seductive act. Balzac's narrator tells the story of Sarrasine in an effort to bring Mme. de Rochefide to bed; Nerval's narrator tells his life story to the women he hopes will "save" him by responding to his love and solving the enigma of his dispersed attachments. But in each case the text specifically distances itself from narration as seduction and claims for itself—implicitly in Balzac's case, explicitly in Nerval's—other powers. The Balzacian narrator appears as a philosopher who expects of his narratee an equivalent degree of philosophical detachment (as opposed to the involvement of seduction); the Nervalian narrator, while also siding with the philosophical against the *romanesque,* asks not for detachment and distance, but for understanding—and the story he tells functions as a way of obtaining from the narratee such sympathetic adherence to an adventure that both narrator and narratee are assumed to perceive as folly. In short, the denial of narrative seduction *in* the texts diverts attention from the seductive program *of* the texts, with their manipulation of the narratee in the name of "understanding" (philosophical or sentimental).

"The Purloined Letter" is not concerned thematically with seduction, but its focus on the fascinating figure of Dupin perhaps works in a similar way to divert attention from the text's own seductive program. Here, too, there is a differentiating technique, Dupin's fascinating discourse being framed by the narration of the story as a whole and to some extent distanced by the play between Dupin's narratorial style and that of the general narration. Although it is thus dissociated from the text as a whole, Dupin's seductive and enigmatic discourse is simultaneously taken up and incorporated into the total narrative project; and this is not simply because the ascendancy Dupin exerts over the other characters, including the narrator (Dupin's nameless friend), is transmitted to the reader through the agency of this latter personage. It is rather that the narratorial advantages of Dupin's style of discourse (what I call "duplicity") are combined, in the narration proper, with the narratorial advantages of another style (that of "self-reflexivity" or self-designation). In short, the issue is complicated, in "The Purloined Letter," by a certain question of disclosure.

If a text relies, for its point, on its artistic ("narratorial") success, the transaction with the reader fails unless the narratee perceives that art is being produced; it becomes necessary, then, for the narrator to divulge the fact that the illocutionary relationship between narrator and narratee involves this new source of "interest."[2] But one of the more durable axioms of Western aesthetics has it that the greatest art lies in the concealment of art and that the production of art—and hence, the gain in narratorial authority—is the greater when the art narrative is apparently nonart, that is, a form of communication concerned principally with its own referent (i.e., "what it is about," the narrative information being divulged). Hence, there is a constant tug-of-war between conflicting strategies—between narrative *self-referentiality* whereby the story draws attention to its status as art and forms of narrative *duplicity* whereby the story pretends to be concerned only with its informational content and yet reveals in unobtrusive ways (usually by slight discrepancies) that this is not so.

Duplicity versus self-reference as artistic modes form the very substance of "The Purloined Letter" when one chooses to read it in terms of narratorial authority, and as a text concerned with its own illocutionary situation. The narratorial mode of Dupin and that of the narration itself represent a range of possibilities as between textual duplicity (with its reliance on the acumen and skilled guesswork of the narratee) and the techniques of self-reflexivity (which still, of course, require a narratee attuned to the literary codes that make self-reference possible). The order of the discussion that follows will suggest a hierarchical order in which the framing (self-referential) narration is seen as commenting, in a sense, on the (duplicitous) narratorial practices demonstrated by Dupin within the narrative, and there is certainly in the text some degree of ironic distancing of this kind. Yet, the total effect is cumulative: although the fascination and sense of enigma produced by Dupin's duplicity are dispelled in the self-revealing artistic reference of the general narration, the two combine in a mutually reinforcing way in supporting the effectiveness of art as the exercise of a "narratorial," not "narrative," authority and hence in promoting a relational, not informational, concept of discourse.

These central questions of situational import, concerning the relationship implied by the text between the text and the reader, can be approached particularly directly in "The Purloined Letter," because the narrative content itself displays an acute awareness of the relational (and therefore situational) character of understanding. Jacques Lacan, the author of the most powerful and influential reading of "The Purloined Letter" in the public domain, was drawn to the text, he says, by the story Dupin tells of the game of "even and odd," which Lacan saw as illustrating the necessary precedence of the *symbolic* (the "signifier") over the subject. The "lucky" schoolboy who wins so frequently at the game by "identifying" with his opponents' thought processes is not, Lacan says, a Kantian subject miraculously identifying with another subject, since

"cette identification se fait non pas à l'adversaire, mais à son raisonne-
ment qu'elle articule (différence au reste qui s'énonce dans le texte)."3 But
the boy's success at identifying with his opponent illustrates not only
Lacan's point about the role of the signifier but also the thematic significance in the text of duplicity and its oppositional correlative, second-
guessing, as a mode of understanding (by contrast with the more simple-
minded attempts at uncomplex and unmediated "identification," such as
the Prefect's straightforward assumptions about the criminal mind he is
dealing with) and hence as a model of communication that perceives it as
a game—a "game of puzzles"—in which one may "win" or "lose."

Jacques Derrida (1975b), in criticizing Lacan's reading for its supposed imposition on the text of a psychoanalytic "meaning" (the interpretation of the story in terms of castration—the letter as that which
"manque à sa place," affirming a *given* in which "le manque a sa place")
seems to miss something of the significance of Lacan's fascination with
this communicational relationship, at once ludic and oppositional, as it is
figured in the text.4 It is true that Lacan's reading is the "analyse fascinée
d'un contenu" (1969, 105) (Why and how does the text so fascinate a
reader like Lacan?) and that it misses the implications of the narrative
framework. But this framework does not have solely the function Derrida
attributes to it, of ensuring textual "dissemination" (the positioning, in
terms of "différence," of "The Purloined Letter" with respect to literature
and the world of discourse at large, and the Dupin trilogy in particular).
The narration also relates in important ways to its content, the *narré,* and
provides in the *narré* significant "clues" (in appropriately detective terminology) or models as to its own functioning as a performative discursive
act: how it is (asking) to be received, what it assumes regarding the
relationship between itself and its readership, what—in short—its point
is as a narrative act. The game of "even and odd" is one such clue.

What is at stake in "The Purloined Letter," then—in "The Purloined
Letter" as a narrative act that describes itself as a "game of puzzles"—is
the gain or loss of narrative/narratorial authority. Consequently, I propose to look first at the thematization of questions of power and authority
in the text, most particularly as they relate to the problem of disclosure.
Derrida has pointed out to what extent the characters are "doubles" of one
another: I propose to exploit this status by examining some of them as
"models" (and "antimodels") of each other, and of the text as a whole, in
terms of the exercise of authority through discourse. The Prefect of Police
will thus be seen as a major foil to Dupin, but not so much in his
detective work as in his prowess as a narrator (the two being, of course,

closely related in any case): his failure in "narrative" authority sets off the success of Dupin's "narratorial" strategies. But the relationship of Dupin to the Minister will then lead me to examine the phenomenon of artistic duplicity as a mode of "narratorial" success, combining concealment with openness, disclosure with covertness, and to compare the different practices of duplicity each character exemplifies. Finally, it will be important to examine the character of the "general narrator" (as Lacan calls him) and his investment in the text as art, his function as the final foil to all the other power holders and narrative/narratorial authorities in the text: here the relationship of self-reflexivity to duplicity will be at the center of the analysis of narratorial authority in the text.[5]

THE PREFECT, THE MINISTER, DUPIN

Possession of "the letter" is possession of (political) power—that is why the Minister steals it from the "personage of most exalted station" (who, for simplicity's sake, will henceforward be referred to as the Queen). But this letter has some peculiar properties. For one thing, its contents are unknown to the reader; they are a secret that is never disclosed. (Is it a love letter? Does it contain evidence of a political plot?) For another, the power the letter confers on the Minister is, precisely, the power to divulge the secret: "The disclosure of the document to a third person, who shall be nameless, would bring in question the honor of a personage of most exalted station; and this fact gives the holder of the document an ascendancy over the illustrious personage whose honor and peace are so jeopardized" (Poe 1978). Moreover, it is (more exactly still) not the divulgence of the letter but its possession, that is, the option of divulging it, that confers the power; and indeed actually to employ the letter in this way would destroy the Minister's "ascendancy." "With the employment the power departs." Hence, the necessary openness of the situation between the blackmailer and his victim: the Minister's ascendancy depends "upon the robber's knowledge of the loser's knowledge of the robber."

The Minister, then, ostentatiously does not disclose and retains power—there is some analogy here with the narrator's position as I have just presented it. That this situation embodies a "law" of the text is confirmed, *a contrario,* by the behavior of the Minister's initial opponents, who are reduced by the weakness of their position to partial (but in fact fairly full) disclosures concerning the letter. The Queen confides to the Prefect "that a certain document of the last importance has been purloined from the royal apartments"; the Prefect, in turn, comes to consult Dupin about the affair, saying "I thought Dupin would like to hear the details of it, because it is so exceedingly *odd*." "Odd" means he has something of value to impart, but it shows, too, that he is an unmasterly narrator, one who does not understand the information he proposes to divulge, who does not truly "possess" it before he dispossesses himself of it. His authority—such authority as he has—derives solely from the political power of the Queen, whose agent he is, a power itself somewhat impaired in the present circumstances. Still, as a potential narrator, he does have information to give, in the form of "details"; and his incaution in thus risking his authority, in the face of the option he has of withholding what he knows, is specifically underlined by the text:

"I will tell you in a few words; but, before I begin, let me caution you that this is an affair demanding the greatest secrecy, and that I should most probably lose the position I now hold, were it known that I confided it to any one."

"Proceed," said I.

"Or not," said Dupin.

"Well, then."

The weak narrative authority of the Prefect is conveyed to the reader in the subsequent section of text through the narrative situation the text enacts. Insensitive to the frame of mind of his hearers, who are of the condescending opinion that "there was nearly half as much of the entertaining as of the contemptible about the man," and oblivious to the irony in their comments and rejoinders, especially those of Dupin, he reveals himself to be as rhetorically deficient, in failing to "admeasure" himself to narratees who are in a clear sense already his "opponents" in a kind of "game," as he is intellectually deficient in perceiving only the details, and not the pattern, of the story he has to tell. His loss of authority to his narratees is consequently twofold: they possess a better understanding than he does of the information he has come to impart (since Dupin at least is able to tell him from the start that the problem lies in his not being able to see the wood for the trees: "perhaps it is the very simplicity of the thing that puts you at fault," and they are able to "admeasure" themselves accurately to his limited intellect in a way that he cannot do to theirs.

In light of this, his childish attempt to salvage some narrative authority by withholding certain information from the pair is merely ludicrous. His would-be discretion is futile, either because he cannot maintain his evasiveness ("a certain document" soon becomes "a letter, to be frank") or because this phraseology is in any case transparent (no one is in any doubt as to who is referred to by phrases such as "the illustrious personage" and "the other exalted personage," or what the issues are—Dupin later reveals that, as a "partisan of the lady concerned" and long-time opponent of the Minister, he is perfectly *au fait* with the political implications of the affair). What, in fact, the Prefect does (in response to a specific invitation: "Suppose you detail," said I, "the particulars of your search") is to "blab": he pours forth a long string of "details" and "particulars"—a discourse that has its exact correlative in the philosophy of "nooks and crannies" and of leaving no stone unturned that presides over his search. Narrative divulgence, which he engages in to the point of indulgence (What is one to think of a police chief so anxious to advertise police methods?), is consequently the reverse of the same coin of which the failed search, and the baffled state of mind it produces is the obverse: each is the sign of the Prefect's lack of authority, the latter with respect to the Minister's superior ingeniousness and the former (as we will see) by contrast with Dupin's combination of acuity and canny narratorial authority.

For these reasons, the Prefect's narrative cannot *advance* (it cannot move toward a culminating "point," since its only point is that he cannot see the point); it can only repeat itself, just as he is condemned to repeat, unproductively, his search. The narrative he proffers on his second visit is the (mercifully abbreviated) repetition of his initial tale: "I made the reexamination, however, as Dupin suggested—but it was all labor lost, as I knew it would be." And his final loss of authority, or admission of defeat, when Dupin produces the purloined letter and claims his reward, is therefore most appropriately signaled by his speechlessness. Without authority, one has nothing to say and no right to speak; and in a text such as this, which is so fundamentally concerned with illocutionary relationships and constructed of two opposed narrative situations (the Prefect's failed narrative about his failure, Dupin's successful narrative about his success), to be deprived of that form of power that is the power to disclose (or the right to narrate) is to disappear from the text. So, "This functionary . . . rushed at length unceremoniously from the room and from the house, without having uttered a syllable since Dupin had requested him to fill up the check."

"When he had gone, my friend entered into some explanations"—the reduction of the Prefect to silence is the sign for Dupin immediately to take up the narrator's role, with a contrast that is, of course, total. The

Prefect's preoccupation with monetary reward reveals his motivation as political (Dupin draws the connection). Dupin, in turn, accepts the Prefect's check, but it seems that his real reward is of a more histrionic kind: it lies in the functionary's discomfiture and in the astonishment induced by his theatrical production of the letter, not only in the Prefect but also in his friend ("I was astounded. The Prefect appeared absolutely thunder-stricken"). This parallel in the reactions of the policeman and the friend is important: it suggests a more hidden parallel between the handing over of the letter to the policeman and the "explanations" Dupin is now about to offer his friend, and it betrays the fact that Dupin's true gain is the production of fascination with, and admiration for, his genius, irrespective of whether this is achieved by narrative as an act of non-disclosure (as is the case with the Prefect) or narrative as an act of disclosure (as with his friend).

This parallel requires some explication, because, on the face of it, Dupin is exerting authority in two different ways, according to his audience. To the Prefect, no disclosure whatsoever is made; moreover, Dupin has already administered him a lesson in the art of maintaining (narrative) authority through nondisclosure by means of an anecdote:

Once upon a time, a certain rich miser conceived the design of spunging upon this Abernethy for a medical opinion. Getting up, for this purpose, an ordinary conversation in a private company, he insinuated his case to the physician, as that of an imaginary individual.

"We will suppose," said the miser, "that his symptoms are such and such; now doctor, what would *you* have directed him to take?"

"Take!" said Abernethy, "why, take *advice,* to be sure."

However, the precondition of *narratorial* authority is that there be some narrative, and indeed, to his friend, Dupin enters at considerable length into a series of "explanations." The word, of course, is in significant contrast with the Prefect's "details" and "particulars": instead of obtuseness and confusion, the narrative this time displays mastery of its information. But it is a form of mastery that allows Dupin to be as prolix and expansive in his discourse as the Prefect himself while maintaining the firmest sense of authority.

He has first of all *chosen* his audience, disdaining the Prefect, who is incapable of understanding his sallies, in favor of the friend who, being more receptive, forms a worthier "opponent" in what is to be for the latter something of a guessing game. In contradistinction to the Prefect, whose methods and thinking are adequate only for dealing with the *mass* of opponents (i.e., in his case, criminals), Dupin, like the Minister, is of the elite and disdainful of the mass—aristocratically, he quotes Chamfort to the effect that *"toute convention reçue est une sottise, car elle a convenu au plus grand nombre."* The friend, then, is a worthy opponent, one capable of "admeasuring" himself to Dupin's mind (as the policeman cannot)—but not one capable of *winning* and hence of depriving him of his authority. The friend's role consists of asking clarifying questions and making corroborative comments or else of expressing surprise and raising easily demolished objections—in short, he is the foil to Dupin's brilliance, which he is there to appreciate and enjoy but not to *see through* (and it is in this latter sense that he is a companion figure to the Prefect).

For Dupin's alleged "explanations" are often closer to being enigmatic *pronouncements,* and they have as much the character of nondisclosure as of disclosure. From the beginning of the story, he has been portrayed not just as a pipe smoker (his friend and the Prefect both puff on meerschaums, also) but more specifically as one who uses clouds of pipe smoke as a measure of concealment: his more outrageous pieces of ironic flattery or of didactic lesson giving are directed at the Prefect "amid a perfect whirlwind of smoke" or "between the whiffs of his meerschaum." But when it comes to his dialogue with his friend, all notations of smoke production disappear from the text, because that function has now been taken over by his discourse itself.[6] His "explanations" are in two parts: theory and practice. The theoretical argument proceeds through clear enough stages: the story of the game of "even and odd" and the principle of identification with the opponent; the Prefect's error in supposing he is dealing with a common opponent and that all poets are fools; the discussion of the limited rationality of mathematics; and finally of the relative invisibility of the simple, the self-evident, the obtrusive. Two characteristics, however, make this argument quite difficult to *penetrate.* First, it takes the apparent form of a series of brilliant divagations on unrelated topics—Dupin disdains to indicate the logical structure, the *enchaînement,* of his argument, which has to be inferred by a hearer whose attention is constantly distracted by the second characteristic: the highly arguable character of propositions that range from the preposterous through the paradoxical to the enigmatic but that are presented with total assurance, as if not open to discussion (in short, as if self-evident).[7] The schoolboy's methods of "guessing" and of identification with the opponent *do not work;* on the other hand, the Prefect's plodding but exhaustive techniques of search *ought to have worked.* The challenge to the rationality of mathematics needs, in order to be coherent, to be complemented by some statement—which, however, is allowed to remain entirely implicit—of the value of the poetic mind. And the whole paragraph preceding the description of the puzzle game with maps and illustrating the invisibility of the evident is so enigmatic as to be itself a "game of puzzles."

Lacan goes so far as to speak of "le sentiment de poudre aux yeux" (1969, 26) Dupin's argument produces—he is "pulling the wool over our eyes." I would prefer to speak of the duplicity of his argumentation, since Dupin is concealing by a smokescreen of words and brilliant paradoxes an unstated but self-evident proposition they nevertheless convey—a proposition concerning the need for, and value of, acumen. It is like the name in wide-spaced letters on the map, writ so large it cannot be discerned amid the mass of fine print. Needless to say, it is no accident that the concealed core of the argument is precisely a doctrine in which acumen and penetration are opposed to the Prefect's thoroughness. The Prefect's narration, it will be recalled, was an uncontrolled mass of details and particulars concerning a method of search that depends on the detailed and particular; Dupin's argument is a series of apparent divagations, covertly controlled by the notion of acumen and consequently requiring acumen in order to grasp their unstated ordering principle. As an exercise in authority maintained through such a combination of disclosure and nondisclosure, it contrasts with the Prefect's demonstration of authority lost while showing clear affinity with the Minister's technique of ostentatious concealment.

But Lacan is right to the extent that Dupin's argument (about acumen) requires two kinds of acumen on the part of the hearer: the acumen to grasp it (which the friend appears to have) and the acumen to see through it (which the friend does not have). The stance of self-evidence he adopts concerning the propositions he is putting forward protects the extreme vulnerability of his argument from the penetration of a critical eye—much as the Minister's employment of ostentation serves as a mode of concealment that is vulnerable only to the acumen of Dupin. One might say that Dupin's argument is all show without real substance, in the way that the Minister's use of the letter as an instrument of power depends on deployment, openness, and visibility, with the letter's actual contents being relegated, as unusable and irrelevant, to silence. The difference is that Dupin's duplicitous discourse, while it is vulnerable, survives the relatively uncritical scrutiny of the friend, and his authority remains intact—whereas the Minister's duplicity is laid bare by Dupin's acumen and his power demolished. Dupin does not use his acumen merely to *grasp* the Minister's maneuvers (as his friend understands his arguments); he uses it also to *penetrate* the Minister's duplicity and to reveal the fraudulence of his techniques. So, between the theory and the practice in Dupin's narrative there is an apparent contrast: his theorizing exercises his friend's acumen (in the first sense), and his practice employs acumen (in the second sense) against the Minister's duplicity. The comparison between Dupin's duplicitous discourse and the Minister's technique of open concealment needs to be balanced, then, by some examination (which the contrast with the Prefect implies) of the correlation between Dupin's successful search procedures and the successful maintenance of authority in his narrative.

What is interesting is that, as a detective, Dupin adopts a practice that pits against the Minister's duplicity a form of duplicity that exactly matches and counters it. Under cover of green glasses, a spurious pretext, an animated conversation on a topic designed to distract the Minister's attention, he penetrates by virtue of his acumen through the smokescreen the Minister himself has set up—the pretense of languor concealing his real energy, the turning of the letter inside out and its disguised external appearance—to the principle of simplicity that controls the whole: concealment through hyperobtrusive display. This penetration, through acumen, of the ingenious Minister's duplicity corresponds exactly to the effort the friend was unable to provide in the case of Dupin's narratorial practice; yet the concealment of acumen beneath a deceptive screen (particularly the screen of words implied by the animated discussion) also matches the actual narratorial practice employed by Dupin in offering his "explanations." Dupin's practice as a detective, the practice of duplicity, is doubly successful: like his narratorial practice, it is not penetrated (by the friend, by the Minister), and it proves superior to the Minister's own practice of concealment, which *is* finally penetrated by one with greater acumen and more successful duplicity than he.

The question of the relationship between Dupin and the Minister, as exemplified by Dupin's coup in discovering and regaining the purloined letter, resolves then into that of the relative success and failure of two closely related, and well-matched, forms of duplicity. And since both Dupin and the Minister are poets, my suggestion will be that the story as a whole can best be understood as an examination of, or let us say a meerschaum meditation on, the advantages and disadvantages, the dangers and benefits of artistic duplicity as a mode of exercising narratorial authority. That artistic authority is superior to the authority of power is the primary tenet of the text: the political figures yield their authority to the poets, first the Queen to the Minister, then the Prefect to Dupin. But finally the Minister yields in turn to Dupin: What, then, of this rivalry between the two poets, their relationship of fraternal enmity (pointed up by the reference to *Atrée and Thyeste*) and the victory of the one (who admits himself "guilty of certain doggerel") over the other (who "as poet *and* mathematician . . . would reason well")?

The essence of the similarity between them lies in the fact that each practices duplicity as the art of substituting an appearance for a reality. For the Queen's letter, the Minister substitutes on her table a "letter somewhat similar to the one in question," a hasty stratagem, but effective enough to deceive the King, who does not perceive the substitution, if not the Queen. He then substitutes for the purloined letter the selfsame letter but turned "as a glove, inside out, redirected and resealed"—the same letter, then, with the external appearance of another. What Dupin substitutes for the Minister's deceptive letter is yet another appearance, a careful *facsimile* (the term in his) that reproduces the externals of the letter (but with a new text). Since the series of substitutions begins with, and is modeled on, the Queen's initial stratagem ("She was forced to place it, open as it was, upon a table. The address, however, was uppermost, and, the contents thus unexposed, the letter escaped notice"), we may say that the art of duplicity involves the production, and indeed the ostentatious display, of a deceptive externality intended to conceal an inner truth, the discovery of which would render the perpetrator vulnerable to loss of honor, dignity, or authority. Indeed, since the contents of the Queen's letter are never known, and even the police description of it consists of "a minute account of the internal, and especially of the external, *appearance* of the missing document" (my emphasis), it is almost as if there is no "inner truth" and certainly as if such truth is irrelevant to the game, in which only appearance counts. "Poudre aux yeux," certainly, wool over the eyes—but the *poudre* and the wool are of the essence.

This being so, what distinguishes Dupin from the Minister lies in the area of the "style" of duplicity each practices. The Minister's duplicity uses openness as its main ploy; Dupin relies much more on concealment. The former's substitution of his own letter for the letter purloined from the Queen is performed in full view of the victim (since his power derives, as we know, from the loser's knowledge of the robber). And in "concealing" the purloined letter, he resorts to what Dupin calls "the comprehensive and sagacious expedient of not attempting to conceal it at all"—

although, as we have seen, he does make a minimal effort at concealment by creating a new external form for the letter he proposes to display in its "hyperobtrusive situation." His, then, is the most audacious form of duplicity, the most breathtaking in its simplicity, but also the most rash, the one that is most at risk of being penetrated and hence of producing the most disastrous loss of authority. For his action to count as duplicity, it must involve a minimum of false appearances (simply to display the Queen's letter in unchanged form would not be duplicitous, it would merely be foolhardy); but such minimal disguise, under the sagacious scrutiny of such a one as Dupin, takes the form of *clues* (Why should its edges be "more chafed than seemed necessary"?) and leads to discovery and discomfiture. In terms of poetics, the Minister's device might be equated with realist texts so successful in imitating "natural" discourse that they *must* leave clues if they are to be deciphered as art ("seen through") at all, and thus benefit from artistic authority.[8] Such texts rely for narratorial effectiveness on a kind of internal inconsistency, the penetrability of their disguise.

By contrast, Dupin's practice of duplicity is more "honest," since it relies much more heavily on covertness. The substitution he performs in the Minister's apartment is done without the Minister's knowledge, and Dupin's power over him depends precisely on his remaining unaware of the deception being practiced on him. This corresponds not only to Dupin's reliance as a detective on green glasses and tactics of diversion, but also to his narratorial practice of the verbal smokescreen. It is not that for Dupin concealment is all: again, the procedure would not be duplicitous but merely self-defeating if the Minister were not to discover the trick and if the narratee were not, at least, to discover behind the smokescreen the doctrine of acumen. But in each case, penetration of the duplicity results not in a loss of authority (narratorial or political) on Dupin's part but in a confirmation and even a reinforcement of that authority. What the Minister discovers in penetrating the trick is a text, in Dupin's recognizable hand, that tells him in effect: "You are outwitted." What the narratee learns is also, in a sense, that he has been outwitted, for the text tells only of what one has already had to practice in reading it, the need for acumen. The "secret" is in the form of the words, writ large there, not somewhere behind that screen in the form of a discrete "message," and this is all the more the case if the spuriousness of the argument has also been detected: the narratee is then sent back to the puzzle of the discourse itself, wherein resides its true (duplicitous) essence—and so long as he puzzles, narratorial authority remains intact. One might think here, in contrast to realism, of the artistic practice of Mallarmé, whose textual obscurity "conceals" a message that is nevertheless "overt," since it is indistinguishable from the textuality itself. This, then, is a *textual* duplicity.

To summarize, it seems that the maintenance of artistic authority in "The Purloined Letter" is dependent on the practice of duplicity as a mode of divulgence and nondivulgence, of openness and covertness, at once. Certain tactical considerations dictate the superiority of a relative degree of covertness (which protects narratorial authority) over the corresponding degree of overtness, which may be brilliantly effective, yet necessarily carries with it a significant flaw by its need to incorporate a certain penetrability. Doubtless it is significant that, although the Minister is described as a poet, he is not given a narrative function in the story, he does not produce discourse as Dupin and the Prefect do. In historical terms, the poetics (or ideology of art) he presides over, that of realistic *mimesis,* owes little to Poe, whereas the lineage of Dupin—the practitioners of text as *écriture* such as Baudelaire, Mallarmé, and Valéry—has steadfastly acknowledged his mastery.

THE GENERAL NARRATION

Yet, two further considerations need to be formulated regarding Dupin's practice of duplicity. The first is that he, too, risks a form of failure should he miscalculate his audience: the type of incomprehension displayed by the Prefect in the early part of the story, oblivious as he is to Dupin's smokescreen and to his irony, suggests that he would not perceive the art in Dupin's later narration, nor consequently would he recognize—that is, authorize—the narratorial authority being exercised. He would simply be confirmed in his view that poets are next to fools, and so Dupin is right not to divulge his secrets to him; but he does thereby miss a chance to exercise artistic authority. Such could be the case also of a narratee more acute than the friend, who might simply dismiss the "explanations" as spurious nonsense, without perceiving their narratorial artistry.

The second consideration is that Dupin's duplicity becomes so blatant in its excess of covertness (as the Minister's is blatant in its excess of overtness) that it begins to border on artistic self-reflexivity: there is something self-denunciatory about the histrionic display in which he delights, under the guise of offering "some explanations," and in the production of a verbose and somewhat self-conscious, if enigmatic and fascinating, text. The self-reference becomes explicit not only in his allusion to a chain of literary figures (La Rochefoucauld, La Bruyère, Machiavelli, Campanella) who have allegedly preceded him in the art of mental identification with an adversary but also in Dupin's admeasurement of himself, the perpetrator of "certain doggerel," with the Minister, who is "poet *and* mathematician"; not to mention, finally, the specific status he achieves as producer of text through his pointed citation of Crébillon at the end.

Self-reflexivity as a mode of exercising narratorial authority has over duplicity the signal advantage that it *cannot* be deceptive: the artistic "ascendancy" being laid claim to cannot be mistaken, even by a narratee as obtuse as the Prefect, for anything but what it is. So, it is significant that the narrative mode adopted by the general narrator of "The Purloined Letter" in the narration for which he takes responsibility, that is, that of the text as a whole, is the mode of self-reflexivity. It is as if, having drawn the lessons of the Minister's superior ascendancy over the Queen and the Prefect, and of Dupin's superior authority over him, it remains for the narrator to incorporate into his own art of narration the advantages of artistic indirection with the certainty of effect inherent in artistic self-designation.

I see a certain distancing on the part of the general narration with respect to Dupin in the slyness of the epigraph attributed to Seneca, which opens the text: *Nil sapientiae odiosius acumine nimio.* As translated by Mabbott in the most recent critical edition (Poe 1978, 993–94), the phrase signifies "Nothing is more hateful to wisdom than too much cunning," and it is assumed to be a comment on the excessive cunning (and insufficient wisdom) of the Prefect, by comparison with Dupin. But the word *acumen* is precisely the word Dupin uses in favorable reference to his own abilities and in direct contrast with the mere "care, patience and determination" of the police. There is a sense, then, in which the Senecan phrase comments on Dupin's excessive subtlety and compares it unfavorably with true wisdom. Yet, at the same time, one needs to remember that the text is at pains to point out that Latin words are sometimes false friends: if, as Dupin says, " 'analysis' conveys 'algebra' about as much as, in Latin, *'ambitus'* implies 'ambition,' *'religio'* 'religion' or *'homines honesti'* a set of *honorable* men," then it is possible that Seneca's *acumen* may not apply after all to Dupin's particular "set of notions regarding human ingenuity."9 In its ambiguity, the epigraph functions then to set up an ironic distance between the narration itself and its principal actors, including Dupin, while in its refusal to divulge a clear meaning, it provides a notable example of the maintenance of narratorial authority through verbal art.

A similar refusal of the text to divulge is, of course, what is signified by the principal self-reflexive device in the tale—the letter, about whose actual and specific contents the reader remains totally uninformed while, as Lacan so clearly saw, its externality undergoes many substitutions. The letter thus signifies a conception of text in which the signifier is subject to constant "drift" while the signified remains elusive, if not altogether absent. 10 The opening paragraph of the text (before the motif of the letter has been introduced) provides corroborative self-reflexive imagery. In the "little back library or book-closet" that signifies the enclosed world of letters, the characters appear "intently and exclusively occupied with the curling eddies of smoke that oppressed the atmosphere of the chamber"—an image that is to take on the meaning of the screen of words as the text develops. However—not behind this screen so much as it is an accompaniment to it—the "luxury" of the meerschaum is doubled (as the signifier is doubled by its signified) by the mental luxury of "meditation"—an intellectual pursuit that does not provide an extralinguistic "meaning" but proves to be itself conducted per medium of language ("I was *mentally discussing* certain topics"; my emphasis) and to refer intertextually—as Derrida points out—to other literary texts: "I mean the affair in the rue Morgue, and the mystery attending the murder of Marie Rogêt" (i.e., the two other items in the Dupin canon). Thus, at the point where the text enacts its own emergence from silence, the narrator's moment of choice between "proceed" "or not" ("for an hour at least we had maintained profound silence"), it does so amid an escort of reminders that significance derives from relations and referrals among signs, and not from the existence of some supposed preexisting content (which might be the narrator's "knowledge," the "information" he proposes to convey). Narrative authority (posited on information to be conveyed) has been replaced here by narratorial authority (based on the "undecidability" inherent in artistic signs), and textual self-reflexivity has less the (narrative) effect of producing information than the (narratorial) effect of confirming the text's elusiveness.

At the close of the tale, another emergence of text is enacted, this time by Dupin's substitution (in his *fac-simile* of the original purloined letter) of a text, in the form of a quotation from Crébillon père, for the blank

that he feels it would be "insulting" to offer his reader, the Minister.
Since the words:

>   ——Un dessein si funeste,
> S'il n'est digne d'Atrée est digne de Thyeste

resume a tragedy of duplicity and second-guessing that turns on the
existence of a compromising letter, the self-reflexive reference to "The
Purloined Letter" itself is unmistakable; as is the inference that, in lieu of
the blank contents of the Queen's letter (the always missing signified),
what we have is the text of the tale itself, the signifier, the "whirling
eddies" of words that signify through their inclusion, by intertextual
referral, in the literary canon. Even the undecidability of such a text is
again conveyed by the citation, for while there is some *équivoque* in Atrée's
words within the context of the play, their exact bearing on the relationship of Dupin to the Minister is more than unclear in the context of
the story. (Which of the two is Atrée? Which Thyeste? Whose *dessein* is
being designated? In what sense is it unworthy of the one but worthy of
the other?)[11]

At the midpoint of the tale, where the Prefect's narrative is in-
terchanged for Dupin's, yet another substitution invites self-referential
interpretation: in return for the Prefect's check, Dupin hands over the
letter. A set of signs is exchanged for another set of signs, a "letter" for a
"figure" (50,000 francs), in an episode that clearly embodies the text's
conception of the relationship between the world of art and the world
designated here as "political," that is, between two different value systems, aesthetic and economic, that both depend on the deployment of
signs. If the handing over of the letter here signifies the exercise of
Dupin's narratorial authority (both by his nondivulgence of "information" to the functionary and by the type of artistic divulgence represented
by his explanations to his friend) and if by self-referential extension it also
stands for the text itself as a whole, what is implied is that the *test* of
narratorial authority is its exchange value against the script that has
currency in the economic domain. That this is something of a fools'
exchange is evident, since what the Prefect acquires is the equivalent of
meerschaum smoke, the letter as signifier (although it is mentioned
precisely here that he "cast a rapid glance at its contents"), while Dupin
makes very clear his disdain for the money the Prefect so much respects
(while pocketing his reward with some satisfaction).

In all these ways, then, the self-referentiality characteristic of the general narration proves to be a narratorial device, producing the text as a phenomenon of dissemination, like Dupin's own "whirling eddies" of words, but doing so in a nonduplicitous way. However, it would be misleading to abandon this discussion of the letter as the empty "place" that enables substitutions and exchanges of signs without pointing out that, for all its insistence on textual drift and the absent signified, "The Purloined Letter" does not deny meaning. Rather, it situates it, not in the domain of signs, but in the world of the relationships that signs serve to mediate.[12] Dupin has "a quarrel on hand . . . with some of the algebraists of Paris," and his disagreement with these specialists in signs (whose discipline depends precisely on the equivalence and substitutibility of signs) stems from the fact that "occasions may occur where $x^2 + px$ is not altogether equal to q" or, in other words, that situations alter the value of signs and meaning is contextual. "What is true of *relation*—of form and quantity—is often grossly false in regard to morals, for example"—that is, in regard to the world of human relationships. The letter about whose contents we learn so little is regularly described as to its address: when the Queen places the letter address uppermost on her table, when the false address to D——on the letter as disguised by the Minister alerts Dupin to the deception, and when Dupin finally makes this false address the true one on the *fac-simile* that contains the text from Crébillon and justifies Lacan's statement of the story's moral, that "*une lettre arrive toujours à destination.*"[13] Hence, the process whereby a letter to the Queen becomes a letter to the Minister through the mediation of a false address forms the subject matter of the tale (its essential narrative reversal), just as much as the process whereby Dupin's text replaces the blank inner page. Not only this, but it is the *combination* of these two processes (the production of text *and* its insertion in a significant relationship) that gives point to Dupin's action in the culminating paragraph of the text. The self-referential point is evident: the meaningfulness of "The Purloined Letter" derives similarly from the substitution of text for absence (the story itself for the undivulged contents of the purloined letter) *and* from the production of a relationship between narrator and narratee that is mediated by the text in the way the relationship between Dupin and the Minister is mediated by Dupin's letter—a relationship, consequently, in which what is at issue is the matter of authority.

That communicational situations make meaning is signified, finally, not only by the insistence on "address" throughout "The Purloined Letter" but also by the motif of signature. The text of Crébillon, which is foreign to the relationship of Dupin and the Minister, is inserted into that relationship and thus acquires its cogency by the fact that, in signing it, Dupin takes responsibility for it and becomes its "author":

So, as I knew he would feel some curiosity in regard to the identity of the person who had outwitted him, I thought it a pity not to give him a clew. He is well acquainted with my MS., and I just copied into the middle of the blank sheet the words. . . .

The Prefect, too, must sign the check he hands over to Dupin in exchange for the lost letter—which signifies that here, too, it is the relationship that gives point to what would otherwise be the exchange of empty signs. If Dupin's signature on the letter to the Minister is a triumphant one, a measure of his success in the guessing game that has pitted him against a worthy opponent, the Prefect's signature is his admission of defeat, of confusion and bafflement in the presence of Dupin's superior genius:

For some minutes he remained speechless and motionless, looking incredulously at my friend with open mouth, and eyes that seemed starting from their sockets; then apparently recovering himself in some measure, he seized a pen, and after several pauses and vacant stares, finally filled up and signed a check for fifty thousand francs, and handed it across the table to Dupin.

In both cases, the act of signature acknowledges the role of authority in the relationships that give point to the deployment of textual signs.

What then, finally, of the signature appended to these pages? In the guessing game by which a critic pits himself against the superior genius, the narratorial authority of a text, does the signing of an essay signify "I have outwitted you" or "I concede defeat"? Am I playing Dupin to Poe's minister, or the Prefect to Poe's Dupin? An interpretive essay has something in common with Dupin's exposure of the Minister's techniques of open concealment; but in the long run—as the form of words that recognizes the value of a literary text in the world of universities and scholarly journals—it is more like the Prefect's check (in the world of economics) than it is like Dupin's missive to the Minister (in the world of "letters"); and in signing the present text I am happy to acknowledge both the relational character of the game of "even and odd" I have been playing with Poe's narrator and the defeat of my poor algebraic analysis as a way of admeasuring my intellect to that of my "opponent." However aware one may be of the ruses and stratagems by which narratorial authority produces and maintains itself, the act of reading can only ever, in the end, produce a kind of dumb homage to that strange ascendancy.

Notes

1. Latin *"narrāre* to relate, recount, supposed to be for **gnārāre,* relates to *gnārus,* knowing, skilled, and thus ultimately allied to KNOW" (*Oxford English Dictionary*).

2. This, of course, presupposes that the text is not prepared to place complete reliance on purely *extratextual* indicators (such as the mode of publications, etc.)—an assumption that nineteenth- and twentieth-century narratives appear to justify.

3. "Le séminaire sur 'La lettre volée,'" in *Ecrits 1,* Coll. "Points" (Paris: Editions du Seuil 1969), 19–75. Future references to Lacan will be indicated by page numbers in the text.

My focus on the text differs from Lacan's, and my debt to him lies principally in his having drawn attention to the features of the text that call for interpretation: the substitution of letter for letter and the substitutability of character for character; the fact that Dupin's substitution of letters only partially "repeats" the Minister's previous act of substitution (the latter being overt, the former covert); and finally the simple infractions of verisimilitude, the fact that the Prefect of Police's exhaustive search methods ought to have turned up the missing letter no less infallibly (perhaps more so) than Dupin's reliance on "acumen," and the fact that the "hyperobtrusive" place is not necessarily the best place to conceal an important document from persistent searchers. ("C'est là un leurre," Lacan says delightfully [1969, 26], "dont pour nous, nous ne recommanderions l'essai à personne, crainte qu'il soit déçu à s'y fier.")

4. For a lucid critical account of the Lacan-Derrida confrontation that incorporates also many suggestive elements for a reading of "The Purloined Letter," see Barbara Johnson (1977) [reprinted here as chap. 10]. Following her, Norman N. Holland (1980) [reprinted here as chap. 14] insists on the relationship between the issue of authority in the text and that in the recent critical writing to which it has given rise.

5. The major trend of Poe criticism has been to give preeminent authority to Dupin, who is seen as a Romantic genius, a figure of "godlike omniscience," while the narrative "I" and the reader are allotted "the role of dull-witted dupes" (Thompson 1973, 174; see also Daniel 1971, 103–10). In distancing myself from this interpretation, I am not attempting to reverse this hierarchical ordering of the *characters* so much as to relate, one to the other, the *narrative instances* involved in the tale. The significance of Lacan's contribution in general has been to demystify the figure of the *"sujet supposé savoir";* and it is in this perspective that I approach Dupin as narrator; but I am less interested in the personages as human "subjects" in either the conventional or the Lacanian sense than I am concerned with the functioning of discourse and discourse relationships.

6. For a look at the smoke/words metaphor in Gautier, Baudelaire, Mallarmé, and Ponge, see my "Le poète fumeur" (1979).

7. Can it be that Lacan's fascination with "The Purloined Letter" does not derive exclusively from the implications of the game of "even and odd"? Dupin's discursive practice offers a recognizable "model" of Lacan's own pedagogical style, with its combination of assurance, formal brilliance, and obscurity. (For acknowledgment of the issues of authority involved in the debate about "The Purloined Letter," see Johnson 1977, but see also Shoshana Felman's very subtle reading of Lacan's pedagogical style [1982], which appeared too late for me to be able to take it into account here.)

8. The "clue" as a claim to authorship, and hence to narratorial authority, is explicitly thematized at the end of "The Purloined Letter" through Dupin's need to let the Minister *know* that he has been duped, and by whom.

9. Lewis and Short (1955) gives as figurative meanings of *acumen:* "A. *Acuteness, shrewdness, keenness, acumen.*" The Seneca quotation has not been traced (probably it is a pseudoquotation), so its reference cannot be checked in the original context.

10. Lacan (1969, 39–40) proposes "La lettre détournée" as a more accurate translation of the title than Baudelaire's "La lettre volée." Equally apt would be "La lettre escamotée," since *escamotage* is the sleight of hand by which an object is made to disappear and (normally) a deceptive object is produced in its place— much as Dupin substitutes a deceptive letter for that addressed to the Queen, and much as, more generally, text substitutes in "The Purloined Letter" for the blank contents of the missing letter.

11. For a discussion of *Atrée and Thyeste,* see also Johnson (1977).

12. For the insight that enables me to make this statement, I am particularly indebted to Charles Altieri (1979, 489–510; 1981, chap. 4).

13. This is the formulation that drew Derrida's ire, as a denial of the phenomenon of dissemination. Barbara Johnson shows it to be more profound (and less univocal) in its implications than Derrida supposes; she interprets it to mean that "the letter's destination is *wherever it is read:* the place it assigns to its reader. . . . The letter's destination is not its literal addressee, nor even whoever possesses it, but whoever is possessed *by* it" (1977, 144). She does not point out, however, that the story in fact enacts this philosophical point in its narrative structure, whereby the loss and return of the Queen's letter (on which Lacan and Derrida focus) appears as merely the occasion for a substitution of addressees (the letter to the Queen becoming Dupin's letter to the Minister in the course of the narrative and by means of the action of the story).

14 ❧ Re-covering "The Purloined Letter": Reading as a Personal Transaction

NORMAN N. HOLLAND

Begin with the text, they say. For me, one central fact about the text is that I am reading this story in Pocketbook No. 39, the copy of Poe I had as a boy—one of the first paperbacks in America. "Kind to your Pocket and your Pocketbook." Hardly a distinguished edition, yet I find myself agreeing with what the man I call Marcel says in the library of the Guermantes: "If I had been tempted to be a book collector, as the Prince deGuermantes was, I would have been one of a very peculiar sort. . . . The first edition of a work would have been more precious to me than the others, but I would have understood by that the edition in which I read it for the first time" (Proust 1932, 2:1007).

The Great Tales and Poems of Edgar Allan Poe. Complete and Unabridged. Bound in Perma-Gloss—and the book is indeed in perfectly respectable shape for a paperback published in 1940. I was thirteen years old then. I am fifty-two now, and I have learned, alas, that I am not bound in Perma-Gloss.

"Re-covering 'The Purloined Letter': Reading as a Personal Transaction," by Norman N. Holland, from Susan R. Suleiman and Inge Crossman, ed., *The Reader in the Text: Essays on Audience and Interpretation*. Copyright © 1980 by Princeton University Press. Reprinted by permission of Princeton University Press.

The book, then, as what? As a part of me from then that is not broken
or worn down. Literature endures, while we change. Yet as we change we
change it, so that this "Purloined Letter" both is and is not the same
"Purloined Letter" I first read almost forty years ago.

"Purloined," that lovely, artificial word, so typically Poe-etic; it comes
from *porloignée*—Norman French or, if you like, Norm's French. When I
studied French in school, my favorite province was, inevitably, Norman-
dy. I feel protective toward that word *purloined*. It is not to be confused (as
Lacan 1966b, for example, does)[1] with words meaning "alongside." This
is truly *porloignée* from *loin,* "far," hence, "to put far away." As the
Minister D—— does. As Dupin himself does.

"Purloined" means the letter was taken from one place to another, in
that shifting of signifiers which first attracted Lacan. Indeed, the whole
story proceeds by the moving of papers from one place to another: the two
letters, the check for 50,000 francs, the third letter containing the two
lines of poetry. A story around the placing of letters. If one found the
letter in concealment, then one would know, *That* is the letter. In the
open, that *cannot* be the letter. A study in contexts. Things are in their
place and therefore not noticeable, or they are out of their place and to be
discovered by the bureaucratic methods of the Prefect of Police. Or so Poe
would have us believe.

Yet the Prefect's techniques of search, as he enumerates them, are
marvelous: the long needles, the microscopes, the grids that account for
every tiny bit of space. "The fiftieth part of a line could not escape us," he
says. Nevertheless, I cannot believe, as Dupin does, that the Prefect's
methods are foolproof. Somewhere, inside the wainscoting, painted under a picture, rolled into a window groove, somewhere in a building as
large and intricate as a French *hôtel particulier,* a person as clever as D——
could hide a single letter so that no police officer, no matter how
painstaking, could discover it.

Therefore, I do not really believe the basic premise of Poe's story. I
believe there is a mechanical solution to the Minister's problem of concealing the letter that would make Dupin's oh-so-clever strategy useless.
In the same way, I disbelieve that, in the Prefect's incredibly expensive
and time-consuming searches, someone would not have examined the
letter in the card case. One's secrets are always found out by the sheer
bigness and brute force of governmental power.

Yet I dare not say so. Poe bullies me by suggesting that only inferior
minds would resort to physical concealment. A trick has been worked—

not just on the Prefect and the Minister—but on me.

Yet my very doubts turn me again to the special sense of space I get in this story: secret, small places, hidden drawers, gimlet holes, microscopic dust on the chair rungs, the little card case. Yet we move by analogy, outward from these tiny concealing spaces to the *troisième arrondissement,* to the schoolyard, to the royal apartments, to an intrigue between Dupin and D—— in (Where else?) Vienna.

The central movement of the story is to turn the letter inside out, to turn the hidden, important inner space outward so that it seems trivial. The Prefect turns the physical surroundings of the Hotel D—— inside out, but that is of no use. Dupin, however, turns the mind inside out. He can bring out into the open one's very thoughts. He moves by analogy, deduction or, as he says, by simile and metaphor, which will actually strengthen an argument as well as merely embellish. The poet thinks this way, rather than the mathematician, he says. But also, I would add, the psychoanalyst.

Dupin turns our narrator's mind inside out when he reveals his inner reverie on the shortness of the actor Chantilly in "The Murders in the Rue Morgue." He turns the mind of D—— inside out by analogizing to his chain of reasoning and realizing the letter must be in plain sight. He turns the letter itself inside out, not by probing into all the secret places the Prefect's needles had probed, but by having a lunatic shout in the street outside.

Dupin turns minds inside out by playing with inside and outside. He quotes the advice of a clever schoolboy who won all the marbles at even and odd: " 'When I wish to find out how wise, or how stupid, or how good, or how wicked is any one, or what are his thoughts at the moment, I fashion the expression of my face as accurately as possible in accordance with the expression of his, and then wait to see what thoughts or sentiments arise in my mind or heart, as if to match or correspond with the expression.' " The outer face turns the inner mind inside out, just as Dupin's substitution of a facsimile for the purloined letter duplicates the Minister's original theft by substituting a trivial letter for the crucial one right out in plain sight.[2] So the story's outside calls forth my inside, and I must bring my doubts outside and take the story inside.

My doubts must be hidden in this story about hiding, which is also about not hiding. Like those lines to conceal the names and dates. 18—. "The Prefect of the Parisian police, G——." "The Minister D——." Does Poe really think he can conceal police chiefs and cabinet ministers by little lines? "The fiftieth part of a line could not escape us." That which is most obviously hidden is most easily discovered—is that not the moral of the story?

That which is most obvious, by contrast, is most hidden. The minor peccadillo covers the greater—the letter in the little feminine hand conceals the greater sin of the greater woman. She is the Queen, some critics say—Lacan does, for example—but the story does not. "A personage of most exalted station" who comes alone to the royal *boudoir,* as, indeed, does the Minister D——. A royal mistress perhaps? A sister? A cousin? We shall never learn her name or her secret. "Questions remain," remarks Harry Levin (1967, 141–42), "which M. Dupin is much too discreet to raise: what was written in that letter? by whom to whom? and how did its temporary disappearance affect the writer and the recipient?" We shall not learn in this story, where brains defer to beauty.

I read this story when I was thirteen and I also had something to hide, something that is perfectly known to anyone who knows anything at all about thirteen-year-old boys. Most obvious, yet most carefully concealed. In the Prefect's phrase, "This is an affair demanding the greatest secrecy, and . . . I should most probably lose the position I now hold were it known that I confided it to any one." Yes, indeed, one must keep up one's position, regardless of what others know about you. Thus, the villainous D—— "is, perhaps, the most really energetic human being now alive—but that is only when nobody sees him." Can a thirteen-year-old boy find something of himself in D——?

Hiding. My scarcely containable pleasure at knowing what others do not know. As a boy playing hide-and-seek, I could barely control my impulse to burst out of my hiding place to shout, Here I am, to reveal my magic secret. Here Dupin tells. I—Kilroy—was here. I took the letter, and I left the MS behind. I got away with *it,* the precious, ambiguous object both male and female, both big and black and small and red, both concealed and unconcealed, that I will tell you no more about. Now I know all their secrets of royal sex and power.

When I talk that way, I must sound like the early "Freudism" of Marie Bonaparte. Everything is open. Let it all hang out. "The Purloined Letter," she says, expresses "regret for the missing maternal penis." The letter hangs over the fireplace just as a female penis (if it existed) would hang over "the cloaca" here represented by the symbol of fireplace or chimney. Not even the clitoris is omitted—it is the little brass knob from which the card rack hangs. The struggle between Dupin and the Minister D—— is an Oedipal struggle between father and son, but of a very archaic kind, a struggle to seize not the mother in her entirety but only her penis, only a part therefore. A Bone-a-part, I suppose.

She then can link the wicked D—— to figures in Poe's life and, of course, to Poe himself, so that the tortured author is here equating himself with the hated but admired father by the same talent he discusses abstractly in the story, identification. Dupin receives the check for 50,000 francs and restores the woman her symbolic letter or missing penis. "Thus, once more," says Bonaparte (1971) "we meet the equation gold = penis. The mother gives her son gold in exchange for the penis he restores" (383–84).

Strange as all this sounds, some of it carries over into Lacan's reading—as Jacques Derrida points out (1975a, 66–71; 1975b, 115–17). Like most readings from first-phase or symbolic Freudianism (Holland 1976a), it costs nothing. It cost me something to admit to you that I masturbated, even thirty-nine years ago and at an age when all boys do. It costs nothing to say a little brass knob stands for the clitoris. It is all "out there," quite external and inhuman, quite, therefore, foreign to the spirit of psychoanalysis as a *science de l'homme,* quite like Dupin's abstract intellect or perhaps Lacan's or Derrida's.

Bonaparte comes closer to a human truth when she talks about Dupin as a young man struggling for a woman against an older man, against three of them in fact. The Prefect G—— is a watcher who, ratlike, ferrets out secrets from tiny hiding places. Clumsy and pompous, he conceals the royal group in a cloud of unknowing. "The disclosure of the document to a third person who shall be nameless would bring in question the honour of a personage of most exalted station." By contrast, the Minister D—— easily learns of sexual, familiar secrets and uses them to hold a woman in thrall. A third father is scarcely mentioned, the royal personage who does not know and cannot aid the royal woman, the perhaps cuckolded, and certainly helpless, monarch.

I feel the presence of various fathers, a cuckolded one, a helpless, impotent one, a clever, dangerous one, and not just the characters of the story—other fathers whom I must outwit are Lacan and Derrida. Is it not natural that I feel like a son? Dupin speaks for me when he says, "I act as a partisan of the lady concerned."

Dupin reminds me even more, though, of Prometheus, whose name means "forethought" and who stole a sacred object, black and red like this royal letter, a fragment of glowing charcoal hidden in a giant fennel stalk. No vulture for this Prometheus, however. He gives the enfolded red and black back to the gods and is given 50,000 francs for his forethought. This Dupin-Prometheus thus restores the connection between the gods and men, between the miraculous and the natural, between man and woman. When I was thirteen I used to do magic tricks for my parents' patient guests: the cut rope restored, the missing ace recovered, the marked penny found inside a little red bag inside a matchbox inside a bigger red box all bound up with rubber bands. And always I was the one who knew the secret, not these adults.

So many magic tricks depend on disappearance or loss recovered in a novel and astounding way. They form an image of human development. In infancy, we give up union with a nurturing other to gain individuality. We give up the freedom of chaos to find autonomy. We give up a mother's supporting hand to stand on our own feet. We lose in order to gain. We lose the card or cut the rope or see the handkerchief disappear to gain new wisdom about human possibilities. The royal lady loses the letter but, thanks to the magician Dupin, gains new power over the villainous D———. As he points out, "She has now him in [her power]—since, being unaware that the letter is not in his possession, he will proceed with his exactions as if it was. Thus will he inevitably commit himself at once to his political destruction."

Dupin and I are Prometheus, Magicians, Rescuers of royal ladies. I also, like Dupin, am a decipherer of texts.[3] When he visits D———, he already knows where to look and what to look for, for he has solved the Prefect's long narration of the theft, the letter, the hiding, and the rest. Similarly, he solved the cases of the Rue Morgue and of Marie Rogêt by interpreting newspaper accounts. I work the same way with his stories, or try to.

Dupin exists in a world of texts, but he himself is not a text to be read. Behind the green spectacles, he sees but is not seen. The story gives no information about the physical appearance of Dupin. He and his friend are only half there.

This is a story of two bachelors enjoying "the twofold luxury of meditation and a meerschaum," in the quiet digs "*au troisième, No. 33.*" Twos and threes. Female twos and male threes in an old symbolism. Odd numbers. I remember the Prefect's "fashion of calling everything 'odd' that was beyond his comprehension."

By contrast, Dupin and narrator enjoy the intellectual pleasures: "I was mentally discussing certain topics which had formed matter for conversation between us at an earlier period of the evening . . . the affair of the Rue Morgue, and the mystery attending the murder of Marie Rogêt." The story is a talking among men and a conflict between two men, a regression to being boys, really. "These characters are a boy's dream of men," says Daniel Hoffman, "because they interact only one-dimensionally, that being in the dimension of the intellect" (1978, 117). They have a boys' relationship like Huck and Tom on the island, sitting and smoking and talking about intellectual issues, or like my roommate and myself in graduate school. Even the adversary is part of this company. Dupin visits him intellectually, through "a topic which I knew well had never failed to interest and excite him."

True, it is only one dimension, yet how vital a dimension it is for me. I share the ambition Poe reveals in Dupin's disquisition on mathematics, the feeling that his own intellect has powers not granted to lesser beings. How intelligent I thought myself when I was reading this story at thirteen; and I am not entirely over that vanity yet, as you can see by my choosing to write about a story that two major French thinkers have analyzed. They are all to be outwitted, all these fathers like the Prefect or the Minister, or, for that matter, Lacan or Derrida. As the easygoing narrator observes, "You have a quarrel on hand . . . with some of the algebraists of Paris." Yes, I do. I am confronting them as Dupin confronts the mysterious D——, through an intellectual "discussion . . . upon a topic which I knew well had never failed to interest and excite him."

We interpreters are all like the boy who won the whole school's marbles playing "even and odd" (that mystery again of the odd male and even female). The aim is to bring hidden information out, and we pride ourselves on our cleverness at being able to do that. Others might be stronger, more capable, more likable—but we are smart. We can bring the secret out from behind one's back.

The intellectual brilliance will hide all those doubts one has of oneself at thirteen (or at fifty-two). Behind green spectacles the thinker will see but not be seen. Madness is outside, a cry in the street. Inside, all is rational, masterful. Atreus, Thyestes, those terrible struggles between the generations will be enfolded in the sleek Alexandrines of Crébillon—only another puzzle. This becomes a story about converting sex, murder, cannibalism, or adultery into an intellectual game.[4] The pure-loined letter.

Inevitably, then, it is also a story about the inadequacy of pure intellect to cover human limitations. The key relation (for me) is that between Dupin and his friend the narrator—the relater (my pun intended). He does not know as much as Dupin and he knows he does not know, but it is all all right. He is secure. He trusts and is trusted. He relates. Holmes and Watson pair off more or less the same way, as do Nero Wolfe and

Archie Goodwin or Lord Peter Wimsey and Bunter: the cool detective and his kindly sidekick. They embody two kinds of relations to the world, the knower and the one who relates to the world more as ordinary people do. He acts. He trusts and believes, often without guile, the way Watson is so conventional.

By contrast the knower needs to see under and through and behind. Behind the green spectacles he knows the guilty secret, but he does not have the empathy that encourages Maigret's criminals to write him even after he has packed them off to prison. This kind of detective is only a knower, only an adversary.

For me, as for Dupin, knowing ' safer. Basic trust is for the Watsons of this world who do not need to know everything. The Dupins, the Holmeses, and the Hollands need to see through everything. We need to know even the contents of our friends' heads, to say nothing of the blackmail schemes of the powerful political fathers and the weaknesses of policemen. Then, sitting over meditation and meerschaums, we can feel secure—because we know.

I love this story, as I love the Holmes stories, because I can be both the Dupin one admires and the relater who loves and is loved of Dupin. I find something of the same satisfaction in teaching, for I hover between teaching "it" and teaching "someone." As a relater, I am the benevolent instructor who wears his authority lightly and tries to be loved by his students. As Dupin, I know and you do not and I am going to show you what I know that you do not, but then you will know and we will be friends again and relate the ways relaters (not Dupins) do. As after a game of hide-and-seek.

Here, Dupin is a teacher to his friend the narrator, but to the mysterious D——, he is an adversary. Men of mind fighting with mind. As Dupin points out, the adversaries here are both poets, so that the core of the story is a contest between two poets which is decided by the quotation of two lines of poetry. Would not Robert Graves see here a battle between two bards for the possession of the magic letter and the protection of the White Goddess? Might not even Northrop Frye see here a flyting? Dunbar and Kennedy alliterating each other into hell itself, or even further in the dark backward and abysm of time, Beowulf and sour-mouthed Unferth, a pair of bearskinned savages hurling sarcasm and litotes and knucklebones at each other across a haunch of beef. How essentially Poetic to mask that primitive, magical contest with the elegance and decadence of his two Paris intellectuals and their embroidery of literary and philosophical allusion. Poe's art is artifice—another kind of hiding, the covering of the opposite.

"But," as D. H. Lawrence says, "Poe is rather a scientist than an artist" (1964, 65). Poe responds to the world through this very tendency to embellishment. He thinks of reality as a solid core under a surface of ornament, and when he writes, he creates artifice in order to break it down. Inside out again. For him, the essence of criticism, politics, mathematics, or philosophy becomes a kind of detection, bringing the correct solution out from under the covering text.

Still deeper within that detection I sense Poe's radically romantic belief that there is in fact a solution to be found. He holds a deep faith that there is some sort of thereness at the core of things, even if it be the beating of a murdered heart beneath the floorboards or the first feeble movements in the hollow coffin in the cellar of the House of Usher. That there be *something* there, something one can identify oneself with, is preferable, no matter how horrible that something, to absence. "When the self is broken," says Lawrence of Poe, "and the mystery of the recognition of *otherness* fails, then the longing for identification with the beloved becomes a lust" (1964, 76). In Poe, it is a desperate hunger, something that goes beyond even the need to know: Poe—my Poe—is the child who must know by mind alone the Other he should have held in his mouth or heart. "To try to *know* any living being is to try to suck the life out of that being," says Lawrence (1964, 70), more psychoanalytic than he knows.

It is through this theme, the contrast between knowing and trusting, between Dupin and his relater, that I can articulate for myself those two shadowy figures lurking through my associations, Lacan and Derrida.

Lacan points to similarities in the two thefts of the fateful letter, its theft by the Minister from the Queen, then its theft by Dupin from the Minister. He finds in this mirroring pattern an instance of the repetition compulsion (or, as he calls it, "automatism"), hence of the "insistence" of the signifier, which is itself "symbol only of an absence."

Thus, in his analysis of the Poe story, as in his other writings, Lacan's theme is absence. I suppose it is the psychoanalysis in me, but I hear in that very preoccupation a longing for presence. Derrida calls it "this rush to truth" (1975a, 57), "la précipitation vers la vérité" (1975b, 11). Lacan seeks, as does Dupin himself, the hermeneutical decoding of the text, but for Lacan it is psychoanalysis—Lacanian psychoanalysis—that occupies the place of Dupin, the detective, the magician, the critic, the analyst. "The purloined letter," he tells us, as Poe himself might, is "like an immense female body," and it is Lacan/Dupin who will undress and possess that body—a conclusion completely Poe-etic.

As Jacques Derrida points out in his brilliant and relentlessly skeptical critique of Lacan's seminar on "The Purloined Letter," Lacan's conclusion springs from a variety of tacit assumptions. He assumes, for example, that the signifier has a proper, preordained trajectory; that a letter cannot be subdivided into parts; that one can ignore the story's formal narrative-within-a-narrative structure; that femaleness is defined by castration, and so on. If the story's theme, for Lacan, is fusion with a body of knowledge, for Derrida it is another major theme I glean from Poe, trust (or, for Derrida, distrust). In a world of deconstructions, the greatest intellectual sin is to try to take a fixed position. Derrida, I think, writes out of a need not to believe, a need to *dis*trust. Yet, as with Lacan, I feel the absence is itself a presence. Disbelief is itself a belief in disbelief. Derrida turns his shiftings and doublings and changes of perspective into a credo and a method to be as automatically applied by his disciples as ever the once-New criticism was or as Lacan's shuffling of signifiers is.

Such disbelief I would expect to mask a disappointed need to believe. It shows, I feel, in Derrida's distinctive ambiguity, as for example, in the opening sentences of his brilliant critique of Lacan's seminar: "La psychanalyse, à supposer, se trouve. Quand on croit la trouver, c'est elle, à supposer, qui se trouve." Derrida provides abstractions—texts usually, but here, "la psychanalyse"—as the subjects for verbs that need physical or animate subjects—here, *se trouver.* For me, the effect is to make concrete and abstract hover between presence and absence, activity and inactivity, animate and inanimate. *A supposer,* I sense, in short, Derrida's own version of Poe's quest and Lacan's for a living and dead—someone.

And what of me? The phrase that first comes to mind is: *I want to place myself* in relation to this story and Derrida and Lacan, and even as I say those words, I realize I am recreating still another motif for "The Purloined Letter": articulating states of mind by physical places and changes of mind by movements from place to place or inside out as in so many of Poe's stories of hiding and burial. Here, I move from the boyish intellections of Dupin and his roommate, out to an active struggle over the possession of a text (and a woman), back again to the quiet, now-prosperous, bachelor apartment. In the same way I now want to retreat from my small skirmish with Lacan and Derrida to larger theoretical concerns.

What have I been doing in a theoretical sense? What kind of a reading is this? I call it *transactive criticism* (Holland 1975, 1976b, 1977a,b, 1978b; Schwartz 1978; Willbern 1979). By that I mean a criticism in which the critic works explicitly from his transaction of the text. Of course, no critic can do anything else, and in that sense, all criticism is at least de facto transactive. It becomes de jure transactive when the critic explicitly builds on his relationship to the text.

When he does so, he aligns himself with what I believe are the true dynamics of the reading transaction. Yes, behind my casual, even reckless associations, there is a model of reading. It begins, like Dupin, with the obvious: the text is the same, but everyone responds to it differently. How do we account for the differences?

Many theorists assume there is some kind of normal response with individual variations. The normal response is the one caused by the text, when it is read in a particular way, variously called the hermeneutic circle (by German critics), or simply the formulation of a centering theme around which all the separate details of the work become relevant. When we read that way, we look at each part to anticipate the whole and then we use our sense of the whole to place each part in a context.

Now let me pose a contrast to that kind of reading, in which one folds the text tightly in on a centering theme. Instead of taking the text as a fixed entity, let us think of it as a process involving a text and a person. Let us open up the text by assuming the person brings to it something extrinsic. It could be information from literary history, biography, or an archaic ritual like the flyting between primitive bards. It could even be some quite personal fact like my reading this story in Pocketbook No. 39 or my finding it at a time in my life when I had something sexual to hide.

It seems to me not only possible but likely that whenever we read, we are associating such extratextual, extraliterary facts to the supposedly fixed text. Now rather than strip those associations away, what will happen if we accept these things outside the text and try to understand the combination of text and personal association? That is what I have been trying to do with you in this essay. That is the first step in transactive criticism. It is also the question that I am posing to Lacan and Derrida. Is not a transactive criticism truer to the human dynamics of literary response than the linguistic glides of a Lacan or the deconstructions of a Derrida? Is it not better to have a literary and especially a psychoanalytic criticism that is grounded in the body and the family?

The question leads to theories of reading. One model assumes that there is a normal response to a text which the text itself causes, and that the differences in people's responses are idiosyncrasies which there is little point in trying to account for. This theory, which I call "text-active," has one basic trouble. It simply does not fit what we know of human perception: namely, that perception is a constructive act in which we impose schemata from our minds on the data of our senses. If it were true that texts in themselves caused responses, reading would be an anomalous procedure, quite different from our other acts of interpreting the world around us.

Consider for a moment what used to be called optical illusions. Equal vertical lines with oppositely pointing arrowheads at their ends appear to be unequal. A flight of stairs seems to flip from right-side up to upside down. A drawing alternately shifts from a vase in silhouette to two human profiles.

Psychologists no longer think of these as "illusions" because they serve instead to demonstrate a fundamental truth about human perception. We see more with our brains than with our eyes. There is no way that two vertical lines of equal length can make you think they are unequal. There is no way a still picture of a flight of steps or of a vase can flip your perception of it first one way, then another. You are doing this to yourself. You are demonstrating over seven decades of psychological research— that perception is a constructive act. When we see those vertical lines, we bring something to bear on them; call it a schema, specifically our schema for recognizing rectangular shapes in perspective. What we perceive is the interaction between the lines, the text, if you will, and the schema. We end up with something more than just what is "there."

To take that extra something into account, we need a more sophisticated theory of response than the first, text-active theory. We need a theory in which a text and its literent (reader, viewer, or hearer) act together to cause the response—call it biactive theory. I think of *Rezeptionsästhetik,*[5] for example, as biactive, or speech-act theory (Ohmann 1973), or Fish's "affective stylistics,"[6] or Riffaterre's collection of selected readers into a "super-reader."[7] In all these theories, the text sets limits, then the literent projects into the text within those limits. You can see this kind of distinction in Hirsch's differentiation between "meaning" and "significance" (1976) or in Iser's notion of determinacy and indeterminacy (1974). The novel may speak of a woman, but it is we who endow her with a broad forehead, an aggressive stride, or whatever. The biactivity shows most clearly, perhaps, in Stanley Fish's stop-motion method of reading (which surely came from watching too much football on television). First we read two lines of Lancelot Andrewes during which the text acts on us. Then we stop and project into the text. Then we read two more words. Then we project—and so on until touchdown.

A biactive theory marks a big step forward over the simple text-active theory. It acknowledges that literents do find more in texts than just what is "there." Further, it admits a more than purely linguistic response. People bring social and historical ideas to bear as well as mere linguistic competence.

Nevertheless, the biactive theory seems to me to have two difficulties. First, it is really two theories, a new theory of reader activity plus the old text-active theory in which the text does something to the reader. The biactive theory builds on the false text-active theory; it thus guarantees it can never be more than half right.

Further, the biactive theory divides responses into two stages, as in Fish's stop-motion reading of sentences. But when I test it against the optical illusions, a two-stage theory does not fit. I do not first see the lines and then decide that I will interpret them as though they were perspectives of rectangles. I do it all in one continuous transaction. I never see the lines without a schema for seeing them.

If so, texts cannot simply cause or even limit response in any direct way independent of our schemata, intellectual, moral, or aesthetic, for reading literature. In fact, if you actually collect people's free responses to texts, they simply do not show a uniform core (from the text) and individual variations (from the people). The responses have practically nothing in common. One has to conclude, I think, that any uniformity we achieve in the classroom comes not from the text but from our own skill and authority as teachers, that is, from agreed-upon (or insisted-upon) methods of teaching.

Therefore, I move on from a biactive theory to a transactive theory in which the literent builds the response, and the text simply changes the consequences of what the literent brings to it. The literent creates meaning and feeling in one continuous and indivisible transaction. One cannot separate, as in the biactive theories, one part coming from the text and another part coming from the literent. In a transactive model, I am engaged in a feedback loop no part of which is independent of the other parts. The schemata, conventions, and codes I bring to bear may be literary, biological, cultural, or the results of economic class, but it is I who bring them to bear with my unique identity. It is I who start the loop and I who sustain it. It is I who ask questions of the text in my personal idiom and I who hear and interpret the answers. It is I who mingle the covering of the purloined letter and the Perma-Gloss of my Pocketbook No. 39.

In short, a transactive theory of response has two advantages over either a text-active theory or a biactive theory. First, it fits what the psychologists tell us about the way we perceive meaning in other contexts besides literature—actively, constructively, if you will, creatively. It does not therefore require literature to be an aberration. Second, a transactive theory will account both for the originality and variety of our responses and for our circumscribing them by conventions. In fact, it will do more. By means of psychoanalytic concepts like identity or fantasy or defense, we can connect literary transactions to personality. Precisely because literary experience is so personal, we can understand it through a technique like free association by which psychoanalysts articulate experience in other contexts. With a transactive theory of response, you can relate the rich variety of literary experience to the rich variety of human beings themselves.

You can, but will you? Is it possible for me to make such highly personal associations as my magic tricks when I was thirteen years old meaningful to you? Can we add them to the text in such a way as to enrich our shared understanding of the story? I think we can, if we go a step beyond the associating I did in the first part of this transacting of "The Purloined Letter."

I can give you my feelings and associations and let you pass them through the story for yourself to see if they enrich your experience. For example, I remember this story in one specific paperback I read when I was thirteen years old. Obviously, you cannot do that, but you can take my association through "The Purloined Letter" by reading the story as a contrast between such tight, spatially defined texts as my paperback or the letter that Dupin physically removes and the indefinite texts of all the different narrations, the Prefect's story, Dupin's story, the narrator's story (which extends outward to include two other Dupin stories) and, I would say, extends even to the Perma-Gloss binding of my thirty-nine-year-old copy. Can you get a richer experience of this story by thinking of it as a prototype of all stories—both physically defined but conceptually and emotionally infinite—open to a million different transactions of it?

Another example: the word purloin cues me to think of this as a story about moving from place to place, a study in the way context changes text and text changes context, so that D——'s open card case becomes a hiding place because of what is inside it, while the most secret and enclosed places in his house are not hiding places at all. The concealed becomes the open and the open becomes the concealed, a sentence that lets me bring to the story a variety of psychological themes: displacement, abreaction, transference, or repression. I can respond to this story as a study in the way we use spatial metaphors for states of mind.

I can also feel in it the exuberance of human development. Like magic tricks, we give up something, the lost card, the cut rope, in order to get something even more precious, the knowledge which is power. Is that a feeling you can take through the story?

For me, this is a story about hiding, especially the hiding of sexual secrets and how painful and costly it is to let another know that kind of secret, how cheap and easy it is to publish other kinds of secrets. I can feel in this story the detective's, the magician's, the critic's, the psycho-analyst's glee, at being able to turn the Perma-Gloss inside out, and at the same time how shameful it can be for the one whose secret is revealed. Like Mario in *Mario and the Magician*.

I sense a similar contrast between the purely intellectual, safe, power-ful kind of knowing practiced by magicians like Dupin and the relating exemplified by the narrator. Intellect is a celibate state of mind to be contrasted with the personal and heterosexual secrets neither Dupin nor the story ever reveals. At that intellectual level, where I am still a graduate student, I can find in this story a flyting: one poet throws lines of poetry at another to win the magic letter and the exalted woman, muse, white goddess, or even the wronged mother. I can read a primitive barbaric magic into the elegant, artistic battle of wits between Dupin and D——, or, for that matter, between Lacan and Derrida (with Hol-land challenging the winner).[8]

That is a purely intellectual kind of knowledge, though, and my associations suggest a more emotional theme: a story about the difference between trusting the world and needing to know it—to know all of it, the under, the behind, the backward, the inside—a theme to which literary critics are surely no strangers. Ordinarily, we try to bring out what my students sometimes call "hidden meanings," although I, at least, used to protest they are "right out there," like the royal letter, to be seen by anyone who knows how to look for them.

The transactive critic tries to bring into the critical arena another kind of obviousness. He wants to use the obvious truth that we each read differently. More orthodox critics sometimes try to hide or get rid of that embarrassing fact by using differences in response as an occasion for eliminating difference. I suggest a movement in the opposite direction. Instead of subtracting readings so as to narrow them down or cancel some, as Lacan and Derrida do, let us use human differences to add response to response, to multiply possibilities, and to enrich the whole experience.[9] That way, we can recover the letter purloined by such abstract, intellectual readings as Lacan's or Derrida's. We can restore stories to their rightful owners—you and me and all of you and me, our emotional as well as our intellectual selves—by recovering reading as a personal transaction.

Notes

1. Lacan misreports the *Oxford English Dictionary* on p. 39 in the French and p. 59 in the English.

2. Lacan attributes the similarity in thefts to the repetition compulsion (which, if used to explain all likenesses, explains none). Daniel Hoffman traces it to the exact identification of Dupin with his foe D—— (1978, 121–22, 131–33). Hoffman's splendidly personal study builds on an associative method like my own. One of the virtues of this kind of "open" criticism is that it permits the cumulation of different readings by different personalities into a larger view of the work. I have gained from Hoffman's associations.

3. Joseph J. Moldenhauer (1968, 284–97, 291), points out that Dupin does what literary critics do: he analyzes texts.

4. Allan Tate speaks of Poe's "intellect moving in isolation from both love and the moral will, whereby it declares itself independent of the human situation in the quest of essential knowledge" (1955, 115).

5. See, for example, Wolfgang Iser (1974), or Hans Robert Jauss (1970). The movement is summarized by Rien T. Segers (1975).

6. Stanley Fish (1970) stated this approach but has modified it since then. See Fish (1976, 191–96), which concludes that all interpretive methods are fictions.

7. See Michael Riffaterre (1966). Riffaterre, in subsequent work, has become more semiotic and hence more of a text-active theorist. See, for example, his analysis of Blake's "The Sick Rose" (1973). At the Modern Language Association Meeting, December 27, 1976, he stated, "It is . . . essential that we underscore how tight is the control, how narrow are the limits imposed by the text upon the reader's reactions to it."

8. After this essay was written, another knight errant entered the lists: Barbara Johnson (1977) wittily and winningly pitted Lacan's and Derrida's essays against each other. Unlike my transactive and psychoanalytic skirmish, however, her "theoretical 'frame of reference' is precisely, to a very large extent, the writings of Lacan and Derrida." It is, of course, no less transactive for that.

9. This new method of reading (deliberately opening a poem outward to include the extratextual) is spelled out in greater detail and with more examples in a collective paper by the seminar English 692 (Holland 1978c). "Poem opening," using the criticism, even the rejected criticism, of others also occurs in Holland (1978a).

15 ❧ The Shadow's Shadow:
The Motif of the Double in Edgar Allan Poe's "The Purloined Letter"

LIAHNA KLENMAN
BABENER

In 1845, Edgar Allan Poe published "The Purloined Letter," his third contribution to the form he had himself invented. While critics of the work have generally recognized its superiority to Poe's other detective stories, particularly in light of its additions to the new genre, few have attributed its merit to factors other than skillful handling of the "ratiocinative" method, or effective rendering of structural unity.[1] But these qualities do not sufficiently account for the distinctive achievement of the work. The author himself admonished against overvaluing his detective tales merely "on account of their method or *air* of method" and encouraged the prudent reader to discover meaning beneath the surface as "an undercurrent of suggestion" (Poe 1966b, 328).

One aspect of the work, often noticed but as yet unexplained, is the pervasive doubling motif[2] which underlies the structure of the tale as a whole and characterizes particularly the relationship between M. Dupin and his rival, the Minister D——. Poe's insistent use of doublings in the story considerably exceeds that which is necessary for presenting Dupin's method of investigation, which in this case stresses detection through psychological identification with an adversary. Rather, the prominent

Reprinted by permission from *Mystery and Detection Annual*, vol. 1 (1972).

pattern of doubles suggests that the protagonist and his foil are moral duplicates and may ultimately be two phases of the same mind.

The double principle informs the basic action of the story, the major event of which is Dupin's retrieval of the purloined letter and consequent triumph over the resourceful D——. The action revolves around Dupin's method of detection, which is based primarily on two logical premises from which he will eventually reason forth the solution to the mystery. One is that the cunning investigator must achieve an "identification of the reasoner's intellect with that of his opponent." The other is the recognition that the truth "may escape observation by dint of being excessively obvious." Both axioms are exemplified by means of an analogy to game strategy. For the first, Dupin describes the familiar schoolboys' game of "even and odd." "One player holds in his hand a number of . . . [marbles], and demands of another whether that number is even or odd. If the guess is right, the guesser wins one; if wrong, he loses one." The shrewder player wins by anticipating the strategy of the other competitor. Dupin illustrates his second postulate with the old sport of locating place names printed on a map. While "a novice in the game generally seeks to embarrass his opponents by giving the most minutely lettered names . . . the adept selects such words as stretch in large characters, from one end of the chart to the other." The prudent player correctly presumes that the other will overlook the larger and more diffused letters in favor of the smaller, more compact words and wins by subverting the expectations of his opponent. It is significant that both of these illustrations incorporate the use of parallel reasoning between contenders, and both epitomize in miniature the primary action of the tale as a whole. Dupin's casual game analogies thus serve as metaphors for the more consequential rivalry between him and D——.

Acting upon these paired axioms, the detective approaches the two-fold problem of the missing letter and the astute thief. Dupin knows that the Minister, who has purportedly stolen the document for purposes of political extortion, must fulfill two requirements if he is ever to utilize his spoils. He must be able to produce the letter at momentary notice, and he must protect it from frequent searches by the police. Given these circumstances, the sleuth reasons that the letter must be secreted on the premises of D——'s lodgings, despite the failure of the Prefect's men to find it. At this point, Dupin applies the first supposition of his method on the basis of a prior knowledge of the character of his adversary and proceeds to recreate the Minister's reasoning in the current situation:

Such a man, I considered, could not fail to be aware of the ordinary policial modes of action. He could not have failed to anticipate . . . the waylayings to which he was subjected. He must have foreseen, I reflected, the secret investigations of his premises. . . . I felt also that the whole train of thought, which I was at some pains in detailing to you just now . . . would necessarily pass through the mind of the Minister. It would imperatively lead him to despise all the ordinary *nooks* of concealment. . . . I saw, in fine, that he would be driven, as a matter of course, to *simplicity,* if not deliberately induced to it as a matter of choice.

In this extract, Dupin is actually reproducing the Minister's own method of reasoning: He "admeasures" the mind of his competitor (as D——— has appraised the intelligence of his police assailants) and predicts his tactics (as D——— has anticipated the tactics of his pursuers). In this way, the detective deduces D———'s plan for concealment of the letter— the paradoxical embodiment of Dupin's own axiom about the difficulty of perceiving the obvious. Like the game players' strategy in his analogies, Dupin's is to outguess his antagonist.

It remains for Dupin, having unriddled the mystery, to verify his solution and to retrieve the letter. He makes an unsolicited visit to the Minister's apartment, where, camouflaged behind a "pair of green spectacles," he scans the room for the letter, which he locates, revamped and resealed, in a letter rack in plain view of the observer. A second visit, on a spurious excuse, furnishes the occasion for a surreptitious exchange of letters, where Dupin, repeating the method used initially by D——— to steal the letter, replaces the original document with a counterfeit one. Dupin describes his replica as "a *fac-simile,* (so far as regards externals) which I had carefully prepared at my lodgings; imitating the D——— cipher, very readily, by means of a seal formed of bread." The vital letter itself is present in two guises. Dupin, studying the one in D———'s letter rack, recognizes that though "it was, to all appearance, radically different from the one of which the Prefect has read us so minute a description," nevertheless this document is the one sought. "It was torn nearly in two, across the middle" and it "had been turned, as a glove, inside out, redirected and re-sealed." So the purloined letter becomes a double of itself. Thus, the entire process of crime solution incorporates a series of noticeable doublings and parallelings: the twin analytical axioms, the pair of game analogies, the two successive intellectual gambols between the police and D——— and between D——— and Dupin, the sequence of mimicked stratagems by which Dupin trips up his enemy, and the twofold nature of the chief clue.

While Poe unquestionably sets up the tale to enable Dupin to demon-strate his imitative method of detection against an antagonist of equal powers, this explanation does not sufficiently account for other insistent uses of the double pattern in the story.

This doubling technique appears especially in the portraits of the two major characters. Dupin's own reasoning processes are frequently de-picted by means of coupled thoughts and parallel ideas. He is particularly fond of elaborate, point-by-point analogies. "The material world," he observes, "abounds with very strict analogies to the immaterial." He is fascinated by semblances and correspondences and often uses them as indirect means of communication. In one occurrence, Dupin induces the Prefect to acknowledge and reward his assistance in the present case by means of the "Abernethy" anecdote. The sleuth recounts the fable of a miser who uses hypothetical questions to maneuver advice from a doctor, and the Prefect, inferring Dupin's point, properly sees in the analogy an image of his own avarice. " 'But,' said the Prefect, a little discomposed, 'I am *perfectly* willing to take advice, and to pay for it. I would *really* give fifty thousand francs to any one who would aid me in the matter,' " and Dupin correspondingly interprets the Prefect's allusion as a reluctant offer of compensation. Dupin's anecdote illustrates again the gaming psychology and emphasizes his tendency to devise fictional doubles as means of expression. Moreover, Dupin himself is often described in terms of paired images. He is first pictured to us relaxing in his secluded quarters, "au troisième, No. 33, Rue Dunôt" (note the repetition of the numbers and the echo of the protagonist's name in that of his street), where he and the nameless narrator enjoy the "twofold luxury of medita-tion and a meerschaum." Correspondingly, the Minister D—— is fre-quently depicted by means of yoked images. The Prefect portrays him as a man who "dares all things, those unbecoming as well as those becoming a man." He practices a thievery "not less ingenious than bold." Dupin knows him as poet and mathematician, courier, and intrigant. D——'s residence, the D—— Hotel, is also a reverberation of his name.

These parallelisms and mated adjectives used to describe the major characters are compounded by an almost compulsive duplication of struc-tural elements in the tale. Nearly every major movement of plot occurs twice. There are two consultations between the Prefect and Dupin. On the occasion of the second call, we are told by the narrator that the Prefect "found us occupied very nearly as before." Both visits are at night, and both times the caller is supplied with pipe and chair. There are two interviews as well between Dupin and D——, and on each occasion they discuss the same subject. There are two major searches of the Minister's apartment by the police. (When the Prefect expresses bewilderment after the first fruitless inspection, Dupin's advice is "to make a thorough research of the premises.") Similarly, we are informed that D—— "has been twice waylaid" in the streets by the inspector's men; both times the men are costumed as thugs, both times the search is executed under the covert supervision of the Prefect himself, and both times D—— is found without the stolen document. There are also two instances of "blackmail": the Minister's against "a personage of most exalted station," and Dupin's of the Prefect to obtain payment for his assistance. There are two rewards paid for the recovery of the letter—both are "very liberal." (The Prefect notes that the prize offered "has been lately doubled.") In addition, there are two instances of papers being purloined, both involving the furtive substitution of the original with a facsimile. Finally, there are two political power struggles, both involving the high deputies of state and both associated with possession of the letter. In the first, D—— plots, and nearly accomplishes, the political collapse of the royal lady; in the second, Dupin extricates the same lady from the grip of her enemies and arranges the downfall of D——.

These numerous and striking instances of mirroring all underscore the paramount doubling in the tale—that between Dupin and the Minister D——. From the perspective of the detective story genre, the two function respectively as sleuth and criminal, protagonist and antagonist. Dupin traps his quarry by adopting his rationale and duplicating his method. But the resemblance between the two far exceeds that which results from Dupin's conscious imitation of his foil, and it renders inapplicable the conventional moral separation between detective and culprit.

The doubling which links Dupin and D—— is readily exhibited by the astonishing similarity of the minds. Both possess the same intellectual capacities and interests. The Minister, author of a treatise on "the differential Calculus," has gained some fame as a mathematician, a subject for which Dupin also demonstrates fondness by his frequent use of mathematical models to illustrate abstract ideas and by his fascination with probabilities. D—— has also "acquired renown as a poet," and Dupin admits to the same talent: "I have been guilty of certain doggerel myself." Dupin clearly recognizes D—— as a like mind: "I knew him . . . as both mathematician and poet," a man of equal mental makeup and a perfect peer.

If Dupin and D—— are intellectual counterparts, they are more significantly moral equivalents, whose motives and methods are equally dubious from an ethical standpoint. While D——'s villainy is never questioned by critics, few regard Dupin as other than an artist, who solves crimes for sheer aesthetic pleasure and hence is exempt from moral scrutiny, or else as a representative of the forces of morality. Neither appraisal is appropriate. Unquestionably, Dupin displays his characteristic preoccupation with sophisticated epistemological puzzles. In this sense, his interest in the case at hand is "artistic," though it does *not* distinguish him from D——, who shares an attraction to the artistic dimension of the problem.

Dupin cannot be regarded simplistically as a moral agent whose able solution of the crime represents a triumph for the cause of virtue. Dupin's mode of procedure, while successful, is nevertheless ethically suspicious; he does, after all, imitate D——'s own tactics, which are clearly pernicious. Both men employ ingenious forms of trickery to execute their plans and to deceive their antagonists. The Minister's talent for duplicity is plain. The letter was first pirated by means of one clever deception and secreted by another "to delude the beholder into an idea of the worthlessness of the document." Once the letter is "hidden," the Minister uses an elaborate ruse to safeguard it. He arranges to be regularly absent from his residence during the evenings in order to facilitate what he knows will be a futile search by the police and thus to convince the Prefect that the letter is not secreted there. During Dupin's visit, the Minister enacts the role of the unsuspecting innocent in order to discourage speculation that he has anything to hide.

Dupin likewise employs deception to confound his opponent. His ostensibly "accidental" call upon D—— is really calculated to gain him entry into the man's lodgings, and once there, he resorts to a series of crafty pretenses to promote his search: he pretends a sight handicap to disguise his survey of the room; he diverts D—— with conversation in order to prolong his inspection; he purposefully leaves behind a snuffbox to provide an excuse for a second visit; he stages a commotion outside the D—— hotel to distract the Minister's attention; and he substitutes a fraudulent letter for the real one in the precise manner that D—— had once used to purloin it himself. He practices a similar kind of deception against the Prefect. Clearly, then, Dupin is not above using the same kind of duplicity practiced by his rival.

While Dupin's methods do not differ materially from those of his adversary, neither, in fact, do his motives. It may be argued that, like D——, Dupin is moved to participate in the affair for reasons which are morally dubious. First, there is the submerged but abiding rivalry with the Prefect, a lesser instance of the more momentous competition with D——. While the Prefect assuredly admires Dupin, he regards the detective as an eccentric and scoffs at his attitudes. For example, he ridicules Dupin's preference for meditation in the dark as "another of your odd notions" and disdainfully equates poets with fools, though he knows Dupin to be a poet himself. His contempt for Dupin's idiosyncrasies induces a subtle competitiveness in Dupin to vindicate himself and to deflate the arrogant inspector. The subdued rivalry between them often takes the form of a flippant banter with a belligerent undercurrent, where the Prefect is frequently outclassed. At the conclusion of one verbal bout between them, heavily interspersed with Dupin's sarcasm, the Prefect laughs, " 'Oh, Dupin, you will be the death of me yet!' " Beneath the superficial levity of the remark is the suggestion of ferocity and violence, and a veiled allusion to the more consequential enmity between Dupin and D——.

Second, there is the matter of the reward. We are told by the "Rue Morgue" narrator that Dupin is a man deprived of his fortune by a "variety of untoward events" and allowed to subsist only "by courtesy of his creditors" (Mabbott 1978, 2:531). The Prefect repeatedly mentions the prize offered for the return of the letter, and each time stresses that it is "enormous"—"I don't like to say how much, precisely." The vagueness of the amount of course augments its value to the hearer. Dupin employs the letter for his own financial intrigue. He promptly demands a large check from the Prefect and withholds the twice-stolen document until the sum is paid. Although it may be considered fair recompense, nevertheless Dupin's little machination is a form of extortion and looks very much like one of D——'s habits.

Third, there is the political turmoil unleashed by the affair of the letter. The Minister has taken it to gain political advantage over the unnamed owner and the interests she represents. The power associated with possession of the letter is frequently underlined by the Prefect as he reveals the story of the theft to Dupin. D—— has been wielding this power "for some months past" "to a dangerous extent," by blackmailing its recipient. This political advantage is not lost upon Dupin, who employs the document for that very purpose when he plots the downfall of D—— and the deliverance of the "illustrious personage" from the hold of her enemies: "You know my political prepossessions. In this matter, I act as a partisan of the lady concerned." Hence, Dupin (like D——) uses the letter to obtain influence and (like D——) to further partisan ends. Moreover, even his ostensibly chivalric rescue of the royal lady in distress is not free from moral ambiguity and possible impropriety, since he is, in effect, assisting her to shelter an illicit romance and to deceive the "other personage from whom it was her wish to conceal it."

Finally, there is the motive of personal revenge against the Minister who "once did [him] an evil turn." Dupin has apparently long nurtured a private vendetta against D——; although he depicts the matter as a kind of amicable contest ("I told him, quite good humoredly, that I should remember"), there is an edge of compulsiveness to his vengeance which is intimated by the epigraph attributed to Seneca: *"Nil sapientiae odiosius acumine nimio"*—"Nothing is so hateful to wisdom as too much sharpness." This implication, that the rivalry is tinged with an element of hate, is reinforced by further evidence of Dupin's vindictiveness, for example his near glee at the prospect of D——'s downfall and his willingness to expose himself to possible injury, even death, to assure such a consequence:

"D——," replied Dupin, "is a desperate man, and a man of nerve. His hotel, too, is not without attendants devoted to his interests. Had I made the wild attempt you suggest [seizing the letter openly], I might never have left the Ministerial presence alive."

The extremity of the danger present, and Dupin's unusual daring in the face of it, emphasizes the viciousness which underlies the personal competition between them. Furthermore, Dupin feels the need to make himself known conclusively to his victim and to invite further reprisals. He inserts tauntingly into the substitute letter an excerpt from Crébillon's *Atrée,* a play which dramatizes the fatal opposition between two brothers. Dupin's quotation recalls the excessive and bloody retaliation of Atreus against the affronts of his brother Thyestes and implies the truly malicious quality of the present revenge.

> ——Un dessein si funeste,
> S'il n'est digne d'Atrée, est digne de Thyeste.

> —A design so deadly,
> If it's not worthy of Atreus, is worthy of Thyestes.

The two characters in the play alluded to are paired by their like capacity for malice and brutality and are implicit counterparts of the detective and his adversary.

Dupin pursues his scheme to promote D———'s downfall in part because he believes the Minister to be a *"monstrum horrendum,* an unprincipled man of genius."* He sees in D———'s example the hazards which
may attend the ascendency of one of exceptional intelligence who uses his
talents for unscrupulous ends. But what really differentiates Dupin from
his opponent? The two are virtual surrogates. Except for the fact that
Dupin is on the side of the established order (and even this is perplexing,
since it is not clear whether he represents the "Queen" or royal figure
against her husband, presumably then the "King," or both of them
together against common conspirators), his own motives are not less
suspect than those of D———, and his methods are cunning and often as
reprehensible as those of his rival. For Dupin, in instigating the over-
throw of such a reprobate as D———, becomes an ethical replica of his
enemy, a *monstrum horrendum* in his own right.

The pattern of the double suggests further possibilities. There is some
implication, for example, that the enigmatic relationship between Dupin and the Minister may be fraternal. A close personal intimacy between
them is clearly alluded to several times. Dupin knows D———'s private
and official dealings almost better than does the Prefect, who has been
following the Minister for several months. It is apparent that the detective has been acquainted with D——— for a considerable time. Dupin
remarks specifically upon a prior encounter "at Vienna, once," and others
are implied. Moreover, the two men are familiar enough that Dupin's
unexpected arrival at D———'s dwelling causes the latter no evident
surprise. Dupin relates that he "maintained a most animated discussion
with the Minister, upon a topic which I knew well had never failed to
interest and excite him." The sleuth knows the idiosyncrasies of his rival
well; there is ample suggestion that some unusual affinity exists between
them. Dupin is so intimate with the workings of D———'s mind that he
anticipates the Minister's thoughts with an almost deterministic certainty and intuits D———'s reasoning patterns in their exact order. Dupin is
also able to penetrate the Minister's various dissemblings. He perceives
that D———'s nightly excursions are calculated "ruses" to fool the police,
and he recognizes that the crumpled letter visible in the letter rack is "so
inconsistent with the *true* methodical habits of D———" that it must be a
disguise for the missing one. This uncanny perceptivity exceeds the kind
of shrewdness which is requisite for detective work.

Poe drops several clues that this strong affiliation between the two
characters is fraternal. Certainly Dupin's choice of the Crébillon quotation referring to the fatal competition between brothers invites such

speculation. The narrator also invokes conjecture that Dupin and D——
may be brothers by his confusion about the reputed accomplishments of
the Minister. " 'But is this really the poet?' I asked. "There are two
brothers, I know; and both have attained reputation in letters.' " Who is
the second brother? He is never identified, for Dupin conspicuously fails
to acknowledge the remark. The mention of an unnamed relation who
mirrors his brother's achievements certainly suggests Dupin. We are also
struck by the fact that Monsieur Dupin and Minister D—— share
phonetically similar names and surnames which begin with the same
letter; the obscurity surrounding the pointedly undisclosed last name
invites some inference that it may be "Dupin."

But Poe's persistent duplication suggests yet another possibility: that
the two characters somehow constitute a single person. Although biographical details in this story are few, those given do tend to underscore
this notion of unanimity. Both men live in relatively secluded quarters.
Dupin's lodgings are located in "a retired and desolate portion of the
Faubourg St. Germain" (Mabbott 1978, 2:532), and the Minister, despite his eminence at Court, prefers a solitary apartment and houses his
servants "at a distance." Also important is the way that the two characters
are counterpoised in time in the story. Dupin, at least in this tale, stays
home at night. The Prefect arranges his visits in the evenings, "just after
dark," because he knows Dupin prefers to deliberate in the dark. Conversely, the Minister has a habit of being "frequently absent from home
all night." In fact, "for three months a night has not passed" that he has
not disappeared to some unstated and unknown location. Dupin's only
outings in the course of the story (his two visits to D——) both occur in
the morning. Significantly, on both occasions he finds the Minister at
home, "yawning, lounging and dawdling as usual." One goes out only at
night and the other leaves only in the daytime. It is almost as if the two
participate cooperatively in some sort of phased existence and one half of
the twosome ceases to exist after nightfall. It is notable that the Minister's presence in the tale is related only by hearsay. We are apprised of his
activities by the Prefect and by Dupin, but they are *never* directly depicted in the story. There is some implication that D—— may not exist
as a separate, independent being at all. D—— figures immediately in
only one episode of the plot, and that is reported, after the fact, solely by
Dupin. Dupin's account of the meeting is sketchy and suspiciously
vague. No dialogue is recorded; for that matter, we are never made to
hear any verbatim statement by D——. Dupin's report focuses almost
entirely on his own undercover inspection of the apartment. The single

reference to D——'s physical appearance is more mystifying than infor-
mative: Dupin depicts D—— in a state of pretended languor and then
remarks: "He is, perhaps, the most really energetic human being now
alive—but that is only when nobody sees him." What does this statement mean? Dupin seems to imply that the Minister is a different person
when he is not being observed, a man with a divided identity which
changes aspect depending on the viewer. Perhaps the comment by Dupin
is a concealed reference to himself. Importantly, the same kind of observation has been made about the detective. The narrator of the "Rue
Morgue" tale observes a potential second self resident within the personality of the detective and often "amused [himself] with the fancy of a
double Dupin" (Mabbott 1978, 2:533). Hence, like D——, Dupin also
has been portrayed as a person of fluctuating identity, and in still another
sense is interchangeable with D——. All of these factors, then, tend to
interfuse the two figures into one singular character whole and point
ultimately to the suggestion that the tale is, in its deepest implications, a
study in the oneness of pursuer and pursued.

Poe's use of the double in "The Purloined Letter" is so pervasive that
it deserves serious scrutiny. I have attempted to demonstrate that Poe
employs the doubling in the tale chiefly to expose a deep affinity between Dupin and his archrival, one which equates them morally and
calls into question the customary ethical norms of the detective tale.
Further, the emphatic double pattern encourages the inference that Dupin and D—— may be brothers and suggests finally that the two may
constitute a singular composite being. In this ultimate sense, then,
"The Purloined Letter" explores the composition of the self, and the
double becomes a metaphor for the variant phases—hunter and hunt-
ed—of the human mind.

NOTES

1. For example, Dorothy L. Sayers (1929, 16) praises the story for its contributions to the new detective story genre (the "method of *psychological deduction*
and solution by the formula of the most *obvious place*"), but her analysis does not
extend much beyond this. Brander Matthews (1966, 85) states the commonly
held attitude that the tale (and all Poe's detective fiction) is noteworthy for its
process of analytical deduction, rather than for any intrinsic interest in the
mystery itself. See also Ellery Queen (1968, ix), T. O. Mabbott (1951, xiv), and
Arthur Hobson Quinn (1941, 421), all of whom evaluate "The Purloined Letter"
as Poe's best detective tale but do little to defend or explain their assessments.

2. Although scholars have frequently observed Poe's propensity for the "double" image in fiction, few have noticed its operation in "The Purloined Letter." Those who mention the idea do little to develop the point. See Howard Haycraft (1946, 174): attempting to identify the historical model for Dupin as one of two illustrious brothers surnamed Dupin, Haycraft comments on the similarity between the fictional Dupin and the Minister D—— and suggests that "in the dual circumstances of Poe's . . . adaptation of the characteristics of the real brothers Dupin" one will readily "scent a highly logical, if possibly unconscious 'transference,'" between hero and foe. See also Alice Chandler (1970), Joseph Moldenhauer (1968, 294), Patrick Quinn (1957, 223–56), and Richard Wilbur (1967, 25–28). Wilbur deals primarily with "The Murders in the Rue Morgue," which he attempts to explicate as a study in the multiple nature of the personality, and he accounts for parallels between Dupin and the other main characters "allegorically as elements of one person." He does not extend his study to "The Purloined Letter."

16   *A Note on Time in "The Purloined Letter"*

FRANÇOIS PERALDI

There are no fewer than forty-six indications of time in Poe's tale. The longest-lasting temporal sequence plunges toward the most distant past, crosses the whole text, and proceeds beyond the narrated story toward a predicted end. We can call it the time of vengeance. It constitutes the temporal axis of the relationship between Dupin and the Minister. Its beginning is the last temporal indication in Poe's text, which comes as a flashback, and it reminds us how fairy tales begin "once upon a time": "D——, at Vienna, once, did me an evil turn." This "once," however, does not indicate the beginning of their relationship, but tells of one in a series of actions that called for vengeance and that finds its resolution, along with its satisfaction, in a probable future, beyond the end of the narrated story: "Thus will he [the Minister] inevitably commit himself, at once, to his political destruction." This destruction is largely due to Dupin's intervention and the concretization of his promise when he told the Minister "quite good-humoredly, that [he] should remember" the evil turn.

Included in the longest-lasting temporal sequence of vengeance, we can find two smaller temporal sequences of unequal length: the sequence of the narrator's narration, which lasts one month, and the sequence of the drama of the letter as it is told by the Prefect (the first part of which was told to the Prefect by the Queen herself) and then by Dupin. Both narrations are reported in direct discourse by the narrator. We have, therefore, two narrations within the narrator's narration, with one of them, the Prefect's, containing the Queen's narration. The drama of the letter has lasted the "eighteen months the Minister has had [the Queen] in his power."

The large temporal sequence of vengeance that encloses all other sequences of the narrated story presents us with some peculiarities. It has a transitional temporal function. First of all, it includes all the temporal aspects of the narrated story as well as the temporal condition of its narration. But it is linked to a completely different temporality: mythical time, which subsumes the temporal sequence of Dupin's vengeance and places it in the almost atemporal myth of the fratricidal vengeance of Atreus and Thyestes. The verses Dupin quotes for the benefit of the Minister are uttered by Atreus when he conceives the menu of the banquet for his brother. Derrida giggles ironically when he underlines Lacan's lapse in substituting *destin* for *dessein* while commenting on Dupin's outburst of rage. But the myth justifies Lacan's transposition, since Atreus's "scheme" is the cause of the tragic "destiny" of his seed. It seems that Thyestes' ineluctable curse never ends and is, indeed, eternal, or that we all are the seed of Atreus. It can be said that Dupin's revenge on the Minister belongs to Atreus's myth. The two men knew each other very well before the Minister did his evil turn to Dupin, since the latter— probably to keep their friendship apparently intact until a suitable time for revenge has come—answered "good-humoredly." The structure of Dupin's vengeance duplicates the original myth explicitly—if not in action, at least in its intention.

The temporality of the tale is a fictional time, despite the verisimilitude conveyed by several indexes of reality: "At Paris, just after dark one gusty evening in the autumn of 18—." But this fictional time touches a historical temporality, a very concrete one, where revenge also takes place and where "real" people—as far as we can distinguish them from fictional subjects—use the purloined letters of "The Purloined Letter" as an indirect means to achieve some personal revenge which, while not as bloody and cruel as Atreus's, is nevertheless fraternal as well as passionate.

I can give two examples from among the commentators. Lacan criticizes Marie Bonaparte's comment about "the little brass knob just beneath the middle of the mantelpiece," saying that the question of deciding its place (beneath or above) "may be abandoned without harm to the inferences of those whose profession is grilling." "And even," he adds in a footnote, "to the cook herself" (1977, 67). Lacan's comment is especially nasty, since Marie Bonaparte, who was frigid, was obsessed by the belief that frigidity was due to a malfunction or a misplacement of the clitoris, to which she compared the little brass knob in her comment on Poe's tale. She suffered several unsuccessful surgical interventions and cauterizing (grilling) of her clitoris in a vain attempt to regain her sexual sensitivity (Bertin 1982). We should note that Lacan was perfectly aware of Marie Bonaparte's obsessions.

We find here the opposition between one who is in the position of seeing (Lacan) and another (Marie Bonaparte) who does not see anything. This is a repetition of the subjective and temporary position assigned to each subject in his turn by the passage of the letter within Poe's story. It appears that even "real people," through the effect of the letter and of the repetition automatism, are partly transformed into fictional subjects. We could also say that the repetition automatism subjects these "real" or "historical" people to the structure of the fiction.

But the effect extends even further, for the theme of fratricidal vengeance also reappears. A bitter dispute had taken place within the French psychoanalytic brotherhood just before Lacan delivered his seminar on "The Purloined Letter." It led to a schism that was, as is often the case in the psychoanalytic community, passionately violent and vile. During the battle for control over the new Institute of Psychoanalysis, Marie Bonaparte's intervention was crucial, probably because she had been Freud's friend for a long time and was therefore his representative, so to speak, in the French milieu. Allied to Lacan at first, she finally joined Sacha Nacht, the hated "brother" and former friend of Lacan (who was Nacht's best man at his marriage), and it ultimately led to Lacan's exclusion from the French psychoanalytic community and to what he calls his "excommunication" by the International Psychoanalytic Association (Turkle 1978).

But there might even be more to it. Marie Bonaparte and Lacan claimed a common object: Freud. Although Lacan professed to promote a return to Freud, he never met him, though he easily could have: curiously enough, he spent some time with Jung. We know that Lacan sent his doctoral thesis on paranoia to Freud in 1932. Freud coldly acknowledged this in a postcard, and that was it (*Ornicar?* [1984], no. 29). When Freud came to Paris in 1938 on his way to London, Lacan did not try to meet him because, he said, he would have to ask the Princess Marie Bonaparte to introduce him, and he did not want to do so (see also Roudinesco 1986, 148).

We turn now to the fratricidal vengeance of Derrida against Lacan. Most elements of the conflict have been exposed by Barbara Johnson in terms of duplication of the relationship between the Queen and the Minister and between the Minister and Dupin, the success of each being due to the other's blind spot. But we have seen that the Queen was a transferential object for both Dupin and the Minister, as Freud was for Lacan and Derrida and (if we want to recall the original myth) as Aerope was for Atreus and Thyestes. If Lacan claimed to be Freud's herald, Derrida would rather be the one who tried to master Freud without having proclaimed any oath of allegiance (i.e., being analyzed). I remember Derrida's rage and his just indignation when I told him that Lacan had stated publicly during one of his seminars, without any evidence, that Derrida had been secretly analyzed and went so far as to give the name of his analyst. An evil turn if ever there was one!

We can undoubtedly agree with Barbara Johnson when she sees in this repetition—namely, "the act of clinching one's triumph by filling in a blank"—the duplication of something that is already inscribed in Poe's text. But the very terms Dupin used to underline the fratricidal nature of his triumph lead us to the conclusion that what was and is at the origin of all the successive repetitions is, in fact, a repetition of the eternal myth of Atreus. I would go so far as to suggest that it is the mythical nature of this particular tale that gives it its power of fascination, the same power Freud found in texts (like Hamlet) that repeated the Oedipus myth in a more or less disguised fashion.

It may be useful to recall the contribution of Lévi-Strauss (1965) to the study of myths in general and of the Oedipus myth in particular. Instead of considering similar myths of different ages as versions of a primitive and originary myth, Lévi-Strauss suggests that we call "myth" all the existing versions of the same mythological structure, all these versions constituting the origins of the myth in question. In this respect Freud's texts on Oedipus, along with Sophocles' play, constitute for Lévi-Strauss the origins of the Oedipus myth. But for us, Lévi-Strauss's readers, his own text on Oedipus takes its place among the origins of this particular myth, and keeping the same principle in mind, we may consider all the texts dealing with "The Purloined Letter," the tale itself, and Crébillon's *Atrée et Thyeste* as the sources of Atreus's myth. According to Lévi-Strauss, the myth of Oedipus is the beginning of the answer to the question: Are we born from one or two persons? And its derivation: Does the same stem from the same or from another? In this context, the myth of Atreus would constitute the beginning of an answer to the question of how two siblings fare who try to seize and enjoy one undifferentiated and therefore pre-oedipal parental figure.

We can distinguish three temporal levels of the repetition of the myth of Atreus: mythical time, in which myths are somehow suspended, awaiting actualization in tales; fictional time, which is the time proper to the actualization of the myth in a tale; historical time, our everyday time in which individuals are subjected to the structure of myths through fictions. We will now attempt to understand fictional time, the temporality of Poe's tale, from the perspective of the three Lacanian registers of the imaginary, the real, and the symbolic.

The first series of temporal indications refers to what can be called a suspended time, a time for reverie or inner discussion. The narrator seems to be entirely caught in a mirror discussion with himself. One does not know what Dupin is doing during the same period, except that "to any casual observer, [he] might have seemed intently and exclusively occupied with the curling eddies of smoke that oppressed the atmosphere of the chamber." But in "The Murders in the Rue Morgue" we are told that once, while his friend the narrator was thus talking silently to himself for fifteen minutes at least, all at once Dupin spoke and showed the extraordinary manner in which he had chimed in with his meditations. He explained that he had only practiced his own method of observation, which could be named, in Lacanian terms, an imaginary identification with his dear friend, his alter ego, guided by a few signifiers he picked up while observing his silent companion. The same method, whose limits have been analyzed by Lacan, is used by the young boy who always won at the game of guessing the odd or even number of marbles held by his playmates. In other words, both the narrator and Dupin were caught in a dual relationship: the narrator was talking to himself, and Dupin, meanwhile, might have very well been identifying with his spiritual twin.

During this kind of temporal sequence, it is worth noting that its duration can be guessed or measured only *afterward*. In other words, while caught in the imaginary, subjects are trapped in an unmeasurable, monotonous time. [1] They know that time exists, but they are not aware of its duration. It resembles the kind of time psychotic subjects are sometimes trapped in for longer or shorter periods, which they can measure, and always do measure, only once they are capable of symbolizing their experience. Mark Vonnegut, in his personal account of a schizophrenic episode, gives a fascinating description of this kind of temporal experience:

It started with pruning the fruit trees. One saw cut would take forever. I was completely absorbed in the sawdust floating gently to the ground, the feel of the saw in my hand, the incredible patterns in the bark, the muscles in my arm pulling back and then pushing forward. Everything stretched infinitely in all directions. Suddenly it seemed as if everything was slowing down and I would never finish sawing the limb. Then by some miracle that branch would be done and I'd have to rest, completely blown out. The same thing kept happening over and over. . . . It seemed I had been working for hours and hours but the sun had not moved at all. (1975, 74)

This is also the kind of unmeasurable time Daniel Schreber (1955) was trapped in during the first part of his psychosis, until he accepted the idea of becoming a woman to bear children for God in order to repopulate the earth. Once he had accepted the representation of foreclosed castration, he was then able to symbolize time again and to reintroduce the past events of the first period of his madness into the flow of time and in a datable perspective, on a temporal axis leading from the past toward the future.

But if the schizophrenic subject finds it difficult to get out of this suspended, unmeasurable, monotonous time, the so-called normal subject can get out of it as soon as something distracts him from the dual relationship he was caught in for a while—something that activates his symbolic activity. This is precisely what happened in the narrator's narration when "the door of our apartment was thrown open," and this sudden interruption disrupts the suspension of time and the narrator's reverie. Again, when Dupin presents the Prefect with the letter, it disrupts the flow of words pouring from his mouth: "The Prefect appeared absolutely thunder-stricken. For some minutes he remained speechless and motionless, looking incredulously at my friend, with open mouth, and eyes that seemed starting from their sockets."

This sudden opening of the door, of the mouth, this sudden disruption of whatever is then taking place, should be carefully distinguished from whatever follows. Something suddenly emerges that at first has no name, for the subject is confronted with the unthinkable, with the real. There is a time proper to the real, owing to its own periodicity, and alien to the subject's memory traces. It is not a lasting time, but rather is a sort of sudden and temporary destruction of the subject's own sense of time by the irruption of a totally different periodicity proper to the outer and as yet unknown world.

Confronted with the unbearable aspect of the nonrepresentable and nonsymbolized real, the subject can either escape in the imaginary world (the only possible escape for a psychotic subject) or can symbolize what at first glance appeared as a nameless "Thing." What appears in the opening of the door is almost instantly recognized, that is, *named* as the Prefect of Police. And what the Prefect of Police is presented with by Dupin is recognized, after several minutes of confrontation with the real—in the time required to recognize it, to understand what it is, to put a name on it—as the stolen letter.

As soon as symbolization occurs, as the real is named and its name linked into the signifying chain, the subject has ready access to the third register of time, symbolic time, the time proper to the symbolic order, to the subjection of the subject (as well as his objects in the outer world) to the linear chains of signifiers. This is the time that can be marked by specific signifiers, dates, that can be measured when talked about, a linear time whose past belongs to the memory traces and whose future is predictable according to the laws of the signifiers that allow Dupin, for example, to predict the inevitable destruction of the Minister, or according to the laws of psychology that allow Lacan, in a very unusual manner, to predict a different future for him.

Keeping in mind these three Lacanian registers, we can review the tale's fictional time, beginning with the indications of the imaginary register. The Queen reads the letter, alone with the image of the Duke S—— and her own reflections; the business transaction and the fifteen-minute conversation between the Minister and the royal couple are mere empty words, whose function is not to symbolize anything but to distract the attention of the King. There is the useless search by the Prefect of Police, who was simply doing what the image of his own profession was telling him to do; in other words, while searching, the Prefect of Police was completely identified with the image of what a Prefect of Police ought to be and to do. There is the dreaming attitude of the Minister when Dupin called one morning at his apartment; the empty speech of Dupin is uttered, here again, only to fascinate the Minister and distract his attention. In all these situations, whether they are alone or caught in a dual relationship, whether they are dreaming or acting, the subjects are trapped in the same monotonous time whose measure is given and can only be given afterward, in the symbolization, the narration of whatever was then happening. In most of these situations the continuity of the imaginary time is suddenly disrupted by a sudden opening, the sudden irruption of the real: the Queen, while reading the duke S———'s letter, is suddenly interrupted by the Minister, whose "lynx eye immediately perceives the paper." At the Minister's hotel, Dupin's eyes fell upon something ("No sooner had [he] glanced . . . "), to be followed the next day by "a loud report" immediately beneath the windows of the hotel, which disrupts the empty discussion with the Minister, who "rushed to a casement, threw it open, and looked out."

The symbolic register appears in the moment of recognition of whatever at first appeared as the real and created a moment of surprise: it is the entry of the King or the immediate recognition of the letter the Minister's lynx eye perceived, for he "recognizes the hand-writing of the address," that is, he can name what it is: a letter from Duke S———. In the Minister's hotel, no sooner had Dupin glanced at the paper than he "concluded it to be that of which [he] was in search." He can name it: despite its deceiving appearance, it is the stolen letter. The loud report is almost immediately named "as if of a pistol" and shortly afterward is recognized by the Minister, who looks out through the open window: "The disturbance in the street had been occasioned by the frantic behavior of a man with a musket."

These registers of fictional time are not simply fictional: they also operate in the time of a psychoanalysis, in which a subject attempts to name the displacements of the letters of his or her life so as to minimize their debilitating effects. Each of us is subjected to his own periodicity, and this is why we can never say how long a psychoanalysis is going to last, how long it will take for a tale to be understood or for a letter to arrive at its destination.

NOTES

1. The monotonous quality of time is attributed by Freud (1887–1902) to the temporal dimension of system *psi*. In his *Project for a Scientific Psychology* (1954b) one could find the seeds of a remarkable psychoanalytic theory of time.

17 Negation in *"The Purloined Letter"*: Hegel, Poe, and Lacan

JOHN MULLER

Ich bin der Geist, der stets verneint!

—Mephisto, Faust, *1. 1338*

In his structuralist reading of "The Purloined Letter," Lacan presents "the intersubjective complex" of "three moments, structuring three glances, borne by three subjects, incarnated each time by different characters" (1972b, 44). Although this stunning triadic paradigm has been of great interest to others (see chapters by Felman, Derrida, Johnson, and Gallop in this book), Lacan's own stated interest lies not in the structure as such but in its movement: "What interests us today is the manner in which the subjects relay each other in their displacement during the intersubjective repetition" (45). Thus it is the repetitive movement or displacement of the subjects that must be explained, and Lacan offers an initial formulation of this process: "We shall see that their displacement is determined by the place which a pure signifier—the purloined letter—comes to occupy in their trio" (45). After examining how the story produces its effects, Lacan returns to "the crossroads at which we had left our drama and its round with the question of the way in which the subjects replace each other in it" (60). He immediately, once again, offers a preliminary basis for the subjects' movement: "Our fable is so constructed as to show that it is the letter and its diversion which governs their entries and roles" (60).

But how are we to take this account? We are to take it, it seems, literally, for "the hero of the drama . . . succumbs . . . because he has shifted to the second position in the triad . . . by virtue of the object of his theft" (60). In a concrete, restricted sense, it is the letter's possession that snares the Minister. But how does the letter have this impact on the Minister? It "benumbs" him into idleness (62) and forgetfulness (65) and, furthermore, "transforms him" into the image of the Queen (65), and therefore he repeats her strategy. Dupin is likewise so transformed by the letter's possession (71).

If we take such an account literally, we remain at a loss to explain the subject's movement through the triadic structure. To say that the letter does such things to people is to read the letter on another level. Thus we can read the letter more broadly as a psychic inscription, a signifier subject to repression (psychological, not physical misplacement) and so understand that "the displacement of the signifier determines the subjects in their acts" (60). In his seminar of 1954–55, Lacan specifies for the subjects that "for each the letter is his unconscious. It is his unconscious with all its consequences; that is to say, that at each moment of the symbolic circuit each becomes another human being" (Lacan 1978b, 231; my translation). But even this account leaves unanswered the question why "the subjects relay each other in their displacement" (1972b, 45). In other words, Why must the subjects, in the letter's possession, shift places in the triadic structure? Can we account for this movement? This chapter will attempt to do so through Hegel's notion of negation, which I will go on to examine in its formal, linguistic aspects as a "pure signifier" precisely insofar as it is nonrepresentable.

NEGATION IN HEGEL'S PHENOMENOLOGY OF SPIRIT

Lacan does not explicitly refer to Hegel in his "Seminar on 'The Purloined Letter,'" but in his year-long seminar of 1954–55, when he initially presented his discussion of Poe's story, he treats Hegel at some length (1978b, 83–97), claiming that "everyone is Hegelian without knowing it" (93; my translation). We shall see to what extent Lacan is Hegelian without saying it in his "Seminar on 'The Purloined Letter.'"

At this point we can also consider whether there are Hegelian aspects in Poe's work. Limon (1983) calls attention to a number of Hegelian influences on Poe's *The Narrative of Arthur Gordon Pym* (1838) and *Eureka* (1848), wherein Poe deals with the relationship of the particular to the universal, matter and spirit, and the antipolar or contradictory aspects of truth. Lacan calls attention (1972b, 66) to Poe's essay "The Philosophy of Furniture," whose first publication in 1840 had the following as its initial paragraph:

"Philosophy," says Hegel, "is utterly useless and fruitless, and *for this very reason,* is the sublimest of all pursuits, the most deserving of our attention, and the most worthy of our zeal"—a somewhat Coleridegy assertion, with a rivulet of deep meaning in a meadow of words. It would be wasting time to disentangle the paradox—and the more so as no one will deny that Philosophy has its merits, and is applicable to an infinity of purposes. (Quoted in Mabbott 1978, 2:495)

This paragraph was dropped by Poe from subsequent reprintings. The contrasts (philosophy as utterly useless and most sublime), the metaphor of meadow and rivulet, the irony ("an infinity of purposes"—Hegel's "bad infinity," no doubt)—all of this is typical of Hegel, as is the prominence given to negation in "The Purloined Letter." The first word, in the epigraph, is "Nil," and the use of the negative, especially in dialogue, is noticeable, as we shall see.

But before examining the texts of Lacan and Poe, we can attempt to gain perspective by considering the role of negation in the *Phenomenology of Spirit* (1977 [1807]), Hegel's elaboration of the journey of human consciousness (*Bewusst-Sein,* being-as-known or conscious being) from pseudosecurity in immediate experience to self-consciousness to social consciousness. Each moment of this complex process is initially given as if its truth were known with certainty; but as the assumed truth is examined, it is incommensurate with ongoing experience, it is negated and given up in dismay, and a new perspective takes its place. Negation characterizes the process whereby consciousness is forced to shift perspective about its own self-certainties as well as the world. But negation is already operative when consciousness limits its perspective by affirming that the individual content in its possession *is* the truth. Thus the discongruence that negates the former perspective operates as the negation of a negation. In this way negation does not merely displace former states of comprehension: the distinctive Hegelian feature of negation is that the truth of what was formerly taken as true, now rejected, is found to be essential to and caught up in the truth of the new perspective (Hegel 1977, 56). This process Hegel calls *Aufheben,* variously translated as "overcoming," "lifting up," "annulling," and "supersession." Hegel writes: "*Supersession* [*Das Aufheben*] exhibits its true twofold meaning which we have seen in the negative: it is at once a *negating* and a *preserving*" (1977, 68).

Hegel presents this dialectical process of *Das Aufheben* as a series of "moments" in a "triadic form" (1977, 29) consisting of "in-itself," "for-itself," and "for-us," or "*an sich,*" "*für sich,*" and "*für uns*" (1977, 52–56). What do these terms mean? The in-itself is the "essence" (1977, 52), or the object as it is: "Consciousness knows *something;* this object is the essence or the *in-itself*" (1977, 55). The object "in-itself" is the object incompletely revealed; the "for-itself" is the object incompletely known but now taken as it is for consciousness, as known by consciousness: "the in-itself becomes a *being-for-consciousness* of the in-itself" (1977, 56). Cognition is "the transforming of that *in-itself* into that which is *for-itself*" (1977, 488). This relationship between the in-itself and the for-itself is always in conflictful tension and therefore always shifting, and as consciousness changes so too does the object of consciousness change. This process of change is what Hegel means by "experience": "*Inasmuch as the new true object issues from it,* this *dialectical* movement which consciousness exercises on itself and which affects both its knowledge and its object, is precisely what is called *experience* [*Erfahrung*]" (1977, 55). But the "new pattern of consciousness" that continually emerges is apparent *as a pattern* only *for us,* "it is not known to the consciousness that we are observing" (1977, 55–56). For the observed consciousness observing its object, "what has thus arisen exists only as an object; *for us,* it appears at the same time as movement and a process of becoming" (1977, 56). Thus the dialectical process, the ongoing shifting discongruence between the in-itself and for-itself, is not what consciousness as *for itself* comprehends: it is we, because we have another standpoint, who are able to see the relationship between in-itself and for-itself. Consciousness as for-us knows experience is dialectical; consciousness as for-itself experiences the dialectic only as a kind of violence: "When consciousness feels this violence, its anxiety may well make it retreat from the truth, and strive to hold on to what it is in danger of losing" (1977, 51). Consciousness is in danger of losing its self-assurance that it has the truth, especially the truth about an other consciousness, when in actuality it has only a one-sided grasp of such truth.

In the face of this danger, this loss of self-assurance, consciousness resists change, and the source of resistance to change, the chief obstacle to further truth, is the ego, which resists giving up "the *fixity* of its self-positing," "the fixity of the pure concrete, which the *I* itself is" (1977, 20). In its fixity, consciousness prefers the familiar:

In ordinary life, consciousness has for its content items of information, experiences, concrete objects of sense, thoughts, basic principles—anything will do as a content, as long as it is ready to hand, or is accepted as a fixed and stable being or essence. Sometimes consciousness follows where this leads, sometimes it breaks the chain, and deals arbitrarily with its content, behaving as if it were determining and manipulating it from outside. It refers the content back to some certainty or other, even if only to the sensation of the moment; and conviction is satisfied when a familiar resting-place is reached. (1977, 29)

When consciousness meets something unfamiliar in itself or in another, "it resists it in order to save its own freedom and its own insight, its own authority, from the alien authority (for this is the guise in which what is newly encountered first appears)" (1977, 35). Consciousness refuses to recognize its comprehension as partial, it refuses to recognize itself "as a moment" (1977, 20) and not the whole. Consciousness, as *Sein-Bewusst*, generalizes from its *an sich* particularity to assume a *für sich* universality as its given nature. In a prevision of Freud's essay "Negation" (Freud 1961 [1925]), Hegel describes how the essential narcissism of consciousness governs its judgments: "Now, self-consciousness holds that object to be good and to possess intrinsic being, in which it finds itself; and that to be bad in which it finds the opposite of itself. Goodness is the likeness of objective reality to it [i.e., to itself], badness, however, their unlikeness" (1977, 302–3). In its narcissistic position, consciousness determines that what is like itself, the familiar, is good, and it resists change. But given the violence that consciousness undergoes in experience, how is it that the lessons of experience are not soon learned? Consciousness is indeed always "learning from experience what is true in it; but equally it is always forgetting it and starting the movement all over again" (1977, 64).[1]

Before moving on to Lacan, whose themes are evidently anticipated here, we must consider the notion of negation, as Hegel does, in its two chief modes of expression—action and language. For Hegel "action is itself nothing else but negativity" (1977, 238), while negativity is "the same as that which is manifested as movement" (1977, 235). Kojève (1969), whose lectures on the *Phenomenology* shaped how Lacan and his generation read Hegel (Miller 1984), emphasizes "the Hegelian conception of Man = Action = Negativity" (Kojève 1969, 155) when he writes: "Thus all action is 'negating.' Far from leaving the given as it is, action destroys it; if not in its being, at least in its given form. And all 'negating-negativity' with respect to the given is necessarily active" (1969, 4). Hegel is most explicit when he writes that action "gives being to a specific content" (1977, 394) and is the necessary condition for self-knowledge: "Accordingly, an individual cannot know what he [really] is until he has made himself a reality through action" (1977, 240). Action negates the individual's previous status and sets up a new tension between the individual as in-itself and the consciousness of the individual or that of an other as for-itself. This does not mean that action is merely an expression of consciousness. Action is related to consciousness as individual to universal, for consciousness "is thus the universal [in relation to] the specific character of [action]" (1977, 241; my translation). But consciousness, purely and simply as universal, has no actuality: "The individual is only what he has done" (1977, 185); and "the true being of man is rather his deed; in this the individual is actual" (1977, 193). Without the specification accomplished in action, consciousness would remain an empty universality.

Speech has the same kind of relation to consciousness as individual to universal, for the power of speech "is the *real existence* [*Dasein*] of the pure self as self; in speech, self-consciousness, qua independent separate individuality, comes as such into existence, so that it exists *for others*. Otherwise the *I*,[2] this pure *I*, is non-existent, is not *there*" (1977, 308). But speech gives existence in the very act of negating former existence:

The *I* is this particular *I*—but equally the universal *I*; its manifesting is also at once the externalization and vanishing of *this* particular *I*, and as a result the *I* remains in its universality. The *I* that utters itself is *heard* or *perceived;* it is an infection [or contagion] in which it has immediately passed into unity with those for whom it is a real existence, and is a universal self-consciousness. That it is *perceived* or *heard* means that its *real existence dies away;* this its otherness has been taken back into itself; and its real existence is just this: that as a self-conscious Now, as a real existence [Dasein], it is *not* a real existence. This vanishing is thus itself at once its abiding; it is its own knowing of itself, and its knowing itself as a self that has passed over into another self that has been perceived and is universal. (1977, 308–9)

Language structures the I as a vanishing self for another, for the particular I manifested in speech passes over into the universal "I" when the speech is heard by an other. We can understand the role of the other here as follows: Language as negation is effective precisely and only in an inter-subjective complex that includes the position of *für uns,* the position of a third for whom the subject gives expression regarding how something in-itself is now for-itself.

We can now make our transition to Lacan if we can specify the relationships between the *an sich* and the real, the *für sich* and the imaginary, and the *für uns* and the symbolic and, following Felman (this volume, chap. 7), map this triadic structure onto "The Purloined Letter" as is show in the accompanying diagram.

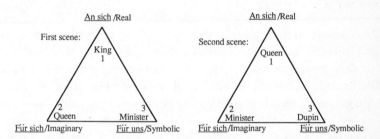

The *an sich* in relation to "the real" is the most obscure region of this map. Hegel describes the *an sich* as standing in an undeveloped, immediate relationship to consciousness (1977, 77); it can be characterized as what "merely is . . . a Thing" [*ein Ding*] about which Hegel says that "consciousness is only actual to itself through the negation and abolition of such a being" (1977, 205). Lacan (1966a) characterizes the real as "the domain of what subsists outside symbolization" (388; my translation), and he approaches the real through "the Thing," which "was there at the beginning, the first thing that was able to separate itself from everything that [the human being] began to name and articulate" (1981a, 1:112).

Lacan draws on Freud's use of "*Das Ding*" in his *Project for a Scientific Psychology* (1954b [1895]) as he attempts to explain how judgments conjoin with memories to yield knowledge. Freud considers the example of a "fellow human being" (*Nebenmensch*) who is the subject's "first satisfying object [*Befriedigungsobjekt*] (and also his first hostile object) as well as his sole assisting force"—that is, the mother. Some of the "perceptual complexes" arising from this object are new, while some are familiar because they "coincide in the subject with his own memory of quite similar visual impressions of his own body—a memory with which will be associated memories of movements experienced by himself." In other words, we know the other, our counterpart, our mother, by reference to our own movements, which take on meaning, in turn, by reference to the other. "For this reason," Freud writes, "it is on his fellow creatures that a human being first learns to cognize," and thus we find in Freud's object relations theory that self and other representations arise together. In any case, Freud concludes:

Thus the complex of a fellow-creature falls into two portions. One of these gives the impression of being a constant structure and remains as a self-contained thing; while the other can be understood by the activity of memory—that is, can be traced back to information about the subject's own body. This process of analyzing a perceptual complex is described as "cognizing" it. (1954b, 393–94)

The first portion, that which is unknown because no attributions can be made about it, "gives the impression of being a constant structure" and "als *Ding* beisammenbleibt," and Freud italicizes *Ding* (1954a, 416). The English translation, "and remains as a coherent 'thing,'" is perverse because Freud is precisely contrasting it to the other "portion" that is coherent, intelligible, cognizable. The phrase "als *Ding* beisammenbleibt" means that a certain "portion" of the *Nebenmensch* remains self-contained, set apart, undifferentiated, undivided, "unassimilable," says Freud (1954b, 423), impervious to our gaze and foreign to our cognition (Lacan 1981a, 1:72). It is the mystery that persists in the object no matter how closely we apprehend it.

   Freud also writes of "*das Ding*" thirty years later in his "Negation" essay (1961 [1925]), and he precisely differentiates it from an object of satisfaction. In the fifth paragraph he elaborates that function of judgment that affirms or disaffirms the possession by a Thing of a particular attribute, where "a Thing" in German is *einem Ding,* and the attribute in question is the primordial "good" or "bad" that determines whether one takes it in or spits it out. In paragraph 6 Freud moves to the judgment of existence that is concerned with the real existence of something of which there is a presentation, the German for which is "*eines vorgestellten Dinges*." Here at issue is not whether or not what has been perceived (a Thing) [*ein Ding*] shall be taken into the ego, but whether something available in representation can be refound in perception. This primordial level of judgment eventually leads to the development (*Entwicklung*) in which experience (*Erfahrung*) has taught that existence must also be considered, and not just the attributes of "a Thing (an object of satisfaction)"; the German is "*ein Ding (Befriedigungsobjekt)*" (1961, 13). Freud is here presenting the transition between *das Ding,* as earliest arena of judgment, and the object as later source of satisfaction. He then *enacts* this transition by no longer referring to *Ding* (as he just has, three times) but instead now refers to "the object" three times: first, to "the external object," *das Objekt drausen,* which is not necessarily present when its representation is reproduced. He goes on to speak of the aim of reality-testing as "not to find an object" (*Objekt*) but to refind it, since "a precondition for the setting up of reality-testing is that objects [*Objekte*] shall have been lost which once brought real satisfaction." Objects exist in the domain of satisfaction-frustration; *das Ding* does not, although it stands in a certain relation to them. We could say that experience constitutes objects precisely by negating *das Ding.* Lacan reiterates this when he writes that "the subject can see it [the real] emerge under the form of a thing which is far from being an object that could satisfy it" (1966a, 389).

The real as *an sich* is the real in our initial moment of contact with it as *das Ding* in the dialectic of experience, logically prior to the status of the *an sich* as object for consciousness. Since the real is unknowable as such, it constitutes an ongoing limit on any comprehension of the *an sich.* Thus *any* position taken by consciousness in a for-itself grasp of the *an sich* must be partial and therefore less than the truth. When consciousness, in the "fixity of its self-positing" (Hegel 1977, 20), assures itself that it has the truth, it engages in a fundamental repression of the limits of its knowledge of *das Ding,* of the unknown in the *an sich.*

The *für sich* is the position of consciousness as knowing an object, or—and this is the same—the *für sich* is the object in its status for-consciousness and thereby as the content of consciousness. In this position (distinct from its position as *für uns*), consciousness is prone to what Hegel calls "picture thinking" (1977, e.g., 35, 203), or representational thinking or thinking in images, in which consciousness reflects the object's visible configurations rather than its structures of meaning. Such "picture-thinking" is associated with the fixity and familiarity maintained by consciousness (1977, 210) and therefore is an essential aspect of its resistance to change and to the truth. The *für sich,* then, bears the features of Lacan's register of the imaginary, including its intrinsically narcissistic features.

The position in which consciousness can comprehend the process as "for us," "*für uns,*" is marked by the dominance of language or the symbolic register. It is from this *für uns* position that, at critical moments, linguistic structures reveal the truth of the impasse in the relationship between *für sich* and *an sich,* as when sense-certainty is ensnared by the effort of an "I" to articulate a "this" in a "here" and "now" (Hegel 1977, 58–66), and it is *we* who "look carefully" (1977, 59), we who "find it" (1977, 59), we who "consider" the true nature of sense-certainty. It is we who "write down," we who "utter" and discover that we cannot express in words "a sensuous being that we *mean*" (1977, 60). In perception it is "for us" that the object's contradictions are already given insofar as the Thing both is "One" and also has many properties (1977, 70). It is only from the place of the *für uns* that we can comprehend that "essentially the True is Subject" (1977, 40) and that in this kind of truth, subjects become their predicates (1977, 39). Intersubjectivity constitutes humanity: "Human nature only really exists in an achieved community of minds" (1977, 43).

The *für uns* moment enables consciousness to comprehend the relationship between the level of appearances (the sensible) and the level of essence (the "supersensible"). This relation is comprehended not in a Kantian dichotomy (we perceive appearances while the essence lies beyond experience), but as a unity. The truth of the essence *is* its appearing: "The supersensible is therefore *appearance qua appearance,*" writes Hegel (1977, 89). In the *für uns* moment we are not captivated by appearances in their immediate effects on us; rather, we comprehend appearance as a revealing. This is precisely the function of Lacan's symbolic register, as Gallop notes when she writes "It is the imaginary *as* imaginary which constitutes the symbolic" (see above, chap. 12; my italics). To be precise, however, it is not the *imaginary* as imaginary that "constitutes" the symbolic, but rather the imaginary *as* imaginary that confirms we are in the symbolic register. From the position of the symbolic register we, as speakers, can grasp this "as" feature because, as Heidegger stresses, language grounds us in an interpretive mode that allows us access to the "existential-hermeneutical 'as' " (1962, 201). Or to put it another way, language, the symbolic order, does not annul the imaginary (which is its content), but rather frames it in a specific manner. As Rosen puts it, "The essence of visibility, the visible as visible, hence as most fully or actually itself, is invisible" (1974, 146). When consciousness insists that the *für sich* and *an sich* are commensurable, it claims a likeness that marks it as operating from the imaginary register. However, when consciousness in the *für uns* moment comprehends the relation between *an sich* and *für sich* as *entspricht* (Hegel 1952, 72; 1977, 54), the relation is not one of likeness but one of discursive correspondence. Verene writes that *entsprechen* "has the sense of answering, suiting, matching, being in accord with, meeting with, corresponding" (1985, 17) that is rooted in language, not perception. But the cor-respondence between *an sich* and *für sich* is continually negated:

Since what first appeared as the object sinks for consciousness to the level of its way of knowing it, and since the in-itself becomes a *being-for consciousness* of the in-itself, the latter is now the new object. Herewith a new pattern of consciousness comes on the scene as well, for which the essence is something different from what it was at the preceding stage. It is this fact that guides the entire series of the patterns of consciousness in their necessary sequence. (Hegel 1977, 56)

These patterns, however, are part of the process that "presents itself to consciousness without its understanding how this happens, which proceeds for us, as it were, behind the back of consciousness" (1977, 56). It proceeds "for us" who look on from the standpoint of the symbolic register.

LACAN'S SEMINAR

We can now attempt to read the "three logical moments" (Lacan 1972b, 43) that Lacan uses to structure Poe's story in terms of the Hegelian moments understood as elaborated above. The first moment "is a glance that sees nothing: The King and the Police" (44). In this first position the King and the police are unable to "read" the letter "because that place entailed blindness" (69). Indeed, according to Dupin, they cannot see it because of "the very simplicity of *the thing*" (my italics). When the Queen calls the police "she is only conforming to her displacement to the next slot in the arrangement of the initial triad in trusting to the very blindness required to occupy that place" (64). This "spot marked by blindness" later comes to be occupied by the Minister (70). Such "blindness" belongs to the *an sich* moment as logically prior to what is available to consciousness; "blindness" also characterizes the real as unknowing and impervious to knowledge or change: "For the real, whatever upheaval we subject it to, is always in its place; it carries it glued to its heel, ignorant of what might exile it from it" (55).

The second moment is "a glance which sees that the first sees nothing and deludes itself as to the secrecy of what it hides: The Queen, then the Minister" (44). This glance has, as its content, another glance: consciousness mirrors consciousness in this second moment, reflecting as its content its object in a dual relationship in which it becomes like its object. The Minister, who "shifted to the second position in the triad," is "immediately captivated by a dual relationship" and is now "trapped in the typically imaginary situation of seeing that he is not seen" by the glance held in his glance and fails to see "the real situation in which he is seen not seeing" by a third who stands outside the dual relationship (60–61). He is so captivated by the dual relation to the Queen that "he is obliged to don the role of the Queen" with its attributes of femininity and concealment. He even repeats her tactical gesture with the letter. She, in turn, confers on him "the position that no one is in fact capable of assuming, since it is imaginary, that of absolute master" (64). We note the allusion to the Hegelian dialectic of master and slave, whose struggle for recognition Lacan sees at the origin of the self-conscious ego. We can also see in this second position "the imaginary import of the character, that is, the narcissistic relation in which the Minister is engaged, this time, no doubt, without knowing it" (63). The Minister also suffers from a forgetfulness that leaves him exposed to an unconscious "return of the repressed" (65). Thus the Minister (and later, Lacan asserts, Dupin as well) is a victim of the fixity of his self-positing. He is betrayed by the familiar, and he forgets the limits of his comprehension: "And what does he fail to see? Precisely the symbolic situation which he himself was so well able to see, and in which he is now seen seeing himself not being seen" by Dupin, who looks on from the *für uns* position (61).

The third moment "sees that the first two glances leave what should be hidden exposed to whomever would seize it: the Minister, and finally Dupin" (44). From this position "the symbolic situation" can be read as one reads names on a map (66). Thus the *für uns* consciousness does not comprehend by means of a "picture thinking" whose content duplicates the observed configuration; rather, it grasps the structure of the observed (the observed consciousness observing another) through "analysis" (50) that is not constrained by substantive content (57).

In Hegelian terms, the three moments are always in process: the *an sich* becomes *an sich–für sich,* which in turn becomes *an sich–für sich–für uns.* That is, what is given at the border of consciousness is taken up as an object for consciousness, and this movement—this coming-into-consciousness of an object, as a structured process—is comprehended in a perspective grounded in the symbolic order. In this way we can say that from the place of *für uns* there is an incessant deconstruction of the *für sich* apprehension of the *an sich.* There is, however, an ongoing undertow of resistance on the part of consciousness that transforms the *für uns* comprehension into a new *für sich* position in relation to the "known" *an sich.*

As Hyppolite puts it, natural consciousness "naturalizes again each truth that it discovers . . . that is to say that there exists a kind of natural transposition of an original discovery which cannot see itself anymore" (1971, 60). Consciousness will find ways to make this new content familiar and is then reluctant to give it up. It suffers from a chronic "forgetfulness" of its experience of the process as the inevitable and only way to approach truth. It assures itself it has found the truth as it insists on the commensurability between *an sich* and *für sich*.

This Hegelian reading (if such it be) of Lacan's Seminar is made in a context in which Lacan has left numerous traces of Hegel. Lacan stresses that "denegation itself" ["*la dénegation* (*Verneinung*) *elle-même*"] is "decisive for the subject" and is a function of language (1972b, 40), for "it is the symbolic order which is constitutive for the subject" (40). But this constituted subject is "traverse(d)" by language (60). Elsewhere Lacan says the subject is subject to a "splitting" (1977, 285) in language so that "the subject designates his being only by barring everything he signifies" (1977, 288); he carries this further and echoes Hegel's notion of the vanishing I when he writes of "the moment of a 'fading' or eclipse of the subject that is closely bound up with the *Spaltung* or splitting that it suffers from its subordination to the signifier" (1977, 313). The signifier, moreover, "materializes the agency of death" for the subject (1972b, 53) insofar as it is the "symbol only of an absence" (1972b, 54). This link between language and death, signification and absence, Lacan expressed elsewhere as follows: "Thus the symbol manifests itself first of all as the murder of the Thing and this death constitutes in the subject the eternalization of his desire" (1977, 104). When language transforms the immediately given Thing into a symbolic presence, it does so through a radical negating that Kojève describes as "equivalent to a murder" (1969, 140).[3] Lacan goes even further and wonders, in his introduction to Jean Hyppolite's commentary on Freud's "Negation" essay, whether death introduces negation into discourse; he specifically asks what non-being as absence, manifested in the symbolic order, owes to the reality of death precisely because the negativity of discourse makes be what is not (Lacan 1966a, 379–80).

Hegelian traces are evident early in the Seminar when Lacan introduces a number of oppositions: the universal versus the particular (46, 48, 50, 55); the issue of necessity versus accident (40, 43, 47); appearance (42, 43, 46) in relation to truth (43, 46, 49, 51); and truth as other than exactitude (47, 49). Regarding mathematical truth, Hegel had written: "For it is only magnitude, the unessential distinction, that mathematics deals with" (1977, 26). Specifically "Hegelian" words (if I may say so) appear in Lacan's text: "dialectic" (1972b, 40); "master [maître]" (1966a, 27; 1972b, 57), "mastery [maîtrise]" (1966a, 31; 1972b, 62), "absolute master [maître absolu]" (1966a, 33; 1972b, 64). The story itself is all about an eighteen-month impasse that Dupin resolves precisely by taking note of apparent "contradictions" (42–43); Lacan himself stresses how "the dialogues themselves, in the opposite use they make of the powers of speech, take on a tension which makes of them a different drama" (1972b, 47). Hegel uses the image of knots: he writes of how "the knowing I" is the "knot" [das Verknüpfen] binding predicates to the subject (1977, 37; see also p. 5 and elsewhere). Lacan, early in the Seminar, writes of how the symbolic chain "binds" [lie] imaginary representations, and near the end he writes of how the signifier "knot[s]" [noue] desire (1966a, 40; 1972b, 71).

Elsewhere Lacan states that he uses Hegel to criticize proponents of post-Freudian psychoanalysis, and he acknowledges his association with "Hegelian" thought.[4] He openly reveals, furthermore, his indebtedness to Hegel, especially when he states that the very principles that govern Freud's speech "are simply the dialectic of the consciousness-of-self, as realized from Socrates to Hegel," and that it is impossible for psychoanalysis "to fail to recognize the structuring moments of the Hegelian phenomenology: in the first place the master-slave dialectic or the dialectic of the belle âme and of the law of the heart, and generally whatever enables us to understand how the constitution of the object is subordinated to the realization of the subject" (Lacan 1977, 79–80). Lacan insists, however, that Freud's decentering of the subject "from the consciousness-of-self" renders "decrepit" Hegel's emphasis on consciousness: to this we may respond that Hegel made allowance for unconscious processes (Hegel 1977, 280, 367, 369, 391, 424). For example, when he discusses Oedipus he writes that "a power which shuns the light of day ensnares the ethical self-consciousness," with the result that "what was locked up in mere possibility has been brought out into the open, hence to link together [verknüpfen, "to knot"] the unconscious and the conscious [das Unbewusste dem Bewussten], non-being with being" (1977, 283). Hyppolite, moreover, in a brilliant essay, argues that the Phenomenology of Spirit has already made a place for psychoanalysis insofar as both deal with the limit of natural consciousness, a limit that opens onto the unconscious: "a natural consciousness which, by the way, cannot help being natural: consciousness ignorant of itself which, in one of its fundamental traits, is radically unconscious" (1971, 59).

Hegel goes on to delineate the "truth" of the split subject: "In this truth, therefore, the deed is brought out into the light of day, as something in which the conscious is bound up with the unconscious, what is one's own with what is alien to it, as an entity divided within itself" (1977, 283–84). Commenting on Sophocles' *Antigone,* Hegel writes of how "from the aspect of knowing, the one character like the other is split up into a conscious and an unconscious part" (1977, 285). But this opening in the Hegelian subject onto an unconscious that renders the subject to itself as split is a condition that may be overcome in Hegel, even if not in history (Kojève 1969), at least in the ideal of absolute knowledge in which *an sich* and *für sich* ultimately coincide in "the indivisible unity of *being-for-self*" (Hegel 1977, 479). For Lacan, however, the split is irreparable, since "the truth discovered by Freud" consists in "the self's radical ex-centricity to itself" (Lacan 1977, 171) so that the notion of an undivided self is no more than "a mirage" (1977, 80), and "it is in this alienation, in this fundamental division, that the dialectic of the subject is established" (1978a, 221).

LINGUISTIC NEGATION

At this point we must consider how this Hegelian reading, even if germane to Lacan's Seminar, is relevant to the Poe text. If negation, in the Hegelian sense, is a determining structure in Poe's short story, then we should be able to find it both in the language and in the action of the story. But before examining Poe's language for the presence of negation, we must determine what negation is, at least in the English language.

When Jespersen wrote that "the chief use of a negative sentence [is] to contradict and to point a contrast" (1966, 4–5), he emphasized the contrapuntal features of negation, either in its "special" form, as "some modification of the word," as in "never," "unhappy," "impossible," "disorder," "nonbelligerent," or as "nexal negation" or the "negative nexus," as in the use of "not" with the verb ("he does not come") (1966, 42). Jespersen also distinguished "indirect negation," involving questioning, ellipsis, conditional clauses, hortatives, and ironical phrases, from what he called "incomplete negation," which uses "approximate negatives" such as "hardly," "restricted negatives" such as "scarcely," "incomplete negatives" such as "little," "few," and "verbs of negative import" such as "deny," "forbid," "hinder," "doubt." In contrast to this wealth of differentiation, Ver Eecke focuses on "the distinction between two kinds of negation," namely "*no* and *not,* that is, the intersubjective and the content negation" (1984, 154). When one says "no" in dialogue, one is presenting a subjective intention or point of view opposed to that of the other; when "not" is used (and the related alternatives that Jespersen calls "indirect"), it is the content of the sentence that is diminished. But Ver Eecke stresses that "no negation [is] capable of destroying the negated content," and because "the linguistic negation in principle does not succeed in destroying the negated content, we must accept the fact that the use of a negation is at least ambivalent" (115–16). Such "ambivalence" is consistent with the fact that the "negation of a content does not destroy this content. In fact, even when the content is negated, one has drawn attention to it" (92). We can go further and say, in Hegelian fashion, that the linguistic negation, precisely while negating the content, preserves it and takes it up in a new way.

A more generalizable linguistic structure of negation has been proposed by Klima, who asks, after reviewing Jespersen's many uses of negation, "Is it the case that a single symbol accounts for certain linguistic facts at the very places where negativeness is intuited?" (1964, 250). Klima's answer, from the viewpoint of generative grammar and following an extended analysis of varying types of negative sentences, is a resounding *yes:*

A single independent negative element, whose simplest reflex is *not,* is found to account for sentence negation; its scope is the whole sentence, but because that element is mobile and capable of fusing with other elements (for example in *nobody*), its ultimate position and form have great latitude. When the negative element originates in other constituents (as for example in the extreme case of *doubt*), the scope of negation is restricted to structures subordinate to those constituents. However, granted the differences due to varying scope, it was found that the phenomena connected with negation could be described grammatically on the basis of a single negative element. (1964, 316)

This "single negative element" ["neg"] reminds us of Freud's "symbol of negation" (1961, 236, 239), which he posits as essential for the development of thinking. Jackendoff further refined Klima's rules of transformation and offered "as a rough semantic test for sentence negation," the following rule: "A sentence $[_sX - \text{neg} - Y_s]$ is an instance of sentence negation if there exists a paraphrase *It is not so* that $[_sX - Y]$" (1969, 218). This position is consistent with the linguistic view of negation as a "mode" applied to a positive proposition. For example, Ducrot and Todorov write:

Furthermore, this modal solution is very close to intuition when the negative utterance is interpreted, psychologically, as the rejection of a prior positive utterance (real or supposed). I only announce to someone that I did not go to Paris if I attribute to him the opinion that I might have gone there. We may describe this phenomenon by saying that the negative utterance takes as its object a positive proposition (the one affirmed in the positive utterance that is being opposed) and affects it with a modality of negation. (1979, 315)

Hagège also emphasizes this dialectical feature of negation (1985, 147, 236). This position likewise finds a place in sociolinguistic discourse analysis: "Negative sentences are typically used to correct or deny false beliefs, and positive sentences therefore make fewer assumptions" (Stubbs 1983, 116). Givón echoes this from the standpoint of pragmatics in stressing "the presuppositionally more marked status of negative sentences," in which "the discourse presupposition of a negative speech act . . . is its corresponding affirmative" (1978, 70). We can delineate, then, a range of intersubjective possibilities that may be operative when a negative sentence is uttered:

1. I dispute what you say.
2. I dispute what I impute to you.
3. I dispute what you pretend to say.
4. I pretend to dispute what you say.
5. I pretend to dispute what I impute to you.
6. I pretend to dispute what you pretend to say.

These positions may be played out not only between speakers in the text, but also between them and the reader as well as between the narrator's narration and the reader. In other words, the negative sentence can be dialectically used in dialogue—in a series of feints and maneuvers to put the other off balance and to disguise the truth.

Negation in "The Purloined Letter"

In examining Poe's text (1978) we can, following Lacan, distinguish two scenes in the story. Let scene 1 include all the text up to page 981 (three lines from the bottom); thus scene 2 begins with the temporal break, "In about a month afterwards he paid us another visit" and includes the rest of the text. In each scene we can distinguish four sources of discourse: the narrator's narration; the narrator in dialogue; the Prefect in dialogue;

Dupin in dialogue. All but the first of these texts, which we can call "narrative," are bracketed by quotation marks.

One way to move through the wealth of negation in Poe's text is to focus not on negative terms but rather on negative sentences by applying Jackendoff's rule. Thus we can count as negative sentences those that can be transformed to take the form: "*It is not so* that X is Y," or, "A (posits) *it is not so* that X is Y." For example, when the Prefect speaks of the Queen's reclaiming her letter he says: "But this, of course, cannot be done openly." We apply the transformation rule to now read: "But [*it is not so* that] this, of course, [can] be done openly." The use of negative constituents severely constrains the rule's application, as when the Prefect elaborates (980), "Any disorder in the glueing—any unusual gaping in the joints—would have sufficed to insure detection." The rule fails when we transform this to read "[*It is not so* that] any order in the glueing." In sentences with double negation, however, the rule's application works very well when applied to the initial negative. The Prefect's assertion at the end of the first scene (981), "I am not more sure that I breathe than I am that the letter is not at the Hotel," becomes: "[*It is not so* that] I am more sure that I breathe than I am that the letter is not at the Hotel." We shall see that this type of negative sentence marked by double negation, wherein the first negative negates the second in a principal or subordinate clause, is prominent in the speech of the Prefect, and even more so in Dupin's speech.

Poe's text contains 332 sentences; of these 118, or 36 percent, contain at least one of three types of negation: (1) 10 sentences (3 percent) are negative questions, and 6 of them are asked by the narrator in dialogue; (2) negative constituents (such as "nameless," "nonsense," "non-appearance") mark 48 sentences (15 percent of the total number of sentences); (3) there are 60 negative sentences (18 percent of the total number of sentences) that are counted according to Jackendoff's rule. When sentence source is examined, there are few differences in the overall use of negation, which ranges from 30 percent for the narrator in dialogue to 40 percent for the Prefect. When type of negation is examined, however, the *negative sentence* (as defined by the Jackendoff rule) is more pronounced in the speech of the Prefect (22 percent) and in Dupin's speech (20 percent), less so in that of the narrator in dialogue (13 percent), and there is only one negative sentence out of 20 in the narration. There is no difference in these percentages when we compare scene 1 with scene 2: in fact, the percentages for the Prefect and Dupin (22 percent and 20 percent) are exactly the same in each scene.[5]

When we look at the frequency of negative sentences with double negation, however, a different pattern emerges. Of the Prefect's 20 negative sentences in scene 1, 5 (or 25 percent) contain double negation, spread across scene 1. In scene 2, on the other hand, the negative sentences with double negation are spoken by Dupin, more than two pages after he begins his "explanations." Of Dupin's 29 negative sentences in scene 2, 41 percent contain double negation. The *only other* such negative sentence with double negation that we find in scene 2 is spoken by the narrator in dialogue with Dupin: "You do not mean to set at nought the well-digested idea of centuries" (986). Dupin does indeed mean to do such a thing, and he achieves his challenging effect partly by the repeated use of negative sentences marked by double negation. Such sentences give him an aura of being a complex thinker (note how often he says "I considered," "I reflected," "I knew well"). Such complexity owes much to the way linguistic negation calls attention to its denied content, which is then openly reaffirmed by the negation of this negation.

In contrast, however, Dupin achieves his effect of being "straightforward" by dropping *all* use of negative terms during those passages in which he "explains" his analytic procedure: when he describes the eight-year-old's process of identification with his opponent (984, the only full page in the story without any negative terms); when he uses the example of large letters on a map (989); when he reports how he identified the stolen letter and seized it (992). In these passages we are given the illusion of a smooth flow in Dupin's explanation, unruffled by negatives, unchallenged by contraries presenting us with assumptions; instead, we are given simply the "objective" facts. This smooth flow is in sharp contrast to the earlier negation-marked descriptions by the Prefect of the events that resulted in impasse (978: "His servants are by no means numerous. . . . For three months a night has not passed during the greater part of which I have not been engaged"). After the Prefect tells how the Minister was waylaid, Dupin imputes a view to the Prefect when he says the Minister "is not altogether a fool, and, if not, must have anticipated these waylayings as a matter of course." The Prefect almost accepts the view Dupin imputes to him when he responds: "Not altogether a fool . . . but then he's a poet, which I take to be only one remove from a fool" (979). Dupin then admits he too is a poet and thereafter falls silent for *two pages* until finally the Prefect asks him what to do: "To make a thorough re-search of the premises," an injunction whose absurdity in the face of impasse elicits from the Prefect the self-assured pronouncement: "That is absolutely needless. . . . I am not more sure that I breathe than I am that the letter is not at the Hotel" (981). This can be heard as the last desperate self-affirmation of the realist's position of sense-certainty, caught in the "fixity of its self-posit-ing" (Hegel 1977, 20). But the presence of the negative terms undercuts the assurance, adds complexity, and sets up the more basic doubt: Does the Prefect have warrant to be sure of himself at all? Dupin confirms this moment of impasse when he answers, "I have no better advice to give you," but then he asks for a description of the letter, almost as an afterthought. We do not, therefore, notice that *for us* no description of the letter is forthcoming.

Dupin's silence as we learn of the Prefect's impasse is crucial for maintaining his position of authority. In his silence he does not indicate how he projects assumptions: neither the assumptions he thinks others make about him nor the assumptions he makes about them—none of this is available, while the Prefect and the narrator in dialogue reveal a variety of assumptions and counterpositions in relation to the other.

Negation in the story's text, then, serves to forward the interaction as a series of impasses and feints and countermoves. We see that negation itself is a form of denial, a type of ruse, perhaps the most deceptive ruse of all used by the "bold intriguant," as Dupin calls the Minister:

Such a man, I considered, could not fail to be aware of the ordinary policial modes of action. He could not have failed to anticipate . . . the waylayings to which he was subjected. He must have foreseen, I re-flected, the secret investigations of his premises. His frequent absences from home at night, which were hailed by the Prefect as certain aids to his success, I regarded only as *ruses*. . . to impress [the police] with the conviction that the letter was not upon the premises. (988)

The Minister's denial of his denial through his apparent vulnerability, his pretended defenselessness, leads to the desired goal: the Prefect's negative judgment about the presence of the letter. Whereas the Prefect comes to believe the Minister's denial ("The letter is not here"), Dupin follows Freud and hears in this negation "It *is* here, somehow" and is not taken in by the Minister's ruse.

The use of negation as a ruse by the Minister is crucial for understand-ing how he achieves his effects; Lacan points to its same use by Dupin: "What could be more convincing, moreover, than the gesture of laying one's cards face-up on the table?" That is, denying that one has anything to hide, posing as one who is open. The Prefect is most vulnerable to this ruse because he is so readily snared by the lures of the imaginary: "My first care was to make thorough search of the Minister's hotel; and here my chief embarrassment lay in the necessity of searching without his knowledge. Beyond all things, I have been warned of the danger which would result from giving him reason to suspect our design" (978). Knowledge, for the Prefect, is a determined content that can be possessed by one individual and denied to another through stealth; what he does not realize is that his "knowledge" about the "danger" that lies in giving another "knowledge" about one's actions is false knowledge planted to snare him. This is similar to the way, as Dupin puts it, "Pagan fables" snare us: "we forget ourselves continually, and make inferences from them as existing realities" (987–88). If this emphasis on forgetfulness of our experience were an insufficient reminder of Hegel, then we cannot fail to be reminded when we then read that to negate accepted truths is to risk violence (988).

The note of negation in "The Purloined Letter" is struck by the first word *"Nil,"* which prepares us for the chorus of negation to come. This non-English *"Nil"* brackets the text together with the final negation as heard in the Crébillon quotation in the story's penultimate line: "S'il n'est digne d'Atrée, est digne de Thyeste" ("If it [the scheme] is not worthy of Atreus, it is worthy of Thyestes"). Poe thus contains, perhaps even causes to be repressed, the function of negation in English by using signifiers that are other, untranslated, apparently left to stand by themselves. Here the "foreign" languages serve as negations of negations by obscuring, in their very freestanding manner, the powerful role of negation in the English text. Here again the cards are left face up on the table with the precise effect that our eyes pass right over them and through them to what they are supposed to signify, to their "translations." In this way the power of the signifier lies in the signifier's transparent materiality, invisible in its very visibility.

The use of *ne,* in the Crébillon quotation, without *pas, point,* or another term may be what Ver Eecke calls "the signifier for a full negation in some archaic expressions" (1984, 108), and therefore the equivalent of *non.* On the other hand, in "formal style, following *si,* the *pas* of the negation is sometimes omitted" (see *Harrap's* 1974, N:5), and in this case it is omitted too for reasons of poetic meter. This *n'* perhaps functions like the "discordantialist" that serves, as Ver Eecke puts it, as "the signifier of the following meaning: There are two opposed movements present or possible" (1984, 102). He goes on to say that *"ne* is the signifier of a split in the subject of the sentence, because *ne* indicates or introduces an alternative and contrary possibility. . . . *Ne* indicates the presence of a

contrary movement" (1984, 110). The quoted lines lead us to pause as *S'*
introduces possibility and *n'* pulls in the contrary movement. The "split"
in the subject *il,* whose antecedent is *dessein,* shows us that the nefarious
character of the deliberate scheme of revenge falls on both brothers. Lacan
further works this split by using *destin* to negate *dessein,* for the unconscious determinations of the signifier establish a destiny that negates our
ego-based designs. The quoted words themselves enact the power of the
signifier: "S'il n'est digne . . . est digne" accomplishes its countermovement with a minimum of typesetting.

The final line of the story affirms the source of the quotation to be
Crébillon, about whom Hoffman writes:

How apt that Dupin should quote Crébillon, who after rivalling Voltaire
with his early tragedies, fell on evil days, the victim of slanders circulated
against him at court, and retired to a garret with his dogs, cats, and
ravens, until, after a seclusion of two decades, he was elected to the
Académie Française and given a pension by Mme. Pompadour. (1978,
129–30)[6]

The ambivalence of the quoted line is firmly and finally put to rest by the
calm, authoritative, positive statement in which Dupin directs us to
Crébillon's text and to the satisfaction of its final negation.

When we examine the story's action from this perspective of negation,
we find that the story proceeds *as* a series of negating actions: that is, each
action is a precise negation of a previous action of another and is, in turn,
negated in the dialectical shifting of actors' positions. But in each negation the truth of the previous position is preserved. The Queen negates
the King's power but preserves its role in her secretiveness as she turns the
letter over and puts it down. The Minister's dramatic action is inaugurated when he perceives the Queen's negation (leaving the letter exposed)
of her negation of the King's sovereignty (through the letter's possession).
By his substitution, the Minister negates the Queen's secrecy but preserves it in his tactic of open concealment. Dupin's speech acts, including
his silence, negate the Prefect's speech acts while holding them in view:
" 'Yes,' said Dupin. 'The measures adopted were not only the best of their
kind, and well executed: Their defect lay in their being inapplicable to
the case, and to the man' " (983–84). Dupin's successful action goes on to
negate the Prefect's failed actions but preserves his motive of monetary
reward. Dupin's retrieval negates the Minister's open tactic but preserves
it in his "MS.," which, in turn, negates the letter's text. His act of

revenge negates the Minister's earlier "evil turn" (993) but retains the element of aggression. Lacan, finally, negates and preserves Dupin's "MS." by conferring a new *"destin"* to the quoted text of Crébillon. The series of negations seems endless as we read the commentaries (especially those of Derrida, Johnson, and Harvey), and this may be due to the dynamic character of the letter as the "pure signifier" of negation.

How can we view the letter in Poe's story as the signifier of negation? Negation, as such, is not representable by an image. Freud (1960b, 57; 1961, 239) stresses that "no" as a linguistic function does not exist in the unconscious, which must utilize sensuous components of the imaginary register to achieve its semiotic effects. Therefore we can state that negation can be performed *only* through the function of a "pure signifier," a signifier ("neg") that has no signified of its own, that is liquid and malleable and so unadulterated by content that it can appear anywhere in a sentence. In this context, the purloined letter derives its power over people, its effect of splitting subjects from one another (splitting the Queen from the King, the Minister from the Queen, Dupin from the Minister, Lacan from Dupin, Derrida from Lacan, and so on) and, through achieving repression, splitting subjects from themselves (the Minister from himself, Dupin from himself, Lacan from Lacan, Derrida from Derrida) precisely from its unique status as pure signifier of negation. The description given us of the purloined letter suggests the process of negation as we have come to see it: "This last was much soiled and crumpled. It was torn nearly in two, across the middle—as if a design, in the first instance, to tear it entirely up as worthless, had been altered, or stayed in the second" (991). This "design" (echoing *dessein*) demonstrates the countermovement of negation, negation at once as repression and as the return of the repressed.

We here encounter, in addition to the Hegelian notion of negation as process and the formal aspects of linguistic negation, a third type of negation as psychological structure. We can say that the letter is the signifier that traverses and splits the subject and also divides the subjects from one another; it is also thereby the signifier of negation whose presence in the negative sentence "is the hall-mark of repression" (Freud 1961, 236). Such a structure of negation preserves what it negates, as Benveniste stresses: "The characteristic of linguistic negation is that it can annul only what has been uttered, which it has to set up for the express purpose of suppressing and that a judgment of nonexistence has necessarily the formal status of a judgment of existence. Thus negation is first acceptance" (1971, 73). But for psychic structure to exist at all, it requires the process of repression whereby experience is preserved precisely by being repressed from consciousness, and for consciousness to be able to function it must be able to say "not." Thus Laplanche and Pontalis stress that "in Freud's view the negation dealt with in psycho-analysis and negation in the logical and linguistic sense—the 'symbol' of negation—share the same origin" (1973, 263). Fisher emphasizes the link between psychological structure and negation when he writes: "The reason personality is so fundamentally involved has to do with the function of negation in defense mechanisms" (1984, 41).

Hegel tells us that "the negative is the self" (1977, 21). Perhaps we can conceive of negation as the very structure that splits the subject, as the bar itself that separates consciousness from what is repressed, that delimits the *für sich* from the *an sich*. This would be the same bar that operates in Lacan's paternal metaphor wherein "Le Nom [Non] du Père" effects the separation from and repression of the totalizing desire of the mother (1966a, 557). This "no" that is homophonous with the patrilineage that names the subject, and therefore designates the subject as limited, is the ongoing structure that prevents psychosis by relativizing every *für sich* position. Consciousness in the psychotic state typically experiences itself as continuous with all others and as influencing or being influenced by all others; it has the truth wholly, immediately, and unqualifiedly. The source of this "no" that relativizes the subject Lacan calls the "Other," the third that enables two to relate without fusion. Two people cannot, without being psychotic, have a dialogue unless they are aware of the Other saying "no," setting limits on the generalizability and grandiosity of their speech.[7] Since negation is a necessary barrier to prevent hallucination, failure of this "no" leads to the collapse of the structure of signification, with its inherent limits and reference to what is absent, with the result that the imaginary dominates the response to the real, whose negation and mediation is now rendered problematic, as presented in Lacan's analysis of Schreber's *Memoirs*. Psychic structure is established only through that negation to which the subject must submit upon entering the register of the symbolic, and this fundamental splitting of the subject into *an sich* and *für sich* may be understood as constituting primary repression.

To posit negation as central to psychic structure is to recognize its specifically human function and its specifically linguistic nature. Ortigues states that the "function of negativity is essential to language"

(1962, 186). Green writes: "Negation does not have a specific place within language; language as a whole is sustained by negation" (1986, 258). Burke argues that "the negative is a purely linguistic resource" (1966, 419), that "the genius of language resides in the genius of the negative" (461), and he states: "The essential distinction between the verbal and the nonverbal is in the fact that language adds the peculiar possibility of the Negative" (420). Just as we can measure the adequacy of any ideology of the human by the place it reserves for negation, so too can we assess any clinical approach in terms of what role is given to the negative. Is negation viewed simply as recalcitrance, to be "modified" through prescribed reward and punishment? Is negation simply perverse refusal on the part of the patient to cooperate with "treatment"? To what extent can we affirm that the moment of negative impasse contains the means of its own resolution? In the very act of negating boundaries, the psychotic patient is attempting to locate existence amid coordinates of space and time; the "negativism" that tests limits does so precisely in order to find them.

Since the power of the negative can be said to come ultimately from the real resisting comprehension, any clinical approach that fashions itself as a masterful agent whose "services" are reimbursed by insurance companies is bound to view the negative with hostility. The ego, furthermore, resists the negative in its pursuit of substantive content and definitive results, what it takes to be the "truth" of its practice. But Hegel alerts us to the dangers inherent in any form of truth as individualistic, as "my" possession. For Hegel, truth is always embedded in a community that rests on the structure of language whose history includes "the seriousness, the suffering, the patience, and the labour of the negative" (1977, 10).

The power of negation in approaching truth permeates Poe's story, a story that shows how self-assurance is repeatedly undermined by negation. Poe's work as a whole can be said to rest on negation. Richard Wilbur states that "Poe's subject matter became the depicted process of negating this world, and his more exciting techniques are techniques of erasure, of explosion, of uncreation" (1975, 5). For Poe—as for Hegel and Lacan—negation is the dynamic corrollary of the ego's self-assured notions about reality. Therefore this is not the last word about "The Purloined Letter," but rather one moment in the commentary that can itself be read as a series of negations. And so the extraordinary power of this story continues even as readers go beyond what is here presented.

NOTES

1. Verene (1985) makes recollection the central task of the *Phenomenology.*

2. Miller has "I" here and in the following lines; the German has *Ich.*

3. In *Marginalia,* Poe had written: "Words—printed ones especially—are murderous things" (1981, 81).

4. In *Ecrits* Lacan wrote in a footnote: "I am referring here to the friend [Jean Wahl] who invited me to this conference [on 'The Dialectic'], having, some months before, revealed to me the reservations that he derived from his personal ontology against 'psychoanalysts' who were too 'Hegelian' for his liking, as if anyone except myself in that assembly could be accused of this" (1966a, 804; 1977, 325).

5. The following table presents the number of negative sentences by scene and by source (P = Prefect, D = Dupin):

	Scene 1		Scene 2	
Source (number of sentences)	P (91)	D (20)	P (9)	D (145)
Number of Negative sentences	20	4	2	29

6. In this final negation of the negation, Poe's own life owes much to the French. Expressing a typically French view of Poe (see Gallop above, chap. 12), Cambiaire writes: "The wish of Baudelaire . . . has been realized. Poe, 'le pauvre Eddie' who was so much maligned and criticized during his life, and even after his death, is now the great Poe, the great poet, the great inspirer of ideas, not only for France, but for the whole world" (1927, 313).

7. This theme has been developed at clinical conferences by Ess A. White, M.D., director of psychotherapy at the Austen Riggs Center.

 *References*

Aarsleff, Hans. 1982. *From Locke to Saussure: Essays on the study of language and intellectual history.* Minneapolis: University of Minnesota Press.

Alexander, Jean A. 1961. Affidavits of genius: French essays on Poe. *Dissertation Abstracts* 22, no. 2:866.

Allouch, Jean. 1983. La "conjecture de Lacan" sur l'origine de l'écriture. *Littoral* 7/8:5–26.

Altieri, Charles. 1979. Presence and reference in a literary text: The example of Williams' "This is just to say." *Critical Inquiry* 5, no. 3:489–510.

———. 1981. *Act and quality: A theory of literary meaning and humanistic understanding.* Amherst: University of Massachusetts Press.

Balakian, Anna. 1971. *André Breton: Magus of surrealism.* New York: Oxford University Press.

Bass, Alan. 1984. "The double game": An introduction. In *Taking chances: Derrida, psychoanalysis, and literature,* ed. Joseph H. Smith and William Kerrigan, 66–85. Baltimore: Johns Hopkins University Press.

Benjamin, Walter. 1969. The storyteller. In *Illuminations,* ed. H. Arendt, 83–109. New York: Schocken Books.

Benveniste, Emile. 1971. *Problems in general linguistics.* Trans. M. Meek. Coral Gables: University of Miami Press. Originally published 1966.

Bertin, Celia. 1982. *Marie Bonaparte: A life.* New York: Harcourt Brace Jovanovich.

Bonaparte, Marie. 1927. Du symbolisme des trophées de tête. *Revue Française de Psychanalyse* 1, no. 4:677–732.

————. 1933. *Edgar Poe: Etude psychanalytique.* Vol. 2. Paris: Denoël et Steele.

————. 1971. *The Life and works of Edgar Allan Poe: A psycho-analytic interpretation.* Trans. John Rodker. New York: Humanities Press. Translation originally published 1949.

Borges, Jorge Luis. 1967. *A personal anthology.* Ed. Anthony Kerrigan. New York: Grove Press. Originally published 1961.

Bowie, Malcolm. 1979. Jacques Lacan. In *Structuralism and since: From Lévi-Strauss to Derrida,* ed. John Sturrock, 116–53. Oxford: Oxford University Press.

Burke, Kenneth. 1966. A dramatist.. view of the origins of language and postscripts on the negative. In *Language as symbolic action: Essays on life, literature, and method,* 419–79. Berkeley and Los Angeles: University of California Press.

Cambiaire, C. P. 1927. *The influence of Edgar Allan Poe in France.* New York: G. E. Stechert.

Carlson, E. W., ed. 1966. *The recognition of Edgar Allan Poe: Selected criticism since 1829.* Ann Arbor: University of Michigan Press.

Chambers, Ross. 1979. Le poète fumeur. *Australian Journal of French Studies* 16, no. 1/2:138–50.

————. 1984. *Story and situation: Narrative seduction and the power of fiction.* Theory and History of Literature, vol. 12. Minneapolis: University of Minnesota Press.

Chandler, Alice. 1970. The visionary race: Poe's attitude toward his dreamers. *Emerson Society Quarterly* 60, pt. 2:73–81.

Clément, Catherine. 1983. *The lives and legends of Jacques Lacan.* Trans. A. Goldhammer. New York: Columbia University Press.

Cooke, P. Pendleton. 1966. Edgar A. Poe (quoting Elizabeth Barrett). In *The recognition of Edgar Allan Poe: Selected criticism since 1829,* ed. E. W. Carlson. Ann Arbor: University of Michigan Press.

Cornford, Francis MacDonald. 1957. *Plato and Parmenides.* New York: Liberal Arts Press.

Cox, Cynthia. 1961. *The enigma of the age: The strange story of the Chevalier d'Eon.* London: Longmans.

Culler, Jonathan. 1979. Jacques Derrida. In *Structuralism and since: From Lévi-Strauss to Derrida,* ed. John Sturrock, 154–80. New York: Oxford University Press.

Daniel, R. 1971. Poe's detective god. In *Twentieth century interpretations of Poe's tales,* ed. W. L. Howarth, 103–10. Englewood Cliffs, N.J.: Prentice-Hall.

de Lauretis, Teresa. 1984. *Alice doesn't: Feminism, semiotics, cinema.* Bloomington: Indiana University Press.

deMan, Paul. 1979. *Allegories of reading: Figural language in Rousseau, Nietzsche, Rilke, and Proust.* New Haven: Yale University Press.

———. 1983. *Blindness and insight: Essays in the rhetoric of contemporary criticism,* 2d ed. Minneapolis: University of Minnesota Press. Originally published 1971.

Derrida, Jacques. 1972. *Positions.* Paris: Editions du Minuit.

———. 1973. *Speech and phenomena: And other essays on Husserl's theory of signs.* Trans. David Allison. Evanston: Northwestern University Press. Originally published 1967.

———. 1974a. *Glas.* Paris: Editions Galilée.

———. 1974b. *Of grammatology.* Trans. Gayatri Spivak. Baltimore: Johns Hopkins University Press. Originally published 1967.

———. 1975a. The purveyor of truth. Trans. Willis Domingo et al. In *Graphesis: Perspectives in literature and philosophy. Yale French Studies* 52:31–113.

———. 1975b. Le facteur de la vérité. *Poétique,* no. 21:96–147.

———. 1976. *L'archéologie du frivole: Lire Condillac.* Paris: Denoël/Gonthier.

———. 1977. *Edmund Husserl's "Origin of geometry": An introduction.* Trans. John P. Leavey. New York: Nicolas Hays. Originally published 1962.

———. 1978a. *Spurs: Nietzsche's styles.* Trans. Barbara Harlow. Chicago: University of Chicago Press. Originally published 1976.

———. 1978b. *La vérité en peinture.* Paris: Flammarion.

———. 1978c. *Writing and difference.* Trans. Alan Bass. Chicago: University of Chicago Press. Originally published 1967.

———. 1980. Le facteur de la vérité. In *La carte postale,* 439–524. Paris: Flammarion.

———. 1981a. *Dissemination.* Trans. Barbara Johnson. Chicago: University of Chicago Press. Originally published 1972.

———. 1981b. *Positions.* Trans. Alan Bass. Chicago: University of Chicago Press. Originally published 1972.

———. 1982. *Margins of philosophy.* Trans. Alan Bass. Chicago: University of Chicago Press. Originally published 1972.

———. 1984. *My chances/Mes chances:* A rendezvous with some Epicurean stereophonies. In *Taking chances: Derrida, psychoanalysis, and literature,* ed. Joseph Smith and William Kerrigan, 1–32. Baltimore: Johns Hopkins University Press.

Dillon, John. 1911. *Edgar Allan Poe: His genius and his character.* New York.

Ducrot, Oswald, and Tzvetan Todorov. 1979. *Encyclopedic dictionary of the sciences of language.* Trans. Catherine Porter. Baltimore: Johns Hopkins University Press. Originally published 1972.

Eco, Umberto, and Thomas A. Sebeok, eds. 1983. *The sign of three: Dupin, Holmes, Peirce.* Bloomington: Indiana University Press.

Eliot, T. S. 1966. From Poe to Valéry. In *The recognition of Edgar Allan Poe: Selected criticism since 1829,* ed. E. W. Carlson. Ann Arbor: University of Michigan Press. Originally published 1949.

Felman, Shoshana. 1977. Turning the screw of interpretation. In *Literature and psychoanalysis: The question of reading—otherwise. Yale French Studies* 55/56:94–138.

————. 1980. On reading poetry: Reflections on the limits and possibilities of psychoanalytical approaches. In *The literary Freud: Mechanisms of defense and the poetic will,* ed. Joseph Smith, 119–48. Psychiatry and the Humanities, vol. 4. New Haven: Yale University Press.

————. 1982. Psychoanalysis and education: Teaching terminable and interminable. *Yale French Studies* 63:21–44.

Fish, Stanley. 1970. Literature in the reader: Affective stylistics. *New Literary History* 2:123–62.

————. 1973. How ordinary is ordinary language? *New Literary History* 5:41–54.

————. 1976. Interpreting "Interpreting the variorum." *Critical Inquiry* 3:191–96.

Fisher, Harwood. 1984. Negation and logic in psychological defenses: A biopsychological perspective. *New Ideas in Psychology* 3, no. 1:39–45.

Freud, Sigmund. 1942. *The interpretation of dreams.* Trans. A. A. Brill. London: Allen and Unwin.

————. 1948a. The antithetical sense of primal words. In *Collected Papers,* vol. 4, trans. Joan Riviere, 184–91. London: Hogarth Press. Originally published 1910.

————. 1948b. The relation of the poet to day-dreaming. In *Collected Papers,* vol. 4, trans. Joan Riviere, 173–82. London: Hogarth Press. Originally published 1908.

————. 1948c. Die Verneinung. In *Gesammelte Werke* 14:11–15. Frankfurt am Main: S. Fischer. Originally published 1925.

————. 1950. *Aus den Aufängen der Psychoanalyse.* Ed. M. Bonaparte, A. Freud, and E. Kris. London: Imago. Originally published 1887–1902.

————. 1953a. Fragment of an analysis of a case of hysteria. In *Standard edition* 7:7–122. London: Hogarth Press. Originally published 1901.

————. 1953b. *The interpretation of dreams.* In *Standard edition,* vols. 4 and 5. London: Hogarth Press. Originally published 1900.

————. 1954a. *The origins of psychoanalysis: Letters to Wilhelm Fliess, drafts and notes.* Ed. M. Bonaparte, A. Freud, and E. Kris, trans. E. Mosbacher and J. Strachey. New York: Basic Books. Originally published 1887–1902.

————. 1954b. *Project for a scientific psychology.* In *The origins of psychoanalysis: Letters to Wilhelm Fliess, drafts and notes.* Ed. M. Bonaparte, A. Freud, and E. Kris, trans. E. Mosbacher and J. Strachey, 355–445. New York: Basic Books. Originally published 1895.

————. 1955a. *Beyond the pleasure principle.* In *Standard edition* 18:7–64. London: Hogarth Press. Originally published 1920.

————. 1955b. *Group psychology and the analysis of the ego.* In *Standard edition* 18:69–143. London: Hogarth Press. Originally published 1921.

————. 1960a. *Jokes and their relation to the unconscious.* In *Standard edition,* vol. 8. London: Hogarth Press. Originally published 1905.

————. 1960b. *The psychopathology of everyday life.* In *Standard edition,* vol. 6. London: Hogarth Press. Originally published 1901.

————. 1961. Negation. In *Standard edition* 19:235–39. London: Hogarth Press. Originally published 1925.

Gallop, Jane. 1982. *The daughter's seduction: Feminism and psychoanalysis.* Ithaca: Cornell University Press.

————. 1985. *Reading Lacan.* Ithaca: Cornell University Press.

Galloway, David, ed. 1967. *Edgar Allan Poe: Selected writings.* New York: Penguin.

Givón, T. 1978. Negation in language: Pragmatics, function, ontology. In *Syntax and semantics,* vol. 9, *Pragmatics,* ed. Peter Cole, 69–112. New York: Academic Press.

Goethe, J. W. von. 1963. *Faust.* The original German and a new translation and introduction by Walter Kaufmann. Part one and sections from part two. Garden City, N.Y.: Anchor Press, Doubleday.

Green, André. 1986. *On private madness.* Madison, Conn.: International Universities Press.

Grice, H. P. 1975. Logic and conversation. In *Speech acts,* ed. P. Cole and J. L. Morgan, 41–58. New York: Academic Press.

Griswold, Rufus W. 1849. The "Ludwig article." *New York Tribune* (evening edition), October 9, 1849 (Virginia Edition, 1:348–59).

————. 1853. *The works of the late Edgar Allan Poe, with a memoir,* vol. 1. New York: Redfield.

Hagège, Claude. 1985. *L'homme de paroles: Contribution linguistique aux sciences humaines.* Paris: Fayard.

Hall, Donald, ed. 1981. *The Oxford book of American literary anecdotes.* New York: Oxford University Press.

Harrap's New Standard French and English Dictionary. 1974. London: Harrap.

Hartman, Geoffrey. 1975. Literature high and low: The case of the mystery story. In *The fate of reading.* Chicago: University of Chicago Press.

Harvey, Irene. 1983. Derrida and the concept of metaphysics. *Research in Phenomenology* 13:113–48.

————. 1985. *Derrida and the economy of différance.* Bloomington: Indiana University Press.

Haycraft, Howard. 1946. Murder for pleasure. In *The art of the mystery story: A collection of critical essays,* ed. Howard Haycraft. New York: Simon and Schuster.

Hegel, Georg W. F. 1952. *Phänomenologie des Geistes*. Hamburg: Felix Meiner. Originally published 1807.

———. 1969. *Science of logic*. Trans. A. V. Miller. New York: Humanities Press. Originally published 1812.

———. 1977. *Phenomenology of spirit*. Trans. A. V. Miller. Oxford: Oxford University Press.

Heidegger, M. 1962. *Being and time*. Trans. J. Macquarrie and E. Robinson. New York: Harper and Row. Originally published 1927.

———. 1969. The onto-theo-logical structure of metaphysics. In *Identity and difference*, trans. J. Stambaugh. New York: Harper and Row. Originally published 1957.

———. 1971. *On the way to language*. Trans. Peter D. Hertz. New York: Harper and Row. Originally published 1959.

———. 1977. *Basic writings*, ed. David F. Krell. New York: Harper and Row.

Higginson, Thomas Wentworth. 1966. Poe. In *The recognition of Edgar Allan Poe: Selected criticism since 1829*, ed. E. W. Carlson. Ann Arbor: University of Michigan Press. Originally published 1879.

Hirsch, E. D., Jr. 1976. *The aims of interpretation*. Chicago: University of Chicago Press.

Hoffman, Daniel. 1978. *Poe Poe Poe Poe Poe Poe Poe*. New York: Avon Books.

Holland, Norman. 1975. Hamlet—my greatest creation. *Journal of the American Academy of Psychoanalysis* 3:419–27.

———. 1976a. Literary interpretation and three phases of psychoanalysis. *Critical Inquiry* 3:221–33.

———. 1976b. Transactive criticism: Re-creation through identity. *Criticism* 18:334–52.

———. (with Leona F. Sherman). 1977a. Gothic possibilities. *New Literary History* 8:279–94.

———. 1977b. Transactive teaching: Cordelia's death. *College English* 39:276–85.

———. 1978a. How do Dr. Johnson's remarks on Cordelia's death add to my own response? In *Psychoanalysis and the question of the text*, ed. Geoffrey Hartman, 18–44. Baltimore: Johns Hopkins University Press.

———. 1978b. Literature as transaction. In *What is literature?* ed. Paul Hernadi, 206–18. Bloomington: Indiana University Press.

———. (with English 692). 1978c. Poem-opening: An invitation to transactive criticism. *College English* 40:2–16.

———. 1980. Re-covering "The purloined letter": Reading as a personal transaction. In *The reader in the text: Essays on audience and interpretation*, ed. J. Suleiman and I. Crosman, 350–70. Princeton: Princeton University Press.

Holquist, Michael. 1983. Whodunit and other questions: Metaphysical detective stories in postwar fiction. In *The poetics of murder: Detective fiction and literary theory,* ed. Glenn W. Most and William W. Stowe, 149–74. New York: Harcourt Brace Jovanovich.

Huxley, Aldous. 1966. Vulgarity in literature. In *The recognition of Edgar Allan Poe: Selected criticism since 1829,* ed. E. W. Carlson. Ann Arbor: University of Michigan Press. Originally published 1949.

Hyppolite, Jean. 1971. Hegel's phenomenology and psychoanalysis. Trans. A. Richer. In *New studies in Hegel's philosophy,* ed. W. Steinkrauss, 57–70. New York: Holt, Rinehart and Winston.

Irigaray, Luce. 1985. *Speculum of the other woman.* Trans. Gillian C. Gill. Ithaca: Cornell University Press. Originally published 1974.

Iser, Wolfgang. 1974. *The implied reader: Patterns of communication in prose fiction from Bunyan to Beckett.* Baltimore: Johns Hopkins University Press.

Jackendoff, Ray. 1969. An interpretive theory of negation. *Foundations of Language* 5:218–41.

Jakobson, Roman (with Krystyna Pomorska). 1983. *Dialogues.* Cambridge: MIT Press.

Jameson, Fredric. 1977. Imaginary and symbolic in Lacan: Marxism, psychoanalytic criticism, and the problem of the subject. *Yale French Studies* 55/56:338–95.

Jauss, Hans Robert. 1970. Literary history as a challenge to literary theory. *New Literary History* 2:7–37.

Jespersen, Otto. 1966. *Negation in English and other languages.* 2d ed. Copenhagen: Ejnar Munksgaard. Originally published 1917.

Johnson, Barbara. 1977. The frame of reference: Poe, Lacan, Derrida. In *Literature and psychoanalysis: The question of reading—otherwise. Yale French Studies* 55/56:457–505.

———. 1980. *The critical difference: Essays in the contemporary rhetoric of reading.* Baltimore: Johns Hopkins University Press.

Julien, Philippe. 1983. Le nom propre et la lettre. *Littoral* 7/8:33–45.

Juranville, A. 1984. *Lacan et la philosophie.* Paris: Presses Universitaires de France.

Kanizsa, Gaetano. 1979. *Organization in vision: Essays on gestalt perception.* New York: Praeger.

Kearney, Richard. 1984. Dialogue with Jacques Derrida. In *Dialogues with contemporary continental thinkers,* 105–26. Manchester: Manchester University Press.

Kirk, G., and J. Raven. 1983. *The Presocratic philosophers.* London: Cambridge University. Originally published 1957.

Klima, Edward S. 1964. Negation in English. In *The structure of language: Readings in the philosophy of language,* ed. J. Fodor and J. Katz, 246–323. Englewood Cliffs, N.J.: Prentice-Hall.

Kojève, Alexandre. 1969. *Introduction to the reading of Hegel: Lectures on the phe-*

nomenology of spirit. Assembled by Raymond Queneau. Ed. A. Bloom, trans. J. Nichols, Jr. New York: Basic Books. Originally published 1947.

Krutch, J. W. 1926. *Edgar Allan Poe: A study in genius.* New York: Knopf.

LaBelle, Maurice Marc. 1980. *Alfred Jarry: Nihilism and the theater of the absurd.* New York: New York University Press.

Lacan, Jacques. 1956. Le séminaire sur "La lettre volée." *Le Psychanalyse* 2:1–44.

———. 1966a. *Ecrits.* Paris: Editions du Seuil.

———. 1966b. Le séminaire sur "La lettre volée." In *Ecrits,* 11–61. Paris: Editions du Seuil. Originally published 1956.

———. 1968. De Rome 53 à Rome 67: La psychanalyse. Raison d'un échec. *Scilicet* 1:42–50.

———. 1969. *Ecrits 1.* Coll. "Points." Paris: Editions du Seuil.

———. 1972a. Of structure as an inmixing of an otherness prerequisite to any subject whatever. In *The structuralist controversy: The languages of criticism and the sciences of man,* ed. Richard Macksey and Eugenio Donato, 186–200. Baltimore: Johns Hopkins University Press.

———. 1972b. Seminar on "The purloined letter." Trans. Jeffrey Mehlman. In *French Freud: Structural studies in psychoanalysis: Yale French Studies* 48:38–72.

———. 1973. *Le séminaire: Livre XI. Les quatre concepts fondamentaux de la psychanalyse.* Ed. Jacques-Alain Miller. Paris: Editions du Seuil. Originally presented 1964.

———. 1975a. *Le séminaire: Livre I. Les écrits techniques de Freud. 1953–1954.* Ed. Jacques-Alain Miller. Paris: Editions du Seuil.

———. 1975b. *Le séminaire: Livre XX. Encore, 1972–1973.* Ed. Jacques-Alain Miller. Paris: Editions du Seuil.

———. 1977. *Ecrits: A selection.* Trans. Alan Sheridan. New York: Norton.

———. 1978a. *The four fundamental concepts of psychoanalysis.* Ed. Jacques-Alain Miller, trans. A. Sheridan. New York: Norton. Originally presented 1964.

———. 1978b. *Le séminaire: Livre II. Le moi dans la théorie de Freud et dans la technique de la psychanalyse. 1954–1955.* Ed. Jacques-Alain Miller. Paris: Editions du Seuil.

———. 1981. *Le séminaire: Livre III. Les psychoses. 1955–1956.* Ed. Jacques-Alain Miller. Paris: Editions du Seuil.

———. 1986. *Le seminaire: Livre VII. L'éthique de la psychanalyse. 1959–1960.* Ed. Jacques-Alain Miller. Paris: Editions du Seuil.

Laplanche, Jean, and J.-B. Pontalis. 1973. *The language of psychoanalysis.* Trans. D. Nicholson-Smith. New York: Norton. Originally published 1967.

Lawrence, D. H. 1964. Edgar Allan Poe. In *Studies in classic American literature.* New York: Viking Press. Originally published 1923.

Le Bon, Gustave. 1960. *The crowd: A study of the popular mind.* New York: Viking Press. Originally published 1895.

Levin, Harry. 1967. *The power of blackness: Hawthorne, Poe, Melville.* New York: Knopf.

Lévi-Strauss, Claude. 1969. *The elementary structures of kinship.* Trans. J. Bell, J. von Sturmer, and R. Needham. Boston: Beacon Press. Originally published 1949.

———. 1963. Language and the analysis of social laws. In *Structural anthropology,* trans. C. Jacobson and B. Schoepf, 55–66. New York: Basic Books. Originally published 1951.

———. 1965. The structural study of myth. In *Reader in comparative religion,* ed. W. A. Lessa and E. Z. Vogt, 2d ed., 502–74. New York: Harper and Row. Originally published 1955.

———. 1978. Preface. In Roman Jakobson, *Six lectures on sound and meaning, 1942–1943,* trans. J. Mepham, xi–xxvi. Cambridge: MIT Press.

Lewis, C. T., and C. Short. 1955. *A Latin dictionary.* Oxford: Clarendon.

Limon, John. 1983. How to place Poe's *Arthur Gordon Pym* in science-dominated intellectual history and how to extract it again. *North Dakota Quarterly* 51, no. 1:31–47.

Lowell, James Russell. 1966. Edgar Allan Poe. In *The recognition of Edgar Allan Poe: Selected criticism since 1829,* ed. E. W. Carlson. Ann Arbor: University of Michigan Press. Originally published 1845.

Mabbott, Thomas O., ed. 1951. *The selected poetry and prose of Edgar Allan Poe.* New York: Modern Library.

———. 1978. *Collected works of Edgar Allan Poe.* Vols. 1–3. Cambridge: Belknap Press of Harvard University Press.

Mallarmé, Stephane. 1945. Scolies. In *Oeuvres complètes,* ed. H. Mondor and G. Jean-Aubry, 445–51. Paris: Gallimard.

Marcus, Maurice G. 1984. Review of *Lacan and language: A reader's guide to Ecrits. International Journal of Psychoanalysis* 65, pt. 2:238–41.

Marks, Elaine, and Isabelle de Courtivron, eds. 1981. *New French feminisms: An anthology.* New York: Schocken Books.

Marks, Jeannet A. 1968. *Genius and disaster: Studies in drugs and genius.* Port Washington, N.Y.: Kennikat Press. Originally published 1925.

Matthews, Brander. 1966. Poe and the detective story. In *The recognition of Edgar Allan Poe: Selected criticism since 1829,* ed. Eric Carlson. Ann Arbor: University of Michigan Press.

Mauclair, Camille. 1925. *Le génie d'Edgar Poe.* Paris: A. Michel.

Mehlman, Jeffrey. 1975. Poe pourri: Lacan's purloined letter. *Semiotexte* 1, no. 3:51–58.

Mencken, H. L., ed. 1942. *A new dictionary of quotations.* New York: Knopf.

Miller, Jacques-Alain. 1984. Jacques Lacan: 1901–1981. Trans. Barbara Guetti and Bruce Fink. *Psychoanalysis and Contemporary Thought* 7:615–28. Originally published 1981.

Mitchell, Juliet, and Jacqueline Rose, eds. 1982. *Feminine sexuality: Jacques Lacan and the école Freudienne.* Trans. Jacqueline Rose. New York: Norton.

Moldenhauer, Joseph J. 1968. Murder as a fine art: Basic connections between

Poe's aesthetics, psychology and moral vision. *PMLA* 83:284–97.

Most, Glenn W. 1983. The Hippocratic smile: John Le Carré and the traditions of the detective novel. In *The poetics of murder: Detective fiction and literary theory,* ed. Glenn W. Most and William W. Stowe, 341–65. New York: Harcourt Brace Jovanovich.

Most, Glenn W., and William W. Stowe, eds. 1983. *The poetics of murder: Detective fiction and literary theory.* New York: Harcourt Brace Jovanovich.

Muller, John P. 1987. Language, psychosis, and spirit. In *The evolution of attachment: Essays in honor of Otto Allen Will, Jr., M.D.,* ed. Yoshiharu Akabane, James L. Sacksteder, and Daniel P. Schwartz. New York: International Universities Press.

Muller, John P., and William J. Richardson. 1982. *Lacan and language: A reader's guide to Ecrits.* New York: International Universities Press.

Ohmann, Richard. 1973. Literature as act. In *Approaches to poetics,* ed. Seymour Chatman, 81–107. New York: Columbia University Press.

Ortigues, Edmund. 1962. *Discours et symbole.* Paris: Editions Aubier Montaigne.

Paz, Octavio. 1981. *The monkey grammarian.* Trans. H. R. Lane. New York: Seaver Books. Originally published 1974.

Pederson-Krag, Geraldine. 1983. Detective stories and the primal scene. In *The poetics of murder: Detective fiction and literary theory,* ed. Glenn W. Most and William W. Stowe, 13–20. New York: Harcourt Brace Jovanovich.

Piaget, Jean. 1970. *Structuralism.* Trans. C. Maschler. New York: Basic Books. Originally published 1968.

Plato. 1963. *The collected dialogues, including the letters.* Ed. E. Hamilton and H. Cairns. Princeton: Princeton University Press.

Poe, Edgar Allan. 1956. *Selected writings of Edgar Allan Poe,* ed. Edward Davidson. Boston: Houghton Mifflin.

———. 1966a. *Complete stories and poems.* New York: Doubleday.

———. 1966b. *The letters of Edgar Allan Poe.* 2d ed. Ed. John Ward Ostrom. New York: Gordian Press.

———. 1967. *Edgar Allan Poe: Selected writings.* Ed. David Galloway. New York: Penguin.

———. 1978. The purloined letter. In *Collected works of Edgar Allan Poe,* vol. 3, *Tales and sketches, 1843–1849,* ed. Thomas O. Mabbott, 972–97. Cambridge: Belknap Press of Harvard University Press. Originally published 1844.

———. 1981. *Marginalia.* Charlottesville: University Press of Virginia. Originally published 1845.

———. 1983. *The other Poe: Comedies and satires.* Ed. David Galloway. New York: Penguin Books.

Pratt, Mary L. 1977. *Towards a speech-act theory of literary discourse.* Bloomington: Indiana University Press.

Proust, Marcel. 1932. *Remembrance of things past.* 7 vols. in 2. Trans. C. K. Scott Moncrieff and F. A. Blossom. New York: Random House.

Queen, Ellery. 1968. Introduction. In *The exploits of the Chevalier Dupin,* by Michael Harrison. Sauk City, Wisc.: Arkham House.

Quinn, Arthur Hobson. 1941. *Edgar Allan Poe: A critical biography.* New York: Appleton-Century.

Quinn, Patrick. 1957. *The French face of Edgar Poe.* Carbondale: Southern Illinois University Press.

Rank, Otto. 1932. *Don Juan: Une étude sur le double.* Trans. S. Lautman. Paris: Denoël and Steele.

―――. 1975. *The Don Juan legend.* Trans. David G. Winter. Princeton: Princeton University Press. Originally published 1924.

Richardson, William J. 1983a. Lacan and the subject of psychoanalysis. In *Interpreting Lacan,* ed. Joseph H. Smith and William Kerrigan, 51–74. Psychiatry and the Humanities, vol. 6. New Haven: Yale University Press.

―――. 1983b. Psychoanalysis and the Being question. In *Interpreting Lacan,* ed. Joseph H. Smith and William Kerrigan, 139–59. Psychiatry and the Humanities, vol. 6. New Haven: Yale University Press.

―――. 1985. Lacanian theory. In *Models of the mind: Their relationships to clinical work,* ed. A. Rothstein, 101–17. Monograph 1, Workshop Series of the American Psychoanalytic Association. New York: International Universities Press.

―――. 1987. Lacan and psychosis. In *Psychosis and sexual identity: Towards a post-analytic view of the Schreber case.* Stony Brook, N.Y.: SUNY Press.

Riffaterre, Michael. 1966. Describing poetic structures: Two approaches to Baudelaire's *Les chats. Yale French Studies* 36/37:200–242.

―――. 1973. The self-sufficient text. *Diacritics* 3, no. 3:39–45.

Robertson, J. M. S. 1926–27. The genius of Poe. *Modern Quarterly* 3:274–84; 4:60–72.

Rosen, Stanley. 1974. *G. W. F. Hegel.* New Haven: Yale University Press.

Roudinesco, Elizabeth. 1986. *La bataille de cent ans: Histoire de la psychanalyse en France: 2. 1925–1985.* Paris: Editions du Seuil.

Rourke, Constance M. 1966. Edgar Allan Poe. In *The recognition of Edgar Allan Poe: Selected criticism since 1829,* ed. E. W. Carlson. Ann Arbor: University of Michigan Press. Originally published 1931.

Saussure, F. de. 1966. *Course in general linguistics.* Ed. C. Bally and A. Sechehaye, trans. W. Baskin. New York: McGraw-Hill. Originally published 1916.

Sayers, Dorothy L. 1929. *The omnibus of crime.* New York: Harcourt Brace.

Schneiderman, Stuart. 1983. *Jacques Lacan: The death of an intellectual hero.* Cambridge: Harvard University Press.

Schreber, Daniel Paul. 1955. *Memoirs of my nervous illness.* Trans. I. Macalpine and R. A. Hunter. London: Dawson and Sons. Originally published 1903.

Schwartz, Murray. 1978. Critic, define thyself. In *Psychoanalysis and the question of the text,* ed. Geoffrey Hartman, 1–17. Baltimore: Johns Hopkins University Press.

Segers, Rien T. 1975. Readers, text and author: Some implications of *Rezeptionsästhetik. Yearbook of Comparative and General Literature* 24:15–23.

Shaw, George Bernard. 1966. Edgar Allan Poe. In *The recognition of Edgar Allan Poe: Selected criticism since 1829,* ed. E. W. Carlson. Ann Arbor: University of Michigan Press. Originally published 1909.

Smith, Joseph H. 1983. Epilogue: Lacan and the subject of American psychoanalysis. In *Interpreting Lacan,* ed. Joseph H. Smith and William Kerrigan, 259–76. Psychiatry and the Humanities, vol. 6. New Haven: Yale University Press.

Stovall, Floyd. 1969. *Edgar Poe the poet: Essays new and old on the man and his work.* Charlottesville: University Press of Virginia.

Stubbs, Michael. 1983. *Discourse analysis: The sociolinguistic analysis of natural language.* Chicago: University of Chicago Press.

Swinburne, A. Charles. 1966. Letter to Sara Sigourney Rice, November 9, 1875. In *The recognition of Edgar Allan Poe: Selected criticism since 1829,* ed. E. W. Carlson. Ann Arbor: University of Michigan Press.

Symons, Julian. 1981. *The tell-tale heart: The life and works of Edgar Allan Poe.* New York: Penguin Books.

Tate, Allen. 1955. The angelic imagination. In *The man of letters in the modern world.* New York: Meridian.

————. 1966. The angelic imagination. In *The recognition of Edgar Allan Poe: Selected criticism since 1829,* ed. E. W. Carlson, 236–54. Ann Arbor: University of Michigan Press.

Taylor, Charles. 1975. *Hegel.* Cambridge: Cambridge University Press.

Thompson, G. R. 1973. *Poe's fiction.* Madison: University of Wisconsin Press.

Thompson, John R. 1929. *The genius and character of Edgar Allan Poe.* Privately printed.

Turkle, Sherry. 1978. *Psychoanalytic politics: Freud's French revolution.* New York: Basic Books.

Ver Eecke, Wilfried. 1984. *Saying "no": Its meaning in child development, psychoanalysis, linguistics, and Hegel.* Pittsburgh: Duquesne University Press.

Verene, Donald P. 1985. *Hegel's recollection: A study of images in the "Phenomenology of spirit."* Albany: State University of New York Press.

Vonnegut, Mark. 1975. *The Eden express.* New York: Praeger.

Wilbur, Richard. 1967. The Poe mystery case. *New York Review of Books* (13 July):25–28.

————. 1975. Interview. *Amherst Student Review* (Amherst College), March 17.

Wilden, Anthony, trans. 1981. *Speech and language in psychoanalysis* by Jacques Lacan. Trans. with notes and commentary. Baltimore: Johns Hopkins University Press. Originally published 1968.

Willbern, David P. 1979. Freud and the inter-penetration of dreams. *Diacritics* 9, no. 1:98–110.

Wilson, Edmund. 1966. Poe at home and abroad. In *The recognition of Edgar Allan Poe: Selected criticism since 1829,* ed. E. W. Carlson, 142–51. Ann Arbor: University of Michigan Press.

Winters, Ivor. 1966. Edgar Allan Poe: A crisis in American obscurantism. In *The recognition of Edgar Allan Poe: Selected criticism since 1829,* ed. E. W. Carlson. Ann Arbor: University of Michigan Press. Originally published 1937.

Wright, Elizabeth. 1984. *Psychoanalytic criticism: Theory in practice.* London: Methuen.

 *Contributors*

LIAHNA KLENMAN BABENER is department head and associate professor of English at Montana State University.

MARIE BONAPARTE was a founder of the Paris Psychoanalytic Society.

ROSS CHAMBERS is Marvin Felheim Distinguished University Professor of French and Comparative Literature at the University of Michigan.

JACQUES DERRIDA is professor of philosophy at the Ecole des Hauts Etudes in Paris.

SHOSHANA FELMAN is the Thomas E. Donnelley Professor of French and Comparative Literature at Yale University.

JANE GALLOP is professor of humanities at Rice University.

IRENE HARVEY is associate professor of philosophy at Pennsylvania State University.

NORMAN N. HOLLAND is the Milbauer Eminent Scholar in English at the University of Florida.

BARBARA JOHNSON is professor of french and comparative literature at Harvard University.

JACQUES LACAN was the leading psychoanalyst in France until his death in 1981.

THOMAS O. MABBOTT was called "the only *total* Poe scholar" by *The Poe Newsletter* before his death in 1968.

JOHN MULLER is a clinical psychologist and member of the senior therapy staff at the Austen Riggs Center.

FRANÇOIS PERALDI is a psychoanalyst and professor of linguistics at the University of Montreal.

WILLIAM RICHARDSON is a psychoanalyst and professor of philosophy at Boston College.

🌿 Index of Authors

✿ Index of Subjects